Keynote

Intermediate
Teacher's Book

Daniel Barber

Communicative Activities by Karen Richardson

Keynote Intermediate
Teacher's Book
Daniel Barber
Karen Richardson

Publisher: Gavin McLean

Publishing Consultant: Karen Spiller

Project Manager: Karen White

Development Editor: Diane Hall

Editorial Manager: Alison Burt

Head of Strategic Marketing ELT: Charlotte Ellis

Senior Content Project Manager: Nick Ventullo

Production Intern: James Richardson

Manufacturing Manager: Eyvett Davis

Cover design: Brenda Carmichael

Text design: MPS North America LLC

Compositor: MPS North America LLC

National Geographic Liaison: Leila Hishmeh

Audio: Tom Dick and Debbie Productions Ltd

DVD: Tom Dick and Debbie Productions Ltd

Cover Photo Caption: Host June Cohen speaks on stage during TED University at TEDGlobal 2012 - June 25–29, 2012, Edinburgh, Scotland. © James Duncan Davidson/TED.

ISBN: 978-1-305-57841-8

National Geographic Learning
Cheriton House, North Way, Andover, Hampshire, SP10 5BE
United Kingdom

Cengage Learning is a leading provider of customized learning solutions with employees residing in nearly 40 different countries and sales in more than 125 countries around the world. Find your local representative at **www.cengage.com**.

Cengage Learning products are represented in Canada by Nelson Education Ltd.

Visit National Geographic Learning online at **ngl.cengage.com**

Visit our corporate website at **www.cengage.com**

CREDITS

The publishers would like to thank TED Staff for their insightful feedback and expert guidance, allowing us to achieve our dual aims of maintaining the integrity of these inspirational TED Talks, while maximising their potential for teaching English.

The publishers would like to thank the following for permission to use copyright material:

Photos

173 (l) © Fernando Madeira/Shutterstock.com; 173 (r) © Dmitry Kalinovsky/Shutterstock.com; 179 (l) © wavebreakmedia/Shutterstock.com; 179 (r) © Ben Blankenburg/Corbis; 188 (l) © Kaspars Grinvalds/Shutterstock.com; 188 (r) © Fuse/Getty Images.

Illustrations by MPS North America LLC

Cover: © James Duncan Davidson/TED.

Printed in Greece by Bakis SA

Print Number: 01   Print Year: 2015

Contents

Introduction

1 What is *Keynote*?

Keynote is a six-level, multi-syllabus English course that takes learners from Elementary level (A1) to Proficient (C2). It is suitable for all adults or young adults in higher education or in work who need English in their professional or personal lives. It is suitable for all teachers, however experienced – extensive teaching notes will help the inexperienced teacher plan lessons, while valuable background information, teaching tips and extension activities will be of great use to even the most experienced teacher.

The units in *Keynote* each take a TED Talk as their point of departure. These talks are given by speakers from all walks of life, countries and fields of work and provide a rich and varied basis for the teaching and learning of authentic English. See section 2 for more about TED.

Each level contains enough material for between 90 and 120 hours' classroom work. Teachers can reduce this time by giving some preparation tasks to students to do at home (such as watching the TED Talks) or extend it with the extra activities in the teaching notes and the photocopiable communicative activities at the back of this book.

What are the components of *Keynote*?

Student's Book

- twelve units of five double-page lessons each (See section 3 below for details.)
- six double-page Review lessons, one after every two units
- a grammar summary and extra exercises to accompany each unit
- audioscripts and TED Talk transcripts
- DVD-Rom with all TED Talks, Vocabulary in context exercises, Presentation skills montages, and recordings for listening and pronunciation exercises

Workbook

- consolidation and extension of all the learning objectives in the Student's Book
- additional TED input via biographical information about the speakers featured in the Student's Book, playlists related to the featured talks and audio of podcasts given by members of the *Keynote* team
- six two-page Writing lessons that provide detailed practice of the kinds of texts that come up in the Cambridge exams. These process-based lessons help students generate ideas, provide them with a model, give them useful language, and help them plan, draft, revise and analyse.

- six two-page Presentation lessons that allow students to practise the presentation skills from the Student's Book and build up a bank of personalized presentation language

Teacher's Book

- full teaching notes for all the units and Review lessons, containing answers, TED Talk and audio transcripts, teaching tips, optional and alternative ways of dealing with the Student's Book exercises, extension activities and background information
- six photocopiable progress tests, with sections looking at the grammar, vocabulary, reading, speaking, writing and often listening presented in the previous two units, with answer key
- twenty-four photocopiable communicative activities, two for each unit, with full teaching notes, containing a variety of activities such as information gap, interactive crosswords and mingling. While most of the worksheets are copied and given to the students, some are to be cut into cards and given to the students. In these cases, it may be best to copy the page onto card (and possibly laminate it), so that the cards are sturdier and can be used several times if necessary.

Website

- video streaming of the TED Talks from the Student's Book, Vocabulary in context and Presentation skill montages
- worksheets organized by industry (e.g. manufacturing, tourism, education) and business function (e.g. human resources, marketing, research and development) that provide highly targeted practice of the language specific to the learners' field of work. They can be used in class or for self study.
- mid- and end-of-year tests
- two bonus grammar lessons (with infographics) to extend the grammar coverage of the B1 level
- Word versions of all the audio/video scripts and reading texts that can be 're-packaged' by teachers to create additional practice material or tests

2 What is TED?

TED is a non-profit organization based on the idea that many people from all areas of life have 'ideas worth spreading', and should be given a platform to spread those ideas. There are currently more than two thousand TED Talks on the TED website, and new talks by leading thinkers and doers across a wide range of fields are constantly being added. TED originated at a conference in 1984 centred on Technology, Entertainment and Design, but the talks now cover far more than those three areas. The talks are given by speakers from across the world, ranging from highly respected business leaders to school students, all of whom have an idea worth spreading. The talks can last as long as eighteen minutes but are generally much shorter. By providing this platform, TED aims to 'make great ideas accessible and spark conversation'. For more on TED, see www.TED.com.

Why are TED Talks great for learning English?

TED Talks feature remarkable people communicating passionately and persuasively, and are a unique source of engaging and often amusing real language. The talks are intrinsically interesting, and are watched by millions of people around the world. In the ELT classroom they provide:

- motivating content that learners choose to watch in their leisure time for entertainment and edification
- educational content, i.e. students learn about the world as well as learning English
- authentic listening input
- exposure to different language varieties: *Keynote* has a mix of talks given by British English, American English, Australian speakers and includes a glossary in each TED Talk lesson to compare and contrast language (See Teaching tip 1 below.)
- exposure to different accents (native, such as British and US, as well as non-native)
- up-to-date language
- ideal material for developing critical thinking skills
- probably the best models in existence for presentation skills

3 How do I teach with *Keynote*?

Unit structure

Each unit in the Student's Book contains five lessons around an overarching theme:

- the first provides an introduction to the TED Talk for the unit, including preparation by pre-teaching key vocabulary and practising skills that will help students when listening to authentic English
- the second is the TED Talk lesson where students watch and listen to the talk, both in its entirety and in short sections, and do further vocabulary work (mining the talk for interesting vocabulary and collocations) as well as work on critical thinking and presentation skills (See Teaching tip 2 below.)
- the third is the grammar lesson, with real input in the form of an infographic that provides a context for the presentation of the grammar and practice, and ends in a spoken output using the new language

- the fourth lesson is based on a reading text, drawn from the theme of the unit and addressing real-life topics, with a variety of comprehension, reading skills and vocabulary exercises
- the last lesson in each unit focuses on functional language, and comprises listening and speaking with accompanying vocabulary work, as well as a section on writing, focusing on text type and writing skills

The grammar, reading and functional lessons in each unit have 21st century outcomes, i.e. the lessons provide and practise the skills and knowledge needed by students to succeed in their professional and personal lives in the 21st century.

The grammar, vocabulary and skills presented in each unit are practised further in the Review lessons after every two units. (See Teaching tip 3 below.)

Grammar

Grammar is presented in a natural and clear context using an infographic, which means that there is not a huge amount of reading for the students to do in order to find the examples of the grammar. Students are led to understanding of the grammatical points through guided discovery, focusing on language from the infographic picked out in one or two grammar boxes, and studied through the use of concept check questions. Students are then directed to the Grammar summary at the back of the book to read about the grammar in more detail. The exercises accompanying the Grammar summaries focus mainly on form and can be done at this point before students tackle the exercises in the unit, which focus more on meaning and use, or they can be done for homework.

The Workbook consolidates the grammar presented in the Student's Book and extends it (often looking at more idiomatic grammar) in the 'Grammar Extra' exercises.

Vocabulary

There are three different categories of vocabulary presentation and practice in *Keynote*:

Key words

The Key words section always appears in the first lesson. In this section some of the words and phrases that are central to the TED Talk are matched with definitions in order to enable students to understand the talk more easily. Note that these words are sometimes above the relevant CEFR level and are not intended for productive use. (See Teaching tip 4 below.)

Vocabulary in context

The Vocabulary in context section always appears in the second lesson, after students have watched the TED Talk. Here, short excerpts which contain useful words, phrases or collocations are repeated and the lexical items are matched with synonyms and then practised in a personalization activity.

Vocabulary development

Further vocabulary work focuses on vocabulary relevant to the theme taken from the reading and listening texts, building on it in the form of work on lexical sets, phrases and collocation.

There is further work on vocabulary in context and the lexical sets of the units in the Workbook. Additionally the Workbook provides more practice of wordbuilding and common collocations of a topic word.

Skills

Reading

Each unit has a reading lesson based on a contemporary and real-world text. The accompanying exercises cover reading comprehension, reading skills and vocabulary work, but also elicit a personal response to the content of the text.

Writing

There is a focus on writing in each final lesson, covering a text type and writing skill, such as using linking words. There are on-page models for students to analyse and follow in their own writing. Writing is further practised in the Workbook where there are six process-based, double-page lessons that provide detailed practice of the kinds of texts that come up in the Cambridge exams (matched to the level of the book).

Listening

Listening is a key component of the course and is dealt with in various ways. To help students deal with the authentic, native speaker-level language of the TED Talks, *Keynote* has a comprehensive authentic listening skills syllabus that – together with a focus on key words from the Talk and background information – allows students to understand listening material which is usually well above their productive level. (See Teaching tip 5 below.) There is often listening in the grammar lessons, consolidating the new language, and there is also graded listening material in the final lesson of each unit, using a wide variety of listening comprehension task types.

Speaking

Each unit has a lesson that focuses specifically on functional and situational language that is relevant to working adults. This is supported by a Useful language box containing a number of expressions relevant to the function or situation. There are also speaking activities throughout the units.

Pronunciation

There is a pronunciation syllabus, integrated with the grammar and speaking lessons where there is a relevant pronunciation area.

4 Teaching tips

The following teaching tips apply throughout the course. There are lesson-specific teaching tips through the units.

Teaching tip 1 Which variety of English?

This deals with the notes comparing North American and British English in the TED Talk lesson. Find out whether your students are interested in learning about the different pronunciation and vocabulary of these two varieties. Ask them what varieties of English they prefer to listen to (native and non-native) and why. Explore any prejudices the class may have around variety. Discuss students' long-term pronunciation goals and whether they hope to sound like native speakers or whether it is better to aim for a clear accent that reflects their identities more accurately. The conclusions to this discussion will determine what you do with the footnotes. If your students are very interested in the two varieties, you may decide to get them practising saying the words in the different accents. Similarly, where the spelling or vocabulary is different, you could encourage students to use the variety they feel most comfortable with in their learning, but ensure that they use one variety consistently.

Where students are interested, you could spend some time investigating the differences further. For example, with spelling differences, you could ask the students to look for patterns (in the glossaries in the book or using online dictionaries). They should be able to identify patterns such as the *-or/-our* ending in North American *color/favor* and British *colour/favour*. With differences in vocabulary, you could encourage students to speculate on how the differences have come about, e.g. is *sidewalk* a more literal word than *pavement*?

Teaching tip 2 Developing presentation skills

After students have watched a TED Talk in each unit, they focus on a particular aspect of presentation skills such as 'using props' or 'audience awareness'. Before embarking on the Presentation skills sections, it's probably worth finding out from your students the kinds of situations when they might have to present (in their first language or in English). Many of your students will need to present information at work and students in academic situations will have to present their research. Even students who don't often give presentations will benefit from presenting in your class because it's an opportunity to build confidence in speaking in English and to develop a key communication skill.

At first, some of your students might not feel comfortable with giving presentations in English. That's why many of the presentations tasks in *Keynote* can be done in pairs, with students taking turns to present to each other. As the course progresses, you could ask students to present to larger groups and once they are more confident, to the whole class.

Remember to allow plenty of preparation time for the presentations. Often it's a good idea to set a presentation task and ask students to work on it for homework before they give their presentation in the next lesson. It's also useful to provide students with preparation strategies such as making notes on pieces of card to refer to, rehearsing in front of a mirror, or presenting to family and friends at home. You will find more tips on setting up and delivering classroom presentations in the relevant part of each unit of this Teacher's Book.

Teaching tip 3 Using the Review lessons

The Review lesson is an opportunity for reflection and consolidation. Encourage students to see the benefits of reviewing recently encountered language as a means to strengthening their learning and for diagnosing which areas they need to study again.

The Review lessons could be set as homework, but by doing them in class you will be available to clarify areas of difficulty, answer questions and see for yourself where students are doing well and where not so well. Ask students how hard they found the exercises as a means of diagnosing what needs reviewing more thoroughly. Also, consider putting students in small groups to work through the grammar, vocabulary, speaking and writing activities on their own while you conduct one-to-one sessions with individuals. Speak to students to find out how they are progressing, what they need to work on, whether they are experiencing any difficulties in the class or any other matters.

Teaching tip 4 Key words

One way of dealing with the Key words activity in the first lesson of each unit is to write the key words on the board. Read out the first definition and nominate a student to say the correct word. If they guess correctly, read out the second definition and nominate another student to guess that word. Continue until they have matched all the words and their definitions in this way. However, whenever a student guesses incorrectly, start from the very beginning again and read out the first definition, nominating a different student each time. The activity ends once the class has correctly matched all the words and definitions in a row without any mistakes.

Teaching tip 5 Dealing with difficult listening activities

The TED Talks are authentic English and may be challenging for some students, which can be a cause of frustration. Here are some ideas to increase your students' ability to deal with authentic language:

- Don't miss out any of the pre-listening exercises in the first lesson, such as Key words or Authentic listening skills. These are designed to make listening easier.

- Students need time before and after listening to prepare and compare: before, to read the task, ask questions and to predict possible answers, and after, to write their answers and to compare them with a partner.

- Time for writing answers is particularly important when watching clips rather than listening because it is hard to watch the video and write at the same time. This is one reason the TED Talks are broken into small segments.

- Let students read the transcript while they listen or watch.

- Isolate the few seconds of the audio or video where the answer to a question lies and let students listen to it a number of times.

- It's hard in long clips to keep concentrating all the time, so pause just before an answer comes up in order to warn students that they should refocus.

- There are ways of changing the speed that video is played back. You may want to investigate how to slow down talks slightly for your students using certain media players.

- If a task is difficult, make it easier. For example, if students have to listen for a word to fill gaps, you could supply the missing words on the board, mixed up, for them to choose.

- Celebrate the successes, however small. If a student hears only one thing, praise them for that. Don't supply extra information which you heard but they did not, unless you have a good reason.

- Remind them now and again of the advice they read about listening to authentic speech in the first lesson of each unit, especially the advice not to try to understand every word, to stay relaxed and to keep listening. Reassure them that listening improves with repeated practice and that the best thing they can do for their listening skills is to persevere.

Unit opener

Three keys to understanding authentic listening input

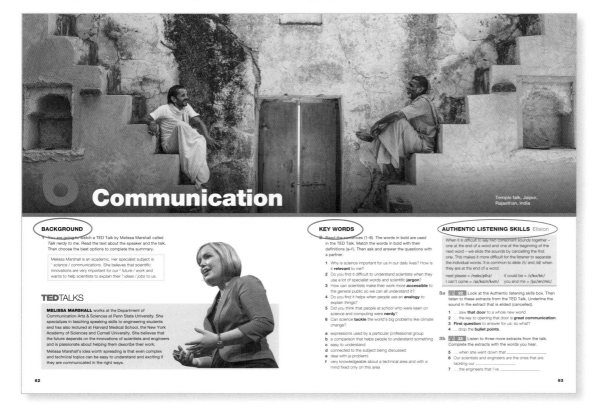

TED Talk lesson

TED Talks
are great for
discussion,
vocabulary,
critical thinking
and presentation
skills

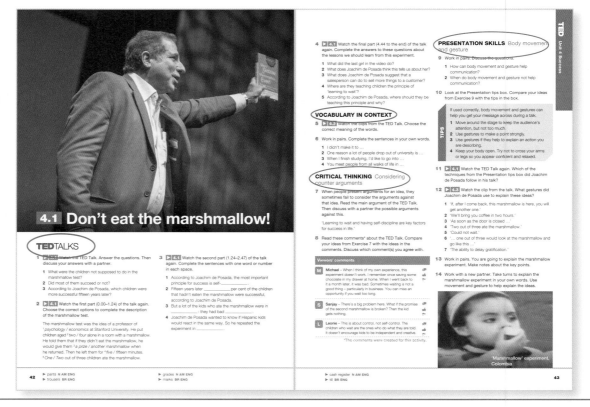

Grammar

Grammar is presented in real-world contexts and practised for real-world outcomes

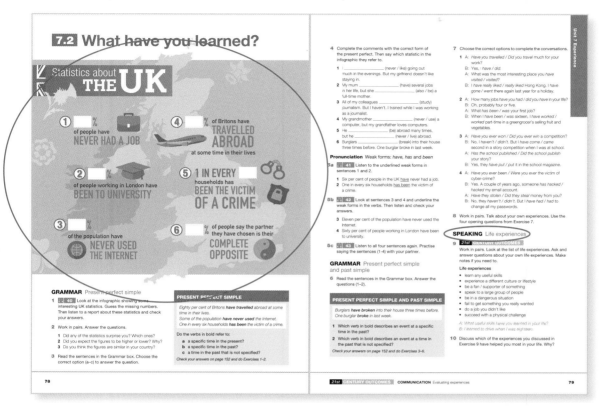

Reading and vocabulary

Contemporary, real-world texts are exploited for reading skills, vocabulary and interest

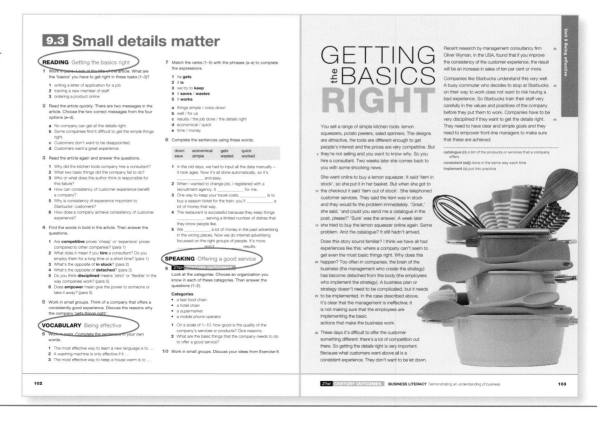

Listening, speaking and writing

Functional language is presented via common, everyday situations where students need to interact in English

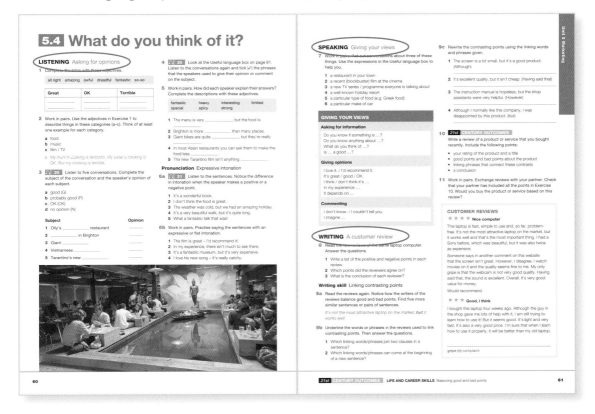

Review

Language and skills are practised via texts about innovative organizations

1 Working life

LEAD IN

• Ask students to open their books and look at the photo on pages 8 and 9.

• Ask questions about the photo and elicit answers from individuals: *Where are these people? What are they doing? How would you describe this job? Who might enjoy a job of this sort? Would you? Why? Why not?*

TEDTALKS
BACKGROUND

1

• Tell the class to read the text about Mark Bezos and his talk. If necessary, clarify the following words:

poverty – the state of being poor

volunteer – someone who does a job for free because they want to

acts of heroism – from *hero*, brave things to do that help others

generosity – if you show generosity, you are happy to give your money or time to someone else for free

• Ask the class what is meant by the TED slogan: *ideas worth spreading.*

• Put students into pairs or threes to discuss the questions. When they are ready, encourage them to share their answers with the class, asking them to justify their ideas.

Answers
1 He worked in advertising before. Now he works for a charity organization and is a volunteer firefighter.
2 Firefighters are highly respected.
3 He is motivated by big and small acts of heroism that he sees every day.

KEY WORDS

2

• **Optional step.** Books closed. Write the seven items of vocabulary on the board in random order. Read out each of the sentences, replacing the words in bold with *beep*. Students call out the word from the board that they think fits the gap. If they get it wrong, shake your head and repeat the sentence. If they get it right, move to the next sentence. If they get this wrong, return to the very beginning, repeating the first sentence and the second. Continue like this until the class confidently fills each gap for sentences 1 to 7 with no errors.

• Books open. Ask students to do Exercise 2 on their own or in pairs. Students match the words in bold with their definitions.

Answers
1 d 2 e 3 c 4 g 5 f 6 b 7 a

• **Optional step.** To further check comprehension, ask follow-up questions: *Does anyone here feel they have a **vocation**. Are you **jealous** of any of your friends or family? Who of you are **homeowners** and who rents? Has anyone been a **volunteer** at a **soup kitchen** or similar charity organization? What should a **witness** do if they see a crime? Would you know what to do if you saw something **in flames**?*

AUTHENTIC LISTENING SKILLS Dealing with new vocabulary

3a

• **Optional step.** After reading the Authentic listening skills box, ask students for their reaction to the advice. Encourage them to describe their experience of listening in English and the difficulties that they have had. Do they normally manage to stay relaxed? Does anyone have any techniques for relaxing into listening?

- **⌂ 1** Write sentence 1 on the board. Play just that sentence and ask them which words were clearest to them and why. Circle the stressed words.

- Instruct them to listen to all three sentences, to circle the stressed words and to underline the words that are repeated. Play the recording.

- Let students compare their answers before sharing with the whole class. Be prepared for differences of opinion; remind them that word stress is not just 'on' or 'off' but that some words are stressed more than others. For this reason, one student may hear stress where another does not. Therefore, the following answers are suggested.

Transcript with suggested answers

1 (Back) in New (York), (I) am the (head) of development for a (non)-profit called (Robin) (Hood).
2 When I'm (not) fighting (poverty), I'm (fighting) (fires) as the assistant (captain) of a volun(teer) (fire) (company).
3 Now in (our) town, where the volunt(eers) (supp)lement a (high)ly (skilled) career (staff), you (have) to (get) to the (fire) scene (pretty) (early) to get (in) on any (action).

3b

- Give students a minute to predict the stressed words and find the repeated words in sentence 4.

- **⌂ 2** Play the recording for students to check.

Transcript with suggested answers

4 ... I am (wit)ness to (acts) of gene(ros)ity and (kind)ness on a monu(men)tal (scale) ... but I'm also (wit)ness to acts of (grace) and (cou)rage on an indi(vid)ual (ba)sis.

1.1 A life lesson from a volunteer firefighter

TEDTALKS

1

- Tell students to look at sentences a–c and decide which lesson they think Mark Bezos wants us to learn. Invite suggestions but don't accept or reject them yet. Ask them to justify their guesses. Before they watch the TED Talk, ask them to read the instruction in Exercise 2 as well.

- ▶ **1.1** Play the whole talk.

Answer

b is the main lesson. (It isn't a because he doesn't mention friends or family, and he talks about helping strangers. It isn't c because he says 'Don't wait until you make your first million to make a difference in somebody's life.')

Transcript

0:13 Back in New York, I am the head of development for a non-profit called Robin Hood. When I'm not fighting poverty, I'm fighting fires as the assistant captain of a volunteer fire company. Now in our town, where the volunteers supplement a highly skilled career staff, you have to get to the fire scene pretty early to get in on any action.

0:32 I remember my first fire. I was the second volunteer on the scene, so there was a pretty good chance I was going to get in. But still it was a real footrace against the other volunteers to get to the captain in charge to find out what our assignments would be. When I found the captain, he was having a very engaging conversation with the homeowner, who was surely having one of the worst days of her life. Here it was, the middle of the night, she was standing outside in the pouring rain, under an umbrella, in her pyjamas, barefoot, while her house was in flames.

1:06 The other volunteer who had arrived just before me – let's call him Lex Luthor – (Laughter) got to the captain first and was asked to go inside and save the homeowner's dog. The dog! I was stunned with jealousy. Here was some lawyer or money manager who, for the rest of his life, gets to tell people that he went into a burning building to save a living creature, just because he beat me by five seconds. Well, I was next. The captain waved me over. He said, 'Bezos, I need you to go into the house. I need you to go upstairs, past the fire, and I need you to get this woman a pair of shoes.' (Laughter) I swear. So, not exactly what I was hoping for, but off I went – up the stairs, down the hall, past the 'real' firefighters, who were pretty much done putting out the fire at this point, into the master bedroom to get a pair of shoes.

2:06 Now I know what you're thinking, but I'm no hero. (Laughter) I carried my payload back downstairs where I met my nemesis and the precious dog by the front door. We took our treasures outside to the homeowner, where, not surprisingly, his received much more attention than did mine. A few weeks later, the department received a letter from the homeowner thanking us for the valiant effort displayed in saving her home. The act of kindness she noted above all others: someone had even gotten her a pair of shoes.

2:46 (Laughter)

2:48 In both my vocation at Robin Hood and my avocation as a volunteer firefighter, I am witness to acts of generosity and kindness on a monumental scale, but I'm also witness to acts of grace and courage on an individual basis. And you know what I've learned? They all matter. So as I look around this room at people who either have achieved, or are on their way to achieving, remarkable levels of success, I would offer this reminder: don't wait. Don't wait until you make your first million to make a difference in somebody's life. If you have something to give, give it now. Serve food at a soup kitchen. Clean up a neighbourhood park. Be a mentor.

3:30 *Not every day is going to offer us a chance to save somebody's life, but every day offers us an opportunity to affect one. So get in the game. Save the shoes.*

3:41 *Thank you. (Applause)*

Background information

Lex Luthor

Lex Luthor is the main enemy of Superman from the original comic strip.

Note the differences in British English and North American English shown at the foot of the spread. In this unit, these focus on pronunciation differences. See Teaching tip 1 on page 6 of the Introduction for ideas on how to present and practise these differences.

2

• Put students in pairs. Get them to discuss their answer to Exercise 1 and the example Mark Bezos gives.

• Invite students to share their thoughts with the whole class. Be generous; even if they understand only the smallest part of the story, praise them for their good listening skills.

Answer

The story of his first fire is a good example of a small act of kindness. The woman really appreciated the fact that he found her some shoes to wear.

3

• Ask students to look at the four sentences.

• ▶1.1 Play the first part of the talk from 0.00-1.06.

• Elicit answers, asking them to justify them if possible.

Answers

1 volunteer   2 second   3 the homeowner   4 night

4

• Let students read the five sentences before watching; they will have to alter *jealousy* to *jealous* and *carried* to *carry* in the task, so ask them to predict the missing words and elicit the part of speech needed to fill the gap.

• ▶1.1 Play the second part of the talk, from 01.06–2.46, again so that students can check their answers.

Answers

1 dog   2 jealous   3 carry/bring   4 homeowner
5 shoes

5

• Again, give students time to read the questions before watching. Suggest that as the answers are more complex, they may prefer to just watch; you will give them time after watching to make notes.

• ▶1.1 Play the third part of the talk (2.46 to the end). Let students make notes after watching. Then put them in pairs to discuss their answers.

Answers

1 He has learned that all the acts of kindness and generosity are important, whether they are big or small.

2 'Don't wait.' If people are waiting to help others once they have made money and live comfortably, they shouldn't, because they have a lot to give already.

3 We can serve food at a soup kitchen. / We can clean a neighbourhood park.

6

• Use the two suggestions Mark Bezos mentions at the end of the talk to start a list on the board of ways we can help our community.

• Students add ideas to this list in pairs. To encourage a flow of ideas, consider getting one or two more ideas from them and adding them to the list before they separate into their pairs.

• Monitor the pairs; make suggestions and be encouraging about their ideas. After a few minutes, get everyone's attention, field their ideas and write them on the board.

• Ask if anyone has done any of these things or knows anyone who does them.

VOCABULARY IN CONTEXT

7

• Explain that students are going to watch some clips from the TED Talk which contain some new words and phrases. They need to choose the correct meaning of the words.

• ▶1.2 Play the clips from the talk. When each multiple-choice question appears, pause the clip so that students can choose the correct definition. Discourage the more confident students from always giving the answer by asking them to raise their hand if they think they know.

• Explore around the words to deepen understanding. For example, tell them that *get in on … action* is normally used with *the*: *get in on **the** action*, and that it is synonymous with *get in on the game*.

Transcript and subtitles

*1 Now in our town, where the volunteers supplement a highly skilled career staff, you have to get to the fire scene pretty early to **get in on any action**.*
    *a **be ready for work***
    *b **avoid doing any work***
    *c **be part of what people are doing***

*2 I was the second volunteer on the scene, so there was **a pretty good chance** I was going to get in.*
    *a **a piece of good luck***
    *b **a strong probability***
    *c **a real danger***

3 *She was standing outside in the pouring rain, under an umbrella, in her pyjamas, **barefoot**, while her house was in flames.*

    a with cold feet

    b with no shoes

    c tired

4 *but off I went – up the stairs, down the hall, past the 'real' firefighters, who were **pretty much done** putting out the fire at this point.*

    a almost finished

    b very tired from

    c having difficulty

5 *I'm also witness to acts of grace and courage on an individual basis. And you know what I've learned? **They all matter.***

    a they are all difficult

    b they are all different

    c they are all important

6 *Not every day is going to offer us a chance to save somebody's life, but every day offers us an opportunity to affect one. So **get in the game**.*

    a become involved

    b get a good job

    c be part of a team

Answers
1 c 2 b 3 b 4 a 5 c 6 a

8

• Ask students to complete the three sentences in their own words so that they are true for them. You could supply examples about yourself to clarify instructions.

• Invite students to read their sentences to the class.

Suggested answers
1 … buy a new car. / … do evening classes.
2 … training for my job. / … depending on my parents for everything.
3 … my family, my friends and my career.

CRITICAL THINKING How a message is delivered

9

• Ask students whether they think Mark Bezos's message was clear, and in pairs to think about the way he got the message across by choosing the best answer: a, b or c.

Answer
c Mark Bezos uses the story of his first fire to illustrate the message.

• **Optional step.** Make sure students realize that the other methods could also be effective ways of getting a message across. Ask them which of the three might be particularly memorable, powerful or emotional.

10

• Tell the students to read the comment and the questions. Elicit one or two opinions from students. If they agree that Mark Bezos' message could make a difference in people's lives, ask them whether they think it might do so in their lives.

Answers
1 It was a short everyday story with a lesson.
2 Students' own answers

PRESENTATION SKILLS Being authentic

11

• **Optional step.** Books closed. Ask students to describe Mark Bezos as a speaker. Write their ideas as adjectives on the board. Suggest an adjective yourself if you need to get ideas flowing. Ask them for other positive qualities in successful speakers. Encourage them by getting them to think of speakers they have heard in the past: at work conferences, on television, comedians, politicians and so on.

• Books open. Students compare their list with that in the book. They decide which qualities are most appealing (attractive) to them.

12

• Ask them to read the Presentation skills box and answer the question. Discuss the answer with the class, exploring the different ways of expressing it. Point out the subheading 'Being authentic'.

Answer
It suggests people like to listen to speakers who are being themselves, using their own words and letting their personality come through.

13

• Ask students to think about Mark Bezos' authenticity as they watch the clip from the TED Talk.

- ▶ 1.3 Play the clip and put them in pairs when it has finished to discuss the questions.
- Get feedback from the class.

14

- Explain that students are going to give a two-minute mini-presentation about their jobs. To do so, they need to make brief notes so that they have things to say. Emphasize the instruction to include information that people may not know, and to mention good and bad points about their work.
- Make sure you include anyone without work; make sure they know they can talk about a job they hope to do in the future or have done in the past.
- Monitor individuals around the room, checking their notes and responding to vocabulary queries.

15

- When students are ready, put them in pairs so that they can do their presentations. Encourage them to be themselves.
- When they have given their presentations, invite them to reflect on each other's talks. What adjectives would they use to describe their partner's presentation style? Did they feel nervous?
- **Optional step.** If giving presentations forms an important part of students' working lives, treat this mini-presentation to a partner as a rehearsal for something bigger: a repeat presentation to bigger groups of people or a rough version of something to be refined and developed. In these cases, get them to think about how they could improve their talk by accentuating its positive aspects.

▶ Set Workbook pages 4–5 for homework.

1.2 What makes a good job?

GRAMMAR Present simple

1

- **Optional step.** Books closed. Tell the class about a job that would interest you if you weren't a teacher, and why you would like it. Give students two minutes to share similar information with a partner, either dreams they had when they were younger or still have now. Then invite volunteers to tell the class what they shared.
- Books open. Tell students to look at the qualities of a good job (a–g) and rank them in order of importance. Then pair them up to compare answers.
- Conclude by doing a brief class survey with a show of hands as to which qualities are seen as most important by the class.

2

- Direct them to the infographic. Ask the class which qualities in Exercise 1 they think are true for occupational therapy.

3

- Explain to students that they are going to listen to an occupational therapist. Ask them to read the questions in preparation. Check that they understand *routine*.
- ▶ 3 Play the recording.

Transcript

I = Interviewer T = Occupational therapist

I: *So what do you do exactly?*

T: *Well, I work as an occupational therapist. We work with people with who have disabilities or when they're recovering after an accident. They just want to have normal lives and to work again. So we help them to do everyday tasks for their jobs or around the house.*

I: *I see, and the patient comes to your clinic, or do you go to them?*

T: *Most days I visit people in their homes and see what they can do and what they can't. I usually advise them about equipment that can help them in the home. People in these situations often have no confidence – they feel anxious. So I always try to make them feel more confident.*

I: *And does that give you a lot of satisfaction?*

T: *Yes, making people feel more confident is the really rewarding part of my job. But I don't spend all my time with patients. You know, as with every job, there are more routine tasks to do. I write reports and attend meetings with other healthcare professionals every day. I rarely get home before 6.30 in the evening, but I love my job.*

- Let them confer in pairs before nominating individuals to share their answers.

4

- **Optional step.** Books closed. If you want to gauge students' prior knowledge of the grammar, dictate (or write on the board) the sentences without the verbs, e.g. *I -BEEP- as an occupational therapist ... What -BEEP- you do exactly?* In pairs, students try to complete the gaps from memory. They then check their answers in the book. This step has the added advantage of making students aware of the need to study the grammar even if they've studied it before.

• Books open. Students read the sentences and answer questions 1–3.

• Students can check their answers and overall understanding of the present simple by turning to the Grammar summary on page 140. If you feel that students need more controlled practice before continuing, they could do one or both of Exercises 1 and 2 in the Grammar summary. Otherwise, you could continue on to Exercise 5 in the unit and set the Grammar summary exercises for homework.

Answers

1 permanent

2 final *-s* on verbs whose subject is in the third person and singular (*he*, *she*, *the patient*, *that*, etc.)

3 do (do, does, don't doesn't)

4 Question 3 is an object question, i.e. the question word *what* is the object of the question, not the subject. Question 6 is a subject question, i.e. the question word *who* is the subject of the question.

Answers to Grammar summary exercises

1

1 has   2 doesn't get   3 loves   4 work   5 does
6 designs   7 gets   8 go   9 have   10 don't find

2

1 A: Does Jess go to university?   B: Yes, she does.
A: Which university does she go to?

2 A: Who likes cake?   B: I don't.   A: Do you want some biscuits instead?

3 A: Do you commute to work by train?   B: Yes, I do.
A: How long does it take?

4 A: Which key opens the front door?

5

• Let students complete the sentences on their own. Monitor carefully to check for understanding.

• Elicit the answers from the class.

Answers

1 do occupational therapists help

2 do they spend, it depends

3 does a therapist see

4 do you have

5 does an occupational therapist earn

6 person helps, do/help, doesn't help

• Ask some concept check questions about the two jobs:

Which job helps you build up your muscles after breaking your leg? (a physiotherapist)

Which helps you to breathe better if your lungs are weak? (a physiotherapist)

Which recommends installing a chair in your shower if you are a wheelchair user? (an occupational therapist)

GRAMMAR Expressions of frequency

6

• **Optional step.** As with the present simple, you may want to gauge students' knowledge of the grammar before doing this exercise. Write the sentences from the grammar box on the board without the expressions of frequency, e.g. *I visit people in their homes.* Write up an adverb or expression of frequency and ask where it can go in the sentence. Repeat for all the expressions of frequency in the examples. This way, you have students' attention at the front of the class, the sentences you are studying are the clear focus, and you can clearly direct the lesson at this crucial presentation stage.

• Put students in pairs to answer the questions and then check their answers on page 140. If you did the Optional step, use the sentences on the board to consolidate the rules with the class.

Answers

1 Adverbs of frequency usually go before the main verb in the present simple (*usually advise*, *often have*)

2 They go after the verb *be* (*are always*).

3 They can go at the beginning of the sentence (*Most days I visit...*) or at the end (*...meetings every day*.).

• Choose from Exercises 3–5 on page 141 according to your students' needs.

Answers to Grammar summary exercises

3

1 It often rains at this time of year.

2 I don't usually take milk with my tea.

3 The trains rarely run on time in England. / In England, the trains rarely run on time.

4 He is always the last person to arrive.

5 We're vegetarians but we sometimes eat fish.

6 There is never enough time to do everything.

4

1 every   2 are   3 Once   4 often   5 most   6 always
7 sell   8 year

5

1 like → likes   2 works → work   3 don't → doesn't
4 He's go → He goes   5 Is → Does   6 eat always → always eat

---

7

- Ask students to put the words in the correct order.
- Don't check the answers yet because students will listen to check in Exercise 8a.

> **Answers**
>
> 1 I'm usually at work by 8.00 in the morning.
> 2 My boss rarely checks my work.
> 3 He sometimes works on the train.
> 4 I always check my emails before I send them.
> 5 People in my country don't usually work late.
> 6 People often wear casual clothes on Fridays.
> 7 I tidy my desk once a month.
> 8 I never take work home with me in the evenings.

Pronunciation Sentence Stress

8a

- 🅰 4 Ask students to listen to the sentences in Exercise 7 and check their answers.
- Students then listen again and decide whether the expressions of frequency are stressed.

> **Answer**
>
> Yes, they are stressed.

8b

- Put students in pairs to practise the sentences with the correct stress. You may want to chorally drill the sentences first.

TEACHING TIP

Pronunciation – back chaining

Saying whole sentences with precision and fluency is difficult. To help, divide the sentences into short phrases. Locate the last stressed syllable in the sentence and drill only from that point to the end. Then locate the penultimate stressed syllable and drill from this new point to the end. Continue until students are saying the whole sentence, e.g: *morning … eight in the morning … work by eight in the morning … usually at work … usually at work by eight in the morning … I'm usually at work by eight in the morning.*

Let them mumble Give the students a minute to practise on their own before whole-class choral drilling. Show them it's OK to say it quietly in their own time, making sure they get the weak forms right.

Listen to your inner voice An even more private technique is to let them imagine themselves saying the sentences out loud, using the voice in their heads to do the speaking.

9

- Take a sentence from Exercise 7 and change it so that it is true for you. Tell students to do the same and to discuss the differences with a partner. They can use the adverbs and expressions in the box to help them.
- After two minutes, stop the class and elicit one or two examples from each pair.

> **Answers**
>
> Students' own answers

10

- Tell students to stay in their pairs and discuss their working day at greater length this time. Point out the discussion questions.
- Go around the class, monitoring to check that they are on task and using the expressions correctly. Make a note of any errors or interesting use of language. Encourage free discussion that is not restricted to the questions in the book.

SPEAKING Best and worst jobs

11 *21st* CENTURY OUTCOMES

- Show students the survey data about best and worst jobs. Put them in groups and ask them to do tasks 1 and 2. Monitor the groups checking that they understand the jobs.
- To encourage students to think critically and evaluate the data, write on the board some extra questions and ask the group to discuss these as well:

  Do you find any of the data surprising? Do you disagree with the positions of any jobs in the list?

  Do you think the results would be similar if the survey was carried out in your country?

  Where do you think this data comes from? What would you like to know about the survey to be sure that the data is accurate?

- In whole-class feedback, let students choose what they would like to share with the class. Ask open questions such as *What did your group talk about?* Encourage discussion of the extra questions, which provide prompts for the 21st CENTURY OUTCOMES aim of evaluating data. Discussion of the origin of the data might raise more questions:

  Who might be interested in collecting data of this type? Is it from a government source or a less serious organization such as a magazine or a publisher?

  How was the survey conducted? Who was asked? How many people were asked? What exactly were they asked?

▶ Photocopiable communicative activity 1.1: Go to page 209 for further practice of present simple and expressions of frequency. The teaching notes are on page 233.

▶ Set Workbook pages 6–7 for homework.

1.3 Have you got what it takes?

READING Skills for the 21st century

1

- Books closed. Write the title of the lesson on the board. Ask students to think about Mark Bezos' profession of firefighter. Ask the class what it takes to be a firefighter and elicit answers. To give them an idea of the meaning of the question, suggest that a firefighter needs to be brave. Ask what else it takes to be one. Ask them if they think they've got what it takes to be one, and if so, what.

- **Optional step.** Put students in pairs. Tell them to discuss what it takes to be a good language learner. Give them a couple of minutes before eliciting answers.

- Tell students that they are going to read an article about what it takes to work in the 21st century. Ask them to look at the list and decide which the key skills are that workers need now.

Answers
Students' own answers

- Put students in pairs to compare their ideas from Exercise 1 and to discuss the questions.

- After a few minutes, round up with a whole-class summary of their opinions.

2

- Show them the article on page 15. Set the two questions and ask them how best to read for this information. Ask them whether it is necessary to understand every word. Set a time limit of five minutes to encourage scan reading for the information they need.

- Give students a chance to compare what they have found with a partner before conducting whole-class feedback.

Answers
1 The author mentions the following skills as important: a Interpersonal skills (line 11)   d Technological knowledge (line 22)   e Critical thinking (line 21)   f Teamwork (line 12) g Organizational skills (line 27)
2 The author also mentions the following skills: understanding of cultural differences and how groups relate (lines 2–5) creativity (line 23)   a desire to learn (line 24)   speed and efficiency (line 26)   ability to prioritize (line 28)

3

- Tell students to read the article again, this time to complete sentences 1–5 with the correct options. Ask them to prepare to justify each answer by noting the line in the article where they read it.

- Give them time to confer before nominating individuals to share answers with the class.

Answers
1 c (lines 1–2)   2 b (lines 7–9)   3 c (lines 15–17) 4 a (lines 19–20)   5 c (lines 27–30)

4

- Staying in their pairs, students discuss to what extent they agree with the article and which ideas seem most true of their work situation, their profession or industry. For students who are currently unemployed or yet to enter a profession, they can think about the article in relation to a profession that they know best or one that they are hoping to enter one day.

5

- Tell students to find the words in the article and choose the correct meaning based on the context.

- When they have finished, go through the answers with the class.

Answers
1 b 2 b 3 a 4 c 5 a 6 c

VOCABULARY Working life collocations (verb + noun)

6

- Explain that students are now going to look for some verb + noun combinations that are often seen together in the context of working life.

- Point out the first collocation in the list: *have a career*, and ask the class to find it in the introductory paragraph of the article. Point out that although the collocation is *have a career*, it appears as *careers that they have*.

- Give them two minutes to find as many of the verbs that go with the nouns as possible. You might set it as a race to see who can find the most.

Answers
b understand cultural differences, technology   c do a job   d attend meetings   e speak (to people) on the phone   f deal with a difficult situation, conflict   g get, process information   h prioritize tasks   i have fun

- Give them a few minutes to record these items in their vocabulary books.

• **Optional step.** Stronger students may be interested in finding more collocations in the article, including but not restricted to verb + noun combinations. These include: *today's workplace, the global economy, think critically, build good relations, appreciate differences*. You could also look at the collocations in the list of skills in Exercise 1 above, e.g. *interpersonal, organizational, management skills*.

7

• Ask students to complete the conversation with the correct verb from Exercise 6. To check their answers, put them in pairs and have them read the dialogue out loud as A and B.

Answers
1 do   2 deal with   3 speak   4 attend   5 process
6 understand   7 have   8 have

Extra activity

Edit the conversation

Have the students edit the conversation so that it describes their own job, or a mystery job that others have to guess.

TEACHING TIP

Spaced repetition

Unless students keep returning to new vocabulary they have studied, they are likely to forget much of it very quickly. To avoid this happening, test them at intervals. It is a good idea to check what they remember by the end of the same lesson, so find two minutes to spare before you finish. Put them in pairs; one student looks at the list while the other is not allowed to look. They take turns to prompt each other with either a verb or a noun. The other has to remember the corresponding noun or verb. Start the next lesson by challenging students to write as many verb + noun collocations about work that they can remember.

SPEAKING My skills

8 `21st` **CENTURY OUTCOMES**

• Explain that understanding your strengths and weaknesses is a key skill in today's workplace. Tell students to write down four skills that are important to them in their work and studies. Offer a personal example about your profession and say that interpersonal skills are essential for teaching.

• For students who are out of work, suggest that they make a list for their studies or for a profession of their choosing.

• Tell them to add two things they expect from their employer. Go around the class checking students' work and making suggestions where appropriate.

9

• Put students in small groups to compare their lists from Exercise 8, answering the questions. In order to fulfil the

21st CENTURY OUTCOME, students can consider what other skills they should have to progress in their career or enter the career of their choice.

• Conduct whole-class feedback. If many students have similar jobs or work in the same profession, ask if classmates agree; if they work in different jobs, treat feedback as a chance to learn about each other's chosen careers.

• **Optional step.** Explain how the information they wrote in Exercise 8 about their skill sets can be used to sell themselves in the jobs market. Ask them to turn to page 83 to look at an example CV and point out the Personal profile section near the start of this CV.

Ask them to think how they could use what they have written in a short passage for their CV. Give them ten minutes to write their Personal profile. Monitor closely, checking for errors and natural use of English. Tell them to file their profiles for future use!

▶ Set Workbook pages 8–9 for homework.

1.4 What do you do?

VOCABULARY Jobs

Extra activity

Guess the job!

Play a game to activate job names. Hand out three small slips of paper per student. Tell them to write, on each slip, the name of a job in English. They should try to avoid writing what other students might be writing by thinking of all sorts of jobs (not just *teacher* or *doctor*!). They should not show anyone.

Split the class into groups of six to eight students. Each group will need a hat or similar for the slips of paper, folded up and mixed together.

Divide these groups further into two teams of three or four students. Explain that each team is going to take turns to try to guess the name of the job. A member of the team takes a slip of paper out of the hat, reads it, and must communicate the job to his or her teammates without saying the name of the job, e.g. *This person works in a hospital but isn't a doctor. (a nurse)*

They continue for one minute (the other team times them), taking slips out and communicating them. Then the opposing team is given a minute to do the same.

When all the slips have been used, each team totals their score, getting one point per job guessed.

1

• Ask students to match the jobs with the photos. Ask them to identify the words used to describe someone who is learning a job.

• On the board, write more collocations: *an apprentice plumber/electrician/carpenter, a trainee nurse/teacher/ accountant, a law/medical student.*

2

• 🔊 5 Tell students to listen to how the jobs in Exercise 1 are pronounced, then to practise in pairs. Play the recording. Pay special attention to word stress in *engineer* and *researcher*, the silent *b* in *plumbing*, the initial schwa /ə/ in *apprentice* and *assistant* and the /ɜː/ sound in *nurse* and *researcher*.

LISTENING Asking about jobs

3

• Explain to students that they are going to listen to a conversation in which Jake is asking Martha about her job. Tell them to read the three questions in preparation for listening.

• 🔊 6 Play the recording.

Transcript

Jake:	*So what do you do?*
Martha:	*I'm an acoustics engineer.*
Jake:	*What's that? Like a sound engineer?*
Martha:	*No, not exactly. We help design spaces like concert halls or conference centres or theatres … spaces where the quality of sound is important.*
Jake:	*So who do you work for?*
Martha:	*I'm a trainee with an international firm of architects.*
Jake:	*Where are you based?*
Martha:	*I'm on a one-year training programme in Frankfurt.*
Jake:	*Wow! What does your job involve then?*
Martha:	*Well, I work on different projects. On each project I work on a different area, like buying materials or budgeting and planning or design.*
Jake:	*Is it a big firm, then?*
Martha:	*Yes, very big but there are only ten of us in the Frankfurt office.*
Jake:	*Do you mind me asking – what kind of contract are you on?*
Martha:	*Well, as I say. It's a one-year contract, but hopefully at the end of the year, they'll give me a permanent job. But I have to do well this year.*
Jake:	*Do you like the job?*
Martha:	*Yeah, it's great. I learn something new every day.*
Jake:	*Oh well, good luck. I hope you get the job.*
Martha:	*Thanks.*

• Give students a minute to confer in pairs. Then nominate individuals to share their answers.

4

• Indicate the table. Give students two minutes to try to formulate the missing words in the questions. You could elicit possible answers for the first question to get them started: *What do you do? What's your job? What do you work as?*

• 🔊 6 Play the recording again. While it is playing, write the incomplete questions on the board.

• When it has finished, invite volunteers to complete the questions on the board. Check that everyone agrees with the answers.

5

• From memory, students make notes about Martha's answers. They compare their answers with a partner. If they need reassurance, or there are gaps in their memory, play the recording one more time for them to check.

Pronunciation Intonation in questions

6a

• 🔊 7 Tell the students to listen to the questions in Exercise 4. Ask them to think about the intonation in the question, where it rises and falls. Let them discuss any rules about intonation that they can see.

6b

• Put students in pairs, allocating the roles of Martha and Jake respectively. They act out the conversation, paying attention to their intonation in the questions.

SPEAKING Talking about jobs and studies

7

• Give students two minutes to make brief notes about their own jobs or their studies. Help them with any unknown vocabulary. Indicate the Useful language box at the top of page 17.

• Put them in pairs again, perhaps with different partners from Exercise 6b. Tell them to interview one another, completing the empty table with the information that they discover.

• Go around the pairs, listening carefully for intonation in questions and any language points that are relevant to their working life.

• When they have finished talking, conclude the activity with feedback. First, elicit what the students have found out. After that, point out and discuss any interesting use of language or errors.

WRITING A formal letter

8

• Ask the class to read the job advertisement quickly. Ask them whether they might be interested in a job like this, and what their reasons would be for or against taking it.

• Ask the students to work in pairs to make a list of questions an applicant might have about the job. To help them with ideas, suggest they look at the conversation between Martha and Jake in the previous section.

• Invite them to ask questions about the job. Write their ideas on the board.

Suggested answers

Who would I be working for? What does the job involve? Where exactly in the South-east is the job based? How long is the job for? What type of contract would I have? Are qualifications or experience in sport necessary? How much travel would there be? What salary can I expect?

9

• Tell students to read the letter and check which questions the writer has about the job and whether any are the same as their questions.

Answers

Stefan asks 'Where exactly in the South-east is the job based?' and 'How long is the job for?'

10

• Ask students to examine the structure of the letter. Tell them to put the functions in the order they appear in the letter. Let students check their ideas with a partner.

• When students tell you the order, ask them to identify the beginning of each function.

Answers

b ('I saw your advertisement …')

d ('I am interested in applying …')

c ('The advertisement says …')

a ('I look forward to hearing from you.')

Writing skill Indirect questions

11a

• Tell students to complete the direct questions based on the polite questions from the letter. You may need to do the first one with the whole class to clarify the exercise.

• As they write, go around and check, focusing particularly on word order. Make sure whole-class feedback is very clear by writing it on the board. Leave a space between the questions.

Answers

1 Where is it?

2 How long does the contract last?

3 Is there a possibility of extending the contract?

• Write the indirect question above the first direct question on the board, making sure that the subject and verb are directly above those of the direct question. Ask the class what they notice about word order. Use arrows crossing over to clearly show the inversion in the direct question and its lack in the indirect question, and point out the use of *does* in 2.

• Ask why the last question is different from the first two and elicit that it is a *yes/no* question. Ask what word replaces *what, where, how long*, and so on in the indirect question, and point out the use of *if*.

• Direct students to page 140 for more information on indirect questions. They can do Exercise 6 in the Grammar summary for more practice.

Answers to Grammar summary exercise

1 When does the bank open?

2 How far is the station from here?

3 What does the job involve?

4 Do you know which company she works for?

5 Can you tell me how I apply for the job?

6 I'd like to know if you offer English courses.

11b

• Ask students to now rewrite in the other 'direction', making direct questions more polite. Remind them to think about the rules they have just looked at in Exercise 11a.

Answers

1 Can you tell me what kind of work it is?

2 Could you tell me where you are based?

3 Can you tell me if it is a big company?

4 I'd like to know what the work involves.

5 Do you know how long the interview usually takes?

6 Can you tell me how often buses go to the business park?

---

12   *21st* CENTURY OUTCOMES

• Ask students to look at the advertisement for film extras. Give them two minutes to decide what two questions they want to ask about it. They should consider the types of question that might be necessary for this job (to fulfil the 21st CENTURY OUTCOME).

• Give them ten minutes to write the letter. Suggest that they use Stefan Krantz's letter as a model, and that they be sure to ask politely!

13

• When they have finished, let them swap letters with a classmate. Instruct them to evaluate each other's letters according to the four-point checklist.

• Ask them whether they feel more capable now of writing a letter to enquire about a job. Ask them whether an email with the same purpose would be any different or not.

▶ Photocopiable communicative activity 1.2: Go to page 210 for further practice of jobs, skills and indirect questions. The teaching notes are on page 233.

▶ Set Workbook pages 10–11 for homework.

▶ Set Workbook Presentation 1 on pages 12–13 for homework.

2 Trends

UNIT AT A GLANCE

THEMES: The processes of change; identifying and instigating new trends

TED TALK: *How to start a movement.* Derek Sivers talk about the different roles in movements and argues that while leaders get the credit for starting a movement, the first followers are often the driving force.

AUTHENTIC LISTENING SKILLS: Content words

CRITICAL THINKING: Extending an argument

PRESENTATION SKILLS: Beginning and ending

GRAMMAR: Present simple and present continuous, Present continuous

VOCABULARY: Verbs describing trends, Relationships

PRONUNCIATION: Stress in everyday phrases

READING: *Identifying trends*

LISTENING: A conference meeting

SPEAKING: General habits and current habits, Describing trends, Meetings and introductions

WRITING: Formal and informal emails

WRITING SKILL: Formal and informal language

LEAD IN

• Ask students to look at the photo. Elicit some ideas about what is shown in the photo (see Background information box).

• Tell students that the TED Talk for this unit is *How to start a movement.* How do they think the photo illustrates that? (The first man is doing a silly walk and the others are following him.)

Background information

The caption states that this photo shows fans of Monty Python celebrating International Silly Walks Day. *Monty Python's Flying Circus* was a British comedy show popular from 1969 to 1974, which made famous a group of comedians who are known to this day, such as Michael Palin and John Cleese. The silly walks come from a sketch in Series 2 (1970) called *The Ministry of Silly Walks*, where John Cleese plays a civil servant walking through London doing a variety of silly walks.

TEDTALKS
BACKGROUND

1

• Tell the class to read the text about Derek Sivers and his talk. If necessary, clarify the following words: *founder* – a person who starts an organization such as a company, *get the credit* – receive recognition as the person who is responsible, *the driving force* – the source of most of the energy for something.

• Put students into pairs or threes to discuss the questions. When they are ready, encourage them to share their answers with the class, asking them to justify their ideas.

Answers

1 He helped to start an Internet music store called CD Baby.

2 Students' own answers. It is suggested that he is a leader because he has started at least two companies.

3 Students' own answers

KEY WORDS

2

• **Optional step.** Books closed. Write on the board the key words in the expressions in which they are found: 'you need guts', 'he is a nut', 'people ... really stand out', 'his was a lone voice', 'people ridiculed her'. Tell them that some of the words are colloquial or slang. Explain what *colloquial* and *slang* mean if necessary (*colloquial* means informal; *slang* is very informal and not appropriate in formal writing or polite conversation). Ask them to identify the less formal words and to justify their ideas. Explain that *guts* and *nut* in these expressions are informal and that informal words are often small words.

• Books open. Put students in pairs. Tell them to cover definitions a–e and to discuss and guess the meanings of the words in bold in sentences 1–5. Give them a couple of minutes for this.

• Ask students to do Exercise 2 on their own or in pairs. Students match the words in bold with their definitions.

Answers

1 c   2 a   3 e   4 b   5 d

• **Optional step.** To further check comprehension, ask follow-up questions: *What jobs/sports do you need to have* ***guts*** *to do? If someone that people think is a* ***nut*** *worked in TV, would they be better as a children's television presenter or a documentary maker? Who* ***stands out*** *at work, and why? What can you say about an accident if there is a* ***lone*** *survivor? Were you or any classmates ever* ***ridiculed*** *at school?*

AUTHENTIC LISTENING SKILLS Content words

3a

- Books closed. Write on the board: *When … listen … authentic speech … not … hear … understand … every … word … Generally … hear … important … content words … clearly … stressed … Try … construct … meaning … content words.*

- Tell the class that this is some advice. Ask the class to try to reconstruct the advice in writing.

- Invite one or two students to say their sentences to the class.

- Books open. Ask students to check their ideas with the Authentic listening skills box on page 19.

- Ask them what types of words are usually content words. Elicit that nouns, verbs, adjectives and adverbs tend to be content words, whereas prepositions, articles, pronouns, conjunctions, etc. tend not to be.

- Tell students to read and listen to the first sentence of the TED Talk. Explain that the content words are the underlined ones.

- 🅰 8 Play the recording. Get students to read the sentence out loud, paying attention to the stress so that it falls on the content words.

3b

- 🅰 9 Indicate sentence 2 from the talk. Play the recording.

- Elicit the missing words from students.

Answers
watch, three, lessons

2.1 How to start a movement

TEDTALKS

1

- Tell students that they are going to watch Derek Sivers' TED Talk. Ask them to read the two questions.

- ▶ 2.1 Play the TED Talk.

- Give students a minute to compare their answers before getting whole-class feedback.

Answers
1 a leader, a first follower, other followers
2 He thinks the first follower is more important (because without him the lone nut would remain a lone nut and not become a leader).

Transcript

0.12 So, ladies and gentlemen, at TED we talk a lot about leadership and how to make a movement. So let's watch a movement happen, start to finish, in under three minutes and dissect some lessons from it.

0.23 First, of course you know, a leader needs the guts to stand out and be ridiculed. But what he's doing is so easy to follow. So here's his first follower with a crucial role; he's going to show everyone else how to follow.

0.36 Now, notice that the leader embraces him as an equal. So, now it's not about the leader any more; it's about them, plural. Now, there he is calling to his friends. Now, if you notice that the first follower is actually an underestimated form of leadership in itself. It takes guts to stand out like that. The first follower is what transforms a lone nut into a leader. (Laughter) (Applause)

1.02 And here comes a second follower. Now it's not a lone nut, it's not two nuts – three is a crowd, and a crowd is news. So a movement must be public. It's important to show not just the leader, but the followers, because you find that new followers emulate the followers, not the leader.

1.19 Now, here come two more people, and immediately after, three more people. Now we've got momentum. This is the tipping point. Now we've got a movement. So, notice that, as more people join in, it's less risky. So those that were sitting on the fence before, now have no reason not to. They won't stand out, they won't be ridiculed, but they will be part of the in-crowd if they hurry. (Laughter) So, over the next minute, you'll see all of those that prefer to stick with the crowd because eventually they would be ridiculed for not joining in. And that's how you make a movement.

1.55 But let's recap some lessons from this. So first, if you are the type like the shirtless dancing guy that is standing alone, remember the importance of nurturing your first few followers as equals so it's clearly about the movement, not you. OK, but we might have missed the real lesson here.

2.13 The biggest lesson, if you noticed – did you catch it? – is that leadership is over-glorified. That, yes, it was the shirtless guy who was first, and he'll get all the credit, but it was really the first follower that transformed the lone nut into a leader. So, as we're told that we should all be leaders, that would be really ineffective.

2.33 If you really care about starting a movement, have the courage to follow and show others how to follow. And when you find a lone nut doing something great, have the guts to be the first one to stand up and join in. And what a perfect place to do that, at TED.

Thanks. (Applause)

Note the differences in British English and North American English shown at the foot of the spread. In this unit, these focus on pronunciation differences and a difference in vocabulary. See Teaching tip 1 on page 6 of the Introduction for ideas on how to present and practise these differences.

2

- Ask the class to look at the four sentences and circle the options they think are correct.

- ▶️2.1 Play the first part of the talk from 0.00–1.02.

- Nominate individuals to share their answers with the class.

Answers

1 guts, ridiculed   2 follow   3 an equal   4 nut

3

- Again, ask the class to attempt the task before they watch, and then to check their answers with the recording.

- ▶️2.1 Play the second part of the talk from 1.02–1.55.

- Ask individuals to read out their completed sentences. They could underline content words first. (See Authentic listening skills on the previous page.)

Answers

1 crowd   2 followers   3 risky   4 movement
5 ridiculed

4

- Put students in pairs to discuss the correct options for questions 1–4.

- ▶️2.1 Play the third part of the talk from 1.55 to the end.

- Together, students check their answers.

Answers

1 b   2 a   3 b   4 a

VOCABULARY IN CONTEXT

5

- ▶️2.2 Play the clips from the talk. When each multiple-choice question appears, students choose the correct definition. Discourage the more confident students from always giving the answer by asking individuals to raise their hand if they think they know.

Transcript and subtitles

*1 So here's his first follower with a **crucial** role; he's going to show everyone else how to follow.*
   a strange
   b very important
   c new

*2 ... the first follower is actually an **underestimated** form of leadership in itself.*
   a not paid well
   b not considered important
   c not official

*3 This is the **tipping point**. Now we've got a movement.*
   a turning point
   b lowest point
   c interesting point

*4 So those that were **sitting on the fence** before, now have no reason not to.*
   a feeling bored
   b not wanting to choose
   c feeling nervous

*5 But let's **recap** some lessons from this.*
   a learn
   b try to find
   c look again at

*6 Remember the importance of **nurturing** your first few followers as equals.*
   a training
   b employing
   c taking care of

Answers

1 b   2 b   3 a   4 b   5 c   6 c

TEACHING TIP

Exploring images behind words' meanings

Some of these words convey interesting images which may make them more memorable to students. Some images can be seen in the etymology of the word: *nurture* means 'to give food needed to live'; it has the same origin as *nurse* and *nourishment*. Mothers nurture their babies. Other expressions can actually be drawn: *tipping point* is arguably more memorable if you draw some scales and slowly add weights to one side until they suddenly tip. *Sitting on the fence* is better understood if you know what a fence looks like. By introducing these images along with vocabulary, you are providing the students with a more memorable learning opportunity.

6

- Give pairs a few minutes to complete the sentences in their own words. Monitor to help them with ideas.

- Give the class an opportunity to share their favourite sentences with one another.

Suggested answers

1 ... use it. / ... practise saying the words.

2 ... how important your colleagues are. / ... first impressions.

3 ... if two friends are arguing, and you don't want to make either friend unhappy, you can sit on the fence and not express your opinion.

4 ... each employee's skills and talents. / ... teamwork.

CRITICAL THINKING Extending an argument

7

- Put students into pairs or small groups to answer the questions. Encourage them to think of more than one answer for each question. Give them a few minutes for this.

> **Suggested answers**
>
> 1 Leaders are important but need followers to start a movement; in a movement, the first follower is at least as important as the leader; the first follower shows people how to follow.
>
> 2 Once a movement has started, it is easy to follow, but the first follower risks being ridiculed, so must be courageous.
>
> 3 It might take courage not to follow when everyone is following, so you risk being isolated. You may need to be courageous if you don't know what the consequences of not following are.

8

- Ask students to read Sun Kim's comment and ask whether anyone in their group shares Sun Kim's feelings.

- Use the post as an opportunity to open the class discussion about following, or deliberately *not* following the crowd, encouraging personal examples from their lives.

> **TEACHING TIP**
>
> **Comment / Tweet / Post**
>
> As well as reading other people's opinions of the TED Talks, why not get students posting their own comments, either for real online or simply handwritten and 'posted' up around the room for classmates to read? Such written comments are personal interpretations of the talk content.
>
> There are various ways of commenting online:
>
> 1 On TED.com. Students will need to sign up, which only takes a minute. Once they have an account, they can comment on this and all future talks they watch on the course.
>
> 2 On a class blog, wiki or forum. Your class or your school may have its own website or blog where students can post their work. If not, consider setting one up for activities such as this.
>
> 3 On the students' own social media, such as Twitter or Facebook.
>
> Students draft a short summary of the discussion they had in Exercise 7. To encourage brevity, limit the number of words to thirty or even less. You could even restrict them to the Twitter 140-character limit. This forces them to prioritize exactly what they want to say about the talk.

PRESENTATION SKILLS Beginning and ending

9

- Put students in pairs. Tell half the pairs to think of as many ways to begin a talk as they can, and the other half to think of ways to end a talk. After a minute or two, bring together pairs that so that they can tell each other their ideas for beginning and ending talks.

- Elicit ideas and put them on the board in two lists.

> **Suggested answers**
>
> 1 You could begin with an anecdote, an example, a joke, a picture, a statement of intention or the objective of the talk, a problem, etc.
>
> 2 You could end with a conclusion, a summary, a question to think about, a recap of what's been said, a directive (as in Derek Sivers' talk), etc.

10

- Tell students to look at the Presentation skills box. Together with the whole class, compare students' answers with those in the box. Did they have different ideas to these ones?

11

- ▷2.3 Play the clips from the talk.

- Ask how Derek Sivers begins and ends his talk.

> **Answer**
>
> He begins by introducing the topic – leadership – and why he is talking about it, which is because on TED they talk about leadership a lot. He ends by emphasizing his main idea one last time, simply and powerfully: 'Have the guts to be the first one to stand up and join in.'

- **Optional step.** Challenge students to remember how Mark Bezos started and ended his talk in Unit 1. He starts by talking about who he is and what his job is. He ends by making a conclusion and issuing a directive: he tells his audience to 'Get in the game' and start helping out.

12

- Tell students to write down the names of any groups that they belong to: clubs, interest groups, online communities, associations, professional organizations, consumer groups, etc. Ask them to choose one group that they could try to persuade people to join.

- Put them in pairs. Tell them to help each other to write a suitable beginning and ending for a talk persuading listeners to join their groups.

13

- Put the students in new pairs (see Teaching tip below). Give them time to each give the beginning and ending of their presentations to one another.

- **Optional step.** Ask students to write the rest of the talk they have started, either in class if there's time, or at home ready to present in the next lesson.

Three ways to pair up students

If students have been working in the same pairs during the lesson, you may decide to change the groupings, for a variety of reasons. Here are some simple techniques for doing this:

1 Imagine these are the pairs: AA BB CC DD EE. Move the first student A to join the last student E. Immediately, everyone is working with a different student, with minimal disruption: AB BC CD DE E<u>A</u>!

2 Use this classroom management issue as an opportunity to recycle language. Before the lesson, prepare sentence halves containing recently learned phrases, e.g.

You need guts …	*… to dance alone.*
People think he is …	*… a nut.*
You really stand …	*… out if you do things differently.*
His was a lone …	*… voice.*
Three is a …	*… crowd.*

Shuffle them, hand out one per person, and ask them to find their new partner. Once they have found each other, ask them to sit down with that person.

3 Assign letters to half the class and repeat the same letters to the other half. Tell them to sit with the person with the same letter as them, i.e. AB CD EF GA BC DE FG → AA BB CC DD EE FF GG.

▶ Set Workbook pages 14–15 for homework.

2.2 Who are you following?

GRAMMAR Present simple and present continuous

1

- **Optional step.** Books closed. Dictate the definition without mentioning *Twitter* or *tweets*. Ask students to write down the definition and guess the missing words. You could replace the missing words with a bird sound!

- Books open. Ask students to answer the questions. Write on the board supplementary questions for pairs to discuss: *Do you know others who use Twitter? Why do people use Twitter? What advantages and disadvantages does it have over other social media such as Facebook and Instagram? What would make you start using Twitter if you haven't already?*

2

- Ask the students to find answers to the questions in the infographic. Field their answers with the class.

Answers

1 645,750,000 active users   2 very fast, by 135,000 every day   3 trending topics   4 individuals, companies and governments (possibly also the 40% of Twitters who just watch other people tweet)

3

- Direct students' attention to the Grammar box and the description of Twitter. Tell them to answer questions 1 and 2.

- Students can check their answers and overall understanding of the present simple and present continuous by turning to the Grammar summary on page 142. If you feel that students need more controlled practice before continuing, they could do Exercise 1 in the Grammar summary. Otherwise, you could continue on to Exercise 4 in the unit and set the Grammar summary exercise for homework.

Answers

1 *Comment* and *follow* describe actions that are generally true.

2 *Are looking* and *are … saying* describe actions that are happening now or around now.

Answers to Grammar summary exercise

1

1 A: Do you smoke?   B: I'm trying

2 A: are you reading   B: writes

3 A: Is anyone sitting   B: He's just getting

4 A: usually take, are doing   B: never take

5 A: does your company do   B: make

4

• Explain that the sentences are related to the infographic. Working on their own, students complete the sentences with either the present simple or the present continuous.

• Let them compare their answers with a partner before inviting one student to read out the whole text while the others listen and check.

Answers

3 send   4 are sending   5 don't tweet   6 look
7 follow*   8 follow*   9 is also growing   10 employs
11 is recruiting

* It is more likely that we would use the simple here, as given, to express a general truth. If a current time adverbial such as *at the moment* were added, these would more likely express trends and the continuous form would be more accurate.

5

• Indicate the Grammar box. Ask students to match the sentences with the uses of the present continuous.

• Again, students can check their answers by turning to the Grammar summary on page 142. If you feel that students need more controlled practice before continuing, they could do Exercises 2–7 in the Grammar summary. Otherwise, you could continue on to Exercise 6 in the unit and set the Grammar summary exercises for homework.

Answers

1 b   2 c   3 a

Answers to Grammar summary exercises

2

1 I'm looking   2 I'm going   3 Is he expecting   4 he's having   5 you're waiting   6 isn't working

3

1 correct   2 don't understand   3 correct   4 want
5 don't have   6 correct   7 know

4

1 are going   2 is increasing   3 is getting   4 are eating
5 is getting   6 are living

5

1 at the moment   2 every day   3 currently   4 this week   5 usually   6 now

6

1 What are you doing at the moment?

2 I'm working as a chef ... but I'm looking for a new job

3 I like the work generally but right now I'm not learning anything new.

4 What do you want to learn?

5 I hope to be a pastry chef ...

6 I'm currently doing a French pastry course.

7 I go to classes every week.*

8 I often think about training … but I never do anything about it

* *I'm going* would also be possible here, following on from *I'm doing* and if the speaker sees the classes as temporary, but the adverbial *every week* suggests the present simple.

7

1 ~~are often eating~~ → often eat   2 ~~only stay~~ → 'm only staying   3 ~~do you do~~ → are you doing   4 ~~are owning~~ → own   5 ~~improve~~ → are improving

6

• Put students in pairs. Tell them to identify the different uses of the present continuous as presented in the Grammar box.

Answers

1 c   2 a   3 a   4 b   5 c   6 b

7

• Ask students to decide whether the sentences are correct, and to correct them if not. Tell them to think of the reason each time, relating it to the information in the Grammar summary.

• In feedback, make sure you ask them why they think it is right or wrong. Don't accept their answer until they have justified it.

8

• Ask students to complete the conversation using the two
verb forms. As they are writing, monitor carefully to check all
students are on task and clear on the distinctions.

• Let them check their answers by reading the dialogue as A
and B.

• In whole-class feedback, ask two volunteers to take the
roles of A and B and to read the dialogue out loud for everyone
to check.

Answers

A: 1 How often do you use Twitter?

B: 2 I read other people's tweets every day, but I don't
tweet.

A: And what is Twitter good for?

B: 3 Well, I'm a scientist and I usually use it for my work.
4 It's very important for me to know what is happening in
my field currently.

A: 5 So who are you following at the moment?

B: 6 Right now, I'm following a conversation between two
scientists in Canada about the environment.

A: And what about other subjects?

B: 7 Sometimes I look at what famous people are saying
at the moment about things in the news. 8 This week a lot
of people are talking about the situation in the Middle East.

Extra activity

Social media interview

Explain to students that they are going to interview one
another in a similar way to the dialogue in Exercise 8. Put
them in groups and tell them to write at least five questions
to ask classmates about their social media habits. Monitor
as they write, ensuring clear use of English and focusing on
use of tenses.

Put students in pairs. Make sure that partners are not from
the same original group. Give them time to interview each
other and encourage follow-up questions.

When they have stopped talking, get some feedback about
students' use of social media by asking them to share
interesting things they found out.

9

• Create two boxes on the board and label them *present
simple* and *present continuous* respectively.

• Ask students to look at the time expressions in the
book. Invite students to come up to the board and write one

expression in either box. When they have written all seven
items on the board, ask the students whether they are right.
Confirm or question their decisions.

Answers

Present simple: every day   sometimes   usually

Present continuous: at the moment   currently   now   this
week

• Ask students if they can think of more expressions to add.
For present simple, they may come up with *never, always,
every week/month/year, most days, occasionally,* etc. For
present continuous, *today, right now, this year,* etc.

10

• Put students in pairs. Ask them to discuss the sentences
and where the expressions in Exercise 9 can go.

Answers

Sometimes,/Every day,/Usually, We sometimes/usually
meet to practise our English together every day.

At the moment,/Currently,/This week, I am currently/now
learning English in evening classes now/at the moment/
this week.

SPEAKING General habits and current habits

11   *21st* CENTURY OUTCOMES

• **Optional step.** To illustrate the next activity, have students
interview you on the topics listed in the book. Elicit the
questions they will need for the first subject, i.e. *What do you
do?* or *What is your work?* and *What are you doing at work at
the moment?* Be prepared to answer questions about the six
different areas of your life.

• Give students a couple of minutes to think and prepare
what they want to say about each area.

• Put students in small groups. Let them ask each other
about their lives, making sure that they talk about what they
normally do and whether they are doing anything different from
normal. Encourage them to explain if they are doing something
different from normal to fulfil the 21st CENTURY OUTCOME of
explaining your habits and motivation.

• Listen in on their conversations, checking for correct use of
English, especially around the use of tense.

• Conclude the lesson by asking students to share anything
interesting that they learned about the members of their group.

▶ Photocopiable communicative activity 2.1: Go to
page 211 for further practice of present simple and present
continuous. The teaching notes are on page 234.

▶ Set Workbook pages 16–17 for homework.

2.3 The next big thing

READING Identifying trends

1

• Put students in pairs. Ask them to read the predictions and decide whether the people were right. Elicit their answers, and any examples they can think of, in a whole-class discussion.

Answers

1 Although he was slightly premature with 2001, many people read newspapers online now. For example, by 2013 more than half of British adults were accessing their news online.

2 Watkins was right that photographs would be sent around the world, but he didn't get the method correct, or the time. Telegraph was the dominant telecommunications system in 1900, and in fact, it was possible even back then to send images in this way. The fax machine had been in existence since 1843, allowing images to be sent long distances. Nowadays, we can share photos with friends online, on sites such as Instagram and Facebook.

3 While there is a great potential for computer technology in classrooms, it is probably untrue that learning and classrooms are 'dominated' by IT, except in a few more privileged parts of the world and wealthy institutions. However, many classrooms are equipped with computers, projectors or interactive whiteboards, and many learners carry their own portable devices which they may or may not use for learning.

Background information

Arthur C Clarke

Clarke was a prolific *futurist*, or person who imagines what life will be like in the future. He famously predicted telecommunications satellites in 1945. Less well known are his predictions of a 'global library' by 2005 (something like the Internet), global positioning technology, satellite television and the mobile phone, which he called a 'personal transceiver'. He wrote that people would 'be able to call a person anywhere on Earth merely by dialling a number'.

2

• Still in pairs, ask students to think about how these people are able to spot such future trends. Give them a minute to discuss the question before opening it up to the whole class.

Suggested answers

They study technology and think about possible applications; they use their imagination; they think about current problems and how technology might solve those problems; they think about what they would like to see in the future (or possibly what they fear!)

3

• Give students five minutes to read the article. They need to compare their ideas in Exercise 2 with the author's.

Answers

The author describes three ways of identifying future trends. You can look at today's trends and where they are leading us, you can look at trends in other sectors or areas of life and apply them to your sector or you can notice how people are playing and the creativity that comes from play.

4

• Show the class the summary of the article and explain that they need to find words and phrases from the article to complete the summary.

• Let them compare their summaries in pairs.

Suggested answers

1 look and listen to what is happening now / keep your eyes and ears open

2 measured the amount of space

3 newspapers

4 (so much) more information to read

5 general trends / trends in everyday life

6 your (own) sector

7 how people are playing / people's hobbies and things they do to have fun

8 free

5

• Tell students to look for examples in the text that illustrate each way of spotting a trend. If you think that they need to read the article again, give them more time to do this. Otherwise, you could discuss the answers together as a whole class.

Answers

First way – Naisbitt made predictions by analysing the amount of space newspapers devoted to certain issues.

Second way – a clothes company could use its observations that in other areas of life people are becoming more active and that companies are collaborating more with other companies to team up with a sports clothing manufacturer to make a new range of clothing.

Third way – Apple and Facebook were both started on the basis of free-time activity by their founders.

6

• Explain that the word *trend* collocates with some adjectives more commonly than others, and that the article contains some common adjective–*trend* collocates.

- Encourage students to look for the adjectives by scanning (see below); set them the challenge to be the first to find all six adjectives in the shortest time.

- When the first student announces they have finished, ask them to give you the six words immediately. Write them on the board. Confirm with the rest of the class that this person has indeed won.

- Now give everyone a minute to match the adjectives to categories 1–4.

Answers

1 emerging (lines 14–15), new (line 21) 2 major (lines 1–2)
3 future (line 8), current (line 28) 4 general (line 20)

7

- Ask students to think of examples of the two trends and discuss them briefly in class.

Suggested answers

1 online payment systems, e.g. PayPal; using contactless debit cards; one-click shopping at large online stores, e.g. Amazon; Bitcoins and other alternative currencies

2 greater numbers of people running; pilates; unusual sports, e.g. Tai chi, Capoeira; diets that involve cutting out gluten or particular sugars, e.g. lactose; fasting one or two days a week

VOCABULARY Verbs describing trends

8

- Tell students to match each verb in bold with its opposite in the box.

Answers

1 growing – shrinking 2 increasing – decreasing
3 improving – getting worse 4 becoming more widespread – becoming less common 5 rising – falling
6 getting richer – getting poorer

- You may be asked about the difference between *get* and *become*. Point out that although the two verbs are often interchangeable, there is a slight change in register, or formality, with *get* being slightly less formal (and more common) than *become*. Also, we can see here that *get* often collocates with shorter comparative adjectives (*get poorer/ richer/worse*) whereas *become* tends to be used with longer comparatives (*become more widespread / less common*).

9

- Put students in pairs. If the class consists of students from the same country, they can all discuss which statements in Exercise 8 they agree with for their country. If the class is multinational, they can tell someone from elsewhere about their country.

- In whole-class feedback, invite students to talk about the most interesting trends in their opinion.

Answers

Students' own answers

10

- Let students work alone to complete the sentences with the verbs and verb phrases from Exercise 8.

- You may decide to write the possible answers on the board for clarity, as some sentences have more than one answer.

SPEAKING Describing trends

11 **21st CENTURY OUTCOMES**

• Ask students to look at the list of areas and to choose one to write about. Tell them to write a sentence on a slip of paper describing a trend in that area.

• Put them in groups of three to five. Tell them to take turns reading each trend and discussing possible reasons for them. Encourage them to think of as many possible reasons as they can in order to fulfil the 21st CENTURY OUTCOME of drawing conclusions about general trends.

• **Optional step.** When they have finished discussing their trends, collect all the slips and redistribute them so that each group has new trends to discuss. This time, however, they try to think of reasons why this trend isn't true or isn't really happening.

Extra activity

The good old days

Explain that they are going to play a game in which they have to complain about modern life. They should imagine that they are grumpy old men or women who remember the past as a wonderful time with none of the problems that exist today.

They play in pairs or small groups. The first person starts by complaining about any aspect of modern life, e.g. *Food is getting more and more expensive.* The next person must complain about something different. They continue until a player can't think of anything to complain about. The last person to fail to think of something bad to say is the winner!

▶ Set Workbook pages 18–19 for homework.

2.4 How are you doing?

VOCABULARY Relationships

1

• Ask students to complete the table with words from the box.

• Draw the table on the board and invite students to help complete it with their answers.

2

• With the class, elicit the informal expressions, encouraging students to guess if they aren't sure.

• **Optional step.** Get students to add more words that they know to the two columns in Exercise 1, e.g. *workmate*, *flatmate*, *boyfriend*.

3

• Put students in pairs. Students choose three people from Exercise 1 to discuss the differences in greetings you would expect with them. You could give an example in front of the class to illustrate the exercise. Use the photograph to teach *bow* if necessary.

Note: In Britain it is usual to shake hands with business colleagues or friends that you don't see every day. People might just smile and say *hello* to colleagues they see every day. With friends and family, it is common to kiss on the cheek, especially with members of the opposite sex. They may just give a nod of the head to neighbours that they don't know very well.

• In feedback, ask students whether they agree with one another. Encourage them to act out the greetings to clarify the actions. Discuss any cultural differences between members of multinational classes, and whether they are aware of differences in other countries.

LISTENING A conference meeting

4

• Set the gist question; tell students to mark with a tick the correct column for each relationship depending on what they hear in the conversation.

• ▣ **10** Play the recording.

• Quickly establish the relationships.

Transcript

J: Hello, Theresa, good to see you. How are you doing?

T: Yeah, things are going very well, thanks. What brings you here?

J: We're here to present our new product.

T: Oh, well, good luck with that. By the way, this is Franco, my marketing assistant.

J: Hi, Franco. Good to meet you. I'm Jim Hyland.

F: Pleased to meet you, Jim.

J: Is it your first conference?

F: Yes, I'm doing an internship at NYT, in Theresa's department.

J: How's it going? Is Theresa working you very hard?

F: Well, yes and no, but I love the job.

T: When's your presentation, Jim?

J: It's tomorrow at 4.30. Please come along.

T: Yes, I'd love to. Well, we have a meeting to go to now, but great to see you and see you tomorrow.

J: Great. See you then. Have a good day.

5

- Tell students that they are going to listen again, this time for the language used. Tell them to choose the phrases that they hear.

- 🅐 10 Play the recording again.

- Students read out the correct phrases to the class.

> #### Answers
>
> 1 How are you doing?   2 Things are going very well, thanks.   3 this is Franco   4 Good to meet you.   5 Pleased to meet you, Jim.   6 How's it going?   7 great to see you

- Ask the class to comment on the level of formality in the conversation. Point out that the phrases Jim uses are quite informal, both with Theresa, who he knows, and to Franco, who he is meeting for the first time. The other phrases in the exercise, which are not spoken, are correct English and would be suitable in formal situations, such as meeting an older person in a more senior position of authority.

> #### Background information
> #### Business English
>
> Most business settings these days are quite informal in nature, certainly in North America and Europe. Generally speaking, business is all about making good, long-lasting relationships with people, so friendliness and a level of relaxed comfort communicating with colleagues and clients is essential.

Pronunciation Stress in everyday phrases

6

- Tell students to listen to and repeat the phrases from Exercise 5. Ask them to pay attention to the stress.

- 🅐 11 Play the recording, ensuring everyone repeats the phrases.

- **Optional step.** Tell students to listen carefully and mark the stress on the phrases in Exercise 5. They can underline the stressed syllables, for example. Play the recording again. Ask them if they notice any repeated stress patterns. On the majority of the phrases there is a repeated pattern of stressed–unstressed–stressed–unstressed, or ● • ● • Let them practise on their own for a minute.

Transcript

The stressed syllables are shown in bold.

1   **How** are you **do**ing?

2   **Things** are going very **well**, thanks.

3   **This** is **Fran**co.

4   Hi, **Fran**co. **Good** to **meet** you.

5   Pleased to **meet** you, **Jim**.

6   **How's** it **go**ing?

7   **Great** to **see** you.

SPEAKING Meetings and introductions

7

- Explain to students that they are going to practise a similar conversation to the one they heard in the previous exercises. Give them a minute to read the roles.

- Put them in groups of three and assign each student a role: A, B or C. Point out the Useful language box on page 27 and ask them to decide if they are going to need more or less formal expressions, and to identify and underline a few phrases that might be useful.

- In their own time, let the students start the role play. Monitor unobtrusively to check that each group is on task and using the language appropriately.

- When they have finished, have them change roles, so that they can practise a different role.

Successful role plays

Why is it that some role plays work fantastically while others fall flat on their face? We must remember that students may be unused to improvising, embarrassed at free speaking in character, challenged by the linguistic demands of thinking on their feet in English and uncomfortable at doing such a strange activity! There's a lot we can do to help.

- Give them the preparation time they need. If necessary, let them make notes, or at least think about the language they will use. Don't rush them!

- Write a suggested first line on the board to get the conversation started. In this role play, for example, you might suggest: *Diane, it is you!* or *Excuse me for a second, but I think I know that man standing over there …*

- Background music hides embarrassed voices. Some quiet music will make students feel less conscious, and also will help set the scene if the role play is set in a restaurant, as it is here.

- Encourage actions and directions, such as having them stand up, shake hands, and so on. Props such as business cards, hats, ties and briefcases can all help students get into character and spark creative improvisation.

- Do the role play more than once. Treat the first one as a rehearsal, a chance to try out the language and make mistakes. Then the second and third times can be performances, possibly even culminating in performing in front of the class.

When students are ready, get them to record the conversation, for their eyes or ears only. They can video themselves on their phone or just record the audio. As well as affording them a chance to check their English, it creates another incentive to perform well.

WRITING Formal and informal emails

8

- Books closed. Tell students that they have just ten seconds to decide which email is more formal and which is informal. Tell them to open their books, time the ten seconds, then tell them to close their books.

- When you confirm the answer with the class, ask them what they saw that led them to that decision.

Answer
Email A is informal, B formal
They are likely to have noticed the contractions and ellipsis in A, and perhaps the greeting.

- Ask the class which email they think is more appropriate, from what we already know about Jim and Theresa (we met them on the previous page). Make sure students are aware of the effect that an overly formal email would likely have on the receiver. The more formal version of the email would probably seem too distant and therefore unfriendly to Jim, who may wonder whether he had said something to Theresa to upset her or make her angry.

Writing skill Formal and informal language

9a

- Put students in pairs. Get them to underline the differences between the two emails.

- Let them compare what they found with another pair.

Answers
Hi / Dear Jim
Good / It was good to see you at the conference last week. **We're / The company is having / organizing** a **party to say goodbye to / farewell party for** Isabelle Jacobs, **who's / who is** leaving at the end of the month **(details attached). Just / I just** wondered if **you'd / you would** like to come. **(The details are attached.)**
Look / I look forward to hearing from you.
All the best / Kind regards
Theresa

- Elicit some of the features of informal email. These include: shortened sentences, with subjects and possibly verbs missing (*Good to see you…*); informal greetings and closing expressions (*Hi, All the best*); informal vocabulary (*having*) and contractions (*you'd*).

9b

- Ask the class to identify the more formal words and expressions in pairs a and b. Do this as a whole class.

Answers
1 b 2 a 3 a 4 b

10

- Show students the email and ask them whether they think that it is written in an appropriate style for the message and the relationship between writer and recipient. Confirm that it is written in an informal style and should be written more formally.

- Give students five minutes to rewrite the email. Monitor attentively to check that students are successfully editing the email and writing it in a more appropriate style.

> **Suggested answer**
>
> Dear Paul,
>
> Thank you for your email about visiting our showroom to look at bathrooms. That is not a problem. We just need to know when is a convenient time for you. We are having some building work in the showroom next week, so I think the following week is probably better.
>
> I look forward to hearing from you.
>
> Kind regards,
>
> Tim
>
> (Customer Services)

11 **21st CENTURY OUTCOMES**

• Working on their own, students write a reply to Tim, thanking him and suggesting when you will visit.

> **Suggested answer**
>
> Dear Tim,
>
> Thank you for your reply. I think that I will be able to visit the showroom on Tuesday 23rd March, if that is convenient for you.
>
> I look forward to hearing from you.
>
> Kind regards,
>
> Paul

12

• Explain that students are going to evaluate each other's emails using the five-point checklist. Ask them to swap their emails with a partner. They should check the emails carefully for the features of formal emails listed in the checklist, in order to fulfil the 21st CENTURY OUTCOMES of Using email to inform, using the appropriate register.

• Give them a minute or two to report what they have noticed back to the writers.

▶ Photocopiable communicative activity 2.2: Go to page 212 for further practice of the language of meetings and introductions. The teaching notes are on page 234.

▶ Set Workbook pages 20–21 for homework.

▶ Set Workbook Writing 1 on pages 22–23 for homework.

LISTENING

▶ Teaching tip 3: Using the Review lessons, Introduction, page 7.

1

• Ask students to read the text about Broken Spoke. (*Spokes* are the thin metal rods that connect the outside of a bicycle wheel to the centre.)

• Put students in pairs to discuss the questions before sharing the answers with the whole class.

Answers
1 People of all ages and backgrounds go to Broken Spoke, including homeless people.
2 Visitors learn how to ride and repair bicycles. They can also learn how to renovate old bikes so that they can be used again.

2

• Tell students that they are going to listen to an interview with one of the founders of Broken Spoke. Let them read the questions first.

• 🔊12 Play the recording.

Transcript

I = *Interviewer*, **E** = *Eleanor*

I: *So, first of all, can you just explain what Broken Spoke does?*

E: *Well, we do three things: we run training courses – how to ride bikes and how to repair them, we sell bicycle parts and we have drop-in workshops where people repair their own bikes with our tools and our help.*

I: *And is it a business or a charity?*

E: *It's a non-profit business.*

I: *Which activity makes the most money?*

E: *Actually, we get equal income from each of the three activities.*

I: *And why did you start it? Did you want people to have a more healthy form of transport? Was it because you love cycling? Or ...*

E: *Yes, it's partly about physical health. Cycling is healthy. But also it's about building community and people sharing what they know with each other. We live in a world where people don't have the skills or knowledge to repair things when they break. I wanted to do something practical and direct about that, something that brings people together, teaches them a skill and helps the environment at the same time.*

I: *And is this a model that you can repeat – it'll work in other situations?*

E: *Oh, yes. There are lots of similar projects – in the UK, the USA and around the world. The problem for us here in Oxford is that renting a workshop is so expensive.*

The business model works, but the difficulty is finding a place with a reasonable rent. We're renting this place now at a low rent but it's only temporary.

I: *Well, I hope you find somewhere more permanent. I think what you're doing is fantastic.*

E: *Thank you.*

• When students have finished listening, let them compare answers with their partners before asking individuals to give them to the whole class.

Answers
1 It's a non-profit business.
2 She hopes it promotes healthy activity, helps build a sense of community and encourages people to share knowledge. (It helps the environment too.)
3 The main problem is finding workshop space with a low rent in the city.

3

• Point out the incomplete notes to students. Explain that they need to complete them with the missing words. Tell them to try to complete the notes individually and then compare their answers in pairs before listening to check.

• 🔊12 Play the recording.

Answers
1 parts 2 workshops 3 healthy 4 community
5 environment 6 USA 7 business

GRAMMAR

4

• Ask students to recall the various areas of grammar that they have studied so far. Ask them which area the next activity is testing (adverbs and expressions of frequency).

• Students work on their own to put the expressions in the correct place. Explain that there is sometimes more than one correct position.

• When they have finished, nominate students to say the answers.

• Gauge how easy or difficult students found the exercise by finding out how many they got correct. Suggest that if they found it hard, they should look again at the rules on page 140.

5

• Put students in pairs to help each other complete the comments using the present simple and present continuous.

• Elicit the answers in whole-class feedback.

VOCABULARY

6

• Decide whether the students can refer to their notes or vocabulary books for this activity. Letting them do so may encourage them to keep written records of the vocabulary they have studied, or you may prefer to treat this as a test.

• Tell them to choose the correct options to complete the text.

• For feedback, nominate students to read out one sentence at a time.

DISCUSSION

7

• Put students in pairs. Tell them to list the ways that Broken Spoke is making a positive contribution to society. Encourage them to look at the indirect effects such as providing people with a sense of purpose, creating a social centre for people with similar interests and so on.

8

• Put pairs together into groups of four. Have them pool their ideas, then tell them that they are going to apply the same non-profit business model to another type of business. Let them choose one of the three types of business themselves, or they could choose another sector entirely. However, they must agree on one.

• Groups discuss how the business runs and how it can benefit society. They make notes.

• As they are talking, write the following questions on the board and tell students to use the questions to guide their discussion.

What does your business do?

Is it a business, a charity, or something else?

Why is it a good idea?

How does it make a positive contribution to society?

• Bring the whole class together to explain their business plans.

• **Optional step**. Have students vote on the business plan that is most likely to already exist; the most imaginative plan; the plan they would most like to develop.

SPEAKING

9

• Put students in pairs and assign each the roles of either Jim or Ursula.

• Decide whether students can complete the conversation orally without writing or not. If you think they can do it without written support, tell them to put their pens down. They should complete the conversation using the prompts orally only. Explain that they can do it slowly the first time, then try again more quickly the second time.

• When they are reasonably fluent at the dialogue, have them swap roles and try again.

- Let them write up the dialogue in the spaces provided. For less confident students or classes, let them write the complete dialogue before reading them out loud.

Answers

1 How do you do, Jim?

2 I'm Ursula.

3 Pleased to meet you, Ursula.

4 Do you work here?

5 I'm currently working as a trainee architect – just for six months.

6 I'm still a student, really.

7 Where are you studying? / Where do you study? *

8 My college is based in Nice in France.

9 And how are you finding / do you find the work here? *

10 It's a very interesting company to work for.

11 Well, it's a pleasure to meet you, Ursula.

12 Nice to meet you too.

* Both the continuous and simple are possible here, depending on whether the speaker views the studying / working as temporary or permanent.

WRITING

10

- Ask students to read the letter and say what the purpose of the letter is and what the problem is. Elicit that it is enquiring about a job but that it is too informal.

- **Optional step**. Get the class to brainstorm the elements of a formal letter. If they can't remember many, tell them to check their notes about the lessons on pages 17 and 27.

- Tell them to rewrite the letter in a more suitable style. As they write, monitor carefully, paying particular attention to formality.

Suggested answers

1 Dear Sir/Madam   2 I just saw   3 news<u>paper</u>   4 <u>I am</u>
5 two points   6 <u>do not</u>   7 <u>does not</u>   8 Could you
tell me w<u>here I can find</u>   9 I <u>look forward</u>   10 Yours
faithfully

11

- When students have finished, tell them to swap letters with their partner and compare the changes they made.

3 Money

UNIT AT A GLANCE

THEMES: Money and its effect on our lives

TED TALK: *An escape from poverty.* Jaqueline Novogratz talks about changing the way we fight poverty.

AUTHENTIC LISTENING SKILLS: Rhythm and stress

CRITICAL THINKING: Reading between the lines

PRESENTATION SKILLS: Persuasion

GRAMMAR: Countable and uncountable nouns, expressions of quantity: *much, many, a lot of, a few, a little; very, too* and *enough*

VOCABULARY: Money

PRONUNCIATION: Questions with *Do you* and *Could you*

READING: *Teaching financial literacy*

LISTENING: Everyday conversations

SPEAKING: Standard of living and quality of life, money quiz, talking about money

WRITING: A report

WRITING SKILL: Writing numbers in a report

LEAD IN

• Books closed. Show students the photo on page 30 of the Student's Book, covering the caption with your hand. Let them have a good look at it.

• While you are showing them the photo, ask them the following questions. They make very brief notes about them:

Where do you think this is?

What might the occasion be?

Who is the woman and why does she have a bank note on her head?

What's happening with the money? Why?

• Put them in pairs to discuss the photo. Give them a minute for this.

• Elicit some of their theories about the woman in the photo. Then tell them to open their books on page 30 and read the caption. (She is the mother of the bride at a wedding reception in Lagos, the biggest city in Nigeria.) Explain that people give money to the mother of the newly married woman as a sign of respect in what is called 'the money dance'.

TEDTALKS

BACKGROUND

1

• Explain to students that they are going to watch a talk called *An escape from poverty.* They read the introduction then get into pairs and discuss questions 1–3. If necessary, explain the meaning of *top-down* in the phrase *top-down aid*: help and money that is given by the most powerful or richest to the least powerful or poorest.

• Use the three questions as a springboard for class discussion about aid in their country, whether they give to any non-profit organizations, and why.

Answers

1 Poor countries receive different types of aid, such as financial assistance (money), food in times of drought and hunger, medical aid, expertise, education and engineering assistance. This is provided by a variety of charities and organizations, as well as governments of developed nations.

2 Acumen helps people with services such as lighting, clean water and housing.

3 It doesn't give money; it supports local organizations.

KEY WORDS

1

• **Optional step.**

▶ Teaching tip: Key words, Introduction, page 7.

• Tell students to cover the definitions a–g, read sentences 1–6 and try to imagine the meaning of the words in bold. If you took the optional step, see if they can remember the definitions.

• Let them uncover the definitions and match them to the words.

Answers

1 f (shack), c (slum)   2 g   3 b   4 e   5 a   6 d

- To check comprehension further, ask follow-up questions: *What do houses have that **shacks** do not? What other countries have lots of **slums**? Are **slums** normally found in the city, near the city or in the country? Can you draw a **sewing machine** on the board? Who do you normally ask for a **loan**? What do people take out **loans** for? If you give $10 to a charity and I **match** that, how much do I give? If you have a **mortgage**, do you have to pay rent? Why might a person need **counselling**?*

▶ Teaching tip: Concept check questions, Unit 12.3, page 163.

AUTHENTIC LISTENING SKILLS Rhythm and stress

3a

- Ask students to read the Authentic listening skills box. Read out the example words in the box (*afford*, etc.), mumbling the unstressed syllables to show that it is still possible to recognize the words by the stressed syllables and the stress pattern alone.

- Write *responsibility* on the board to show primary and secondary stress: *res,ponsi'bility*. Drill the stress pattern of the word: *da-DA-da-**DA**-da-da*. Point out to the students the stress marks placed before the syllables to indicate primary and secondary stress.

- Tell them to look and listen to the first three sentences of the TED Talk, notice the syllables that are stressed in the first sentence (1), and underline the syllables that are stressed in the italicized words in the second and third (2).

- ⬛ 13 Play the recording.

- As you get the answers from the class, drill the words so that students get to hear themselves saying the words correctly.

> ### Answers
> 2 And yet the com<u>plex</u>ity of <u>pov</u>erty really has to look at <u>in</u>come as only one <u>var</u>iable. Because really, it's a con<u>di</u>tion about choice, and the <u>lack</u> of <u>free</u>dom.

3b

- If you want to test students' awareness of the stress patterns of the words before letting them listen, tell them to mark in pencil where they think the stress lies.

- ⬛ 14 Play the recording.

- Let them check with a partner before sharing their answers with the class.

- Ask if they notice any patterns in common. Elicit the commonalities between the words in each column. Ask whether they can make any rules about word stress in English, and whether they can think of any exceptions to the rule. (See answers below for the patterns)

> ### Answers
> A: <u>free</u>dom, <u>doc</u>tor, <u>girl</u>friend, <u>busi</u>ness and <u>in</u>come all have stress on the first syllable. Possible rule: Many two-syllable words have stress on the first syllable (though there are many exceptions, especially in verbs, e.g. al<u>low</u>, col<u>lect</u>, per<u>form</u>).
>
> B: ex<u>peri</u>ence, de<u>velop</u>ment, <u>fam</u>ily, <u>cus</u>tomer and op<u>por</u>tunity all have stress on the antepenultimate syllable (third from last). Possible rule: Many multi-syllabic words have stress on the antepenultimate syllable unless another rule takes priority (see Column C words, for example).
>
> C: gene<u>ra</u>tion, defi<u>ni</u>tion, con<u>di</u>tion, de<u>ci</u>sion and organi<u>za</u>tion all have stress on the penultimate syllable. Rule: Words ending in *-tion/-sion* have stress on the syllable before this ending. There are very few exceptions to this rule.

3.1 An escape from poverty

TEDTALKS

▶ Teaching tip: Dealing with difficult listening activities, Introduction page 7.

1

- Tell the class that they are going to hear about a woman called Jane, who comes from a slum in the Mathare Valley near Nairobi in Kenya. Explain that the first time they watch, they should try to understand the general story: how Jane escaped from poverty. Point out questions 1–3.

- ▶ 3.1 Play the TED Talk.

- Give students time to check their ideas with a partner.

> ### Answers
> 1 He left her.   2 She sells dresses.   3 It is outside Nairobi away from the slum.

Transcript

0.12 *I've been working on issues of poverty for more than twenty years, and so it's ironic that the problem that and question that I most grapple with is how you actually define poverty. What does it mean? So often, we look at dollar terms – people making less than a dollar or two or three a day. And yet the complexity of poverty really has to look at income as only one variable. Because really, it's a condition about choice, and the lack of freedom.*

0.40 *And I had an experience that really deepened and elucidated for me the understanding that I have. It was* *in Kenya, and I want to share it with you. I was with my friend Susan Meiselas, the photographer, in the Mathare Valley slums. Now, Mathare Valley is one of the oldest slums in Africa. It's about three miles out of Nairobi, and it's a mile long and about two-tenths of a mile wide, where over half a million people live crammed in these little tin shacks, generation after generation, renting them, often eight or ten people to a room.*

1.10 *And it was here that I met Jane. I was struck immediately by the kindness and the gentleness in her face, and I asked her to tell me her story. She started off by telling me her dream. She said, 'I had two. My first dream was to be a doctor, and the second was to marry a good man who would stay with me and my family, because my mother was a single mom, and couldn't afford to pay for school fees. So I had to give up the first dream, and I focused on the second.' She got married when she was 18, had a baby right away. And when she turned twenty, found herself pregnant with a second child, her mom died and her husband left her – married another woman. So she was again in Mathare, with no income, no skill set, no money.*

1.53 *In 2001, her life changed. She had a girlfriend who had heard about this organization, Jamii Bora, that would lend money to people no matter how poor you were, as long as you provided a commensurate amount in savings. And so she spent a year to save 50 dollars, and started borrowing, and over time she was able to buy a sewing machine. She started tailoring. And that turned into what she does now, which is to go into the second-hand clothing markets, and for about three dollars and 25 cents she buys an old ball gown. Some of them might be ones you gave. And she repurposes them with frills and ribbons, and makes these frothy confections that she sells to women for their daughter's Sweet 16 or first Holy Communion – those milestones in a life that people want to celebrate all along the economic spectrum. And she does really good business. In fact, I watched her walk through the streets hawking. And before you knew it, there was a crowd of women around her, buying these dresses.*

2.55 *And I reflected, as I was watching her sell the dresses, and also the jewellery that she makes, that now Jane makes more than four dollars a day. And by many definitions she is no longer poor. But she still lives in Mathare Valley. And so she can't move out.*

3.12 *Jamii Bora understands that and understands that when we're talking about poverty, we've got to look at people all along the economic spectrum. And so with patient capital from Acumen and other organizations, loans and investments that will go the long term with them, they built a low-cost housing development, about an hour outside Nairobi central. And they designed it from the perspective of customers like Jane herself, insisting on responsibility and accountability. So she has to give ten per cent of the*

mortgage – of the total value, or about 400 dollars in savings. And then they match her mortgage to what she paid in rent for her little shanty. And in the next couple of weeks, she's going to be among the first 200 families to move into this development.

4.00 *I said, 'Well what about your dreams?' And she said, 'Well, you know, my dreams don't look exactly like I thought they would when I was a little girl. But if I think about it, I thought I wanted a husband, but what I really wanted was a family that was loving. And I fiercely love my children, and they love me back.' She said, 'I thought that I wanted to be a doctor, but what I really wanted to be was somebody who served and healed and cured. And so I feel so blessed with everything that I have, that two days a week I go and I counsel HIV patients. And I say, "Look at me. You are not dead. You are still alive. And if you are still alive you have to serve."' And she said, 'I'm not a doctor who gives out pills. But maybe me, I give out something better because I give them hope.'*

4.49 *And in the middle of this economic crisis, where so many of us are inclined to pull in with fear, I think we're well suited to take a cue from Jane and reach out, recognizing that being poor doesn't mean being ordinary. Because when systems are broken, like the ones that we're seeing around the world, it's an opportunity for invention and for innovation. It's an opportunity to truly build a world where we can extend services and products to all human beings, so that they can make decisions and choices for themselves. I truly believe it's where dignity starts. We owe it to the Janes of the world. And just as important, we owe it to ourselves.*

5.33 *Thank you.*

Note the differences in British English and North American English shown at the foot of the spread. In this unit, these focus on spelling and vocabulary differences. See Teaching tip 1 on page 6 of the Introduction for ideas on how to present and practise these differences.

2

• Ask students to read the six sentences before they watch the first part of the talk again.

• **Optional step**. Get students to guess the answers. Conduct a class poll to see how many people think the first word is correct and how many the second.

• ▶ 3.1 Play the first part of the talk from 0.00–1.53.

• Ask individuals to give their answers.

Answers
1 freedom   2 slums   3 half   4 doctor   5 two children
6 skills

• Ask them if they know anyone like Jane, with similar dreams or a similar family situation.

3

• Ask what the missing words in the next exercise have in common (they are all verbs used to talk about money). Check understanding by asking questions:

Which two verbs take place in a shop? (buy and sell)

What does the shop customer do? (buy)

Which does the shop assistant do? (sell)

What other verb describes what the shop assistant is doing while working? (making money)

Which verbs usually take place in a bank (lend and save)

What does the bank do? (lend money)

Where does money go when we want to save it? (in a bank account)

• Tell students to complete the paragraph with the missing words before they listen.

• ▷3.1 Play the second part of the talk from 1.53–3.12.

Answers
1 lends   2 save   3 buys   4 sells   5 makes

4

• Make sure students have time to read the sentences before they listen.

• ▷3.1 Play the third part of the talk from 3.12–4.00.

• Confirm the correct answers with the whole class.

Answers
1 housing   2 customers   3 400   4 rent

5

• Explain that students are going to listen to the conclusion of the talk. Tell them to decide whether sentences 1–4 are true or false.

• ▷3.1 Play the fourth part of the talk from 4.00 to the end.

• For variety, conduct whole class feedback with a show of hands, i.e. *Number 1. Hands up who thinks it is true.*

Answers
1 F (They haven't, but she feels as fulfilled as if they had.)
2 T (She loves her children and they love her.)
3 F (She says that really she wanted to be someone who served and healed and cured, which she does in voluntary work counselling HIV patients.)
4 T (She thinks we should build a world where people like Jane can make decisions and choices for themselves.)

VOCABULARY IN CONTEXT

6

• ▷3.2 Play the clips from the talk. When each multiple-choice question appears, students choose the correct definition. Discourage the more confident students from always giving the answer by asking people to raise their hand if they think they know.

Transcript and subtitles

*1 … this organization, Jamii Bora, that would lend money to people **no matter** how poor you were, as long as you provided a commensurate amount in savings.*
　a and they didn't know
　b and it wasn't important
　c and it was clear

*2 She started tailoring. And that **turned into** what she does now, which is to go into the second-hand clothing markets …*
　a became
　b changed
　c helped

*3 She sells to women for their daughter's Sweet 16 or first Holy Communion – those **milestones** in a life that people want to celebrate all along the economic spectrum.*
　a signs
　b unusual events
　c important moments

*4 And she **does** really **good business**.*
　a is a good business woman
　b sells a lot
　c sells good products

*5 I watched her walk through the streets hawking. And **before you knew it**, there was a crowd of women around her, buying these dresses.*
　a very soon
　b after a time
　c before she noticed

Answers
1 b   2 a   3 c   4 b   5 a

7

• Get students into pairs to complete the sentences with their own words. Let them compare their sentences with those of other pairs.

Suggested answers
1 … offices. / … an apartment block.
2 … the bakery. They always have lots of customers.
3 … passing my driving test. / … leaving university. / … getting married.

• **Optional step**. Brainstorm important milestones in people's lives.

CRITICAL THINKING Reading between the lines

8

• Put students in pairs. Ask them to discuss the statements with regard to Jacqueline Novogratz's talk and answer the question.

> **Answer**
>
> b – It is clear from the anecdote about Jane that she believes poverty has a solution and that the money needed can come from poor people's earning power, not rich people.

9

• Ask students to read the comment.

• Ask them to *take their stand*! Have them stand up and position themselves at one end of the room (you decide which) if they strongly agree with Thibault, at the opposite end of the room if they strongly disagree, and at a point somewhere in between if they believe something different.

• Ask individuals to justify their stand. Ask those standing at either extreme first. Encourage different points of view by challenging them to think of different types of aid. You could mention charities which take a different approach to Acumen, like GiveDirectly.org, which gives money directly to people in poor countries rather than spending the money on their behalf. After several students have justified their position, ask if any students have changed their opinion, and to move to a point that indicates their new position.

• **Optional step**. Have students write their own comment in response to the talk.

▶ Teaching tip: Comment / Tweet / Post, Unit 2.1, page 26.

PRESENTATION SKILLS Persuasion

10

• Ask students to read the Presentation tips box and answer the question.

11

• Tell students to identify the facts and real-life examples Jacqueline Novogratz uses to persuade us of her expertise.

• ▶ 3.3 Play the clip.

> **Answers**
>
> Jane uses facts about poverty, i.e. that it is not just a problem of living on two or three dollars a day, and she backs this up with her experiences in the Mathare Valley in Kenya.

12

• Tell students to work in pairs. Assign each member of the pairs as either Student A or B and tell them to turn to pages 171 and 172 respectively.

• Give students time to memorize their facts.

13

• Before students give the beginnings of their presentations to their partners, encourage them to be passionate when they give their facts, emphasizing key information.

• Let students practise with their partner, focusing on being persuasive.

▶ Set Workbook pages 24–25 for homework.

3.2 The money in your pocket

GRAMMAR Countable and uncountable nouns

1

• Put students in pairs to discuss the questions. The meaning of *standard of living* should be clear from context, but if students ask, tell them it is how much money and material comfort that people have.

• Elicit answers from the whole class. Start by asking for a show of hands: *Hands up who thinks people have a higher standard of living now?* etc.

• Be prepared for a variety of points of view about question 2. There are many factors such as globalization, job security and the environment which may affect life in the next fifty years.

> **Answers**
>
> Students' own answers

2

• Still in their pairs, students look at the infographic and answer the questions. (Note that the bars on the infographic aren't to scale.)

• Nominate individuals to share their answers with the class. Ask students if they think the objects here are representative of the standard of living, and whether they can think of other products that would better represent their standard of living.

> **Answers**
>
> 1 All are easier to buy.
>
> 2 The chair was and still is the easiest item to buy.
>
> 3 The piano is still very expensive.

Extra activity

Reasons, reasons

Put students in teams of three or four. Explain that you know four reasons why many things are cheaper today than they were in the past. Explain that teams can win points if they can guess the reasons you know, but they can also win points for thinking of other reasons.

Give them three minutes to quietly decide on reasons in their teams.

Bring the class together. Teams take turns to say one reason for today's cheap products. If their ideas coincide with the ones listed below, they get a point. If they come up with alternatives, ask the rest of the class if that is a valid reason, and give your opinion, too. Award extra points as appropriate.

Your four reasons are:

- Mass production. The unit price of goods has decreased as more units are produced.
- Globalization. Goods can be manufactured in countries where labour is cheap.
- Automation. Machines make production quicker and more efficient.
- The development of cheap materials such as plastics. Expensive materials can be replaced without losing quality.

3

- Explain to students that they are going to listen to an interview with an economist about the standard of living. Tell them to read questions 1–3.
- 🅰 **15** Play the recording.

Transcript

P = Presenter, L = Professor Long

P: *Now … we haven't had any good news about the economy lately, but here is some positive information – some facts that will perhaps make you feel better about the money in your pocket. In the studio today, we have an economist, Professor David Long, who claims that we are lucky compared to people living one hundred years ago – people who didn't have any hopes of buying the things that we can afford today. So we should be grateful, Professor.*

L: *Absolutely. Most middle-class people in Europe now have a better standard of living than a king living 300 years ago or a rich person 120 years ago. Most people were poor 120 years ago. They didn't have many possessions. They didn't have much food. They worked long hours and only had a little time for leisure. For example, in 1895 a person had to work 24 hours to earn the money to buy an office chair. Now a person only has to work two hours to do the same. Of course there are still a lot of poor people in the world and a few countries have very low economic growth, but even in these less developed countries the standard of living is rising fast compared to 120 years ago.*

- Give students a minute to compare answers with a partner. Then invite students to share answers with the class.

> **Answers**
>
> 1 He claims we should feel lucky compared to people living one hundred years ago.
>
> 2 Most middle class people in Europe have a better standard of living than a king 300 years ago.
>
> 3 For most people it is going up quickly, even in less developed countries.

- Ask students whether they agree with Professor Long.

4

- Direct students' attention to the Grammar box. Tell them to answer questions 1 and 2.
- Students can check their answers and overall understanding of countable and uncountable nouns by turning to the Grammar summary on page 144. If you feel that students need more controlled practice before continuing, they could do one or all of Exercises 1–4 in the Grammar summary. Otherwise, you could continue on to Exercise 5 in the unit and set the Grammar summary exercises for homework.

> **Answers**
>
> 1 a person   b hours   c money
>
> 2
>
> a We use *a(n)* and *the* before a singular countable noun.
>
> b We use *the, some* and *any* before an uncountable or a plural countable noun.

> **Answers to Grammar summary exercises**
>
> 1
>
> Countable: biscuit, chair, dollar, job, party, river, song
>
> Uncountable: food, fun, furniture, money, music, water, work
>
> 2
>
> 2 suitcase**s**   3 suggestion**s**   5 question**s**   6 banana**s**
>
> 3
>
> 1 any   2 a   3 some   4 a   5 some   6 any   7 is
> 8 any   9 some   10 a
>
> 4
>
> 1 any / some   2 no   3 some   4 any   5 any   6 no

5

- Ask students to choose the correct options to complete the sentences on their own. Answer any doubts they may have.
- Let them check with a partner before conducting whole-class feedback.

6

• Put students in pairs to rewrite the sentences in Exercise 5 so that the other option fits grammatically. Model the activity on the board using the first one or two sentences as examples.

• Elicit answers.

7

• Ask students to put the notes into full sentences, using the determiners as necessary. Monitor to check individuals' progress.

GRAMMAR Expressions of quantity: *much, many, a lot of, a few, a little*

8

• Explain to students that they are going to listen to an extract from the interview with Professor Long to decide whether the statements are true or false. Give them time to read the statements.

• 🔊 16 Play the recording.

Transcript

(See Professor Long's speech in the transcript for Exercise 3 above.)

• **Optional step**. Books closed. Tell students to listen again to write down the sentences that told them whether the statements are true or false. Give a student control of the audio controls and explain that they can ask him or her to stop and rewind as many times as they need to complete the sentences. When they have finished, ask them to open their books and find some of the sentences in the Grammar box at the top of page 35.

9

• If they haven't done the **Optional step** in Exercise 8, ask students to read the sentences in the Grammar box and answer questions 1–3. If they have, they can just answer the questions.

• Students can check their answers and overall understanding of expressions of quantity by turning to the Grammar summary on page 144. If you feel that students need more controlled practice before continuing, they could do Exercises 5–7 in the Grammar summary. Otherwise, you could continue on to Exercise 10 in the unit and set the Grammar summary exercises for homework. Note that the Grammar summary also includes some information on the use of *too*, *very* and *enough*, and Exercise 8 practises this.

• **Optional step**. Students describe the classroom and things that they can see using the expressions of quantity: *some, any, the, a, much, many, a lot of, a few, a little*. Write these on the board and start off with some examples, e.g. *There aren't many students here today. We have a lot of posters on the wall.*

10

• Students choose the correct options to complete the conversations.

• When they have finished, put them in pairs to read out the dialogues and compare answers.

• **Optional step**. Get students to alter the sentences so that they are true for them.

> **Answers**
>
> 1 many, a few   2 much, a lot of   3 a little, a few
> 4 much, a few

SPEAKING Standard of living and quality of life

11   *21st* CENTURY OUTCOMES

• Explain that students are going to discuss and compare their standard of living and quality of life. Briefly discuss the difference in meaning between the two phrases. For example, you could say that some people with a low standard of living may still have a good quality of life.

• Show them the list and make sure they can formulate questions using the prompts, e.g. *How much sleep do you get each night?* (Or *How many hours sleep …?*).

• Put them in pairs to ask and answer the questions. As they speak, go around the classroom paying attention to their use of countable and uncountable quantifiers.

• Stop them after a few minutes and make any comments and corrections you have about their use of English.

12

• Tell students to look at the information they have collected about their classmates and using the data, try to evaluate their standard of living and quality of life.

• Put students in new pairs.

▶ Teaching tip: Three ways to pair up students, Unit 2.1, page 27.

• Tell them to report to their new partners about their old partners' standard of living and quality of life.

• In whole-class feedback, ask who has a very good standard of living, who has a good quality of life, and why. Try to draw out any conclusions students may have.

▶ Photocopiable communicative activity 3.1: Go to page 213 for further practice of quantifiers. The teaching notes are on page 235.

▶ Set Workbook pages 26–27 for homework.

3.3 How to manage your money

READING Teaching financial literacy

1

• Put students in groups of three to five. They answer the questions. Monitor their discussion.

• Elect representatives from each group to report back to the class.

> **Suggested answers**
>
> 1 a, c, d and e are all ways of being 'good with money'; b and f don't necessarily mean a person is good with money, but they may be indications.
> 2–4 Students' own answers

2

• Conclude the whole-class discussion by asking whether students believe it is important to teach financial skills to children. Make sure they state why they think so and how old children should be when they learn these things.

3

• Ask students to read the article on page 37. They should look for answers to the questions in Exercise 2.

• When they report what they have found, make sure they state where in the article the answers are given.

> **Answers**
>
> According to the article, it is important to teach financial skills because the use of credit cards and online banking these days makes money seem less real (lines 14–16) and because borrowing is easier so there is more danger that people will get into debt (lines 16–18). The article recommends starting this education at an 'early age' (line 13); the use of fairy tales, quizzes and games implies that this should start with young children.

4

• Tell students to read the first two paragraphs of the article again to complete the facts with one word from the text. Note that one word (question 5) will need to change form.

• Have students read out their completed facts to the class.

> **Answers**
>
> 1 enjoyment   2 financial   3 plastic   4 online
> 5 borrow   6 challenge

5

- Tell students to read the rest of the article to match the teaching tools (1–4) with the descriptions (a–d).

- Let them check their answers with a partner.

Answers

1 c   2 d   3 b   4 a

6

- In their pairs, students discuss their answers to questions 1 and 2.

Answers

Students' own answers

(Other fairy stories with a possible financial message include: *The Goose that Laid the Golden Egg*, which promotes holding on to things that provide an income rather than sacrificing them for short-term benefit, and *The Little Red Hen*, which teaches us not to expect to gain the benefits of something we have not contributed towards.)

VOCABULARY Money

7

- Students choose the correct options to complete the descriptions of three people's financial situations.

- Read out the descriptions, pausing at each option for students to call out the correct answer.

Answers

1 invested, earn   2 borrowed, owes   3 spends, makes, afford

- **Optional step**. Ask them which of the three people are good with money (Graham and Florence are managing OK). Find out which of them they relate to most and why. Also ask which of the tools mentioned in the article they might benefit from.

8

- Explain that there are some useful nouns related to money in the descriptions in Exercise 7. Tell them to find them and match them to their definitions (1–5).

Answers

1 savings   2 debts   3 loan   4 salary   5 income

TEACHING TIP

Help students organize vocabulary notes

Learners need guidance in organizing vocabulary so that they can learn it reliably and thoroughly. The students have studied a number of words and phrases concerning money, so now is a good moment to consolidate learning by bringing the vocabulary together.

Ask students to brainstorm all the money words they have learned recently. Remind them of the verbs they used in Exercise 3 on page 33, for example, and such phrases as 'standard of living' on page 34. Invite them to contribute other related words they know. Put them in groups to discuss the best ways to record and present this vocabulary on one page of their vocabulary notebooks. Let them share their ideas.

A visual means of organizing this vocabulary is with a spidergram. Notice how words are organized according to part of speech; nouns are indicated by *a/an* + noun. Collocations are given, such as *invest **in***.

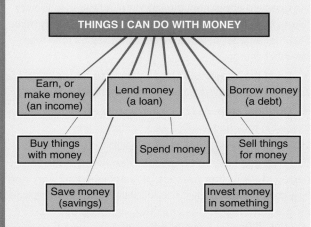

Encourage students to record words in example sentences that help them remember their meaning and use. Make sure students leave space for more words and phrases that they might learn in the future.

9

- Tell students to use the words studied in Exercises 7 and 8 to write sentences about themselves. Monitor as they write, checking accuracy and appropriacy.

- Put them in pairs to discuss their sentences. Encourage them to ask each other follow-up questions.

- If you have followed the Teaching tip, you could tell them to write up their sentences in their vocabulary books.

SPEAKING Money quiz

10

• Tell students to read the statements and award each one a '5' if they totally agree, '0' if they disagree, or any number in between.

• Put students in pairs to compare their attitudes to the statements. Encourage them to provide supporting examples by offering one or two of your own before they discuss theirs. For example, to illustrate the first point, talk about someone you know who is careful with money and never goes on holiday or has much fun. Or conversely, someone who has hundreds of pairs of shoes but hasn't started a pension yet.

Answer
Students' own answers

• Discuss students' answers in the class, and why they agreed / disagreed with the statements. Ask them to state what they think are sensible financial decisions.

11

• Use whole-class feedback from Exercise 10 to lead into the question about how the students' attitudes to money differs from those of their parents. Ask whether they think they make better or worse financial decisions than their parents have done.

• Bring the lesson to a close by drawing any conclusions about how attitudes to money have changed in general.

• **Optional step**. Ask students what lesson about money they wish they had learned as a child and why.

▶ Photocopiable communicative activity 3.2: Go to page 214 for further practice of financial vocabulary and *how much / how many*? The teaching notes are on page 235.

▶ Set Workbook pages 28–29 for homework.

3.4 Have you got any change?

LISTENING Everyday conversations

1

• Ask students to look at the photos. Ask them to think of other situations where they might talk about money. Also ask which of these situations they might find themselves speaking English in.

• Tell them to match the photos to questions a–e. Don't confirm answers yet as these are checked in Exercise 2.

2

• 🔊 17 Play the recording for students to check their answers.

Answers
1 d 2 e 3 c 4 a 5 b

Transcript

1

A: I'd like $200 in Swiss Francs, please. What's the rate today?

B: OK. $200 buys you 181 Swiss Francs.

A: Do you charge commission?

B: No, it's commission-free.

2

A: OK. That's $16.80, please.

B: Thanks. Here's $20. Please keep the change.

A: Thank you.

B: Oh, and can I have a receipt, please?

3

A: Excuse me. Do you have change for a £10 note?

B: Sorry, I don't, but you can get coins from the change machine.

A: OK Thanks.

4

A: Thanks, that was delicious. Could you bring us the bill?

B: Certainly … Here you are.

A: Thanks. Is service included?

B: No, it isn't.

5

A: Could you lend me £5 to get some lunch?

B: Sure.

A: I'll pay you back when I go to the bank.

B: OK – no hurry.

Background information
British and American differences
Americans use the word *bill* to refer to what Britons call a *note*, e.g. *a ten dollar bill*. In the United States, a restaurant bill is known as a *check*, e.g. *Could I have the check, please?*

3

• Tell students to complete the everyday conversations with the missing words.

• 🔊 17 Play the recording again for students to check.

- **Optional step.** Students read out their dialogues.

SPEAKING Talking about money

Pronunciation Questions with *Do you* and *Could you*

> **TEACHING TIP**
>
> **Receptive or productive?**
>
> In the past, the model for good pronunciation for learners of English was native speakers of English (NSs). Today we understand that expecting learners to speak like NSs is not just unrealistic, it may not be the best model to aim for. This is because there are features of connected speech that NSs use that can make it difficult to understand, such as the /dʒ/ sound in *Do you* /dʒə/.
>
> It's important for learners to understand the fast, natural speech of NSs, so they need to practise listening to these features of connected speech (receptive). But do they need to learn how to speak like this (productive practice)? Ask yourself whether students will be easier to understand if they say 'Do you…?' /də juː/ or /dʒə/. Ask students, too, whether they want to sound like native speakers of English or clear speakers of English as a global language.

4a

- Ask the class to listen to the sentences.
- 🔊 18 Play the recording.
- Ask them how the underlined words are pronounced. Point out that *Do you* and *Could you* sound like one word and contain a /dʒ/ sound.
- Let them listen again and repeat the sentences.

4b

- Tell them to identify whether each question starts with *Do you* or *Could you*.
- 🔊 19 Play the recording. Ask students to listen carefully.

Answer

Questions 1 and 3 start with *Could you* and questions 2 and 4 with *Do you*.

- **Optional step.** Students listen again and write the four questions, as a dictation.

Memorizing dialogues

Some very common, formulaic everyday dialogues such as these may be worth memorizing by heart for instant recall in real-life situations. Tell students that they are going to learn the dialogues by practising in pairs. Let them read through them several times, then tell them to close their books and try to remember every word. They can take turns, one reading and prompting while the other tries to remember his or her lines. Offer memorization support in the form of prompts on the board. For example, for the first dialogue, write:

> I'd like … in … , please. What's … today?
>
> OK. $200 … 181…
>
> Do you … commission?
>
> No, it's …

As they begin to learn it by heart, increase the challenge by gradually rubbing out words until there are few or no words left. Exercise 5 develops this further by varying the dialogue and adding complications.

5

- Put students in pairs. Tell them to look at the photos and questions in Exercise 1. Explain that they are going to act out similar conversations to the ones in Exercises 1–4.
- Point out the new situations (1–4). Check that students understand that they have to practise similar conversations using the new information. Give them a minute to predict which useful expressions from the box they can use for each conversation. Make sure they understand that the words and figures in blue are the ones they need to change.
- Give them several minutes to practise all four conversations at least once. You could encourage further practice by having them swap roles. Monitor, listening carefully for good use of English.
- Provide the class with feedback about their performance and use of English, correcting notable errors and evaluating overall competence.
- **Optional step.** Pairs write new situations based on the conversations for other pairs to perform.

WRITING A report

6

- Ask students to quickly read the report and explain who the writer might be and why they are writing the report. Elicit that the writer is a member of a group considering opening a French restaurant somewhere in the city. The report is to help them decide whether the proposed restaurant is likely to be a success.
- Tell them to read it again and answer questions 1–3.

Answer
1 The sentences are short.
2 It contains more facts than opinions.
3 It ends with the next step.

Writing skill Writing numbers in a report

7a

• Explain the difference between a number written as a number (e.g. *1*) and a number written as a word (e.g. *one*).

• Tell students to read the report again to see whether the different types of number (1–7) is written as a number or a word. Have them write *N* for number and *W* for word.

• In feedback list the numbers written as numbers and words respectively.

Answers
1 N   2 W   3 N   4 W   5 W   6 N   7 N   8 N

7b

• Tell them to punctuate the four numbers using the report as a guide.

Answers
1 9.30 a.m.   2 450   3 $12.99   4 30,000

• Ask whether English has the same punctuation rules for numbers as their own language.

7c

• Explain that the report about Slovenia contains many numbers but they are all written in words. Students write the words as numbers where necessary.

• Let them compare answers with a partner before nominating individuals to share with the class.

Answers
two point one million → 2.1 million or 2,100,000
fifty-five per cent → 55%
first of May two thousand and four → 1st May 2004
two thousand and four → 2004
two thousand and seven → 2007
Fifty dollars ✓
forty-three dollars → $43
two hours ✓

8 *21st* CENTURY OUTCOMES

• Students write a similar report to the one about Slovenia but about Ireland this time. They use the notes and figures in the box.

• Go around the class checking students' writing. Pay particular attention to their sentence length and expression of numbers.

9

• When everyone has finished writing, tell them to exchange reports with a partner. Ask them to use the checklist to assess their partners' report.

• They should ensure that their partner has recorded all the facts accurately and written the numbers correctly, to fulfil the 21st CENTURY OUTCOME of Presenting information accurately.

Suggested answer
Ireland is a country with beautiful countryside. It has a population of 4.6 million. Twenty-five per cent of the population live in the Dublin area. It joined the European Union in 1973 and enjoyed a period of fast economic growth between 1995 and 2007.
Dublin is quite an expensive city for the visitor. It will cost you a minimum of $150 per day to stay there. One thing you should certainly do is buy a Dublin sightseeing pass. It costs €60 for a two-day pass and gives you entrance to 32 different museums and sights.

• **Optional step**. Students write a similar report about their own country. First, they should make some notes and include figures about the population, cost of living, history and tips for the visitor.

▶ Set Workbook pages 30–31 for homework.

▶ Set Workbook Presentation 2 on pages 32–33 for homework.

4 Success

LEAD IN

• Books closed. Write *success* on the board and ask the class to write a personal definition. Offer your own example to clarify what you mean, e.g. *Success for me is getting up in the morning and going for a run.* Let students compare their definitions in pairs or groups.

• Tell students to open their books on page 40. Ask: *Where are these people? What goal have they just achieved? What personal qualities do you think they possess?*

• Open the whole class discussion up with the question: *What do you think are the ingredients to a successful life?*

TEDTALKS
BACKGROUND

1

• Explain to students that they are going to watch a talk called *Don't eat the marshmallow!* They read the introduction then get into pairs and discuss questions 1–3. If necessary, explain the meaning of *predictor* first: something that shows what something will be like in the future.

• Nominate individuals to share answers with the class.

> **Answers**
>
> 1 He helped* companies and teams to find deep and lasting reasons to succeed.
>
> *Joachim de Posada died in June 2015.
>
> 2 Coaches are employed to help people realize different goals: in sports, business and personal health. There are also life coaches and language coaches!
>
> 3 Students' own answers. (Marshmallows are soft sweets; children sometimes cook them over fires when they go camping. Piranhas are fish with sharp teeth that live in South America and eat meat.)

KEY WORDS

2

• Tell students that they are going to learn some important words from the talk. They should read the sentences and guess the meanings of the words in bold. Have them cover up the definitions to encourage guesswork. Then let them match the words and definitions (a–f).

> **Answers**
>
> 1 b 2 c 3 e 4 d 5 a 6 f

• **Optional step**. Students rewrite the sentences so that they mean the same but without using the words in bold or their synonyms in the definitions, e.g. *5 I did very well in my maths and science exams because I studied hard.*

AUTHENTIC LISTENING SKILLS Dealing with accents

3a

• Let students read the Authentic listening skills box.

• **Optional step**. Dictate or write on the board a series of awareness-raising questions about accent:

> *What differences do you notice between your own accent and other accents in your language?*
>
> *Are there any accents that you find hard to understand in your own language? Why?*
>
> *What about English? What accents do you hear? E.g. American, British, your own accent, French, Japanese, etc.*
>
> *Which accents, both native and non-native English, are important for you to practise listening to?*

Put students in groups of three or four and give them time to discuss the questions. Then draw conclusions with the whole class.

- Tell them to listen to the sentence from the TED Talk. They should pay attention to the way the underlined words are pronounced.

- 🔊 20 Play the recording. Then elicit any differences they notice.

> **Answer**
>
> *Come* and *another* contain the /ʌ/ sound in British English. Joachim de Posada pronounces them /kɒm/ and /anɒðər/, replacing the /ʌ/ with /ɒ/

3b

- Students read and listen to the sentences, focusing on Joachim de Posada's pronunciation of the underlined words.

- 🔊 21 Play the recording. Then elicit the pronunciation.

> **Answers**
>
> The main difference between all these words is that the /ʌ/ sound in British English is replaced by /ɒ/.
>
> British /trʌbl/, Joachim de Posada (J de P) /trɒbl/ British /sʌm/, J de P /sɒm/ British /kəlʌmbɪə/, J de P /kɒlɒmbɪə/ British /fʌni/, J de P /fɒni/ British /ʌðə/, J de P /ɒðər/

- Explain that this is a common difference with Spanish speakers of English. Ask students if they can explain some of the pronunciation differences for speakers of their language. If they are Spanish speakers, find out if they know more differences.

4.1 Don't eat the marshmallow!

TEDTALKS

1

- Tell students they are going to watch the TED Talk. Ask them to read questions 1–3.

- ▶ 4.1 Play the whole talk.

Transcript

0.12 I'm here because I have a very important message: I think we have found the most important factor for success. And it was found close to here, Stanford. Psychology professor took kids that were four years old and put them in a room all by themselves. And he would tell the child, a four-year-old kid, 'Johnny, I am going to leave you here with a marshmallow for fifteen minutes. If, after I come back, this marshmallow is here, you will get another one. So you will have two.' To tell a four-year-old kid to wait fifteen minutes for something that they like, is equivalent to telling us, 'We'll bring you coffee in two hours.' (Laughter) Exact equivalent.

1.01 So what happened when the professor left the room? As soon as the door closed … two out of three ate the marshmallow. Five seconds, ten seconds, 40 seconds, 50 seconds, two minutes, four minutes, eight minutes. Some lasted fourteen-and-a-half minutes. (Laughter) Couldn't do it. Could not wait. What's interesting is that one out of three would look at the marshmallow and go like this … Would look at it. Put it back. They would walk around. They would play with their skirts and pants.

1.42 That child already, at four, understood the most important principle for success, which is the ability to delay gratification. Self-discipline: the most important factor for success. Fifteen years later, fourteen or fifteen years later, follow-up study. What did they find? They went to look for these kids who were now eighteen and nineteen. And they found that 100 per cent of the children that had not eaten the marshmallow were successful. They had good grades. They were doing wonderful.[1] They were happy. They had their plans. They had good relationships with the teachers, students. They were doing fine.

2.23 A great percentage of the kids that ate the marshmallow, they were in trouble. They did not make it to university. They had bad grades. Some of them dropped out. A few were still there with bad grades. A few had good grades.

2.35 I had a question in my mind: Would Hispanic kids react the same way as the American kids? So I went to Colombia. And I reproduced the experiment. And it was very funny. I used four, five and six years old kids.[2] And let me show you what happened.

(Spanish) (Laughter)

4.44 So what happened in Colombia? Hispanic kids, two out of three ate the marshmallow; one out of three did not. This little girl was interesting; she ate the inside of the marshmallow. (Laughter) In other words, she wanted us to think that she had not eaten it, so she would get two. But she ate it. So we know she'll be successful. But we have to watch her. (Laughter) She should not go into banking, for example, or work in[3] a cash register. But she will be successful.

5.13 And this applies for everything.[4] Even in sales. The sales person that – the customer says, 'I want that.' And the person says, 'OK, here you are.' That person ate the marshmallow. If the sales person says, 'Wait a second. Let me ask you a few questions to see if this is a good choice.' Then you sell a lot more. So this has applications in all walks of life.

5.35 I end with – the Koreans did this. You know what? This is so good that we want a marshmallow book for children. We did one for children. And now it is all over Korea. They are teaching these kids exactly this principle. And we need to learn that principle here in the States, because we have a big debt. We are eating more marshmallows than we are producing. Thank you so much.

(1) In British English this would be better expressed as *They were doing wonderfully*. Sometimes in English adjectives can be used as adverbs, especially in American English, e.g. *Drive **safe**, He's doing **great***. In British English, these would be *Drive safe**ly**, He's doing **well***.

(2) Normally *six-year-old kids*.

(3) Normally ***at** a cash register*.

(4) Normally *applies **to** everything*.

Note the differences in British English and North American English shown at the foot of the spread. In this unit, these focus on vocabulary differences. See Teaching tip 1 on page 6 of the Introduction for ideas on how to present and practise these differences.

• Give students time to compare their answers with a partner before eliciting answers from the class.

Answers

1 eat the marshmallow   2 Most of them didn't succeed.
3 those who didn't eat the marshmallow

• **Optional step**. Put students in pairs. Ask them to devise a similar test for adults. Pairs share their ideas with the class. Vote for the best idea.

Background information

Psychology tests on young babies

The 'Marshmallow test' is famous for what it can predict about the children's futures but also for its ingenious simplicity. However, testing children is usually much more difficult. For example, it must be impossible to test young babies, before they can communicate. So how did psychologists find out that babies just a few months old can distinguish similar sounds?

In 1971, Peter D Eimas and colleagues from Brown University designed a clever experiment which measured how interested babies were in what they could hear by how quickly they sucked on an artificial nipple. The quicker the sucking, the more interested the babies were, they assumed. They found that babies as young as one to four months showed increased interest when a repeated /b/ sound changed to /p/ and vice versa.

2

• Tell the class that they are going to watch the first part of the talk again. They need to choose the correct options to complete the description of the marshmallow test. Give them a minute to read it.

• ▶4.1 Play the first part of the talk from 0.00–1.24.

• Again, let students confer before nominating individuals to share answers with the class.

Answers

1 psychology   2 four   3 another marshmallow
4 fifteen   5 Two

3

• Tell them that for the next section of the talk, they should complete sentences 1–4 with one word or number.

• ▶4.1 Play the second part of the talk from 1.24–2.47. Elicit answers.

Answers

1 discipline   2 100   3 trouble, grades   4 Colombia

4

• Ask students to read questions 1–5 and see if they can remember any answers.

• ▶4.1 Play the third part of the talk from 4.44 to the end.

• Give them a couple of minutes to discuss their answers in pairs. Then open the discussion to the whole class.

Answers

1 The girl ate the inside of the marshmallow. She tried to trick them into thinking she had not eaten it.

2 He thinks she will be successful (but that she needs to be watched!).

3 They can ask the customer questions to encourage them to buy more from them.

4 Korea

5 He thinks they should teach this principle in the United States because they are using more resources than they can produce.

VOCABULARY IN CONTEXT

5

• ▶4.2 Play the clips from the talk. When each multiple-choice question appears, students choose the correct definition. Discourage the more confident students from always giving the answer by asking individuals to raise their hand if they think they know.

Transcript and subtitles

*1 Psychology professor took kids that were four years old and put them in a room **all by themselves**.*
  a completely alone
  b together

*2 They did not **make it to** university.*
  a manage to go to
  b want to go to

*3 Some of them **dropped out**.*
  a failed their exams
  b left before the end of the course

*4 She should not **go into** banking, for example, or work in a cash register.*
  a study a course in
  b follow a career in

5 *So this has applications in **all walks of life**.*
   a different situations
   b different countries

Answers
1 a 2 a 3 b 4 b 5 a

6

• Put students in pairs. Tell them to complete the sentences in their own words.

• Elicit a few examples of each sentence so that students can compare ideas.

Suggested answers
1 … the party last night. / … the supermarket. I had too many things to do. 2 … because they run out of money. / … because they lose interest in their course. 3 … education. / … web design. / … I.T. 4 … running clubs. / … the entertainment business.

CRITICAL THINKING Considering counter arguments

7

• Explain the meaning of *counter arguments* – the arguments against an idea. Read out the summary of the main argument and ask students whether Joachim de Posada presents any counter arguments in his TED Talk. (He does not.)

• Put students in pairs to think of a counter argument for this statement. If you think students will struggle to come up with one, write on the board the following questions: *Is waiting and self-control always the right approach? In what ways does the marshmallow test reflect real life? Is it a good test of self-control? What does success really mean?*

• Elicit any ideas the class has and encourage others to respond.

Answer
Students' own answers

8

• Ask the students to read the comments, compare them with their ideas from Exercise 7 and decide which comments they agree with.

• Elicit their responses to the posts.

• **Optional step**. Students write their own comments.

▶ Teaching tip: Comment / Tweet / Post, Unit 2.1, page 26.

PRESENTATION SKILLS Body movement and gesture

9

• Ask students to discuss the questions in pairs. They could also think about whether body movement and gestures help or hinder intercultural communication.

10

• Tell them to compare their ideas with those in the Presentation tips box. Ask if they had any different ideas.

11

• Tell them to watch the TED Talk again, identifying any tips that Joachim de Posada followed in his talk.

• ▶4.1 Play the talk again.

Answer
He follows all the techniques mentioned in the box, although you may feel that perhaps he moves around the stage a little too much (technique 1).

12

• Explain to students that they are now going to look more closely at the gestures Joachim de Posada uses in a clip from the talk. Prepare them by asking them to read the lines they need to look out for.

• ▶4.3 Play the clip from the talk.

• Give students a minute to compare and describe the gestures they noticed with a partner, then nominate individuals for the answers.

Answers
1 He pulls a second marshmallow from his pocket. 2 He holds up two fingers. 3 He mimes quickly eating a marshmallow. 4 He holds up the marshmallow. 5 He holds up his hand with palm facing out in a 'Wait' gesture. 6 He mimes the children's gestures: he puts his hand to his head, then over his mouth. 7 He emphasizes this key phrase by 'punctuating' each word with a hand gesture.

13

• Explain that students are going to practise using gesture to present the marshmallow experiment. With a partner, students make notes about the key points of the experiment.

14

• Put them into new pairs.

▶ Teaching tip: Three ways to pair up students, Unit 2.1, page 27.

• Tell them to take turns explaining the experiment, using movement and gesture to help explain the ideas.

- While they watch their new partners, students should pay attention to the specific gestures used. When they have finished, they can provide one another with feedback.

▶ Set Workbook pages 34–35 for homework.

4.2 The road to success

GRAMMAR Past simple and past continuous

Extra activity

Think of someone who ...

Tell students to write the names of people they know who fulfil the following criteria. Tell them they don't have to write a name for all criteria. They can use friends, family members, colleagues, famous people, or themselves. Read slowly, pausing to give students time to think.

Someone ...

- *who loves their job*
- *who isn't happy at work and this affects their life outside work*
- *who changed career late in life*
- *who didn't go to university but wishes they had gone*
- *who did go to university but didn't need to for the job they currently do.*

Put them in small groups of three or four and tell them to show the names they have written. The others in the group ask questions about the people and the reasons the student wrote their names.

1

- Show students statements 1–4 and ask them to decide how much they agree.
- Put them in pairs to discuss their answers.
- Ask for a show of hands as to who agrees with each statement. Invite comments from the class.

2

- Tell students to look at the infographic about the career of Simon Sinek and answer the questions.
- Nominate students to tell the class their answers.

Answers
1 His first job was in an advertising company in New York. He now teaches at Columbia University and is a successful public speaker.
2 Ideas 1, 2 and 4

3

- Direct students' attention to the Grammar box. Tell them to answer questions 1 and 2.

- Students can check their answers and overall understanding of the present simple and present continuous by turning to the Grammar summary on page 146. If you feel that students need more controlled practice before continuing, they could do Exercise 1 and 2 in the Grammar summary. Otherwise, you could continue on to Exercise 4 in the unit and set the Grammar summary exercises for homework.

Answers
1 lived, went, graduated, went, became, started, decided, didn't finish, left, moved, got   2 was studying

Answers to Grammar summary exercises
1
1 Did you see   2 I didn't   3 Was it   4 explained 5 made   6 changed   7 interviewed   8 asked 9 was   10 replied   11 didn't think   12 wanted
2
1 was sitting, flew, stole   2 had, was walking   3 left, were still discussing   4 left, ended   5 didn't get, were playing   6 didn't know, were waiting   7 drove, took 8 Did you stay, had

4

- Tell students to complete the rest of Simon Sinek's story. They use the correct form of the past simple or continuous.
- Invite volunteers to read out parts of the passage to the class. Make sure that you correct any mispronunciations of the past forms.

Answers
1 set   2 worked   3 built   4 was working   5 wasn't feeling   6 asked   7 found   8 changed   9 published 10 was

- **Optional step.** Check that students can form the past simple orally as well as in written form. Drill the infinitive and past simple forms of the verbs.

5

- If students did well in Exercise 4 and seem confident, have them do this exercise orally, without writing. Put them in pairs, instruct them to put their pens down, and ask them to take turns to say each sentence correctly.

Answers
1 became, was studying   2 moved, was going   3 went, didn't get   4 left, didn't like   5 interrupted, were having 6 fell, weren't sitting

- Let them cross out the wrong answers if they haven't already done so.

Pronunciation Weak forms: *was* and *were*

6

• Tell students to listen to the sentences and identify the stressed words.

• ⟨🔊 22⟩ Play the recording.

• Ask them to listen again, this time paying attention to the pronunciation of *was*, *were*, *wasn't* and *weren't*.

• Write the sentences on the board for clarity (or better, ask volunteers to do so). Have them mark the stressed words.

Answers

1 I <u>learned</u> to speak <u>Spa</u>nish while I was <u>work</u>ing in <u>Spain</u>.

2 Did you de<u>cide</u> to be a poli<u>ti</u>cian while you were <u>study</u>ing?

3 <u>Sorry</u>. What did you <u>say</u>? I <u>wasn't</u> <u>lis</u>tening.

4 We weren't ex<u>pec</u>ting you, but we're very <u>happy</u> you <u>came</u>.

was is pronounced /wəz/   *were* is pronounced /wə/
wasn't is pronounced /wɒznt/   *weren't* is pronounced /wɜːnt /

• Point out that in affirmative sentences, auxiliary verbs tend not to be stressed, but we do sometimes stress negative auxiliary verbs.

• Drill the sentences, isolating the verbs and back chaining so that they can practise in manageable chunks.

▶ Teaching tip: Pronunciation – backchaining, Unit 1.2, page 17.

• **Optional step**. Say the sentences in random order but replacing each syllable with *MMM* or *mm*, e.g. sentence 3 would be: *MMMmm. mm mm mm MMM? mm MMMmm MMMmm-mm*. Students say which sentence you said. They then do the same in pairs, testing each other.

7

• Tell students to use their own words to complete the sentences. Elicit a few examples for sentence 1 to get them started, encouraging them to use the past continuous.

• When they have completed all the sentences, put them in pairs to compare their sentences.

• Elicit a few suggestions for each from the class. Check the pronunciation of the weak forms of *was* and *were*. Ask if anyone has written any sentences that are true. Ask them about their experiences.

Suggested answers

1 I decided to change job because I wasn't enjoying it much.

2 I met a lot of interesting people when I was working in customer services.

3 I took a part-time job while I was studying.

4 I met my boyfriend when I was travelling.

5 I moved to the country because I was keen to have a change.

6 I didn't have the time or energy to study while I was working as a waiter.

GRAMMAR Past perfect

8

• Point out the description of Yvonne Cortez. Ask students to find her first job and her profession now.

Answer

Her first job was as a door-to-door salesperson. She is now a professional singer.

9

• Tell students that they are going to listen to an interview with Yvonne. They prepare for listening by reading the two questions.

• ⟨🔊 23⟩ Play the recording.

Transcript

I = Interviewer, Y = Yvonne Cortez

I: *So, Yvonne. Why did you decide to leave school at seventeen? Why didn't you go on to college at that point?*

Y: *Well, I guess like a lot of kids I had studied for long enough. I wanted to get out and see life and earn some money.*

I: *And did you hope to become a professional singer then?*

Y: *Umm … well, yes and no. I had done some concerts at school and a lot of people had said I was good, but for me, I hadn't thought about it as a career – it* *was still just a hobby. I didn't think I was ready to be a professional. So I took a job as a door-to-door salesperson. I hadn't had any sales experience – it was just to earn money, really.*

- Instead of eliciting answers from the class, you could move on to Exercise 10 and let them check their answers with the sentences in the Grammar box.

> **Answers**
>
> 1 She felt that she had studied for long enough and she wanted to see life and earn money.
>
> 2 'Yes and no'. People had said she was good, but it was still just a hobby. She didn't think she was ready to be a professional.

10

- If you have not already done so, direct students' attention to the Grammar box. Tell them to answer questions 1–3.

- Students can check their answers and overall understanding of the past perfect by turning to the Grammar summary on page 146. If you feel that students need more controlled practice before continuing, they could do Exercise 3–6 in the Grammar summary. Otherwise, you could continue on to Exercise 11 in the unit and set the Grammar summary exercises for homework.

> **Answers**
>
> 1 The underlined verb (*took*) happened after Yvonne left school. The verbs in bold happened before she left school.
>
> 2 The past perfect is used.
>
> 3 It is formed with the auxiliary verb *had* + past participle (*studied*, *done*, *said, thought*).

> **Answers to Grammar summary exercises**
>
> **3**
>
> 1 correct   2 incorrect – ate   3 correct   4 correct
> 5 incorrect – Did you get it?   6 incorrect – didn't answer
>
> **4**
>
> 1 They arrived at about 8 pm.
>
> 2 They arrived late, at about 8.30 p.m.
>
> 3 They arrived very late, at about 9 p.m.
>
> **5**
>
> 2 wanted   3 knew   4 didn't want   5 did   6 had
> 7 were walking   8 saw   9 liked   10 had decided
> 11 went   12 waited   13 came   14 had sold
>
> **6**
>
> 1 ~~were you training~~ → did you train   2 ~~played~~ → was playing   3 ~~was thinking~~ → thought   4 ~~had forgotten~~ → forgot   5 ~~already left~~ → had already left   6 ~~did you parked~~ → did you park

Pronunciation *had* and *hadn't*

11

- Tell students to listen to the sentences with *had* and *hadn't* from the Grammar box to find out how *had* is pronounced. After each sentence pause the recording for students to repeat, focusing on the pronunciation of *had*.

- 🔊 24 Play the recording.

> **Answer**
>
> Like *was* and *were* in Exercise 6, *had* can be pronounced as a weak form: /həd/ or fully contracted *'d*. In the sentences here it is contracted, although it is pronounced strongly in the negative *hadn't* /hædnt/. As in Exercise 6, don't focus on the isolated word; make sure students practise it in the context of the phrase or sentence.

12

- Tell students to complete the sentences by choosing the correct options.

- Elicit the sentences from individuals to confirm the answers, checking pronunciation of *had*.

> **Answers**
>
> 1 hadn't decided   2 had had   3 hadn't arrived
> 4 didn't eat   5 took   6 had done

SPEAKING My career path

13 21st CENTURY OUTCOMES

- Draw a time line of your own career path, from your schooldays and education through to the present day. Present it by describing the events and the reasons for the path you took.

- **Optional step**. Discuss the metaphors we use to describe the series of events in our lives. Explain that *career path* is a common metaphor, but there are other ways of representing a time line. Elicit a few from students, such as a river, a road, a train line, stepping stones and so on. Let students decide how they want to represent their time lines in the next step. At the end of the exercise, ask them why they chose that metaphor.

- Tell students to make a similar time line to yours. Give them a few minutes for this. While they are busy, suggest some landmarks they might like to include, such as leaving school, graduation, first jobs, changes to the direction of the path and so on.

- Indicate the 21st CENTURY OUTCOME at the foot of the page. Present a few ways on the board of explaining reasons for things that happened and decisions you made, e.g.

    I decided to … because …

    I'm not sure why …

    I was thinking of … when I …

• Put them in pairs to show each other their timelines and explain it. As they talk, monitor, carefully noting good and bad uses of narrative tenses. Check that they are explaining their reasons for their actions clearly.

• **Optional step**. For homework, have them swap time lines, take each other's home and write a biography of their classmates. They can present them as gifts to one another at the beginning of the next lesson.

▶ Photocopiable communicative activity 4.1: Go to page 215 for further practice of the narrative tenses. The teaching notes are on page 236.

▶ Set Workbook pages 36–37 for homework.

4.3 I didn't do it for the money …

READING Paid to succeed

1

• Ask students to read the statement about motivation, think about the meaning of the words in bold and think of an example for each.

• Invite students to say whether they agree with the statement and justify their point of view.

> **Answer**
>
> If you reward someone, you give them something good, such as money or praise because they have done something good, e.g. you thank someone for helping you.
>
> If you punish someone, you give them something bad because they have done something bad, e.g. you have to pay a fine for parking illegally.

• **Optional step**. Draw a donkey, a carrot and a stick on the board. Ask students which is the reward (the carrot) and which the punishment (the stick). Point out the nouns *reward* and *punishment*.

2

• Put students in pairs to discuss the different motivations they had as children from parents and their school and whether they worked.

• Elicit some examples of rewards and punishments. Discuss as a class the effectiveness of each.

3

• Tell students to read the article and choose the statement that best summarizes Gorard's idea. Make sure that they justify their answers by finding evidence in the article.

4

• Ask students to read the article again, this time searching
for evidence supporting options a–c in sentences 1–4.

• When they have finished reading, let them discuss their
answers in pairs.

• **Optional step**. In pairs, students make notes of reasons
why the correct answers are correct and the other options are
incorrect.

Answers

1 b (lines 3–6. There is no evidence for a or c.)

2 c (lines 13–16. There is no evidence for a or b.)

3 c (lines 24–27. There is no evidence for a, and option b
isn't correct because in lines 23–24 it says 'test results did
not greatly improve'.)

4 b (lines 36–38. There is no discussion of the teacher–
student relationship mentioned in option a; option c is
incorrect because it doesn't explain why giving praise
would cost money.)

5

• Explain that words 1–5 can be found in the article. Tell
students to find them and use the context to match them to
the words with similar meanings.

Answers

1 (line 1) rich   2 (line 6) reward   3 (line 10) hard work
4 (line 14) goals   5 (line 31) results

VOCABULARY Success and rewards

6

• Ask students to choose the best option for each sentence.
Tell them that all the words can be found in the article.

• Nominate individuals for the answers.

Answers

1 reward   2 incentives   3 motivate   4 praise
5 passed   6 set   7 succeeded   8 achieve

• Ask the class the following questions to consolidate
understanding:

*What are the two possible results of taking a test? (You
can pass or fail)*

What verbs collocate with a target? (set and achieve)

*Who sets targets, the company or the employee? (the
company)*

Which verb is often followed by 'in'? (succeed)

*What phrase means money as a reward? (a financial
incentive)*

*When you praise someone, what can you say? (e.g. Well
done! Good job! You did really well, etc.)*

*Which verb has no object (i.e. it is intransitive): succeed or
achieve? (succeed)*

7

• Tell students to use words from Exercise 6 in the correct
form to complete the text.

• When they have finished, put them in pairs to check their
answers.

Answers

1 reward   2 pass   3 motivates   4 succeed
5 achieve   6 praise   7 fail   8 incentives

8

• Put students in pairs so that they can discuss which of the
views in Exercise 7 they agree with.

• Elicit whole-class discussion and encourage an exchange
of views.

Background information

How the brain rewards itself

Perhaps you have this expression in your language:
Learning is its own reward. Well, we now understand
that this may be literally true, neurologically speaking.
Money may motivate, but curiosity is what really interests
the brain in learning. When a person is more interested
in something, such as when they know a little about
something but there is a gap in their knowledge, their
brains produce more of a chemical called dopamine. This
strengthens the memory involved in learning, so they
learn better. Dopamine is what you get after feeding an
addiction like chocolate. It's the brain's way of rewarding
itself!

SPEAKING Incentives at work

9   *21st* **CENTURY OUTCOMES**

• Put students in small groups. Ask them to look at the
list of common incentives that employers use to motivate
employees. Tell them to discuss and decide which incentives
cost most, are most effective and which they personally
respond to best.

• While they are talking, listen carefully to their ideas and
the language they use. Make a note of good uses of the target
vocabulary as well as any errors.

- Nominate a spokesperson for each group to summarize their conclusions to the class. Invite further comments where there is disagreement.

10

- Ask the class if, during the discussion, they thought of any other incentives for the workplace which are cheap and can be effective.

Suggested answers

small personal gifts, e.g. chocolates, flowers, pens; vouchers for a local department store; holding meetings outside on sunny days

---

▶ Set Workbook pages 38–39 for homework.

4.4 Sorry, I did my best

VOCABULARY Prepositional phrases

1

- Tell students to match the phrases in the box with their meanings (1–5).

Answers

1 be out of practice   2 be in a hurry   3 have an off day
4 have a day off   5 be on a call

Note that *to be on a call* is different from *to be on call*. If a doctor, for example, is *on call*, she is available in case she is needed at work.

2

- Put students in pairs. Tell them to discuss questions 1–4.

Answers

Students' own answers

LISTENING Office conversations

3

- Explain to students that they are going to hear six short conversations that take place in an office. They need to complete the subject of each conversation.

- 🔊 25 Play the recording.

Transcript

1

A: *Did you post my letter?*

B: *Oh, I'm sorry. I was having an off day yesterday. I forgot.*

2

A: *Can I just ask – why did you book a table for only four people? There are six of us.*

B: *Oh, sorry. You were on a call and I did it without checking with you first.*

3

A: *Did you finish writing the report for Sarah?*

B: *No, sorry. I had a day off yesterday and I didn't realize it was urgent.*

4

A: *Did you translate the letter to Hans Ulrich?*

B: *I did my best. But I'm a bit out of practice with my German, I'm afraid.*

5

A: *Why did you order so much paper? We have nowhere to put it.*

B: *Oh, sorry. It seemed like a good idea at the time. It was really cheap.*

6

A: *Did you book our plane tickets?*

B: *No, sorry. I was in a hurry and I forgot.*

- Let students compare with a partner before eliciting the answers.

Answers

1 posting   2 table   3 report   4 translating   5 paper
6 (plane) tickets

4

- Ask students to try to remember with their partner what happened in each conversation.

- Tell them to listen again to check. They write the number of the conversation (1–6) next to the reasons given (a–f)

- 🔊 25 Play the recording again.

Answers

a 4   b 1   c 2   d 3   e 6   f 5

5

- Point out the Useful language box. Ask students to match the reasons in Exercise 4 (a–f) with expressions in the Useful language box. Explain that they will not need all the phrases in the box. Do the first as an example to clarify instructions.

- Elicit answers from the students.

Answers

a I did my best.

b I was having an off day.

c I did it without checking.

---

d I didn't realize it was urgent.

e I was in a hurry.

f I did it without thinking.

Pronunciation *Sorry*

6a

• Tell students to listen to three different ways of saying sorry. As they listen, they should match the ways with its function (a–c).

• ▶26 Play the recording. Elicit the answers.

Answers
1 b   2 c   3 a

• Get students in pairs to practise saying sorry in these three ways.

6b

• Tell students they are going to listen to the office conversations from Exercise 3 again. Instruct them to label each conversation with the way that *sorry* was used (1–3).

• ▶25 Play the recording.

• Either simply elicit the answers, or tell students to find the conversation transcript on page 166 and practise reading them out loud with their partner. They should pay special attention to the way they say *sorry*.

Answer
The people in conversations 1, 2 and 5 used intonation 3; the people in conversations 3 and 6 used intonation 2. (There is no *sorry* in conversation 4.)

Extra activity

One word role play – *Sorry!*

Explain that you are going to describe different situations and students have to act out the response. Their response should consist of one word only: *sorry*. Tell students to stand up to encourage freer gesture and body language.

Read out the following situations one at a time, pausing between each to let them say *sorry*!

Your brother asks you if he can borrow £100.

Your neighbour tells you that her cat died yesterday.

A friend tells you that they're going to be in a new Hollywood film.

You spill coffee on your mother's sofa.

Your friend says something to you but you are listening to music on your phone.

You accidentally knock into an old man in the street. He falls over.

Someone in the street asks you for a light for their cigarette. You don't smoke.

You forgot to bring your books to class.

You're dancing with a friend in a disco and they shout a question to you.

Ask students to sit down. If they are enjoying the activity, have them think of a new situation each where *sorry* might be an appropriate response. When they stand up a second time, join the class yourself by standing up. Wait for volunteers to take the teacher's role, describing situations to the class, who then say *Sorry!*

SPEAKING Giving reasons for actions

7

• Put students in pairs. Tell them to choose three of the situations and to act out the conversations. Make sure they are aware of the expressions in the Useful language box.

• Monitor carefully, making suggestions and corrections where appropriate.

• **Optional step**. The conversations in Exercise 7 are quick, so do them as a mingling activity. Label students on one side of the class *A* and those on the other side *B*. Explain that the As pair up with a B and start a conversation with a suitable question, e.g. *Why didn't you stay until the end of the meeting?* The Bs respond. Then you shout *Change!*, at which point the As find a new B to practise another conversation with. As should make sure that they practise all five situations. Tell the whole class to stand up and get started. Shout *Change!* after only a few seconds. Keep making them change partners until they have all practised the five conversations at least once.

WRITING Messaging

8

• Tell students to read messages 1–9. Explain that some are messages of congratulations, some of sympathy and some are messages of explanation. Check that they understand *sympathy* (a response to bad news). They need to categorize them accordingly (C, S or E).

• Let them compare their answers with a partner before eliciting the messages in groups.

Answers
1 S   2 S   3 E   4 C   5 C   6 E   7 C   8 E   9 S

9

• **Optional step**. Present the verb patterns used with the three verbs *sympathize*, *explain* and *congratulate*: *sympathize with s.o. (who…)* , *explain why…*, *congratulate s.o. on (verb + -ing …*

• Put students in pairs to discuss possible reasons for writing each message.

• Elicit answers from the class.

10

• Ask the class if they notice anything unusual about the sentences in the messages in Exercise 8. Amongst the ideas you discuss, make sure they mention the fact that words are often missed out.

• Ask them to identify the missing words in sentences 1–4. You could do this together with the class as a whole.

Writing skill Prepositions in messages

11

• Tell students to quickly underline all the prepositions in the messages in Exercise 8.

• Ask them to complete the sentences with the correct preposition: either *about*, *for* or *on*.

12   *21st* CENTURY OUTCOMES

• Explain to students that they are going to practise writing messages to their partner. Show students the three subjects they will write about.

• Tell them to add a fourth subject of their choice. To help them think of one, tell them to get out their mobile phones if they have them, open a messaging app that they often use, and read through some recent messages for inspiration.

• Tell students to write the four messages to their partner. As they write, go around the room, checking on their English, paying attention to use of prepositions. Remind them that we use either a noun or the *-ing* form of a verb after prepositions.

13

• Pairs now exchange messages. Tell them to use the four-point checklist to evaluate their partners' messages and check that they are appropriate for the situations.

• **Optional step.** If students are happy to share contact details, or already have a group for the class established on a messaging app such as WhatsApp, a Facebook group or a class forum, they may wish to write the messages on their phones and send them digitally. This may be a suitable moment to create an online class group to which everyone can write, multiplying the communication possibilities. Once students have practised the messages in Exercise 12, they can write personalized messages to individuals in the class.

TEACHING TIP

An online social media class group

There are many benefits to creating an online group for you and your class. As well as administrative advantages, such as letting students inform you of absence or letting you remind students of homework, it opens up all sorts of possibilities for encouraging students to study and use English in a variety of ways outside of class hours. The skill of messaging will certainly get lots of practice, for example, among other things.

There are potential drawbacks to giving students your contact details, which you should think about carefully before starting. If used well, though, an online continuation of the class adds a dimension to students' learning and brings English closer to their everyday lives.

▶ Photocopiable communicative activity 4.2: Go to page 216 for further practice of prepositional phrases and past simple and continuous. The teaching notes are on page 236.

▶ Set Workbook pages 40–41 for homework.

▶ Set Workbook Writing 2 on pages 42–43 for homework.

REVIEW 2 | UNITS 3 AND 4

READING

1

• Tell students to read the article about M-Pesa and answer questions 1–5.

• Let students discuss their answers in pairs before conducting whole-class feedback.

> **Answers**
>
> 1 'Mobile money' in Swahili
>
> 2 a revolution in the way people receive money, make payments and transfer money from place to place
>
> 3 cheap, convenient
>
> 4 service points, or 'outlets', usually in petrol stations and shops
>
> 5 It has motivated a new generation of Kenyan entrepreneurs to develop new technologies to help people in developing countries.

GRAMMAR

2

• Students choose the correct options to complete the summary.

• Nominate individuals to share answers with the class.

> **Answers**
>
> 1 many   2 a lot of   3 –   4 a   5 a few   6 any
> 7 no   8 a

3

• Explain that the next passage describes how M-Pesa began. Tell them to complete it with the verbs in brackets in the correct past tense form.

• Elicit the three forms students have been studying (past simple, past continuous, past perfect).

> **Answers**
>
> 1 came   2 noticed   3 were sending   4 used
> 5 sold   6 met   7 had already started   8 launched

VOCABULARY

4

• Tell students to choose the correct options to complete the sentences about M-Pesa.

• To check their answers, they look up any they are unsure about in their vocabulary notebooks.

> **Answers**
>
> 1 borrow   2 earn   3 income   4 invest   5 savings
> 6 rewards   7 achieve   8 incentive   9 set   10 succeed

5

• Tell students to complete the account. They should use the words in the box.

> **Answers**
>
> 1 loan   2 succeeding   3 save   4 payment   5 afford
> 6 lent   7 achieving   8 made

DISCUSSION

6

• Put students in pairs or small groups. Direct their attention to the three discussion questions.

• Let them talk for a few minutes. Ensure that they make notes as they go along. Listen out for interesting use of English in their discussions, such as use of recently learned grammar and vocabulary, or notable errors.

• Put pairs or small groups together to share and compare their ideas.

• Elicit some ideas for whole-class discussion. Give feedback on their discussion.

▶ Teaching tip: Correcting speaking activities, Unit 4.2, page 58.

> **Suggested answers**
>
> 1 Students' own answers
>
> 2 M-Pesa is used in Kenya, Tanzania, South Africa, Afghanistan, India and Romania. These are all developing countries at different levels of development; all have populations with limited access to computers, but where mobile telecommunications are affordable to many and play a big part in daily life.
>
> 3 Possible areas where technology is adapted to particular situations include: those adapted for people with physical disabilities, such as messaging for the deaf community; technologies that can go to places that humans cannot, such as robots in radioactive places or probes in space; translation software that allows people to understand other languages. Areas where it is adapted to particular countries include: the wind-up radio for developing countries with no electricity, invented by Trevor Baylis; genetically modified 'golden rice' which contains high amounts of vitamin A for children in India; and the development of different renewable energy projects for different countries.

Extra activity

Poster presentation

Students work in groups to plan an infographic or poster presentation about a subject that emerges from their discussion, e.g. technology in developing countries, popular technologies in their local areas, uses of mobile technology. First, they research the topic online. They design a poster to present the information in graphic form. When the posters have been prepared, they are displayed around the room. Students go around the poster 'exhibition', asking questions about each other's posters.

SPEAKING

7

• Ask students to take turns in pairs to say the parts of either Jonny or the interlocutor (the cashier, waiter, Wilson or David).

• Tell them to put their pens down. They should complete the conversation using the prompts orally only. Explain that they can do it slowly the first time, then try again more quickly the second time.

Answers

1

J: Hello. I'd like to change €200 into Kenyan shillings. What's the rate today?

C: It's 110 shillings for 1 euro.

J: OK. Do you charge commission?

C: Yes, two per cent.

J: That's fine. Can I have a receipt, please?

2

J: Sorry. I'm in a hurry. Can I have the bill, please?

W: Yes, here you are. It's 230 shillings.

J: Is service included?

W: No, sir.

J: Here's 300 shillings. Please keep the change.

3

W: So, Jonny, what did you do on your day off yesterday?

J: I went on a city tour, but the guide spoke Swahili.

W: How is your Swahili these days?

J: I'm a bit out of practice. But I did my best.

4

J: I tried to contact you earlier, David. Did you get my message about printing the new contracts?

D: Oh, yes. Sorry. I was on a call. But I got the message.

J: So, did you print them?

D: No, sorry. I didn't realize it was urgent.

• To consolidate, let them write up the dialogues in the spaces provided.

8

• Tell students to act out the dialogues from memory.

▶ Extra activity: Memorizing dialogues, Unit 3.4, page 49.

• Ask for volunteers to perform the dialogues in front of the class.

WRITING

9

• Put students in pairs. Explain that they are going to write three short messages to their partner, who will then reply to them. Point out the three subjects (1–3). Give them two minutes to write the messages. Ask them to leave a space under each message for a reply.

10

• Tell them to swap messages. In the spaces that their partner has left, they write responses.

11

• Let them compare answers to see whether they used the same phrases to congratulate, explain and show sympathy.

Suggested answers

1 A Guess what! DEC Electronics has just offered me a job as a manager in their factory in Kenya. Isn't that exciting?

  B That's great news! I'm really pleased for you.

2 A Can you meet me after work for a coffee this evening? There's something I'd like to ask you.

  B I can't, I'm afraid. I have to pick the kids up from school today.

3 A I missed the flight home. The taxi was late and the traffic was terrible!

  B Sorry to hear that. Can you get another flight straight away?

---

5 Marketing

UNIT AT A GLANCE

THEMES: Marketing and branding, companies' relationships with customers

TED TALK: *3 ways to (usefully) lose control of your brand.* Tim Leberecht talks about building a stronger brand by handing over control to customers and employees.

AUTHENTIC LISTENING SKILLS: Understanding contrasts

CRITICAL THINKING: Supporting evidence

PRESENTATION SKILLS: Using presentation slides

GRAMMAR: Comparatives and superlatives

VOCABULARY: Marketing collocations

PRONUNCIATION: Expressive intonation

READING: *The power of the crowd*

LISTENING: Asking for opinions

SPEAKING: Comparing the market, Effective marketing, Giving your views

WRITING: A customer review

WRITING SKILL: Linking contrasting points

LEAD IN

• Put students in pairs. Tell students to open books on page 52, look at the photo and read the caption. They discuss who the people on the ground might be in the photo and what the project might be about.

• Elicit ideas in whole-class discussion. Read students the background information.

Background information

JR

In 2013, French street artist JR invited New Yorkers to take self-portraits in a photo booth (a small cabin where you can have your photograph taken) in Times Square. The world's first ever photo booth had been installed there almost 100 years ago. The first portraits were of New Yorkers whose lives were affected by Hurricane Sandy. Later, schools, neighbourhood groups and community organizations were invited to come. In a TED Talk, JR asks: Can art change the world?

• Ask whether they believe art such as this can change the world, and if so, how.

TEDTALKS
BACKGROUND

1

• Tell the class that they are going to watch some of a TED Talk called *3 ways to (usefully) lose control of your brand*, by Tim Leberecht. Check students' understanding of *brand*. Ask the following questions:

What famous brands can you think of? (e.g. Intel, Mercedes-Benz, Lego, Canon, Coca-Cola)

What's the difference between a brand and a product? (See Exercise 2 for a definition of *brand*.)

Extra activity

Whose logo?

Search online for a 'famous brand quiz'. These are series of images of logos with the name deleted. Flash them up on a projector or screen to test students on 'brand awareness'. After the quiz, ask which brands they know best and why.

• Ask students to read the text in pairs, then discuss the questions.

• Ask students to share their answers with the class.

Suggested answers

1 / 2 Students' own answers

3 Many brands sell online, where potential customers read people's comments about brands and their products. These comments might recommend or warn against it. A famous example of a customer comment harming sales happened when United Airlines broke the guitar of musician Dave Carroll on a flight and refused to pay for a new one. He wrote a song called *United breaks guitars* and posted the video on YouTube. After more than 14 million hits, the video did considerable damage to United's brand image.

KEY WORDS

2

• Instruct students to cover up definitions a–g. They read sentences 1–6 and guess the meanings of the words in bold, then write their guesses next to the words.

• Elicit ideas before letting them uncover the definitions and match them to the words.

Answers

1 e   2 c (loyal), g (brand)   3 f   4 a   5 d   6 b

AUTHENTIC LISTENING
SKILLS Understanding contrasts

3a

- **Optional step.** Books closed. Write on the board: *I like tea _____ I don't like coffee*. Students fill the gap in as many ways as they can. Be careful with necessary punctuation:

  *I like tea **but** I don't like coffee.*

  *I like tea. **However,** I don't like coffee.*

- Students read the Authentic listening skills box. Tell them to read the two pairs of contrasting ideas (1–2) from the beginning of the TED Talk and fill in the gaps as they listen.

- 🎧 **27** Play the recording.

Answers
1 However   2 But

3b

- Ask students to write the missing contrasting ideas in two more sentences from the talk.

- 🎧 **28** Play the recording. Ask students if they would like to hear the sentences again.

Answers
3 the offer was exclusive, (and only stood for a limited period of time).
4 builds lasting, long-term

3c

- Tell students to listen and repeat to practise saying the sentences.

- 🎧 **29** Play the recording.

5.1 3 ways to (usefully) lose control of your brand

TEDTALKS

1

- Explain that Tim Leberecht is interested in how companies communicate with customers and employees. While students watch an edited version of his TED Talk, tell them to write down the companies and products he mentions.

- ▶ **5.1** Play the whole talk.

Transcript

0.13 *Companies are losing control. What happens on Wall Street no longer stays on Wall Street. What happens*

in Vegas ends up on YouTube. (Laughter) Reputations are volatile. Loyalties are fickle. Management teams seem increasingly disconnected from their staff. (Laughter) A recent survey said that 27 per cent of bosses believe their employees are inspired by their firm. However, in the same survey, only four per cent of employees agreed. Companies are losing control of their customers and their employees. But are they really?

0.53 *I'm a marketer, and as a marketer, I know that I've never really been in control. Your brand is what other people say about you when you're not in the room, the saying goes. Hyperconnectivity and transparency allow companies to be in that room now, 24/7. They can listen and join the conversation. In fact, they have more control over the loss of control than ever before. They can design for it. But how?*

1.23 *First of all, they can give employees and customers more control. They can collaborate with them on the creation of ideas, knowledge, content, designs and product. They can give them more control over pricing, which is what the band Radiohead did with its pay-as-you-like online release of its album 'In Rainbows'. Buyers could determine the price, but the offer was exclusive, and only stood for a limited period of time. The album sold more copies than previous releases of the band. The Danish chocolate company Anthon Berg opened a so-called 'generous store' in Copenhagen. It asked customers to purchase chocolate with the promise of good deeds towards loved ones. It turned transactions into interactions, and generosity into a currency.*

2.11 *The ultimate empowerment of customers is to ask them not to buy. Outdoor clothier Patagonia encouraged prospective buyers to check out eBay for its used products and to resole their shoes before purchasing new ones. In an even more radical stance against consumerism, the company placed a 'Don't Buy This Jacket' advertisement during the peak of shopping season. It may have jeopardized short-term sales, but it built lasting, long-term loyalty based on shared values.*

2.44 *Research has shown that giving employees more control over their work makes them happier and more productive. The Brazilian company Semco Group famously lets employees set their own work schedules and even their salaries.*

3.00 *Companies can give people more control, but they can also give them less control. Take the travel service Nextpedition. Nextpedition turns the trip into a game, with surprising twists and turns along the way. It does not tell the traveller where she's going until the very last minute, and information is provided just in time. Similarly, Dutch airline KLM launched a surprise campaign, seemingly randomly handing out small gifts to travellers en route to their destination.*

3.36 *Is there anything companies can do to make their employees feel less pressed for time? Yes. Force them to help others. A recent study suggests that having employees complete occasional altruistic tasks throughout the day increases their sense of overall productivity. At Frog, the company I work for, we hold internal speed meet sessions that connect old and new employees, helping them get to know each other fast. By applying a strict process, we give them less control, less choice, but we enable more and richer social interactions.*

4.15 *At the end of the day, as hyperconnectivity and transparency expose companies' behaviour in broad daylight, staying true to their true selves is the only sustainable value proposition. Or as the ballet dancer Alonzo King said, 'What''s interesting about you is you.' For the true selves of companies to come through, openness is paramount, but radical openness is not a solution, because when everything is open, nothing is open. 'A smile is a door that is half open and half closed,' the author Jennifer Egan wrote. Companies can give their employees and customers more control or less. They can worry about how much openness is good for them, and what needs to stay closed. Or they can simply smile, and remain open to all possibilities. Thank you. (Applause)*

Note the differences in British English and North American English shown at the foot of the spread. In this unit, these focus on spelling and vocabulary differences. See Teaching tip 1 on page 6 of the Introduction for ideas on how to present and practise these differences.

Answers
Anthon Berg – chocolate
Patagonia – outdoor clothing, e.g. jackets
Brazilian company Semco Group – no product mentioned
Nextpedition – travel services
Dutch airline KLM – no product mentioned
Frog – no product mentioned

2

• Put students in small groups. Tell them to compare notes from Exercise 1 and discuss why (any) one of the companies was interesting to Tim Leberecht.

• Don't expect much information after only the first listening. Whatever information they can share with the group is worthy of praise.

3

• Give students time to read statements 1–4 before watching the first part of the talk again.

• ▶ **5.1** Play the first part of the talk from 0.00–1.18.

• Let them check with a partner before eliciting answers.

Answers
1 control   2 disconnected from   3 say   4 companies

4

• Ask students to read the examples (1–6) of companies giving more or less control.

• Tell students to match the examples with the companies (a–f) during the second part of the talk.

• ▶ **5.1** Play the second part of the talk from 1.18–3.36.

• Let them check answers with a partner, then elicit answers.

Answers
1 b   2 d   3 a   4 c   5 f   6 e

5

• Tell students to complete the sentences with words from the box then listen to check.

• ▶ **5.1** Play the third part of the talk from 3.36 to the end.

Answers
1 help, connect   2 true   3 open, smile

VOCABULARY IN CONTEXT

6

• ▶ **5.2** Play the clips from the talk. When each multiple-choice question appears, students choose the correct definition. Discourage the more confident students from always giving the answer by asking individuals to raise their hand if they think they know.

Transcript and subtitles

*1 It asked customers to **purchase** chocolate with the promise of good deeds towards loved ones.*
  a eat
  b exchange
  c buy

*2 Outdoor clothier Patagonia encouraged prospective buyers to check out eBay for its **used** products and to resole their shoes before purchasing new ones.*
  a not new
  b out-of-date
  c useful

*3 In an even more radical stance against consumerism, the company placed a 'Don't Buy This Jacket' advertisement during the **peak** of shopping season.*
  a the low point
  b the middle
  c the high point

4 *The Brazilian company Semco Group famously lets employees **set** their own work schedules and even their salaries.*

    a discuss
    b know
    c decide

5 *Is there anything companies can do to make their employees feel less **pressed for time**?*

    a in a hurry
    b stressed
    c tired

6 At the end of the day, *... staying true to their true selves is the only sustainable value proposition.*

    a in the evening
    b in the end
    c at the last moment

Answers

1 c 2 a 3 c 4 c 5 a 6 b

7

- Ask students to complete the sentences in pairs. After they've done this, elicit examples of each for students to compare.

Suggested answers

1 ... video games ... books. / ... furniture ... clothes.

2 ... summer and Christmas. / ... New Year and Carnival.

3 ... develop good relations with colleagues. / ... make money!

CRITICAL THINKING Supporting evidence

8

- Read out the rubric, then ask students to look at each example (a–c) in pairs and decide how it supported Leberecht's message.

Suggested answers

a They gave customers more control over the price of the product.

b By forcing employees to attend 'speed meet' sessions, they give employees no choice in who they talk to, where or when.

c Patagonia encourages more customer control by reminding them of greener options to buy second-hand Patagonia products.

9

- Still in pairs, students share their opinions about these practices and the others in the talk. Write on the board two more discussion points:

    What are the advantages and disadvantages to the companies of these practices?

What other examples can you think of to support Tim Leberecht's argument?

Suggested answers

The advantages include a closer relationship with customers, better industrial relations with staff and good publicity, since some of these ideas attract media attention. Disadvantages include the possibility of customers and employees taking advantage of the greater control they have been given.

10

- Ask students to read Mike's comment. Invite whole-class discussion in reaction. Encourage participation by introducing the other practices mentioned in the talk and any others the students might have brought up. Ask them whether they think these ideas are genuinely open gestures or cynical marketing strategies.

PRESENTATION SKILLS Using presentation slides

11

- **Optional step.** Write on the board: *Death by PowerPoint!* Ask the class what PowerPoint is (software which lets people display visual presentations). Ask if anyone has used PowerPoint or a similar programme. Invite suggestions as to what the phrase means. If they do not know, explain that it refers to the poor use, or over-use, of such software so that it makes listeners bored.

- Put students in pairs to discuss the questions. Encourage them to draw on personal experience and mention any effective or ineffective presentations they have attended.

- After a couple of minutes, ask them to share their ideas with the rest of the class.

12

- Students compare their ideas from Exercise 11 with the points in the Presentation tips box. Elicit any extra tips they thought of.

Answer

Students' own answers

13

- Explain to students that they are going to watch some clips from the talk. Ask them to note the images and the number of words Tim Leberecht typically used in his slides.

- ▶ 5.3 Play the clips.

- Nominate students to describe what they saw.

14

• Explain that students are now going to illustrate an idea with one or more slides of their own choosing.

• Put students in pairs. If students don't have access to a computer, they can sketch the slides or describe them as they imagine them. With Internet access, they can source the images using image searches and copy them to a presentation programme if they have one.

15

• Put pairs together in groups of four. Let them present their slide or slides. Find out whose ideas were similar or different.

Extra activities

Make a Powerful Point

Either

Put students in groups. Hand out the talk transcript from Unit 1 (Mark Bezos). Remind students that this had no visuals. Tell them to plan slides for his talk, using advice from the Presentation tips box as a guide. When they have finished, have them present their ideas to the class.

or

Put students in groups. Remind students of Jacqueline Novogratz's talk from Unit 3 about changing the way we fight poverty. In their groups, students make a list of all the images that they remember from the talk. Replay the talk to refresh their memory. Then tell them to discuss how effective her images were in conveying her message. When they have finished, elicit answers in whole-class discussion.

▶ Set Workbook pages 44–45 for homework.

5.2 What are you looking for?

GRAMMAR Comparatives and superlatives

1

• **Optional step.** Bring to class two simple products that you might buy in the supermarket, such as two bottles of shampoo. Hold them both up and ask the class which they would buy and why. Ask how customers can compare them. Elicit ideas such as by reading the labels or by buying both and trying them at home.

• Put students in pairs to discuss questions 1 and 2.

• In feedback, find out: who does a lot of window shopping before buying, who carefully reads labels, who makes quicker impulse buys without thinking, who sticks to the same brands, who uses the Internet to compare similar products.

2

• Direct students' attention to the infographic. Ask them to read it to find out why the cars are covered and no brands are given.

3

• Tell students to decide which car, A, B or C, answers each of the questions in the infographic.

4

• Direct students' attention to the Grammar box. Tell them to answer questions a–c.

• Students can check their answers and overall understanding of comparatives and superlatives by turning to the Grammar summary on page 148. If you feel that students need more controlled practice before continuing, they could do Exercises 1–6 in the Grammar summary. Otherwise, you could continue on to Exercise 5 in the unit and set the Grammar summary exercises for homework.

Answers

a 3 and 4   b 2   c 1

Answers to Grammar summary exercises

1

1 quickest   2 cheaper   3 more rewarding
4 most expensive   5 simpler   6 healthier
7 prettiest   8 most difficult

2

1 Silver is less expensive than gold.

2 Flying business class is more comfortable than flying economy.

3 The problem is more difficult than you think.

4 She's the oldest of four daughters.

5 Your first idea is not always your best. (Also possible: Your first is not always your best idea. / Your best idea is not always your first.)

3

2 worst   3 more   4 less   5 worse   6 best
7 least   8 most

4

1 correct   2 incorrect – the most interesting   3 correct
4 incorrect – the worst   5 incorrect – earlier
6 incorrect – less   7 correct   8 incorrect – as angry as

5

2 than   3 most   4 as   5 as   6 more   7 as
8 more   9 than   10 most   11 the   12 from /
to   13 not   14 as

6

1 ~~that~~ → than   2 ~~happier~~ → happiest   3 ~~a more easier~~ →
an easier   4 ~~than~~ → from / to   5 ~~most bad~~ → worst
6 ~~the best~~ → better

Extra activity

Paper, scissors, stone

The rules of this well-known game (called 'Rock, paper, scissors' in the United States), in case you aren't sure, are simple: two players simultaneously present one of three gestures to their opponent, symbolizing either paper, scissors or stone. By choosing paper (indicated by a flat hand gesture), player A can beat player B if B chooses stone, but will risk losing if B chooses scissors. By choosing stone (a closed fist), A beats scissors but loses to paper. By choosing scissors (the index and middle fingers together forming a 'V'), A beats paper but loses to stone.

The game is easily adapted to give students practice in grammar and vocabulary. For the winner of each turn to get a point, they must test their opponent with a language challenge; only if the opponent gets it wrong do they get a point.

Play the game as normal, but whoever wins a round says an adjective. Their opponent must say (and spell) the comparative and superlative forms of the adjective or else the winner gets his or her point.

Demonstrate with a volunteer at the front of the class, then put students in pairs to play. The first to three points is the winner.

5

• Tell students to refer to the infographic to find the information they need.

Answers

1 the safest   2 more comfortable   3 the most expensive   4 the worst   5 the least practical
6 lower, as low as

6

• Ask students to discuss in pairs which car is best according to the infographic. They should be able to recall most of the information, so, to encourage communication and greater use of the comparative structures, consider asking them to close their books for this discussion.

• Invite students to share their opinions with the rest of the class.

• **Optional step.** Ask the class to discuss which car would be best for a family, for a travelling businessman, for a young person who has just passed their test or as a taxi.

7

• Give students time to look at the infographic and complete the facts about cars in the UK.

• Get them to read the answers out to the class. (See the first step in Exercise 8 below.)

Answers

1 than   2 More (*less* is not possible with countable nouns – the correct form is *fewer*)   3 most   4 the
5 most, least   6 less   7 as, as   8 as

8

• As you go through the answers in Exercise 7, invite opinions about the facts: which are surprising? Which are true for them? Which are true in their country?

• **Optional step.** Put students in pairs to discuss possible reasons these facts might be true. Then collectively discuss their theories.

9

- Briefly ask the class what factors would help them decide when choosing a new camera. Elicit a few ideas.

- Tell them to read the question and complete each response with the correct option.

Answers

1 most, the   2 as   3 best   4 than   5 from
6 most, more

10

- Students discuss in pairs the statements in Exercise 9 that describe them and their shopping habits. Let them compare these with others in the class.

SPEAKING Comparing the market

11   *21st* **CENTURY OUTCOMES**

- Put students in pairs and allocate A/B roles. Tell them that they are going to ask and answers questions to complete a table and that they have different information; Students A should go to page 171 and Students B to page 172. Tell them not to look at each other's information.

- Elicit the first question that they will need, i.e. *How many stars has The Five Palms got?* Also remind them how to practise the grammar they have been studying with this information. For example, elicit the sentence *The Five Palms is as comfortable/luxurious as the Astra.*

- Depending on the strengths of the class, consider eliciting the other adjectives they will need.

- Give them a few minutes in their pairs to complete the task and share information.

12

- Still in their pairs, students make comparisons between the hotels and tell each other their preferred hotels and why. Monitor their conversations, checking for good use of comparative structures.

- After a few minutes, regain students' attention to find out who preferred which hotel. They should give their reasons for their preference, using the facts they have, to fulfil the 21st CENTURY OUTCOME.

- Give any necessary correction concerning comparative structures.

▶ Photocopiable communicative activity 5.1: Go to page 217 for further practice of comparative structures. The teaching notes are on page 237.

▶ Set Workbook pages 46–47 for homework.

5.3 Help is out there

READING The power of the crowd

1

- Elicit types of advert: TV, Internet adverts, trailers for films, posters in streets and shops, etc. Put students in pairs to discuss the questions then invite feedback to the class.

2

- Students read the article and choose the options (a–c) that best describe the main ideas in the article. Remind them to note where the information is that helps them decide.

Answers

1 c (Lays and Ford are examples of this; a isn't mentioned; paragraph 2 says that online advertising doesn't work, contradicting b)

2 b (lines 33–34; not a because 'this was not a way of saving money'; not c because bad publicity is not mentioned)

3

- Tell them to read the article again and match the paragraphs with the headings.

- Give students time to compare then elicit answers.

Answers

1 D   2 A   3 E   4 C   5 B

4

- Ask students to complete sentences 1–5 with one word from each paragraph. Give a time limit to encourage scan reading.

▶ Teaching tip: Scan reading, Unit 2.2, page 31.

Answers

1 chat   2 interruption   3 appeal   4 submitted
5 engage

5

- Use the whole-class feedback in Exercise 4 to explore whether students agree or disagree with sentences 2 and 5.

Answers

Students' own answers

VOCABULARY Marketing collocations

6

• **Optional step.** Books closed. Write the completed steps in the sequence on the board in random order. Invite students to number the steps in the correct sequential order. When they have finished, rub out the verbs in each step, in preparation for Exercise 6.

• Books open. Tell students to complete the sequence with the missing verbs from the box. If you took the Optional step, use this stage for them to check their ideas.

> **Answers**
> 2 listen 3 understand 4 develop 5 launch 6 run
> 7 promote 8 measure

7

• Pairs. Students discuss which parts of the sequence in Exercise 6 Lays and Ford did.

> **Answer**
> According to the article, Lays did market research and listened to their customers via the Facebook campaign, then launched the product. Ford ran an advertising campaign before launching the product.

8

• Explain that both options are possible according to each student's point of view. They compare their answers and justify their views with a partner.

> **Answers**
> Students' own answers.

SPEAKING Effective marketing

9 **21st CENTURY OUTCOMES**

• Ask students to look at the list of different kinds of promotion or recommendation. They think of examples of at least three that have caught their attention in a positive or negative way.

• Put students in small groups to tell each other their examples.

• Tell them to decide which ways of promoting or recommending things seem most effective according to their examples. (This fulfils the 21st CENTURY OUTCOME of evaluating different means of communication.)

Extra activity

Search terms

Invite volunteers to describe to the whole class adverts they have seen online. Tell listeners to write down the search terms they would need to use to find the adverts themselves. Follow up the next lesson by asking whether they found any of the adverts and what they thought of them.

▶ Set Workbook pages 48–49 for homework.

5.4 What do you think of it?

LISTENING Asking for opinions

1

• Tell students to complete the table with the adjectives. Elicit answers.

> **Answers**
> Great – amazing, fantastic
> OK – all right, so-so
> Terrible – awful, dreadful

• Quickly drill the adjectives with suitably expressive intonation.

2

• Put students in pairs to describe things in categories a–c using the adjectives from Exercise 1. They should think of at least one thing for each category.

• When they have finished, elicit a couple of examples of each category.

> **Answers**
> Students' own answers

3

• Explain to the class that they are going to listen to five conversations. As they listen, they must complete the subject of each conversation and the speakers' opinions.

• 🔊 **30** Play the recording.

Transcript

1

A: Do you know the new Thai restaurant round the corner?

B: Olly's Thai? Yeah, we went there last week.

A: What do you think of it?

B: Yeah, I'd recommend it. The menu's very limited, but the food is fantastic.

2

A: Is Brighton a good town for shopping?

B: I don't know. But I imagine it's more interesting than many places, because it has a lot of independent shops.

3

A: I'm thinking of buying a new bike. Do you know anything about Giant bikes?

B: Yes. I've got one myself. I love it, but it depends on what you're looking for.

A: What do you mean?

B: Well. They're generally quite heavy bikes, but they're really strong. That's important for me, because I'm quite hard on bikes.

4

A: We're going to a Vietnamese restaurant tonight. Do you know if the food is good?

B: I couldn't tell you, really.

A: Is it spicy?

B: In my experience, in most Asian restaurants you can just ask the waiter to make the dish less spicy.

5

A: What do you think of Tarantino's new film?

B: It's OK. I don't think it's anything special.

• Let students check their answers with a partner before conducting whole-class feedback.

> **Answers**
> 1 Thai – G   2 shopping – P   3 bikes – G   4 restaurant – N   5 film – OK

4

• Point out the Useful language box on page 61. Tell students to listen again to the conversations and tick the phrases the speakers use to comment.

• 🎧 30 Play the recording again. Ask the class for the phrases they heard.

> **Answers**
> Conversation 1 – What do you think of…?, I'd recommend it.
> Conversation 2 – Is … a good …?, I don't know, I imagine …
> Conversation 3 – Do you know anything about …?, I love it, It depends on …
> Conversation 4 – Do you know if something is …?, I couldn't tell you, In my experience …
> Conversation 5 – What do you think of …?, I don't think it's …

5

• Put students in pairs to try to remember which adjectives the speakers used to explain their answers. Tell them to complete the descriptions.

• Elicit answers from the class or play the recording again for students to check.

> **Answers**
> 1 limited, fantastic   2 interesting   3 heavy, strong   4 spicy   5 special

Pronunciation Expressive intonation

6a

• Tell students to listen to the sentences and focus on the differences in intonation when the speaker makes a positive or negative point.

• 🎧 31 Play the recording.

> **Answer**
> The intonation when making positive points is expressive, with a wide pitch range and heavy stress on the main syllable of the word carrying the positive opinion. In negative points, it is less expressive, with a flatter range.

6b

• Ask students to practise saying the sentences in pairs, with appropriate intonation. Listen carefully for natural-sounding intonation.

> **TEACHING TIP**
>
> **Intonation**
>
> Intonation patterns vary from language to language. To some learners, for example, male English speakers can sound effeminate because their intonation uses a wider pitch range than men in their language typically use. Some students may enjoy exaggerating expressive intonation for comic effect, but be aware that others may be reluctant to mimic these patterns. Conversely, they may be interested to know that a flat intonation can suggest boredom or lack of interest to the listener, so more natural English intonation patterns may be something to consider adopting.

SPEAKING Giving your views

7

- Tell students that they are going to practise giving their views. Ask them to work in pairs to choose three things to talk about from the list. Make sure they have specific restaurants, films and so on in mind. Remind them not to write anything, but to improvise using the expressions in the Useful language box.

- As they act out the dialogues, listen for correct use of English, appropriate intonation and a wide range of adjectives in their views.

- **Optional step.** Invite volunteer pairs to act out dialogues in front of the class. They should not mention the name of the thing they are commenting on, though, replacing giveaway words with *BEEP*, e.g. *Do you know anything about the new BEEP in town?* The rest of the class have to guess what they are talking about.

- Go through any interesting language points you want to bring to the students' attention, such as common errors.

▶ Teaching tip: Correcting speaking activities, Unit 4.2, page 58.

If there is time, instruct students to act out two more conversations.

WRITING A customer review

8

- Ask students to read the customer reviews and to answer the questions. Suggest they make lists of the positive and negative points in their notebooks.

- Elicit points from students for whole-class feedback.

Answers

1 First review: Positive: fast, simple to use, problem-free, works well, screen quality fine, sound excellent, good value for money. Negative points: not very attractive, webcam not good quality.

Second review: Positive: light, fast and good price. Negative: the customer finding it difficult to learn to use. It is not clear whether this is because the computer is complicated or the customer not very computer literate!

2 They agree that it is fast and good value for money.

3 They both recommend the laptop.

Writing skill Linking contrasting points

9a

- Tell students to look for contrasting points in the reviews. Show them how the contrasting ideas can be in the same sentence or in adjacent sentences.

Answers

I had a Sony before, which was beautiful, <u>but</u> it was also twice as expensive.

Someone says in another comment on this website that the screen isn't great. <u>However</u>, I disagree.

My only gripe is that the webcam is not very good quality. <u>Having said that</u>, the sound is excellent.

<u>Although</u> the guy in the shop gave me lots of help with it, I am still trying to learn how to use it! <u>But</u> it seems good.

9b

- Ask students to underline the word and phrases used to link contrasting points, then answer the questions.

Answers

1 but, although   2 Although, However, Having said that, But

- **Optional step.** Remind them of the Authentic listening skills section on page 53. Elicit other ways of linking contrasting points.

Note: in some texts, such as formal letters and academic essays, *but* should not be used at the start of sentences.

9c

• Ask students to rewrite the contrasting points using the words and phrases given. Monitor carefully, checking for accurate punctuation. Stronger students may appreciate seeing alternatives to the word order, as shown in brackets below.

Answers

1 Although the screen is a bit small, it's a good product. (It's a good product, although the screen …)

2 It's excellent quality. Having said that, it isn't cheap.

3 The instruction manual is hopeless. However, the shop assistants were very helpful. (The shop assistants were very helpful, however.)

4 I normally like this company, but I was disappointed by this product. (…company. But I was…)

---

10   *21st* CENTURY OUTCOMES

• Tell students to write a review of something they have bought recently, using the bullet points to guide them.

• Monitor closely while they write, checking that students are writing balanced reviews, including a range of suitable linking words and a clear conclusion.

11

• Tell students to swap reviews with a partner and check that they have included the points from Exercise 10. Ensure that they have included the good and bad points as instructed, and balanced the two, i.e. that the review is fair (to fulfil 21st CENTURY OUTCOMES).

• In feedback, ask students whether they would buy the product or service based on their partners' reviews.

• **Optional step.** If students bought the product online, ask them whether the website where they bought it has customer reviews. Students may be motivated to write their reviews online.

▶ Teaching tip: Comment / Tweet / Post, Unit 2.1, page 26.

▶ Photocopiable communicative activity 5.2: Go to page 218 for further practice of the language of giving opinion, comparative structures and adjectives. The teaching notes are on page 238.

▶ Set Workbook pages 50–51 for homework.

▶ Set Workbook Presentation 3 on pages 52–53 for homework.

6 Communication

LEAD IN

• Books closed. Show the class one or two of the photos introducing Units 1–5. Tell them the title of the next unit: *Communication*. Ask students, in pairs, to come up with an idea for a photo to illustrate the theme and to discuss the message behind their choice of photo.

• Alternatively, you could ask students at the end of the previous lesson to bring in a photo that illustrates communication. If they have Internet access, they can source an image online.

• After a couple of minutes, elicit some ideas and discuss the different messages behind each image.

• Tell students to open their books on pages 62-3 to look at the photo. In their pairs, they discuss the following questions:

Where are the men? What are they doing?

What message does this photo communicate to you?

TEDTALKS
BACKGROUND

1

• Tell students to read the text about the speaker and the talk and to complete the summary with the correct options.

Answers
1 communications   2 future   3 ideas

KEY WORDS

2

• Ask students to read sentences 1–6, matching the words in bold to their definitions.

Answers
1 d   2 a   3 c   4 b   5 f   6 e

• If necessary, check comprehension further by asking follow-up questions: *What natural phenomenon is explained by this **analogy**?* (draw a greenhouse and the sun's rays entering as an analogy for global warming) *Why is global warming especially **relevant** to small island communities in the Pacific?* (The sea level may go up because of global warming, and this may affect them) *What other areas does the world need to **tackle**?* (e.g. poverty, waste management, disease) *Which areas of science are not **accessible** to normal people, in your opinion?* (e.g. theoretical physics, quantum theory, neuroscience) *What **jargon** is there in your profession? Were you or anyone in your class at school **nerdy**? What were they interested in?*

• Put students in pairs to ask each other the questions. After a couple of minutes, elicit ideas for each.

AUTHENTIC LISTENING SKILLS Elision

3a

• Ask students to read the Authentic listening skills box. Read out the example phrases in the box (*next please*, etc). Say the connected phrase, e.g. /nekspliːz/ then say the words distinctly /nekst pliːz/. Point out the elision of the /t/ sound. Make students copy you each step of the way so that they can feel and hear the difference themselves.

• Tell students to listen to four extracts from the TED Talk and underline the sound that is elided.

• ⌂ 32 Play the recording.

• Let students compare answers with a partner before asking them to share with the class.

3b

- Tell students to listen carefully for the missing words in three more extracts.

- ⏵ **33** Play the recording twice.

Background information

Formally recognized elision

People may say *nex_ please* and *the firs_ question*, but that doesn't mean you should write it like this. However, it is acceptable to write a few examples of elision. That's what contractions are. *They've* and *What's* are simply spoken elisions that are formally recognized in writing. Notice that in the most formal writing contexts, such as business letters, contractions are considered inappropriate.

But what about the following contractions? In what writing types might they be acceptable?

What've you been doing? (*What have*)

rock 'n' roll (rock *and* roll)

It's a beautiful day, innit? (*isn't it*)

I like it 'cos it's fun. (*because*)

In some informal writing such as text messages between friends it is acceptable to use such contractions, but you need to be careful using them in other contexts. They may look uneducated or rude. What other examples of elision in writing have you seen?

6.1 Talk nerdy to me

TEDTALKS

1

- Explain to students that they are going to listen to the TED Talk for the main ideas. Indicate the questions.

- ⏵ **6.1** Play the TED Talk.

Transcript

0.13 Five years ago, I experienced a bit of what it must have been like to be Alice in Wonderland. Penn State asked me, a communications teacher, to teach a communications class for engineering students. And I was scared. (Laughter) Really scared. Scared of these students with their big brains and their big books and their big, unfamiliar words. But as these conversations unfolded, I experienced what Alice must have when she went down that rabbit hole and saw that door to a whole new world. That's just how I felt as I had those conversations with the students. I was amazed at the ideas that they had, and I wanted others to experience this wonderland as well. And I believe the key to opening that door is great communication.

1.00 We desperately need great communication from our scientists and engineers in order to change the world. Our scientists and engineers are the ones that are tackling our grandest challenges, from energy to environment to health care, among others, and if we don't know about it and understand it, then the work isn't done, and I believe it's our responsibility as non-scientists to have these interactions. But these great conversations can't occur if our scientists and engineers don't invite us in to see their wonderland. So scientists and engineers, please, talk nerdy to us.

1.36 I want to share a few keys on how you can do that to make sure that we can see that your science is sexy and that your engineering is engaging. First question to answer for us: so what? Tell us why your science is relevant to us. Don't just tell me that you study trabeculae, but tell me that you study trabeculae, which is the mesh-like structure of our bones because it's important to understanding and treating osteoporosis.

2.04 And when you're describing your science, beware of jargon. Jargon is a barrier to our understanding of your ideas. Sure, you can say 'spatial and temporal' but why not just say 'space and time', which is so much more accessible to us? And making your ideas accessible is not the same as dumbing it down. Instead, as Einstein said, make everything as simple as possible, but no simpler. You can clearly communicate your science without compromising the ideas. A few things to consider are having examples, stories and analogies. Those are ways to engage and excite us about your content. And when presenting your work, drop the bullet points. Have you ever wondered why they're called bullet points? (Laughter) What do bullets do? Bullets kill, and they will kill your presentation. A slide like this is not only boring, but it relies too much on the language area of our brain, and causes us to become overwhelmed. Instead, this example slide by Genevieve Brown is much more effective. It's showing that the special structure of trabeculae are so strong that they actually inspired the unique design of the Eiffel Tower. And the trick here is to use a single, readable sentence that the audience can key into if they get a bit lost, and then provide visuals which appeal to our other senses and create a deeper sense of understanding of what's being described.

3.33 So I think these are just a few keys that can help the rest of us to open that door and see the wonderland that is science and engineering. And because the engineers that I've worked with have taught me to become really in touch with my inner nerd, I want to summarize with an equation. (Laughter) Take your science, subtract your bullet points and your jargon, divide by relevance, meaning share what's relevant to the audience, and multiply it by the passion that you have for this incredible work that you're doing, and that is going to equal incredible interactions that are full of understanding. And so, scientists and engineers, when you've solved this equation, by all means, talk nerdy to me. (Laughter) Thank you. (Applause)

Note the differences in British English and North American English shown at the foot of the spread. In this unit, these focus on pronunciation differences. See Teaching tip 1 on page 6 of the Introduction for ideas on how to present and practise these differences.

• Let students check in pairs before eliciting answers.

Answers
1 the world of science and engineering
2 by helping scientists communicate their ideas

2

• Ask students to choose the correct options to complete the description.

• ▶ 6.1 Play the first part of the talk (0.00–1.36). Go through the answers with the class.

Answers
1 engineering 2 scared 3 amazed 4 wonderland
5 health care

3

• Students focus on the steps scientists should take in the second part of the talk. Tell them to complete the sentences with one word.

• ▶ 6.1 Play the second part of the talk from 1.36–3.33.

Answers
1 relevant 2 jargon 3 simpler 4 bullet 5 visuals

• **Optional step.** Ask if students can think of other advice they would give to people wanting to present complex ideas clearly. Remind them of the Presentation tips in previous units. Extra ideas could include: staying focused on one big idea (from Unit 3), using stories that engage audiences emotionally (Unit 3), using gestures to help get meaning across (Unit 4), not reading from your slides (Unit 5).

4

• Remind students that Melissa Marshall uses an equation at the end of her talk. Tell them to watch and complete the equation using the words in the box.

• ▶ 6.1 Play the third part of the talk from 3.33 to the end.

• Ask students to discuss what the equation means in pairs. Elicit their ideas.

Answers
1 subtract 2 divide 3 multiply 4 equal
The equation means scientists should present their ideas without lots of difficult words but showing their passion for the topic and making it relevant to their audience.

VOCABULARY IN CONTEXT

5

• ▶ 6.2 Play the clips from the talk. When each multiple-choice question appears, students choose the correct definition. Discourage the more confident students from always giving the answer by asking individuals to raise their hand if they think they know.

Transcript and subtitles

1 And I believe the **key** to opening that door is great communication.
- *a* solution
- *b* difficulty
- *c* result

2 But these great conversations can't **occur** if our scientists and engineers don't invite us in.
- *a* start
- *b* stop
- *c* happen

3 And when you're describing your science, **beware of** jargon.
- *a* try to use
- *b* be careful of
- *c* be frightened of

4 Jargon **is a barrier to** our understanding of your ideas.
- *a* stops
- *b* helps
- *c* improves

5 And the **trick** here is to use a single, readable sentence that the audience can key into.
- *a* joke
- *b* skill
- *c* disadvantage

Answers

1 a   2 c   3 b   4 a   5 b

6

• Ask students in pairs to complete the sentences in their own words. Elicit some answers.

Suggested answers

1 … brevity (keeping it short) / … listening to the other person / … patience.

2 … cultural differences because polite gestures in one language might be rude in others.

3 … higher education / … employment / … global understanding.

CRITICAL THINKING Demonstrating your argument

7

• Ask the class to discuss in pairs whether they thought Melissa Marshall followed her own recommendations in preparing and giving her talk. Tell them to discuss her ways for explaining her ideas in a clear way.

• Discuss as a whole class the techniques she uses to communicate.

Suggested answers

She did follow her own recommendations, by using these techniques: a visual presentation with slides containing no bullet points; repeating her main line (*Talk nerdy to me*); contrasting a poor slide with bullets and jargon with a good, visual slide; using an analogy with a familiar story (*Alice in Wonderland*); mentioning science's relevance to us; making it personal, recounting her personal experience with engineers.

8

• Ask students to read the comment and answer the first question about who else should follow their own advice.

Answers

Teachers, doctors, employers, bankers (and anyone who instructs others) should follow their advice when they tell us how to be healthy, how to work efficiently, how to be careful with money, etc.

• Invite the class to discuss whether they agree and to suggest other professionals who could benefit from the advice.

• Ask whether students agree with Melissa Marshall that scientists need help communicating their ideas.

Answers

Students' own answers

9

• Give students a couple of minutes to think of any professionals they have met who were good communicators. They can then compare their experiences with a partner. If they have difficulty with this, you can offer some suggestions from the answers below.

• Invite individuals to share their ideas in whole-class feedback.

Suggested answers

Most students will have had experience of e.g. teachers, medical professionals, sports instructors, technology advisers, tour guides.

PRESENTATION SKILLS Engaging with your audience

10

• Ask students to discuss in pairs how good presenters can make presentations seem like conversations.

Suggested answers

Not reading from a script; making eye contact with the audience; using informal language, gestures and humour to mimic conversation with friends; asking questions.

11

• Get students to read the Presentation tips and compare with their own ideas.

• Ask the class which ideas were similar, and whether they had other ideas not mentioned in the box.

12

• Explain that as students watch a clip from the talk, they should note any techniques used which are mentioned in the Presentation tips box.

• ▶ 6.3 Play the clip.

> **Answers**
>
> She uses all of the techniques mentioned in the tips box. She also uses informal language, e.g. **Sure**, you can say …, **drop** the bullet points.

13

• Tell students to prepare a two-minute mini-presentation on an idea or concept they are knowledgeable about. Encourage them to explore various areas for the topic: professional life, home life, studies or free time. Alternatively, they could re-use and develop a presentation that they have prepared in a previous unit.

• As students make notes, monitor, offering suggestions and corrections. They should think what questions they can ask to involve the audience in the 'conversation'. Remind them of relevant advice from earlier units.

14

• Let students practise on each other in pairs, focusing on the techniques from the Presentation tips box.

• When they have practised for a while, change pairs for them to give their presentations to new partners. Instruct partners to give feedback based on the tips.

▶ Teaching tip: Three ways to pair up students, Unit 2.1, page 27.

• **Optional step**. To round off the lesson, invite volunteers to the front of the class to do their presentations in front of everyone.

▶ Set Workbook pages 54–55 for homework.

6.2 How do you communicate?

GRAMMAR Verb patterns with infinitive and -ing

1

• Books closed. Put students in pairs. Tell them to make a list of ways that people communicate. Avoid giving them examples at this stage to encourage a free interpretation of the question.

• Ask them to divide the list in two: written and spoken forms of communication. Students may need a miscellaneous category for other means of communication.

• Invite students to write their ideas on the board, organized in lists.

> **Suggested answers**
>
> Written forms of communication: letters, emails, text messages, social media messages such as tweets, newspaper articles, blogs, notes, signs and notices, poetry and prose, etc.
>
> Spoken forms of communication: face-to-face communication, phone calls, online video calls, speeches, TV and radio shows, movies, theatre, etc.
>
> Other: gestures, hand movements, facial expressions, through visual means such as signs and posters, codes, art

2

• Still with their books closed, students in pairs get together to form groups of four. Tell them to decide which forms of communication are the most and least personal, and to justify their opinions. Again, leave the students to define *personal* themselves.

• Elect a spokesperson for each group to summarize their discussion for the whole class.

> **Answers**
>
> Students' own answers

3

• Give students two minutes to do the quiz on their own. Monitor in case students need help understanding some less frequent words such as *avoid, linked, to post, unread, voicemail*.

• When they have finished, find out the number of 'texters', 'networkers', 'callers' and 'emailers' with a show of hands.

4

• Ask individuals if they agree with the result of the quiz and why.

Background information

Texting is the business!

Do you think email is to business life what texting is to social life? Think again. Texting is quickly replacing email in the workplace for many tasks which email has been responsible for over the last twenty years, from reminding people to attend meetings all the way to closing large business deals. While it may be seen as rude to check your emails on your mobile phone in the middle of a meeting, checking a quick text is less likely to offend. Of course, email is still the best medium for long, detailed messages and for attaching documents, but if an email is urgent, people often send a text just to let someone know that they have sent them an email!

However, be careful using texts in business. Think carefully about whether adding an emoji to a text to make it funny or light-hearted is appropriate in a professional setting. Also, while we text at all hours to our family and friends, your work colleagues will appreciate you sending them work messages only during office hours.

5

• Direct students' attention to the Grammar box. Tell them to answer questions 1–3.

• Tell them to find two more examples of verbs followed by *to* + infinitive and the *-ing* form in the quiz.

Answers

1 try, wants   2 avoid, hate   3 allows

a *to* + infinitive: *hope, decide*

b *-ing* form: *spend (time), like, enjoy*

• Students can check their answers and overall understanding of verb patterns by turning to the Grammar summary on page 150. If you feel that students need more controlled practice before continuing, they could do one or both of Exercises 1–2 in the Grammar summary. Otherwise, you could continue on to Exercise 6 in the unit and set the Grammar summary exercises for homework.

Answers to Grammar summary exercises

1

1 to fix   2 to help   3 to make   4 speaking   5 giving
6 standing   7 to give   8 to do   9 to have   10 renting
11 to come   12 looking   13 paying   14 to do   15 to be   16 paying

2

2 Can you tell him to call me?

3 Do you want me to go to the bank?

4 I hope not to be late.

5 I agreed to pay her £12 per hour.

6 I hate not knowing the answer.

7 She encouraged me to apply for the job.

8 I asked her to book two tickets.

6

• As students complete the texts with the correct form of the verbs, monitor carefully, checking all are clear on the rules.

• For feedback, ask students to read out one sentence at a time.

Answers

Text 1

1 to use   2 using   3 to say   4 apologizing   5 to send

Text 2

1 to answer   2 writing   3 writing   4 doing

• **Optional step**. Ask students which person they sympathize with most in 1 and 2. Can they think of other problems they experience with communication?

7

• Ask students to complete the sentences in ways that are true for them. Ensure that they use the verb forms correctly.

• Students compare their answers in pairs.

Suggested answers

1 … listening to callers who try to sell me something.

2 … checking and rechecking my emails when it isn't necessary.

3 … to write to my grandmother more often. She doesn't have email.

4 … watching presentations with lots of bullet points.

5 … talking to my family on WhatsApp.

Extra activity

Top five Communication Gripes

Tell the class about something that annoys you about modern communication, such as your mobile phone's battery life, poor punctuation in texts or animated emoticons. Teach them the phrases: *The thing I really hate about… is…*; *I can't stand…* and *I hate the way…*

Put students in groups. Ask them to discuss the things that annoy them most about modern communication, their 'gripes' or complaints. Tell them to decide on the worst five. They should reach a decision in about ten minutes.

Reorganize them so that they are talking to people from other groups, i.e. AAA BBB CCC → ABC ABC ABC. Tell them to share and compare their groups' gripes.

GRAMMAR Infinitive and -ing clauses

8

• Students answer questions 1 and 2 in the Grammar box, then turn to page 150 to check their answers. If appropriate, they complete Exercises 3–5 of the Grammar summary.

Answers

1 The first sentence uses *to* + infinitive, the second uses the *-ing* form of the verb.

2 There is no difference in meaning; any difference is stylistic or a shift in emphasis.

Answers to Grammar summary exercises

3

1 Changing jobs can be stressful.

2 It's essential to know the right person to contact.

3 It's very rewarding to help people with their problems.

4 Seeing him again after so many years was strange.

5 It's easier to walk downhill than (to walk) uphill.

6 Not having the right information was embarrassing.

7 It takes a long time to plan a big event.

8 Spending time with my family was great.

4

2 It isn't easy to write poetry. / Writing poetry isn't easy.

3 It's tiring to work twelve hours per day. / Working twelve hours per day is tiring.

4 It's a bad idea to go for a run without a bottle of water. / Going for a run without a bottle of water is a bad idea.

5 It's sensible to book tickets in advance. / Booking tickets in advance is sensible.

6 It isn't polite to phone people after 9 p.m. / Phoning people after 9 p.m. isn't polite.

5

1 ~~to listen~~ → listening   2 ~~wait~~ → waiting   3 ~~finding~~ → find / to find   4 ~~told to~~ → told me to   5 ~~to not~~ → not to   6 ~~To work~~ → Working

9

• If students have done the exercises from the Grammar summary, let them do this exercise orally, as suggested in the Teaching tip below.

Answers

2 Calling him late at night was a bad idea.

3 It's very important to write clearly.

4 Looking at a computer all day is tiring.

5 Hearing different points of view is always useful.

6 It's sometimes difficult to know the right means of communication to use.

7 It's lazy to text rather than to phone.

8 It's hard to write a good letter.

SPEAKING Means of communication

10   *21st* CENTURY OUTCOMES

• Show the class the four messages that need to be sent. Explain that students need to decide the best way to send the messages and to briefly describe what they would say.

• Also ask them to consider what possible consequences there would be of choosing the *wrong* means of communication.

• Put the students in pairs for the discussion, monitoring them to check they are on task and adding details. Ask them to justify their choice of means of communication for each situation and what they think would happen if they got it wrong.

• Put pairs together to share their ideas and compare.

• In feedback, ask if pairs had any differences of opinion.

Suggested answers

1 A card or letter offering congratulations is a suitable response. Sending flowers with the message is very popular, too. If they are not close friends, an email or Facebook message may also be acceptable. A text may cause offence for being too casual.

---

2 It is important that the customer feels you really care about the problem and that your apology is serious, so a formal email or letter is appropriate. A quick email or text would not be appropriate. It might read: 'I would like to apologize for sending you incorrect information about …'.

3 The only appropriate means to do this is face-to-face in a private place such as your office. A letter or email suggests that you don't care enough about something which is going to seriously affect the employee's life. You might say: 'Belinda, I'm afraid I have some bad news. You've probably heard that the office is closing? Well, we're going to have to reduce the staff, and I'm sorry to say that we have to let you go.'

4 You could share a link to the song on Spotify or Facebook, either via these sites or by email, etc. You might accompany the link with a short phrase like: 'Fantastic song!'

- **Optional step**. Students write a fifth message for classmates to comment on and discuss.

▶ Photocopiable communicative activity 6.1: Go to page 219 for further practice of verb + infinitive or -ing form structures. The teaching notes are on page 238.

▶ Set Workbook pages 56–57 for homework.

6.3 Good communication

READING Why we don't listen any more

1

- Put students in pairs. Give them two minutes to think of two people they enjoy listening to and two they don't. Make sure they discuss their reasons for liking or not liking them.
- Let students share and compare their ideas.

2

- Ask students to read the article. The first time they read they should focus on the reasons the writer says we have stopped listening to our leaders. Set a time limit to encourage skim reading.

Answer
He says that we have stopped listening to our leaders because they do not speak from the heart and because their actions don't match what they say they are going to do.

3

- Ask them to read the article again and choose the correct answers to the questions. Remind them to look for evidence to support their answers.
- In feedback, ask them to justify their answers.

Answers
1 b (line 5) 2 a (lines 5–7) 3 c (lines 7–8) 4 b (line 17) 5 b (lines 26–7) 6 a (lines 28–9) 7 b (lines 30–34) 8 c (lines 40–41)

4

- Tell students that the words and expressions needed to complete the sentences are in order through the article.

▶ Teaching tip: Scan reading, Unit 2.3, page 31.

- Ask individual students to read out each completed sentence to the class.

Answers
1 reliable 2 defend 3 the heart 4 match 5 trust

- Make sure students record the new words and phrases in their vocabulary books: *a reliable transport system / person, to defend your argument / point of view, speak from the heart, keep promises, lose trust in*.

5

- Ask students to work in pairs to choose the two most important lessons from the article, using the list in Exercise 4.
- Open the floor for whole-class discussion.

Answers
Students' own answers

VOCABULARY Communication collocations

6

- Write the six verbs from box A on the board with space for the collocations. Demonstrate the activity with the whole class by eliciting the collocation with *have* from box B (*a meeting*). Tell them some verbs have more than one collocation and some phrases in box B collocate with more than one verb.
- Put students in pairs to do the exercise.
- Let pairs check answers with another pair before eliciting answers from the class.

Answers
have a meeting **give** a presentation / a speech **make** a comment / a phone call / a speech **post** a comment / a letter **send** an email / a letter / a text message **write** a comment / an email / a letter / a presentation / a report / a speech / a message

- Check that students understand that politicians and Oscar winners *give speeches*, while *presentations* are given at conferences and in meetings. Point out that you *give a presentation* or *a speech*, but that you don't *make a presentation*, only *make a speech*. Point out also that *making a comment* means speaking, while *posting a comment* means writing.

7

- Students complete the sentences with the collocations from Exercise 6. Warn them that they may sometimes need to change the form and that there is usually more than one answer.

- Let students discuss with another student when they have finished.

> **Answers**
>
> 1 make a phone call   2 give a presentation / make/ give a speech   3 posted/wrote a comment   4 sent him an email / text message   5 'm having / have a meeting   6 write the report/presentation/speech/letter, wrote/made a few comments   7 post/send/write her a letter

8

- Ask students in pairs to tell each other which of the things in Exercise 6 they did in the last week. Ask them to say what the subject was for each one. Encourage further practice of the collocations by asking them to tell their partners when they last did the other things in Exercise 6.

> **Answers**
>
> Students' own answers

SPEAKING Communication skills

9   *21st* **CENTURY OUTCOMES**

- Put students in small groups to discuss the professions and the most important communication skills to them. Encourage them to specify subskills, such as doctors needing to speak sensitively about people's illnesses.

- Ask spokespeople from each group to present their ideas to the class.

> **Answers**
>
> Students' own answers

10

- Now ask students to tell each other (in their groups) about their jobs or jobs they know and the communication skills required to do them well. This fulfils the 21st CENTURY OUTCOME of understanding the importance of communication skills.

Extra activity

Pop quiz

If you have any spare time at the end of the lesson, use it to reinforce the language learned that day. Tell students to close their books and get out a piece of paper and a pen. Tell them to write down the following (answers in brackets):

- an adjective to describe a transport system that you can trust (*reliable* – 1 point)

- a phrase that means to say something you really believe in (*speak from the heart* – 1 point)

- the missing preposition in the phrase *to lose trust BEEP someone.* (*in* – 1 point)

- two reasons we don't listen to authority figures any more (see Exercise 2 – 2 points)

- two professions who need good listening skills (see Exercise 9 – 2 points)

- as many communication collocations as they remember for the verbs *have*, *give*, *make*, *post*, *send* and *write* (see Exercise 6 – max 18 points)

Students award themselves a mark out of 25.

If you don't have time at the end of this lesson, you could leave the quiz until the start of the next lesson. This type of quiz can of course be done after any lesson.

▶ Set Workbook pages 58–59 for homework.

6.4 Is it your first time here?

VOCABULARY Small talk phrases

Extra activity

Central Park

Books closed. Sketch a city park scene with park bench on the board. If you have online access, put on some 'city park sound effects'. As you sketch ask the class: *Where are we? What time is it? What's the weather like?* to elicit the setting. Draw two people at either end of the bench – stick figures are fine! Ask: *What are they doing?* Let students decide the details, but establish that the two people are strangers.

Put students in groups of three. Explain that two of each group are the people in the park. The third is a silent observer. Have one of the people already sitting on the bench. The other sits down to start the scene.

Take observers to one side and quietly explain their role, which is to find out whether the strangers speak, who speaks first, exactly what they say to begin the conversation, and what their body language says about them.

Tell students to start. Leave students to improvise for as long as it takes for any conversations to start, but stop the activity after three or four minutes.

Ask the observers to report on the scenes they witnessed. Ask them whether the strangers spoke, what they spoke about and whether body language suggested that they were happy to talk to one another.

1

• Books open. Show students the two photos and ask which scenario, A or B, is more probable where they live. Elicit possible reasons people do or don't talk to one another.

2

• Put students in pairs to discuss where people sometimes talk to strangers and what topics they commonly talk about. Be sure to also personalize the topic by asking them to think about their attitudes to small talk. Do they do it? Where? When? Why? Why not?

Answers
Students' own answers

3

• Ask students to read the explanation and decide which opening sentences are good examples of small talk. If they did the Extra activity, they can compare these opening lines with what they said.

Suggested answers
Topics acceptable as small talk may differ from country to country, but in general, sentences 1–6 are all good examples of small talk, although sentence 5 could be slightly inappropriate in some situations. Sentence 7 is opinionated and negative and invites disagreement, even potentially causing offence. Sentence 8 is an unsuitable first topic of conversation; it is not light or friendly. Like sentence 7, there is a good chance the two people won't find things in common in this area.

4

• Tell students to match answers a–h to the opening sentences 1–8 in Exercise 3.

• Conduct whole-class feedback as dialogues, with one student providing the opener and another the answer.

Answers
1 b 2 c 3 e 4 a 5 f 6 h 7 d 8 g

LISTENING Follow-up questions

5

• Put students in pairs to continue conversations 1–6 from Exercises 3 and 4 by thinking of follow-up questions or comments. They should do this orally without writing anything, and only continue for two or three lines.

• Tell them to listen to the conversations and compare these conversations with theirs.

• 🅐 34 Play the recording.

Transcript

1

A: Do you come from Spain?

B: Yes, I do. How did you know?

A: It was your accent. Whereabouts in Spain are you from?

B: From Madrid. Do you know it?

2

A: Is it your first time in Vienna?

B: Yes, it is. I really like it.

A: Have you visited the Schönbrunn Palace yet?

B: No, I haven't, but it's on my to-do list.

3

A: Can you believe this weather we're having?

B: I know, it's amazing. A bit hot for work, though.

A: That's true. Do you have a holiday coming up soon?

B: No, unfortunately not.

4

A: I love the food in this hotel.

B: Yes, it's great.

A: I know. I have to be careful I don't eat too much.

B: Oh, I don't worry about that.

5

A: I like your jacket. It's a really nice colour.

B: Thanks. I just bought it yesterday, actually.

A: Oh, where did you get it?

B: At Mango.

6

A: Oh, you're reading 'Wonder'. I really enjoyed that book.

B: Yes, I've only just started it, but I can't put it down.

A: Have you read her other book?

B: No, what's that called?

• Ask students if their follow-up questions and comments were similar or very different.

Pronunciation Sentence stress

6a

• Tell students to complete the answers with the words in the box.

• Conduct feedback as a dialogue, with different students reading out the openers and responses.

Answers
1 actually   2 great   3 so   4 really   5 do

6b

• 🔊 35 Play the recording for students to check their answers.

• 🔊 35 Play the recording a second time. This time students underline the words that are stressed in each answer.

• Let them check with another student before eliciting answers.

Answers
1 <u>No</u>, we're on <u>ho</u>liday, actually.
2 <u>Yes</u>, it's <u>great</u>.
3 <u>Yes</u>, so would <u>I</u>.
4 <u>No</u>, not <u>rea</u>lly. Just a <u>few</u> <u>words</u>.
5 <u>Yes</u>, I <u>do</u>. It's fan<u>tas</u>tic.

6c

• Chorally drill the phrases in short, manageable chunks, paying attention to stress.

• Students practise saying the conversations in pairs.

• **Optional step.** Give students practice at manipulating the grammar of short responses so that they can respond more spontaneously. Point out that we use *so* to agree to an affirmative sentence and *neither* to agree to a negative sentence. Elicit the short answer to *I like chocolate.* (*So do I.*) and *We don't live here.* (*Neither do we.*) Read out the following, eliciting short answer responses each time: *I love this weather.* (*So do I.*) *I'm from Argentina.* (*So am I.*) *I'm enjoying the festival.* (*So am I.*) *We aren't staying in the city.* (*Neither are we.*) *I can't wait until her next book comes out.* (*Neither can I.*) *I'd like to come to the conference again.* (*So would I.*) *I haven't seen her before.* (*Neither have I.*)

SPEAKING Small talk

7

• Explain that students are now going to practise what they have learned. Ask them to imagine they are at a conference, it is lunchtime and they sit down next to someone they don't know.

• Nominate students to provide details about the conference. Ask: *What city is the conference in? What is it about? Who is the main speaker? What is the weather like? What type of food are they serving?* Accept whatever answers the students give.

• Ask students to form pairs to practise small talk, using the expressions in the Useful language box to help. Listen carefully to their openers and responses. Pay attention to the appropriacy of the questions and topics.

• Provide any feedback about the language used and the appropriacy of their small talk. Then get them to change partners and act out another conversation.

WRITING Short emails

8

• Ask students to read short emails A–E and match them to the subjects. Point out the subject lines are empty to ensure understanding.

Answers
1 B   2 D   3 C   4 A   5 E

Writing skill Reasons for writing

9a

• Ask students to find and note the different elements in each email. Using that information they decide which emails are formal and which are less formal.

• Let them discuss before sharing answers.

Answers
Email A – Greeting: *Hi …,* reason for writing: *I'm just writing to ask if …* , action wanted: *… if you could send me …* , ending: *Thanks and best wishes.* A is a less formal email.
Email B – Greeting: *Hi …* , reason for writing: *Just a quick note to say …* , action wanted: none, ending: just his name. B is an informal email.

Email C – Greeting: *Dear …* , reason for writing: *I apologize for …* , action wanted: none; ending: *Kind regards*. C is a formal email.

Email D – Greeting: *Dear …* , reason for writing: *This is to confirm that …* , action wanted: none, ending: *Yours sincerely …* . D is a formal email.

Email E – Greeting: *Hello*, reason for writing: *I am writing to enquire …* , action wanted: *Please can you call me …* , ending: *Thanks*. E is a slightly formal email.

9b

- Students choose the correct words to complete the sentences.

Answers

1 for   2 about   3 for   4 if   5 that

10 *21st* CENTURY OUTCOMES

- Put students in pairs and allocate letter A and B to the students in each pair. Tell them to read the details of their respective situations, then to write an email.

- As you monitor their writing, check that the register is suitable and the use of expressions from Exercise 9 is correct.

11

- Have them exchange emails with their partner. Students should check that their partner has started and ended appropriately, and given a reason for writing, i.e. explained their purpose effectively.

Suggested answers

A

Hello / Dear Sir or Madam

I am writing to enquire about the possibility of staying in your hotel for two nights, from the 18th to the 20th of next month. I will need a single room. Please could you let me know if a room is available?

Yours,

David Ferran

B

Hi Jake,

How are you? I'm just writing to apologize for not replying to your email two weeks ago. I spoke to the Human Resources department but unfortunately there aren't any positions available at the moment.

Good luck looking for a job, and best wishes,

Joanna

12

- Give students a few minutes to write a short reply to their partner's email.

Extra activity

Writing for real

Ask students to imagine that they are planning a short city break. Each student should choose a different city if possible. Tell them to think of all the things that they might do there, where they could stay and how they might get around. Ask them to make a list of possible questions that they might have when planning their trip, such as museum opening times, room prices in hotels, typical taxi fares and so on.

Tell them that they are going to write an email of enquiry to the city's tourist office. Decide whether you think students should actually send the email or not. If you decide to let them send their emails, show them how to search for the relevant website and where to go to leave an email. Recommend that they prepare the email first then copy and paste it into the webpage. If students send the emails, tell them to bring any replies they receive over the following lessons to read out to the class.

▶ Photocopiable communicative activity 6.2: Go to page 220 for further practice of the language of small talk. The teaching notes are on page 239.

▶ Set Workbook pages 60–61 for homework.

▶ Set Workbook Writing 3 on pages 62–63 for homework.

REVIEW 3 | UNITS 5 AND 6

READING

1

- Books closed. Write the name of the organization on the board. If necessary, check understanding of *moral* (if something is done morally, it is based on what the person believes is right thing to do). Put students in pairs to discuss what the organization might do.

- Elicit their ideas about *Morally Marketed* but don't tell them whether they are right or wrong.

- Let them read the article to find out what it does.

> **Answer**
>
> *Morally Marketed* promotes honesty and openness in marketing and encourages discussion about what is right and wrong in marketing.

2

- Ask students to read the article again and decide whether the sentences are true or false.

> **Answers**
>
> 1 F (Ralph believes marketing has more influence on us than we think.)
>
> 2 T ('... in their advertisements, companies often communicate messages that are misleading.')
>
> 3 F ('*Morally Marketed* encourages an open conversation about what is good and bad practice ...')
>
> 4 T ('Its aims are to get marketers to promote positive values in society ...')
>
> 5 F (It shows children asking for a light, not actually smoking.)

GRAMMAR

3

- Make sure students understand that they must use two words to complete each space.

> **Answers**
>
> 1 more honest   2 the best   3 more careful   4 as easy
> 5 faster than

4

- Tell students to complete the comments with the given verb in the correct form.

> **Answers**
>
> 1 watching   2 to be, to smoke   3 to smoke / smoking
> 4 stopping, to stop   5 thinking

VOCABULARY

5

- Ask students to complete the text with the words.

> **Answers**
>
> 1 wrote   2 did   3 listened   4 developed   5 launched
> 6 had   7 promote   8 run   9 posted   10 send

DISCUSSION

6

- Put students in pairs to think of two adverts and to describe them to each other. One should be for a product that is good for us (or should be), such as yoghurt, exercise machines; and another is for something fun, such as chocolate, fizzy drinks. They should discuss how honest and open they think the adverts are.

- Ask students to share their adverts and opinions with the rest of the class.

7

- Ask students to write two more truthful slogans about other products, like the examples in the text in Exercise 5.

- Invite students to read their slogans out for the rest of the class to guess the product.

SPEAKING

8

- Put students in pairs. Tell them to read the conversations, which practise the speaking skills introduced on page 61.

- Decide whether students can complete the conversations orally without writing or not. If you think they can do them without written support, tell them to put their pens down. They should complete the conversations using the prompts orally only. Explain that they can do it slowly the first time, then try again more quickly the second time.

- When they are reasonably fluent at the conversations, have them swap roles and try again.

- Let them write up the conversations in the spaces provided. For less confident students or classes, let them write the complete conversations before reading them out loud.

Answers

1

A: Do you know anything about advertising on the Internet?

B: It depends on what you mean by advertising.

A: Well, I just want more people to find our website.

B: Oh, I see. Well, in my experience, it is / might be / can be a good idea to get an expert to advise you on that.

2

A: What do you think of the new Marks and Spencer advertisement?

B: I couldn't tell you. I haven't seen it.

3

A: Do you know if Lowe Alpine make good winter jackets?

B: Yes, they're great. I've got one myself. I'd recommend them.

9

• Put students in pairs to practise their small talk skills (introduced on page 70) using the four opening sentences. Remind them of the need to ask follow-up questions to show interest and keep the conversations going.

• **Optional step**. Invite volunteers to perform their mini-dialogues in front of the class.

10

• Tell students to listen and compare their conversations in Exercise 9 with those on the recording.

• ⌂ 36 Play the recording.

• Tell students to write as much of each dialogue as they can remember, either on their own or in pairs to help each other.

• ⌂ 36 Play the recording again for students to check and complete the dialogues.

Transcript

1

A: Where are you from?

B: I'm from Italy.

A: Whereabouts in Italy?

B: Milan. Do you know it?

2

A: I like your jacket.

B: Thanks.

A: Where did you get it?

B: From a vintage clothes shop in Brighton.

3

A: Is it your first time here?

B: Yes, it is. It's great.

A: Have you visited the Rijksmuseum?

B: Not yet, but I'd like to.

4

A: I can't believe this hot weather we're having.

B: I know. It's incredible.

A: What's the weather like in England at the moment?

B: It's the same, actually.

WRITING A customer review

11

• Ask students to read the review and complete the sentences with their own ideas. Do not check answers yet; this will be done after Exercise 12.

12

• Let students compare their reviews in pairs to see whether their ideas are similar or different.

Suggested answers

1 … they are definitely worth it. / … they are excellent quality.

2 I wore them in the rain and my feet were completely dry.

3 … they don't really feel heavy when you have them on your feet.

7 Experience

THEMES: Life experiences and their effect on who we are now

TED TALK: *What I've learned from my autistic brothers.* Faith Jegede talks about her experiences growing up with two autistic brothers and what they have taught her about 'normality' and being 'extraordinary'.

AUTHENTIC LISTENING SKILLS: Weak forms

CRITICAL THINKING: A speaker's authority

PRESENTATION SKILLS: Being concise

GRAMMAR: Present perfect simple, present perfect simple and past simple, Extension: present perfect continuous

VOCABULARY: Personal qualities

PRONUNCIATION: Weak forms: *have*, *has* and *been*, Linking words

READING: France's new CV law

LISTENING: A job interview

SPEAKING: Life experiences, Diversity at work, Describing skills and interests

WRITING: A CV

WRITING SKILL: Verb forms

LEAD IN

• Ask students to open their books and look at the photo on page 74.

• Ask questions about the photo and elicit answers from individuals: *What is she doing? How does the photo illustrate the theme of experience? What image would you choose to illustrate the theme?*

TEDTALKS
BACKGROUND

1

• Tell the class to read the text about Faith Jegede and her talk. If necessary, check the meaning of the following words:

truth seeker – someone who looks for what is true

believe in a cause – if you believe in a cause, you think that something is important enough to work hard to achieve

awareness – understanding of an issue or subject

standing out – being noticeable and impressive

• **Optional step.** Drill the pronunciation of autism /ˈɔːtɪzm/ and autistic /ɔːˈtɪstɪk/. Even if they are cognates, the initial vowel sound is likely to be different in the students' first language. Emphasize the shift in word stress between the noun and adjective: *autism* Ooo, *autistic* oOo.

• In pairs or threes, students discuss the questions. Monitor groups closely and check with anyone talking about personal experiences in their groups that they would be happy to share this with the whole class.

• Encourage them to share their answers with the class, asking them to justify their ideas.

Answers
Students' own answers

TEACHING TIP

A sensitive subject?

The word *autism* is a cognate in many languages but students may not be aware of the nature of the condition. On the other hand, some class members *may* have experience of autism in their families. If you know of anyone like this, don't assume they will be happy to talk about it in front of the class. Consider asking them *before* the lesson whether they would be willing.

Write *autism (n)* and *autistic (adj)* on the board and check understanding: *If a person has autism, can they walk and talk and use their muscles?* (Yes) *Is it always easy to see if a person has autism?* (No) *Is there a solution to the condition? Can an autistic person ever stop having autism?* (Not at the moment) *Might an autistic person have problems at a party?* (Yes) *What kind of problems?* (They would find it difficult to talk to people and relate to them).

KEY WORDS

2

• Ask students to guess the meaning of the words in bold, covering up definitions a–f. Then have them match the words with their definitions.

Answers
1 d   2 a   3 f   4 b   5 e   6 c

• To further check comprehension, ask follow-up questions: *What situations do **hyperactive** children find difficult? When is it acceptable to **tell a lie**? What is the best way to deal with a child who is **having a tantrum**? Is it **greedy** to want a big salary? What is **unique** about your country? Do you know a good **cure** for a cold?*

AUTHENTIC LISTENING SKILLS
Weak forms

3a

- **Optional step**. Books closed. Write on the board a sentence from the previous activity:

  My brother was born with a bone disease that has no cure.

- Tell the class that you are going to say it out loud twice and ask them to tell you what difference they notice between the two versions. The first time, give every word the same time duration and emphasis, with no stress or weak forms. Then say it naturally, emphasizing the content words and ensuring you use weak forms of *was*, *a* and *that*.

- Elicit the differences between the two versions, i.e. in the second version you 'swallowed' the function (grammatical) words. Ask a student to come to the board and underline the weak forms in the sentence.

  My brother <u>was</u> born with <u>a</u> bone disease <u>that</u> has no cure.

- Ask students to read the Authentic listening skills box, then to guess which words in Exercise 3a will be in their weak forms. Elicit answers without saying whether they are correct or not.

- ▶ Teaching tip: Don't stress!, Unit 4.2, page 56.

- 🔊 37 Play the recording. Students underline the weak forms.

- Copy the sentences on the board so volunteers can underline the weak forms for everyone to see.

Answers

1 Now, I'd like <u>to</u> introduce you to my brothers.

2 Remi is 22, tall <u>and</u> very handsome.

Note that the second *to* in sentence 1 is pronounced with the full form. This is probably because of the hesitation at that point.

3b

- Have students underline weak forms in these two sentences in pairs.

- 🔊 38 Play the recording, twice if necessary.

- Invite a student to underline the weak forms on the board. There is likely to be some disagreement, for example, some people may hear the word *but* as a weak form /bət/ while others may say it is just spoken very quickly.

Answers

3 He's speechless, <u>but</u> he communicates joy in a way <u>that</u> some <u>of</u> the best orators cannot.

4 He remembers the year <u>of</u> release <u>for</u> every song on my iPod.

- Note that some of the words are barely audible. It may be worth mentioning that proficient speakers often don't hear words, but reconstruct the sentence from the clearly spoken words and the meaning, imagining the words that must be there.

3c

- 🔊 39 Play the recording, the four sentences, again, pausing between each one to give the students time to say the sentences out loud.

- Monitor, correct and drill the weak forms.

▶ Teaching tip: Pronunciation – backchaining, Unit 1.2, page 17.

Let the students decide

TEACHING TIP

Students need to recognize weak forms and understand them in connected speech, but it is less certain that they need to produce them in speech. Weak forms could make them harder to understand. Talk about these issues with the class and let students decide: do they want to practise weak forms to sound more natural, or is being clear in English more important to them?

7.1 What I've learned from my autistic brothers
TEDTALKS

1

- Tell students to read questions 1 and 2. Ask them for an antonym for *ordinary*. Ask if anyone can describe typical autistic behaviour. Don't accept or correct their ideas.

- ▶ 7.1 Play the whole talk.

Transcript

0:14 Today I have just one request. Please don't tell me I'm normal.

0:20 Now I'd like to introduce you to my brothers. Remi is 22, tall and very handsome. He's speechless, but he communicates joy in a way that some of the best orators cannot. Remi knows what love is. He shares it unconditionally and he shares it regardless. He's not greedy. He doesn't see skin colour. He doesn't care about religious differences, and get this: he has never told a lie. When he sings songs from our childhood, attempting words that not even I could remember, he reminds me of one thing: how little we know about the mind, and how wonderful the unknown must be.

1:09 Samuel is 16. He's tall. He's very handsome. He has the most impeccable memory. He has a selective one, though. He doesn't remember if he stole my chocolate bar, but he remembers the year of release for every song on my iPod, conversations we had when he was four, weeing on my arm on the first ever episode of Teletubbies, and Lady Gaga's birthday.

1:37 *Don't they sound incredible? But most people don't agree. And in fact, because their minds don't fit into society's version of normal, they're often bypassed and misunderstood.*

1:52 *But what lifted my heart and strengthened my soul was that even though this was the case, although they were not seen as ordinary, this could only mean one thing: that they were extraordinary -- autistic and extraordinary.*

2:11 *Now, for you who may be less familiar with the term 'autism', it's a complex brain disorder that affects social communication, learning and sometimes physical skills. It manifests in each individual differently, hence why Remi is so different from Sam. And across the world, every twenty minutes, one new person is diagnosed with autism, and although it's one of the fastest-growing developmental disorders in the world, there is no known cause or cure.*

2:40 *And I cannot remember the first moment I encountered autism, but I cannot recall a day without it. I was just three years old when my brother came along, and I was so excited that I had a new being in my life. And after a few months went by, I realized that he was different. He screamed a lot. He didn't want to play like the other babies did, and in fact, he didn't seem very interested in me whatsoever. Remi lived and reigned in his own world, with his own rules, and he found pleasure in the smallest things, like lining up cars around the room and staring at the washing machine and eating anything that came in between. And as he grew older, he grew more different, and the differences became more obvious. Yet beyond the tantrums and the frustration and the never-ending hyperactivity was something really unique: a pure and innocent nature, a boy who saw the world without prejudice, a human who had never lied. Extraordinary.*

3:51 *Now, I cannot deny that there have been some challenging moments in my family, moments where I've wished that they were just like me. But I cast my mind back to the things that they've taught me about individuality and communication and love, and I realize that these are things that I wouldn't want to change with normality. Normality overlooks the beauty that differences give us, and the fact that we are different doesn't mean that one of us is wrong. It just means that there's a different kind of right. And if I could communicate just one thing to Remi and to Sam and to you, it would be that you don't have to be normal. You can be extraordinary. Because autistic or not, the differences that we have – We've got a gift! Everyone's got a gift inside of us, and in all honesty, the pursuit of normality is the ultimate sacrifice of potential. The chance for greatness, for progress and for change dies the moment we try to be like someone else.*

5:04 *Please – don't tell me I'm normal. Thank you. (Applause)*

- In small groups, students compare what they heard before you elicit answers.

Answers
1 *extraordinary*, she describes her brothers in this way
2 Remi doesn't talk but he communicates joy in other ways, he shares his love with everyone, he isn't greedy, he doesn't discriminate, he never lies, Samuel has an excellent memory.

Note the differences in British English and North American English shown at the foot of the spread. In this unit, these focus on vocabulary differences. See Teaching tip 1 on page 6 of the Introduction for ideas on how to present and practise these differences. Point out that Faith Jegede uses the British English *chocolate bar* and *washing machine*, but an American speaker would say *candy bar* and *(clothes) washer*.

2

- Show students the table and ask them to fill in any gaps from memory that they can.

- ▶️ 7.1 Play the first part of the talk (0.00–1.52) for students to check and complete the table.

- When the clip has finished, elicit the answers.

Answers
1 tall   2 very handsome   3 love   4 lie   5 16   6 tall
7 very handsome   8 memory

3

- For the next part of the talk, students choose the correct option to complete the sentences. Ask them to read the five sentences before they watch and predict the correct answers.

TEACHING TIP

Turn listening into checking

Students often find fast, natural speech difficult to understand, even though the tasks are designed to be within the abilities of this level. In many listening activities, prediction work can make understanding much easier. By encouraging students to think of possible answers, you focus their attention on the task. If the class is struggling to understand the speaker, you could even discuss likely answers as a class, sharing around more confident class members' ideas. Listening then becomes a matter of confirming group ideas rather than distinguishing them alone.

- ▶️ 7.1 Play the second part of the talk from 1.52–3.51. When it has finished, ask individual students to read out the answers.

Answers
1 different   2 common   3 excited   4 world   5 pure and innocent

4

• Put the students in pairs to complete Faith Jegede's ideas with the words in the box.

• ▶ 7.1 Play the third part of the talk (3.51 to the end) for students to check their answers.

> **Answers**
> 1 beauty   2 wrong, different   3 extraordinary
> 4 progress   5 normal

5

• Tell students in pairs to discuss the questions.

• Give them a couple of minutes for this. Nominate individuals to share their discussion points with the class.

VOCABULARY IN CONTEXT

6

• ▶ 7.2 Play the clips from the talk. When each multiple-choice question appears, students choose the correct definition. Discourage the more confident students from always giving the answer by asking individuals to raise their hand if they think they know.

Transcript and subtitles

1 He doesn't care about religious differences, and **get this***: He has never told a lie.*
  a listen to this
  b answer this
  c solve this

2 Now, for you who may **be** *less* **familiar with** *the term 'autism', it's a complex brain disorder that affects social communication.*
  a use often
  b like
  c know well

3 And I cannot remember the first moment I encountered autism, but I cannot **recall** *a day without it.*
  a imagine
  b remember
  c name

4 … he found pleasure in the smallest things, like lining up cars around the room and **staring at** *the washing machine.*
  a talking to
  b listening to
  c looking hard at

5 Now, I cannot deny that there have been some **challenging** *moments in my family, moments where I've wished that they were just like me.*
  a horrible
  b not easy
  c exciting

6 Yet beyond the tantrums and the frustration and the **never-ending** *hyperactivity was something really unique*
  a very great
  b continuous
  c very annoying

> **Answers**
> 1 a   2 c   3 b   4 c   5 b   6 b

Extra activity

Ask for more!

When the clip has finished, test the students' memory of the words by reading out the sentences in random order but replacing the words in bold with a 'beep', creating a spoken gap fill. The whole class fills the gaps by calling out the word, e.g. *Now, I cannot deny that there have been some BEEP moments in my family. – Challenging.* Repeat the sentences until you are confident that most of the students know which word fits in each sentence. This also gets them repeating the words so that you can check pronunciation. You could also say the synonyms as prompts for the words, e.g. *continuous – never-ending.*

7

• Give students a few minutes to complete the four sentences on their own. Make sure that they understand that the sentences should be true for them. Give examples from your own life to make this clear.

• Monitor as they write, suggesting corrections where necessary.

• Tell them to compare their sentences with a partner or in small groups.

> **Suggested answers**
> 1 … passed my teaching course. / … celebrated my 16th birthday.
> 2 … Adobe Photoshop. / … Schubert's music.
> 3 economics / philosophy / linguistics / pure maths
> 4 … chocolate! / … matching socks!

CRITICAL THINKING A speaker's authority

8

• **Optional step**. Books closed. Ask students to imagine that they are in a large lecture hall with lots of people. Ask them to imagine the hall, the people, the noise and so on, and to describe in their minds the speaker at the front. Make sure they decide on the speaker's age, sex, clothes and profession. Now ask several students to describe their speaker to the whole class. Ask what it is that gives that person the authority to be listened to by so many people. Encourage different answers, such as the person's age and experience, their expertise and knowledge in the area, their presentation skills and ability to entertain. Ask whether the person would have as much authority if they were younger/older, male/female, wearing jeans, or less experienced.

- **Books open.** Ask students to work on their own before eliciting the correct answer.

Answer
b

9
- Ask students to read the comment and answer the question.

Answer
The viewer also has an autistic brother. The viewer and Faith have learned to understand and appreciate autistic behaviour by seeing things from their brothers' point of view, appreciating differences and what that brings to their experience of the world.

10
- Put students in pairs. Tell them to try and remember the positive and negative aspects about Faith's experience with her brothers.
- After a couple of minutes, group each pair with a neighbouring pair and ask them to compare their answers.

Suggested answers
Positive points include: Remi's happiness and love, his lack of prejudice, his innocence, the fact that he never lies, the sense of wonder at the mind; Samuel's amazing memory; above all, it has taught her not to try to be normal but to be extraordinary like her brothers.

Negative points might include: the fact that many people don't understand how incredible her brothers are; that autism affects social communication, learning and sometimes physical skills; Remi's screaming as a baby, and his tantrums and hyperactivity; his lack of social skills or interest in his big sister; the challenging moments when she wished her brothers were more normal.

- **Optional step.** Students identify the things they would feel confident enough to talk about, whether personal or professional, and share with a partner where they think that confidence comes from in each case.

PRESENTATION SKILLS Being concise

11
- Books closed. Ask for a definition or synonyms for *concise* (short, brief, saying things quickly and simply, etc.).
- Books open. Give the students a minute to read the Tips box about being concise.
- Elicit a few ideas as to why concision in presentations is a good quality.

Suggested answers
Listeners won't get bored; main ideas will be clear if you don't try to convey lots of other ideas at the same time; if you interest people with a powerful idea straight away, they will listen to all of your talk; deciding beforehand about what to include forces you to focus on the most important information.

- Ask them how long most presentations they have attended are (e.g. typically, business presentations might last thirty minutes to an hour).

12
- Explain that students are going to watch some clips from the talk. They should think about which tips Faith Jegede follows.
- ▶ 7.3 Play the clips.

Answer
She follows all of them – she express ideas in a short, simple way, she focuses on two or three main points, she leaves out unnecessary details, she gets to the point quickly.

13
- Students are required to prioritize information and simplify longer sentences in order to edit the texts. If this a skill the class can do well, they can work individually. However, if students need support, let them work in small groups.
- Direct half of the students (A) to page 171 and half (B) to page 172, where they will find the texts.
- Tell them to make the information as concise as possible, just two or three short sentences.

Suggested answers
Student A – Autism in adults

Autism affects adults and children. People learn that they have autism in different ways. Autism is not an illness, it is a condition that affects the way you see the world.

Student B – Understanding what it is like to be autistic

Autistic people often feel that their senses are under attack. For example, they can't block out sounds like most people can, and almost feel pain trying to deal with all the noise. If they seem angry or upset, people without autism need to be patient and sympathetic with them.

- When all the groups have finished, divide the class into pairs of one A and one B student.
- Explain that they are going to tell each other the information about autism that they have just learned.
- Give them a couple of minutes to share their information.

▶ Set Workbook pages 64–65 for homework.

7.2 What have you learned?

GRAMMAR Present perfect simple

1

- Show students the infographic about the UK. Discuss the first statistic with the whole class to clarify what they have to do. Ask them to think about what they know about the UK and to guess whether they think Britain has a lot of jobs and low unemployment or not many jobs and high unemployment.

- Invite suggestions as to the percentage of Britons who have never had a job. Write the range of answers on the board under the number '1' (e.g. if students have said 3%, 10%, 40% and 15%, write 3%–40%).

- Put the students in small groups and ask them to discuss the other statistics (2–6) on the infographic.

- After two minutes, regain class attention and collect guesses. Write them on the board.

- Now tell the class to listen to find out the actual statistics.

- 🔊 40 Play the recording.

Answers
1 6%   2 60%   3 11%   4 80%   5 one in every six 6 50

TEACHING TIP

Easy listening? Give the answers!

If your class has been struggling a little with listening tasks, provide them with the answers on the board, but mixed up. The students can then see the information they are listening for and match it to the correct statistic, an easier task than listening without the options.

Transcript

Meanwhile back at home, new statistics just published show that while unemployment is down, there are still six per cent of people in the UK who have never had a job. London remains the highest skilled workforce – sixty per cent of those working in London have been to university. In technology, 73 per cent of us now use the Internet every day, but eleven per cent of Britons have never used it. Other highlights show that eighty per cent of Britons have travelled abroad at some time in their lives and one in six households have been the victim of a crime. Lastly, in our relationships it seems that we can't make up our minds if we want to be with someone who is similar or very different. Fifty per cent of people say the partner they have chosen is their complete opposite.

2

- Ask students to discuss the statistics in relation to questions 1–3 in pairs. These questions may generate a lot of discussion, especially question 3, so remind them to speak in English.

- In whole-class feedback, make sure that students justify their guesses for question 3. Ask questions that personalize the topic: *Do you know anyone who has never had a job / used the Internet / has been the victim of a crime? Have you travelled abroad?*

Answer
Students' own answers

- **Optional step.** Ask students to find out the information about their country/ies for question 3 on the Internet, either in class or for homework.

- If you wish, ask the class about the nature of the information itself: *Where do they think this information comes from? How easy it is to find? Do they think it is accurate? Why might the figures be too high or too low?* etc. (All the data is from the Office for National Statistics, a government department in the UK, amongst other sources.)

3

- Tell the students to answer the question about the sentences in the Grammar box.

- Students can check their answers and overall understanding of the present perfect simple by turning to the Grammar summary on page 152. If students need more controlled practice before continuing, they could do Exercises 1 and 2 in the Grammar summary. Otherwise, continue on to Exercise 4 in the unit and set the Grammar summary exercises for homework.

Answer
c

Answers to Grammar summary exercises
1 1 have looked   2 Have you had   3 have owned 4 have also helped   5 haven't worked   6 has also owned   7 has sold   8 has it taught   9 have learned   10 has also given **2** 1 ~~just been~~ → just gone   2 correct   3 ~~have gone~~ → have been   4 ~~has been~~ → has gone

- Ask the class more questions to focus on the present perfect:

    What is the verb structure in the three sentences called? (the present perfect)

    What time do they all refer to (a time in the past that is not specified)

What auxiliary verb is used to form the present perfect?
(*have* or *has*)

What form of the verb is used after the auxiliary? (the past participle)

- To further clarify the function, or meaning, of the present perfect, draw a time line for the first sentence:

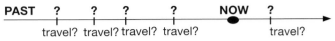

| PAST | ? | ? | ? | ? | NOW | ? |

travel? travel? travel? travel?   travel?

**80% of Britons have travelled
abroad at some time in their lives**

- Ask: *Have 80% of Britons been abroad before now?* (Yes) *Do we know when?* (No) *Is it possible that they will also travel abroad in the future?* (Yes)

4

- Tell students to complete the comments with the correct form of the present perfect. Elicit the irregular verbs in the exercise and their past participles before students begin.
- When they have finished, get students to share answers.

Answers

1 have never liked   2 has had, has also been   3 have studied   4 has never used   5 has been, has never lived   6 have broken

---

- Ask students to say which statistics in the infographic the completed sentences refer to.

Answers

1 statistic 6   2 statistic 1   3 statistic 2   4 statistic 3
5 statistic 4   6 statistic 5

Pronunciation Weak forms: *have, has* and *been*

5a

- Remind students of what they learned about the pronunciation of auxiliary verbs on page 75 (they often have weak forms). Point out that the auxiliary *have* and the participle *been* also have weak forms.
- Ask students to look at the sentences in Exercise 5a while they listen.
- ⟨41⟩ Play the recording once or twice and ask them how the underlined words are pronounced.
- Show on the board the phonetic transcription of the weak forms /əv/ and /əz bɪn/ but don't drill them in isolation. Instead, drill the sentences as a whole, making sure you only stress the important words:

  1 **Six** *per cent of* **pe**ople *in the* **UK** *have* **nev**er had a **job**.

  2 **One** *in every* **six house**holds *has been the* **vic**tim of a **crime**.

▶ Teaching tip: Don't stress!, Unit 4.2, page 56.

5b

- Ask students to underline the weak forms in the verbs.
- ⟨42⟩ Play the recording for them to check.

Answers

3 Eleven per cent of the population <u>have</u> never used the Internet.

4 Sixty per cent of people working in London <u>have</u> <u>been</u> to university.

5c

- Finally, ask students to listen and repeat all the sentences.
- ⟨43⟩ Play the recording.
- Let them practise in pairs in their own time for a minute.
- **Optional step.** Students underline all weak forms in sentences 1–4 to review the earlier lesson on weak forms.

GRAMMAR Present perfect simple and past simple

6

- Tell students to look at the Grammar box.
- Put them in pairs to discuss questions 1 and 2 and to check their answers in the Grammar summary on page 152. Then confirm the answers with the whole class.
- Let students do some or all of Exercises 3–6 in the Grammar summary if they need more controlled practice, or continue on to Exercise 7 in the unit and set the Grammar summary exercises for homework. Note that the present perfect continuous is also explained in the Grammar summary on page 152. Exercise 7 on page 153 practises the form. There is a full Grammar extension lesson to teach this structure on the *Keynote* website. To access this lesson, go to ngl .cengage.com/keynote and use the password printed on the title page of this Teacher's Book.

Answers

1 *broke* relates to an event at a specific time in the past.

2 *have broken* relates to an event at a time in the past that is not specified.

Answers to Grammar summary exercises

3

1 we've met   2 left   3 has painted   4 I've had
5 hasn't seen   6 didn't see   7 broke   8 Did you call

4

1 Have you ever seen   2 I've already eaten   3 He's never had   4 replied to your letter yet?   5 Has she ever worked   6 look at your report yet.

5

1 've lost   2 did you lose   3 left   4 've never done
5 've just missed   6 went   7 Did he say   8 hasn't
finished   9 've booked   10 didn't have

6

1 Did you ever have → Have you ever had   2 have
seen → saw   3 gone → been   4 yet arrived → arrived
yet   5 have met → met   6 Have you wrote → Did you
write

7

1 have you been doing   2 've been getting   3 's been
trying   4 has he been going   5 's been working

- **Optional step.** You could further illustrate the distinction
with any personal experiences that the class has discussed,
e.g. *Joaquin **has been** skiing many times. He last **went** in
January.*

7

- Ask students to choose the correct options to complete
the conversations.

- Let them compare answers by putting them in pairs and
reading conversations out as dialogues.

- For whole-class feedback, nominate students from
different pairs to read the dialogues out loud.

Answers

1 A: have you travelled   B: have   A: visited   B: really
liked, went

2 A: have you had   A: was   B: was, worked

3 A: Have you ever won   B: haven't, came   A: Did the
school publish   B: put

4 A: Have you ever been   B: hacked   A: Did they steal
B: didn't, had

Note that the past simple would be possible for the first
exchange of all of these dialogues if the situation no
longer exists, for example, if in number 1 the person no
longer works.

8

- Have students talk about their own experiences in pairs
by asking each other the same four questions that begin each
mini dialogue, starting with *Have you travelled much?*

- Give them a few minutes for this. Go around the room,
visiting the pairs and listening to their experiences. Make sure
that they use the tenses correctly.

- For feedback, nominate individuals to share one interesting
thing that they learned about their partner with the rest of the
class.

SPEAKING Life experiences

9   `21st` **CENTURY OUTCOMES**

- **Optional step.** Before the lesson, make notes of
experiences you have had for each of the categories in the list.
Invite students to ask you about your life experiences, using the
list to prompt questions. Make sure they form correct questions,
e.g. *What useful skills have you learned?* Respond. Invite follow
up questions, making sure they use the past simple where
appropriate, e.g. *When did you do this?* Did you enjoy it? etc.

- In pairs, students ask and answer each other's questions.
Monitor their conversations and collect good and bad
examples of their use of tense and other interesting language
used.

- After a few minutes, stop the activity and invite volunteers
to share with the whole class some interesting things that they
learned about their partners.

- Point out any useful errors or interesting language that you
heard them use.

10

- Point out the 21st CENTURY OUTCOMES skill at the foot
of the page. Write on the board the following questions to
encourage evaluation of the experiences:

   *Which experiences have helped you most in your
   working/personal life?*

   *Which experiences have helped you find new friends?
   / were the most fun? / taught you something about
   yourself? / showed you a point of view you had never
   realized?*

- Put students into small groups to discuss which of the
experiences discussed in Exercise 9 have helped them most.
Tell them to also use the questions on the board to evaluate
their experiences.

▶ Photocopiable communicative activity 7.1: Go to
page 221 for further practice of the present perfect and past
simple. The teaching notes are on page 239.

▶ Set Workbook pages 66–67 for homework.

7.3 Encouraging diversity

READING France's new CV law

1

- Books closed. Ask students which of them has written a
CV in their first language and other languages. Ask what the
abbreviation CV stands for (*curriculum vitae*) and whether
anyone knows what the Americans call a CV (a *resumé*,
pronounced /ˈrezjuːmeɪ/).

- Briefly ask what type of information they include in their CVs and note it on the board.

- Books open. Ask students to look at the list of items in Exercise 1 and compare it with their ideas on the board.

- Have them tick the items to include on a CV in their country/ies. Check if there is anything in the list that they wouldn't include, and discuss why. Conversely, are there items on typical CVs from their countries that are absent from the list, e.g. a photo of the applicant?

- Now ask students what a CV doesn't tell you about the person. They can discuss this in pairs.

Note: Bear in mind that there may be disagreement, especially between people from different countries, because the conventions for CV writing vary from country to country, and from industry to industry.

Answers
1 Students' own answers
2 (suggested answers) personality, communication skills, appearance (unless a photo is provided)

- Check their understanding of some of the more difficult headings, e.g. *Marital status* and *Ethnic origin*. Do this by eliciting what they would write under these categories.

2

- Tell students to stay in pairs. Read out the definition of *anonymous*. Check understanding by asking if anyone has an anonymous avatar on their social media page (i.e. a head-and-shoulders silhouette instead of a photo of them).

- Discuss in class why an anonymous CV might be useful or beneficial.

- Tell them to read the article to find out. Give them just three minutes to encourage skim reading for this gist task.

- When they have finished, elicit the answer.

Answer
They are designed to stop employers discriminating against candidates on the basis of their age, sex or ethnic origin.

3

- Ask students to read the article more carefully to decide whether statements 1 to 8 are true or false. Remind them to identify where in the text they found the information so that they can show their evidence.

- When they have finished reading, let them confer in pairs to compare answers before whole-class feedback. Ask students to say what tells them the answer.

Answers
1 T (lines 5–7)   2 F (lines 8–10)   3 T (lines 14–15)
4 F (lines 20–23)   5 F (lines 25–30)   6 T (lines 31–34)
7 T (lines 34–35)   8 F (lines 40–41)

4

- Explain that students are going to look closer at vocabulary in the article. Ask them to look at the definitions and make sure they understand that the words are found in paragraphs 1 and 2 only.

- Put the students in pairs to work together on finding the missing words.

Answers
1 applicant (line 3)   2 employee (line 6)   3 employer (line 8)   4 workforce (line 13)

5

- **Optional step.** Ask students to read through the sentences and see if they can complete any of them before checking with the text.

- Tell students to look at the article to complete the sentences or check their answers. Point out that the paragraph number for each word is given.

Answers
1 implement   2 discriminate   3 tell   4 frustrated
5 diversity

6

- Put students in small groups. Ask them to discuss the questions and try to find solutions to the problems mentioned in the article.

- Give them a few minutes. If groups are struggling to come up with ideas, help by asking, e.g: *Is there a problem taking the dates off a CV completely? How could a candidate show the amount of experience they have had without dates? What sensible ways of maintaining anonymity are there?*

- **Optional step.** Regroup students so they can share their ideas: put one person from each group together. An easy way is to give everyone in each group a letter, then say: *All the As over here, all the Bs over there*, etc. (i.e. ABCD ABCD ABCD → AAA BBB CCC DDD).

- Ask them to pool all their ideas and decide on the best solutions to each problem.

- When they have finished talking, draw some conclusions as a whole class. Find out which ideas were the most popular for each problem listed.

Suggested answers
Perhaps dates could be left off as long as education, experience and qualifications are given in chronological order; interviews could be done by telephone or online without video; make the job description more attractive to certain parts of the workforce, e.g. for younger women, include childcare incentives.

VOCABULARY Personal qualities

7

- **Optional step**. Books closed. Ask students what jobs they do or plan to do for a living. Elicit some personal and professional qualities necessary to do these jobs. Check understanding by asking each time a student suggests a quality why it is important for that profession. Write the qualities on the the board, differentiating between adjectives (e.g. *patient*) and nouns (*a lot of patience*).

- Books open. Tell students to look at the words in the box and if necessary check they understand their meanings by asking questions, e.g.

  If you are determined to succeed and get a very good job or lots of money, how could you be described? (ambitious)

  Name some caring jobs. (nurse, social worker, nursery school teacher, etc.)

  The opposite of nervous and stressed? (easy-going)

  A synonym for enthusiastic? (excited, interested, keen, etc.)

  Do you need to be hard-working in your job?

  If you can work on your own without too much help from your boss, how could you be described? (independent)

  I plan my life carefully and effectively. I am … . (organized)

  Which word describes someone who says they will do something today and they do it today? (reliable)

  Which word describes someone who likes talking to new people and makes friends easily? (sociable)

  Can you be a team-player if you don't play sport? (yes)

- Give students a minute on their own to decide which adjectives describe them very well, well or not very well.

- **Optional step.** If your students know each other well, ask them to do the same for their partner or someone else in the room. They can then compare.

8

- Ask students to talk in pairs about the use of these words in CVs and to decide which words should not be included in a CV.

> **Suggested answers**
>
> *Ambitious* suggests that you want to get to the top, which may be unsuitable if the job has a low level of pay or is not considered an aspirational job.
>
> *Easy-going* could be seen as the same as lazy, or not hard-working. While this is not necessarily true, it might be better to say *I stay calm under pressure* or similar.
>
> An *independent* person may not fit in to a team where there is a lot of dependence on the other members. It could be understood to mean that you prefer to work alone.

Extra activity

Personal profile

Tell the students to write a one-sentence summary, or Personal profile to put at the beginning of their CV. Write on the board an example for your own CV, e.g. *I am a caring and hard-working English teacher looking to work in a friendly school with similar enthusiastic professionals.*

SPEAKING Diversity at work

9 21st CENTURY OUTCOMES

- Explain that students are going to imagine a professional situation and tell them to read the instructions.

- Ask them whether they are surprised that only seven per cent of the students are women. Invite students to suggest reasons, e.g. the profession is traditionally seen as a man's job, girls are discouraged from studying science, girls are naturally more interested in arts and humanities than technical subjects, there are few examples of women in these roles so few women consider it as a career, women might feel uncomfortable studying with no one of their own gender.

- Ask the class whether they think this lack of diversity is a problem, and if so, why. Encourage students to think about job opportunities for women as well as the possible benefits that women may bring to engineering.

- Tell students that they are teachers and managers at the college. Put them into groups of between four and six.

- Point out the proposals and explain that they should discuss them, thinking of more if they can.

> **Suggested answers**
>
> Other ideas might include: running a promotional campaign to encourage women to enter the profession, actively promoting junior female academic staff to more senior roles within the university, including female members of staff in the university admissions department.

10

- Still in their groups, students list the advantages and disadvantages of each idea. They then decide on a plan of action.

- Give them ten minutes for this. Ask a spokesperson from each group to explain their plan of action to the class.

- Ask the class whether there is a lack of diversity (of gender, race, age, disabilities, etc.) in their professions or other professions they know. Ask whether they think this is a problem, and whether they can see ways of changing the situation.

▶ Set Workbook pages 68–69 for homework.

7.4 I love a challenge

LISTENING A job interview

1

• Books closed. In pairs, students write four questions they would expect to hear at a job interview.

• Give them two minutes for this. Then get each pair to join up with another to compare questions. Tell them to discuss which question would be hardest to answer, and why.

Answer
Students' own answers

2

• Books open. Have students read the description of RSQ to find out what people in this organization do.

Answer
organize media campaigns, work with animals in the field, raise money

• If necessary, explain the following expressions:

an **endangered animal** – an animal that may soon become extinct and disappear

a **charity** – an organization that helps animals or disadvantaged people by collecting money from the public.

raise money – to collect money for a specific reason

a **media campaign** – a programme of events such as television appearances, posters or social media posting designed to encourage people to do something

in the field – in the places where the action is, not in the office

• **Optional step.** Ask them whether they would be interested in working for such an organization, and why.

3

• Explain that students are going to listen to a job interview for a position at RSQ, and focus attention on the four questions.

• Ask whether students thought of these questions in Exercise 1. Check understanding.

• ⓐ44 Play the recording.

Transcript

I = Interviewer, H = Harry

I: *Hi, please come in and take a seat. Sorry to keep you waiting.*

H: *That's all right.*

I: *So, I understand you graduated recently and you're looking for work with a charitable organization. What attracted you to this job in particular?*

H: *Well, the main thing is that I'm very interested in working in the field, in countries where animals are in*

danger. I mean, I understand that the job also involves desk work …

I: *Well, that depends on the job …*

H: *OK and well … I love what RSQ is doing too.*

I: *Thank you … we're very proud of our work too. You're a graduate in economics. What are your long-term ambitions – to work in a bank, perhaps?*

H: *No. A lot of my friends have taken jobs in the City but as I said I'm keen on doing something practical and more … useful, I guess. I'd like to do a job where I'm helping the environment.*

I: *OK and what can you do, practically?*

H: *I'm good with my hands. I help my father a lot with building jobs.*

I: *Do you have experience of foreign countries?*

H: *Mmm … I haven't worked abroad before, but, I've travelled a lot and I'm very willing to learn.*

I: *Uh-huh … I see. Do you have any experience of working with animals?*

H: *Yes, horses and cows and pigs. I've worked on a farm most of my life. My parents are farmers.*

I: *OK. And what other experience do you have that's relevant to this position?*

H: *Well, at uni I worked on a campaign, an environmental campaign, helping to save a local green area from development. There was a lot of wildlife there – birds and so on – and the council was going to build some flats there.*

I: *Oh, that's interesting. Did the campaign succeed?*

H: *Yes, we persuaded the council to use only thirty per cent of the land for development. So we saved the rest. I think I'm good at persuading people. Also, I really love a challenge and I'm not afraid of taking risks.*

I: *OK, and what about …*

• Give students a minute to compare their answers with a partner before nominating people to share answers with the class.

Answers
1 He's interested in working in the field, in countries where animals are in danger. He loves what RSQ is doing.
2 He'd like to work in a job helping the environment.
3 He's good with his hands. He helps his father a lot with building jobs. He is used to working with animals.
4 He worked on an (environmental) campaign at university.

4

• Ask students to try to add the missing words, in their pairs.

• ⓐ44 Play the recording again for students to check their answers and complete the sentences. Note that different numbers of words are needed in the answers.

• Write on the board the collocations: *interested* _____,
keen _____, *would like to* _____, *good* _____, *love
a* _____, *afraid* _____. Invite students to come up to the
board and fill in the gaps.

5

• Ask students to raise their hands if they believe Harry will
get the job. Ask them to justify their opinions.

Pronunciation Linking words

6

• Ask everyone to repeat after you: *din ... interested in ...
min ... minterested in ... I'm interested in.*

• Explain that when we speak normally, we often join words
together. If the last sound of a word is a vowel and the first
sound of the next word is a consonant, or vice versa, we
usually connect them as if they were part of the same word.

• Tell students to read the four sentences to find places
where the sounds link from word to word.

• While they are working, write the sentences on the board.

• 🔊 45 Play the recording for them to check. Ask for the
answers, encouraging them to say the words linked. Show the
links on the board for clarity.

• Students practise saying the sentences in pairs, alternating
and checking each other's pronunciation.

Extra activity

Guess the writer

Using the collocations that you wrote on the board earlier,
have the students practise using some of the new language.
Tell them to complete (some of) the following sentences
on a piece of paper so that they say something true about
themselves.

I'm (not) interested in ...

I'm (not very) keen on ...

I'm (not very) good at ...

I'm (not) afraid of ...

I'd like to ...

I love a ...

Do the same yourself. Make sure everyone writes their
names on the piece of paper, then collect them in, shuffle

them, and redistribute them in random order, keeping one
person's for yourself. Explain that everyone is going to read
out the sentences and that the others in the class must try
to guess whose sentences they are. As an example, read
out the paper that you have kept and ask the class to guess
who wrote those sentences. Tell them if they are right. In
large classes, get them into groups of six or so to do the
activity.

SPEAKING Describing skills and interests

7

• Explain that RSQ is interested in employing some new
members of the team.

• **Optional step.** Brainstorm possible interview questions
and add new ones to those already on the board along with
the ones from Exercise 3.

• Have students read the three jobs (a–c) and make sure that
they understand what the jobs entail; ask for possible tasks
that would be done in each one.

• Give individuals a few minutes to decide which job they
would be most suited to, how their experience will help (they
can of course invent previous relevant work experience if they
prefer), and what they would like to say in the interview. Refer
them to the expressions in the functions box.

• Now put students in pairs and tell them to take turns at
interviewing each other, using the questions on the board, or
in Exercise 3 if you haven't got any on the board.

• Allow ten minutes for this stage, five per interview. Monitor
the interviews carefully, listening out for the recent vocabulary
and grammar studied.

• Ask individual students if they would give their partners the
jobs, and to explain why / why not.

WRITING A CV

8

• Books closed. Ask students whether they think an English
CV could be useful to them now or in the future, and why.

• Together, brainstorm any advice that they would give
someone about to write their CV. Note down ideas on the
board.

• Books open. Ask students to read the sentences and to
decide whether they are true or false. Check their answers.

9

• Ask students to read Jessica's CV quickly and decide
which job from Exercise 7 Jessica is applying for. (She is
applying to be a fundraiser.)

- Students identify the points in Exercise 8 that Jessica has included.

Answer

All of them, but we can't know about 3.

- **Optional step.** Ask students to discuss how the details in the CV should change to be relevant for jobs a and b.

Writing skill Verb forms

10

- Point to the first sentence of the Personal profile and ask students to find the verb. When they realize there isn't one, ask them what the full sentence should be (*I am a hard-working and …*) and why it is written like this (for brevity and to make the important information stand out more).

- Ask them to look at the rest of the profile and find what tense it is in (present tense).

- Now tell them to look at the other sections of Jessica's CV and identify the different verb forms used.

Answers

a 3 b 2 c 1 (no subject *I*)

d 1 (past used where a specific past event is mentioned)

e 1, 2 (*-ing* form for activities and past tense for specific events)

11

- Tell students to work on their own to rewrite the sections so that they match Jessica's style.

- Make sure they understand that this style is one suggested approach only. There are other formats for CVs, but this is a very common one.

Suggested answers

Personal profile - ~~I am a~~**A**n organized and hard-working IT engineer. ~~The~~**My** key skills ~~I have~~ are a knowledge of Microsoft products and of security software.

Responsibilities - ~~I had to v~~ **V**isiting clients, ~~and~~ install**ing** new software. ~~I also~~ **H**elp**ing** clients ~~to~~ solve their IT problems.

Achievements - ~~I~~ **A**chieved a customer satisfaction rating of 96%. ~~and I w~~ **W**on a prize for best customer service.

12   21st CENTURY OUTCOMES

- Tell students that they are going to prepare a CV for the job of field worker in Exercise 7. If you did the optional step in Exercise 9, they will already have thought about this. If not, brainstorm relevant education, employment and skills information before students write.

- Point out that although they will be writing this CV for an imaginary job with RSQ, the basic text and format will be easy to adapt to a real job of their choice, so this is a valuable exercise.

Suggest that they write their CV on a piece of paper so that they can give it to you for correction to help them in job-seeking.

- If students did the Extra activity in the previous lesson ('Personal Profile' on page 99) they could include their profiles into their CVs.

- **Optional step.** If students can write directly into a word processor, they could email their CV to you or print it out for you. You could also suggest that they look for professional CV templates online so that they look elegant and professional.

13

- When most students have finished, have them swap CVs with a partner.

- Each student uses the checklist to ensure their partner's CV is well-written and assesses how well their partner has presented themselves professionally, according to the 21st CENTURY OUTCOME.

Background information

The Common European Framework of Reference for Languages

An essential section in international CVs is one on languages. Applicants should be positive about their linguistic abilities but realistic about what they can and cannot do. They also need a suitable way to describe their language skills. The Common European Framework of Reference for Languages provides a way of describing these systematically. Search online for the *Common European Framework of Reference for Languages descriptors*.

▶ Photocopiable communicative activity 7.2: Go to page 222 for further practice of personal qualities and expressions from 7.4. The teaching notes are on page 240.

▶ Set Workbook pages 70–71 for homework.

▶ Set Workbook Presentation 4 on pages 72–73 for homework.

8 Seeing the future

LEAD IN

- Books closed. Show students the main photo on pages 84–5 without letting them see the caption. Ask them what they think it is, and elicit ideas.

- Books open. Tell them to check their ideas against the caption. Ask them:

  What do you think the sculpture represents?

  What are the themes of the unit, according to the image?

  Would you like to see it? What do you think you would see that you can't in the photo?

  Do you imagine cities in the future looking like this? Why? Why not?

  Is this a positive or negative vision of the future, in your opinion? Why?

- **Optional step**. If you have access to the Internet, find a video of the sculpture by Chris Burden at work and show the class.

Background information

Chris Burden

The creator of Metropolis II, who died in May 2015, studied what it was like to live in the modern cities of today. He was a very interesting artist, who did some extraordinary things to explore the power, machinery and architecture of urban life. Early in his career, 'works of art' included: being shot in the arm by a friend, hijacking a television station, staying in bed in an art gallery for 22 days, pretending to be the victim of a car accident and firing a gun at an aeroplane. His art was always controversial and shocking. He was a major influence on modern artists today.

TEDTALKS
BACKGROUND

- Put students in pairs. Tell the class to read the text about the TED Talk and the speaker, then to discuss the questions.

- Check understanding of *commute* (to travel regularly to work using a form of transport) and *eco-friendly* (something that doesn't harm the environment is described in this way).

- Exploit whole-class feedback as an opportunity to personalize the themes of the unit.

Suggested answers

1 skateboard, bicycle, train, underground, tram

2 & 3 Students' own answers

KEY WORDS

2

- **Optional step.** Books closed. Write the eight words in bold on the board in random order. Read out the description, replacing the words in bold with *BEEP*. Students call out the word from the board that they think fits the gap. If they get it wrong, shake your head and repeat the sentence. If they get it right, move to the next sentence. If they get this wrong, return to the very beginning, repeating the first sentence and the second. Continue like this until the class confidently fills each gap with no errors.

- Ask students to read the description of the car, first to guess the meaning of the words, then to match them to the definitions (a–h).

Answers

1 d   2 e   3 h   4 a   5 b   6 f   7 c   8 g

- To further check comprehension, ask follow-up questions: *What other devices are sometimes **portable**?* (e.g. TVs, computers, camping showers), *What devices typically have a **remote control**?* (e.g. TVs, toy helicopters, military drones, air conditioning units), *What **range** do most Wi-Fi routers have?* (about 20 metres), *What **sustainable** sources of energy are there?* (e.g. wind power, hydroelectricity), *What do you have to* *regularly **charge**?* (e.g. mobile phone, electric shaver)*, Which pedal on the car is the **accelerator**?* (left) *And the **brake**?* (middle)

AUTHENTIC LISTENING
SKILLS Prediction

3a

- Tell students to read the Authentic listening skills box.

- Ask students to discuss in pairs what they think Sanjay Dastoor is going to talk about. Then tell them to look at the first sentence from the TED Talk and predict the missing words.

- Elicit a few ideas for each gap so that students can compare ideas.

- 🔲 46 Play the recording so that students complete the first part of the sentence.

Answers
1 show   2 electric   3 vehicle   4 less   5 bicycle

- Ask students how well they predicted the words. Ask for a show of hands of those who managed to predict one, two, three, four or even all five words correctly. Congratulate them on their success.

3b

- In pairs, students predict what Sanjay Dastoor might say next about the vehicle.

- After a minute, elicit some of their ideas about content.

- 🔲 47 Play the recording so that students can compare their answers with what he actually says.

- Let them check their answers with the audio transcript on page 167. (See the first sentence of the Talk transcript below.)

8.1 A skateboard, with a boost

TEDTALKS

1

- Explain that the class is now going to watch Sanjay Dastoor's talk. As they watch, they should think about the way the skateboard works and what some of its advantages are.

- ▷ 8.1 Play the whole talk.

Transcript

0.14   Today I'm going to show you an electric vehicle that weighs less than a bicycle, that you can carry with you anywhere, that you can charge off a normal wall outlet in fifteen minutes, and you can run it for 1,000 kilometres on about a dollar of electricity. But

when I say the word electric vehicle, people think about vehicles. They think about cars and motorcycles and bicycles, and the vehicles that you use every day. But if you come about it from a different perspective, you can create some more interesting, more novel concepts.

0.50   So we built something. I've got some of the pieces in my pocket here. So this is the motor. This motor has enough power to take you up the hills of San Francisco at about twenty miles per hour, about thirty kilometres an hour, and this battery, this battery right here has about six miles of range, or ten kilometres, which is enough to cover about half of the car trips in the US alone. But the best part about these components is that we bought them at a toy store. These are from remote control airplanes. And the performance of these things has gotten so good that if you think about vehicles a little bit differently, you can really change things.

1.30   So today we're going to show you one example of how you can use this. Pay attention to not only how fun this thing is, but also how the portability that comes with this can totally change the way you interact with a city like San Francisco.

1.44   (Music) [6 Mile Range] [Top Speed Near 20mph] [Uphill Climbing] [Regenerative Braking]

2.51   (Applause) (Cheers)

3.02   So we're going to show you what this thing can do. It's really manoeuvrable. You have a hand-held remote, so you can pretty easily control acceleration, braking, go in reverse if you like, also have braking. It's incredible just how light this thing is. I mean, this is something you can pick up and carry with you anywhere you go.

3.29   So I'll leave you with one of the most compelling facts about this technology and these kinds of vehicles. This uses twenty times less energy for every mile or kilometre that you travel than a car, which means not only is this thing fast to charge and really cheap to build, but it also reduces the footprint of your energy use in terms of your transportation. So instead of looking at large amounts of energy needed for each person in this room to get around in a city, now you can look at much smaller amounts and more sustainable transportation.

4.02   So next time you think about a vehicle, I hope, like us, you're thinking about something new.

4.07   Thank you.

Note the differences in British English and North American English shown at the foot of the spread. In this unit, these focus on vocabulary and spelling differences. See Teaching tip 1 on page 6 of the Introduction for ideas on how to present and practise these differences.

- Put students in pairs to discuss how the skateboard works and its advantages over other forms of transport.

- Get the class to share ideas.

2

• Tell students to watch the first part of the talk again and complete the facts about the skateboard.

• ▶ 8.1 Play the first part of the talk from 0.00–1.16.

Answers

1 less than   2 15   3 1   4 30   5 10   6 half

3

• Ask students to discuss the question in pairs then nominate a student to share with the class.

Answer

cars, bicycles, motorcycles, other forms of transport that are used every day

4

• Tell students to watch the next part of the talk and answer questions 1 and 2.

• ▶ 8.1 Play the second part of the talk from 1.16–1.44.

• Let students discuss their answers before whole-class feedback.

Answers

1 They are from toy stores. He emphasizes the quality of these cheap products and the ease with which you can adapt them for alternative uses.

2 It is fun and because it is so light, it can change the way you move around the city.

5

• Tell students to watch the third part of the talk and identify the images that accompany each of the four subtitles.

• ▶ 8.1 Play the third part of the talk from 1.44–2.51.

• In pairs, students discuss what they saw and what each subtitle means.

Answers

Image of:

1 a person skateboarding around a corner. *6 Mile Range* is the distance the skateboards can go.

2 a person going fast on the skateboard. *Top Speed Near 20 mph* is the fastest it can go.

3 a person going up a hill on the skateboard. *Uphill Climbing* refers to the skateboard's ability to go up steep hills.

4 a person slowing to a stop then starting again. *Regenerative Braking* refers to the skateboard's ability to reuse the energy it loses when it slows or stops.

6

• Tell students to watch the fourth part of the talk and to complete the sentences with the words in the box.

• ▶ 8.1 Play the fourth part of the talk from 2.51 to the end.

Answers

1 remote control   2 carry   3 twenty   4 cheap
5 footprint   6 new

VOCABULARY IN CONTEXT

7

• ▶ 8.2 Play the clips from the talk. When each multiple-choice question appears, students choose the correct definition. Discourage the more confident students from always giving the answer by asking individuals to raise their hand if they think they know.

Transcript and subtitles

*1 But if you come about it from a different perspective, you can create some more interesting, more **novel** concepts.*
  a cheap
  b simple
  c original

*2 But the best part about these **components** is that we bought them at a toy store.*
  a parts
  b toys
  c motors

*3 So I'll leave you with one of the most **compelling** facts about this technology and these kinds of vehicles.*
  a serious
  b unusual
  c powerful

*4 ... which means not only is this thing fast to charge and really cheap to build, but it also reduces the **footprint** of your energy use in terms of your transportation.*
  a pollution
  b amount
  c effect on nature

*5 So instead of looking at large amounts of energy needed for each person in this room to **get around** in a city ...*
  a travel about
  b keep warm
  c commute

Answers

1 c   2 a   3 c   4 c   5 a

8

- Ask students to think of examples for the ideas in pairs.
- Invite suggestions from the whole class.

> **Suggested answers**
>
> 1 Taking the underground or bus may be cheap. A bicycle or motorbike may be quicker than a car. Walking may be the best way to get around if the city is small.
>
> 2 private helicopter, jet pack, canoe (if there is a river), on horseback, by Internet (i.e. working from home)
>
> 3 computers, cars (vehicles in general), mobile phones, televisions, radios, food processors, sewing machines, satellites, photocopiers . . .

Extra activity

'I watched this really interesting talk the other day . . .'

Ask students if they sometimes describe talks, YouTube clips and other things they have seen on the Internet to their friends. Explain that this activity gets students practising this real-world conversation. Write on the board the following useful expressions:

> *I watched this really interesting/funny/crazy talk / YouTube clip / advert / short film the other day . . .*
>
> *It's about . . .*
>
> *The woman's/man's name is . . .*
>
> *You'll find it if you search for . . .*

Put students in pairs. Tell them to imagine that one of them hasn't seen the TED Talk and the student who did is telling them about it. Practise the conversation. Give the class time for both students in each pair to practise.

Ask them to think of other talks, YouTube clips, adverts or short films they have seen recently. Give them time to tell each other about those clips.

CRITICAL THINKING Evaluating claims

9

- Ask students what forms of transport Sanjay Dastoor compares his skateboards to (cars, bicycles and motorcycles).
- Put students in pairs. Get them to make a list of the advantages of the electric skateboard over these other vehicles.
- Have them now think of any possible disadvantages of the skateboards.

> **Suggested answers**
>
> Advantages: see answers to Exercise 1 above.
>
> Disadvantages: limited to short distances, risk of running out of power far from home, could easily break, limited to smooth surfaces, risk of injury to rider or pedestrians on pavements, risk to riders on roads (no lanes in the street

dedicated to skateboards), may be expensive for what it is, not ideal to use in bad weather, limited to one rider only, not as healthy to use as a bicycle or going on foot.

10

- Ask students to read the comments in pairs and compare the ideas there to their ideas in Exercise 9. Ask them whether they think they are good comments.
- **Optional step.** Let students respond to the talk with their own comments.

▶ Teaching tip: Comment / Tweet / Post, Unit 2.1, page 26.

11

- Ask the class to summarize by saying what they think the most important arguments for and against the electric skateboard are.

> **Answers**
>
> Students' own answers

- Ask the class whether Sanjay Dastoor is right not to mention any disadvantages in his talk. Make sure they justify their opinions.

PRESENTATION SKILLS Signposting

12

- Draw a signpost on the board. Put students in pairs to discuss what signposts are for on the road and what they are in a talk or presentation.

13

- Ask students to read the Presentation tips box to check that they were correct.
- After reading, students can tell you who signposts are useful for.

> **Answer**
>
> Signposting in talks is useful for the audience because it tells them the direction of the talk, or the section of the talk.

14

- Explain to students that they are going to watch some clips from the TED Talk. They should note down phrases that Sanjay Dastoor uses at the four stages of the talk.

- ▶ 8.3 Play the clips from the talk.
- Give students the opportunity to watch again if you see that they have not written all the phrases, and time to confer with a neighbour before directing them to the TED Talk transcript on pages 177–178 to check.

Answers

1 Starting: *Today I'm going to show you (an electric vehicle …)*

2 Moving on: *So today we're going to show you (one example of how you can use this).*

3 The demonstration: *So we're going to show you (what this thing can do).*

4 Concluding: *So I'll leave you with (one of the most compelling facts …)*

15

- Tell students that they are going to prepare a short presentation in pairs about the best form of transport in your country or area. Ask them to discuss some ideas about what to say.
- Ask them now to prepare the opening paragraph and to plan the structure of the presentation. Insist that they write into the plan signposting language to describe to the audience what the presentation is going to focus on.
- Make sure that both students in each pair are making notes.

16

- Put students in new pairs.

▶ Teaching tip: Three ways to pair up students, Unit 2.1, page 27.

- Students take turns to introduce their presentations to each other. Point out the questions for the listeners.

- When all students have given their introductions, nominate some of them to tell the class what language they and their partners used and whether it was effective.

Suggested introduction

Today I'm going to talk about the best form of transport in my country. It's the fastest way to get between cities, and although it is expensive, I believe that it provides the most comfortable way to travel. I'm talking about the intercity train services, of course. **First I'm going to give you** some facts about intercity trains that I hope will convince you that it is the best form of transport …

- **Optional step.** Students can apply what they have learned about signposting language to previous presentations they have worked on in Units 1 to 7. They can look at ways of signposting at the start of their presentations but also later when they want to move on, go back or conclude.

▶ Teaching tip 2: Developing presentation skills, Introduction page 6.

▶ Set Workbook pages 74–75 for homework.

8.2 The future of transport

GRAMMAR Predictions with *will* and *might*

1

- Books closed. Draw the following table on the board. Ask students to copy it in their notebooks:

Form of transport	traffic congestion	delays	high cost	lack of comfort	poor connections	safety
cars	✓					
buses						
trains						
underground trains						
bicycles						
air travel						

- Tell students to tick the boxes to show the main problems with each modern transport system. Do one as an example to clarify.
- In pairs, students compare their answers.

Answers

Students' own answers

Be sensitive to local differences

Clearly some places have worse transport systems than others. One city might have an excellent bus network but a poor record when it comes to bicycle safety. Also, recent scandals or disasters in a country may influence how students perceive the safety or reliability of that system.

Respect students' opinions even if they do not reflect global trends. In multilingual classes, exploit these differences as an opportunity to encourage genuine communication; let students talk about the transport systems they know. In monolingual classes, you could compare the systems of different cities that the students know about.

2

• Books open. Still in pairs, students discuss the question.

• Elicit their predictions, making sure they justify their answers.

3

• Ask students to look at the infographic and answer the questions.

• Let them compare answers with a partner before sharing with the whole class.

Answers

1 cars – over 100%   2 high-speed trains
3 in airports   4 congestion on the roads

4

• Tell the students to answer the question about the sentences in the Grammar box.

• Students can check their answers and overall understanding of predictions with *will* and *might* by turning to the Grammar summary on page 154. If students need more controlled practice before continuing, they could do Exercises 1 and 2 in the Grammar summary. Otherwise, continue on to Exercise 5 in the unit and set the Grammar summary exercises for homework.

Answers

1 future   2 might   3 won't

Answers to Grammar summary exercises

1

1 When will you be home tonight? I hope I'll be home by 6.30.

2 The Green Party won't win the election. No, but they might get a lot of votes.

3 It might rain this afternoon. Oh dear. Will it rain very heavily?

4 Do you think she'll like her present? Yes, she'll love it.

2

1 might spend   2 won't take   3 'll get   4 will/might go   5 might not be   6 'll leave

5

• Ask students to find one more example each of *will* and *might* in the infographic. Ask them to identify the prediction which is less sure.

Answers

will: (students can select any of these) *The number of high speed rail passengers will increase ..., ... the market for electric bicycles will grow ..., Global air travel will grow ..., The fastest growth will be in East Asia. This will encourage people ..., ... more transport will take to the air ...*

might: *... we might see more moving walkways ...*

6

• Tell students to complete the predictions using *will* or *might*. Make it clear that sometimes both verbs are possible.

Answers

1 will certainly be   2 will be   3 will use   4 might encourage   5 will/might grow   6 won't / might not see 7 might/will mean   8 won't be

---

Pronunciation *want* /wɒnt/ and *won't* /wəʊnt/

7

• **Optional step**. Books closed. Tell students to write the sentences they hear. Play the recording (🎧48) as a dictation. Put them in small groups. Tell them to compare their sentences. Find out whether they heard the same as each other, and whether people sometimes confused *want* and *won't*. If you take this step, drill *want* and *won't* before playing the recording with books open.

• Books open. Ask students to listen to the sentences and underline the one they hear.

• 🎧48 Play the recording once only.

• In feedback ask for a show of hands to see who heard the first sentence or the second. Then give the answers.

Answers

3 They want to go by car.
4 I won't know the answer before Tuesday.
5 I won't tell him.
6 They want to leave here before 11 o'clock.
7 She won't come.
8 They want to do business with us.

• Ask students how many they got correct. If they got them all correct, go to Exercise 8. If most students got some wrong, continue.

- Drill the two words. Drill the first two sentences in Exercise 7: *I won't help. / I want to help.* Point out that the pronunciation of *want to* is not very different from *won't* because *to* is said in its weak form /tə/.

- **Optional step**. In pairs, students test each other by saying one of each pair of sentences randomly. Their partner tries to distinguish which they said.

8

- Put students in small groups. Ask them to think of other ideas that might be in the future of transport. Remind them to use *will*, *won't* and *might*.

- As they talk, listen in to the conversation, noting any good expression of future time.

▶ Teaching tip: Correcting speaking activities, Unit 4.2, page 58.

> **Suggested answers**
>
> Students might talk about futuristic means of transport impossible with current technology such as levitation devices, teleportation machines and flying cars. Or they might discuss forms of transport that already exist, such as motorized scooters, hovercraft, microlights and other light aircraft.

GRAMMAR Decisions with *going to*

9

- Explain to students that they are going to listen to a city councillor talking about plans for solving traffic problems. Clarify the meaning of city councillor by asking: *Where does a city councillor work? (In the city hall)*. Tell them to complete the names of the three plans she mentions.

- 🎧 49 Play the recording.

Transcript

I = Interviewer, C = Councillor

I: *Look – I think everyone agrees that the traffic situation in our city can't continue as it is. What are you planning to do about it?*

C: *You're right. There's already too much traffic congestion and, without action, the problem will just get worse. So we have to get people out of their cars and onto other forms of transport.*

I: *OK. How are you going to do that?*

C: *Well, first we have to make other forms of transport more attractive. We're going to introduce a City Bicycle scheme – a fleet of bicycles that people can pick up and drop off at different locations around the city. Also, we're going to create special Park and Ride car parks around the city where car drivers will be able to park their car for free and then travel into the city by bus.*

I: *OK – that sounds very positive. Anything else?*

C: *Yes, we're going to make parking in the city easier, but much more expensive, because ...*

I: *I'm not sure that will be popular.*

C: *Maybe not, but it's necessary. We're going to introduce smart parking meters so you can pay for your parking with your phone. It will cost you significantly more than before. However, you won't have to worry always about having the right change or about going back to the meter to put more money in.*

I: *OK, thank you. And just on another subject ...*

- Let students compare answers with a partner before asking them to share with the class.

> **Answers**
>
> 1 Bicycle   2 Ride   3 parking

10

- Tell students to listen to the councillor again, this time to complete the descriptions of how the ideas will work.

- 🎧 49 Play the recording again.

- Ask students to compare their answers in pairs, then discuss their opinions about these ideas.

- Ensure everyone understands the three ideas and encourage a variety of responses to them.

> **Answers**
>
> 1 pick up and drop off (bicycles)
> 2 travel into the city by bus
> 3 with their phone, (much) more expensive

11

- Tell the students to answer the questions about the sentences in the Grammar box.

- Students can check their answers and overall understanding of decisions with *going to* by turning to the Grammar summary on page 154. If students need more controlled practice before continuing, they could do Exercise 3 in the Grammar summary. Otherwise, continue on to Exercise 12 in the unit and set the Grammar summary exercise for homework.

> **Answers**
>
> 1 future   2 already decided

> **Answers to Grammar summary exercise**
>
> 3
>
> 2 are going to save   3 'm going to do   4 Is John going to stop   5 's going to lose   6 Are you going to eat   7 isn't going to work   8 're going to travel

12

- Tell students to complete the texts with the correct form of *will* or *going to*.

- Let them check in pairs then ask them to share their answers.

Answers
1 're going to have   2 are going to take   3 are also going to ask   4 will save   5 will be   6 'm going to start 7 will help   8 will probably save   9 'm going to get

SPEAKING Transport options

13   21st **CENTURY OUTCOMES**

- Explain to students that they are going to show the different transport options in their city or in a city they know well. To do this they must work out a route from one side of the city to the other using at least four forms of transport.

- Point out the 21st CENTURY OUTCOMES skill at the foot of the page. Explain that in order to choose a good way across the city, they need to analyse the transport system and evaluate how effective each form of transport is.

- Elicit the criteria they should consider. These must include the time it takes, the cost and the impact on the environment but they may include other factors such as comfort and safety.

- As they are planning their routes, monitor, checking that they are using a variety of forms of transport.

14

- Tell students to change partners and to describe what they have decided. Remind them of the usefulness of *going to* to do this.

- Write on the board: *How integrated is the transport system in your city?* Explain that *integrated* means all working together as one efficient system. Tell them to discuss the good and bad things about transport in the city and to answer the question on the board.

- Invite students to share their opinions with the class. Prompt them to explain which elements of the transport system in their city are more or less integrated and why that is. In particular, ask them how it impacts them and people they know.

▶ Photocopiable communicative activity 8.1 Go to page 223 for further practice of predictions with *will* and *might*. The teaching notes are on page 240.

▶ Set Workbook pages 76–77 for homework.

8.3 This might be the answer

READING Our pick – new gadgets

1

- **Optional step**. At the end of the previous lesson ask students to bring in an interesting gadget from home. Start today's lesson with a show and tell where each student shows the class their gadget and tells them what it does and why they like it. Have the class vote for their favourite gadget.

- Give students three minutes to discuss the questions in pairs. Then elicit answers from the whole class.

Suggested answers
1 & 2 Students' own answers
3 tying your shoe laces, drying dishes, cleaning your glasses, looking after small children, locking all the doors and windows, taking the tea bag from a hot cup of tea

2

- Ask students to read the article and complete the table. Make sure they understand they answer according to what they think.

- Put students in pairs to compare opinions.

Answers
Students' own answers

3

- Tell them to read the article again to decide which gadget each statement is true for. Make sure they know that they can choose two of the gadgets, or even all three.

- Nominate students for answers.

Answers
1 N, G, P   2 N, P   3 G, P   4 G, P   5 N   6 N, P 7 G   8 G, N

4

- Ask students to find the words in bold in the article. Using the context, they choose the correct synonym, a or b.

Answers
1 a   2 a   3 a   4 a   5 a   6 b

5

• Put students in groups to answer the questions. Make sure they justify their opinion to one another.

• Elect spokespersons to summarize each group's thoughts to the whole class.

Answer
Students' own answers

VOCABULARY Describing devices

6

• Explain that one of the aims of the lesson is to practise ways of talking about gadgets and other products, and they are going to mine the article for useful language to do this.

• Show them the ten categories and accompanying sentences from the article. Tell them they have two minutes to find as many useful words as possible.

▶ Teaching tip: Scan reading, Unit 2.3, page 31.

• Let them scan the text for two minutes, then stop them and let them compare in pairs before eliciting answers.

Answers
2 made   3 weighs   4 measures   5 costs   6 runs 7 store   8 need   9 looks   10 comes

• **Optional step**. Put students in small groups. They either get any gadgets they have with them out of their bags or think of a gadget they have at home. They describe the gadgets using the new expressions.

7

• Books closed. Write on the board: *The camera measures 11 centimetres in diameter.* Underneath, write: *centimetres is   11   across   it .*

• Ask students to use the words to make a sentence that means the same as the first. Elicit: *It is 11 centimetres across.* Underline *in diameter* and *across* as synonymous.

• Books open. Tell students to complete sentences 2–5 using the words given.

Answers
2 length   3 high   4 width   5 deep

• Ask students which words are nouns (*diameter*, *length*, *height*, *width*, *depth*) and which are adjectives (*long*, *high*, *wide*, *deep*; *across* is an adverb). Elicit the preposition which introduces the nouns (*in*: *in diameter*, *in length*, etc.).

• Drill the words, paying attention to the consonant clusters with /θ/ in *length*, *width* and *depth*.

8

• Show the class the two gadgets shown in the photos. Explain that half the class are going to talk about gadget A and half about gadget B.

• Put students in pairs, then assign one from each pair A and one B. Tell the As to go to page 171 and the Bs to go to page 172.

• Tell them to read and memorize the specifications for their gadget. Tell them they can make a note of any numbers they need to know, but cannot write any words. They must not show their partners their page.

• Remind them the aim of this speaking activity and ask them to imagine what they are going to say about their gadget using the new expressions from Exercises 7 and 8.

• When they are ready, tell them to return to page 90 and take turns to present their gadgets.

• Monitor carefully, making a note of good and bad use of the expressions.

• When students have finished, point out any common errors and ask the class which gadget they would prefer and why.

SPEAKING Can I live without it?

9 *21st* **CENTURY OUTCOMES**

• Books closed. Put students in groups of three to five. Vary the make-up of the groups as much as possible in terms of age, gender, nationality and so on. This will make different opinions and priorities more likely in the discussion.

• Explain that together they must make a group decision about which gadgets and machines from a list they will keep. Ask them to first discuss how they are going to reach agreement. Elicit some ideas from the groups and share these with the class. They could, for example:

discuss the advantages of each gadget

eliminate any gadgets that they can all agree on

vote for each gadget democratically

assign a chairperson to make a final decision

make difficult decisions by choosing randomly, such as with the toss of a coin

• Books open. Tell them to look at the eight machines and gadgets and decide which four to keep. Give them five minutes to reach a decision.

• **Optional step.** If groups reach an agreement quickly, tell them to reduce the number of gadgets to just three.

10

• Put groups together to compare their decisions.

• Conclude the lesson by finding out which gadgets the class in general found most and least essential.

▶ Photocopiable communicative activity 8.2 Go to page 224 for further practice of describing gadgets. The teaching notes are on page 241.

▶ Set Workbook pages 78–79 for homework.

8.4 Speak after the tone

LISTENING Phrases in telephoning

1

• Ask students to complete the recorded voicemail message.

• Ask the whole class to read out the text chorally to check answers.

Answers
1 voicemail   2 available   3 call   4 message   5 tone

• **Optional step.** Give students a minute to try to memorize this very familiar text so that they can say it from memory.

2

• Put students in pairs to note down the information you need to give when leaving a message.

• Elicit answers from the class.

Suggested answers
You usually need to give your name, your number, the time of the call (though the last two aren't always necessary as many phones record them anyway), the reason for calling and what you want to happen.

3

• Ask the class to map their answers from Exercise 2 onto the table (the first and third columns refer to the reason for calling and the fourth to what you want to happen).

• Tell them to listen to four messages on John's voicemail and complete the table. Reassure them that they will hear each message twice.

• 🎧 50   Play the recording.

Transcript

This is the voicemail of John Waterfield. I'm sorry I'm not available to take your call. Please leave a message. Speak after the tone.

1

P: *Oh, hi, John. This is Pete. I'm just calling about the film later. What time are we going to meet? Let me know. You can just send a text, if you like. OK. See you later.*

2

T: *Hello. It's Thomas Clark here from KM Digital. I'm calling about the proposal that you asked for. No need to call back. I'll send you all the information in an email.*

3

W: *Hi, it's me again. Sorry to bother you at work. The dog's not well. I'm going to take him to the vet. I'll let you know what happens.*

4

B: *John. Hi, it's Bianca from HSBC. Sorry I missed your call. I was in a meeting. Um, yes, please call me back on this number. I'll be in the office this afternoon.*

4

• Let students compare answers in pairs before getting whole-class feedback. Ask the class who they think the third caller is and why.

Answers				
	Work (W) or personal (P)	Name of caller	Subject (1–3 words)	Next step
1	P	Pete	Film (later)	Send a text with a time to meet.
2	W	Thomas Clark	(KM Digital) Proposal	Wait for email.
3	P	Not given – 'me'	Dog unwell	Wait for more news.
4	W	Bianca	Missed call	Call her.

The third caller is probably John's wife, girlfriend or someone that he lives with. He knows her very well so she doesn't need to give her name.

5

• In pairs, students answer the questions about the language used in the messages.

- Let them share their answers as a class but don't confirm them yet. Let them listen to the messages to check.

- 🔊 50 Play the recording again.

Pronunciation Contraction '*ll*

6a

- Tell students to listen to and repeat the two sentences, paying particular attention to the way '*ll* is pronounced.

- 🔊 51 Play the recording.

- Ask whether '*ll* is stressed (no it isn't). Let students hear and say the sentences with and without '*ll*: *I let… I'll let… I send… I'll send*.

6b

- In pairs, students practise saying the four sentences. Monitor carefully, checking for clear pronunciation of '*ll*.

- **Optional step**. In pairs, students test one another by reading out the following sentences, which you write on the board. Each time, they choose either with or without *will*; their partner listens and tries to discriminate.

  I see / I'll see him on Monday.

  They get / They'll get there before us.

  He arrives / He'll arrive soon.

SPEAKING Leaving messages

7

- **Optional step**. Ask students to reread the Grammar summary on page 154 about using *will* for spontaneous decisions. If they need practice in this structure, they can do Exercises 4 and 5 now.

Answers to Grammar summary exercises

4

1 I'll see   2 I'll call   3 I'll tell   4 I'm going to fix   5 I'll call   6 I'll   7 we'll have   8 I'll take   9 I'm going to catch

5

1 ~~We'll~~ → We're going to   2 ~~rains~~ → rain   3 ~~might to cancel~~ → might cancel   4 ~~I'm going to~~ → I'll   5 ~~we'll to see~~ → we'll see   6 ~~Marco will move~~ → Marco is going to move

- Divide the class in two: Students A and B. Ask As to turn to page 171 and Bs to 172.

- Explain that they are going to practise leaving messages on each other's voicemail. Tell them to read the instructions for the two messages and choose some of the expressions in the Useful language box that can help.

- Tell them to use their inner voice to practise leaving the message (see Teaching tip below).

- Put As and Bs together in pairs. Tell them to sit with their chairs back to back. Make sure that they note the details of the voicemails that they 'receive'.

- **Optional step**. If everyone has a smartphone, they can record their messages as sound files, or even as voicemails on their partner's phone, to make the task more realistic.

- When they have left all four messages, students check their notes with their partner.

Suggested answers

Student A, Message 1: Hi. It's [name]. I'm just calling to ask if you want to come for dinner on Friday. Please let me know. You can call me back or send a text if you like.

Student A, Message 2: Hello. This is Asha Lamb. I'm calling from Cover insurance company to arrange a meeting. No need to call back. I'll send you an email with more information. Thanks!

Student B, Message 1: Yes, hello. This is [name] from the Regency Hotel. Sorry to bother you, but you made a reservation earlier and I need to confirm: did you reserve a single or double room? Can you call me back, please?

Student B, Message 2: Hi, It's [name] here. I'm just calling about our meeting. I'm sorry about this, but I'm going to be thirty minutes late. I'll call you if that changes.

TEACHING TIP

Using your inner voice

It isn't true that you need a friend to practise speaking. Or even that you need to speak! Many language learners practise what they are going to say using their 'inner voice'.

Tell students that you are going to tell them a number which they must write down, but not immediately. They must remember the number until you let them write. Say the number twice: *5–9–2–2–1*. After ten seconds, tell them to write it down. Ask them how they remembered the number. Explain that the voice they heard repeating the number inside their heads is called the 'inner voice'.

Ask if any of them use their inner voice to help them with English. Find out how. Explain that they can use their inner voice to prepare for speaking activities and even to practise pronunciation silently!

WRITING Short emails

8

• **Optional step**. Review the lesson about short emails on page 71. Ask if anyone remembers the aspect of emails they practised then (giving your reasons for writing). Ask them for different ways to introduce your reasons. If they can't think of any, jog their memory with prompts on the board and a few scenarios: you want someone to send you a link, you want to thank friends for dinner, you want to tell a client they have a room reserved at your hotel.

I'm just ... Just a quick ... This is ...

• Tell students to read emails A–D and match them to the responses 1–4.

> **Answers**
>
> A 3 B 4 C 1 D 2

9

• Ask students to match the underlined phrases in responses 1–4 in Exercise 8 with meanings 1–4.

> **Answers**
>
> a I'll get back to you   b I'll look into it   c I'll have a look
> d We'll let you know

Writing skill Reported speech

10a

• Show students the reported statement from email A in Exercise 8 and how it reports what Bill actually said. Elicit the differences between the original statement and the reported statement. These include: the addition of a reporting verb to introduce the statement (*He said that ...*), the verb shifted back a tense (*is → was*) and a change of reference pronoun (*me → him*).

• Tell students to write the direct speech for reported statements 2–5. Consider putting students in pairs if you feel they may need support doing this.

• Elicit answers from the class.

> **Answers**
>
> 2 'Can/Could you look at my report?'
> 3 'It will take two working days.'
> 4 'I've had another job offer.'
> 5 'I need to give the other company an answer.'

• Students can check their answers and overall understanding of reported speech by turning to the Grammar summary on page 154. If students need more controlled practice before continuing, they could do Exercise 6 in the Grammar summary.

> **Answers to Grammar summary exercise**
>
> 6
> 1 ... would send the email again.
> 2 ... hadn't really answered his question.
> 3 ... could call Barbara back later.
> 4 ... was a bit annoyed about the delay.
> 5 ... they had posted it on Tuesday by express post.
> 6 ... wanted to check the quote before he sent it.

10b

• Ask student to report the direct speech in 1–8 by completing the sentences.

• While it is sometimes possible not to put the verb one step back in the past, this exercise focuses on doing so. Check that students are using backshift as they do the exercise.

> **Answers**
>
> 1 ... was the best day for her.
> 2 ... had postponed the meeting.
> 3 ... could let me know by the end of the week.
> 4 ... would pick me up from the airport.
> 5 ... did not accept returns.
> 6 ... would read it when you had a moment.
> 7 ... was happy with the changes.
> 8 ... had left the parcel at reception.

Extra activity

What she said!

Before the lesson, write some sentences on separate pieces of paper that one student could say to another in class, e.g. *'Yuki, did you do your homework?'*, *'Joao, I like your t-shirt'*, *'Frank, there's a fly on your head'*. Using the students' names and making them silly helps make the activity engaging. Hand out the slips of paper. Tell students that they are going to dictate the sentences to the class, and everyone writes the reported version of what they hear.

Invite one student to read their sentence out loud to the class. Elicit the reported speech on the board, e.g. *Kanji asked Yuki if she had done her homework*. Repeat this with another sentence to ensure that students have seen an example of a reported question and a statement (with *told*), making sure that students write the sentences down.

Now invite students to read out their sentences, one after another, to let the others in the class write them down in reported form. Do the same yourself so that you have a record of the correct sentences. Students will need to do this in groups if there are more than about twelve students in the class. When everyone has read out their sentences, elicit the correct reported sentences by asking, for example, *What did Kanji say?*

11

- Ask students to look at the full reply to email B. Tell them to identify the three elements in the email. You may want to clarify that the subject is what should be written in the 'subject' box, but can be found in the body of the email.

- Let them compare answers with a partner before sharing with the whole class.

Answers

Subject: report. Explanation: I've been really busy.

Next steps: I'll have a look today and send you my comments.

---

12   `21st` `CENTURY OUTCOMES`

- Ask students to look again at email C in Exercise 8. Explain that they are going to write a reply. They will need to apologize and explain that the chair is from a new supplier that promised delivery in three to five days. Make sure that they incorporate the elements in Exercise 11.

- While students are writing, monitor carefully, using the checklist in Exercise 13 below to evaluate progress and make suggestions for improvement.

13

- Ask students to identify any formal emails on the page. Elicit that emails D and 2 in Exercise 8 sound formal. Elicit reasons why they sound formal. These include lack of contractions, such as *had had another job offer*, formal vocabulary such as *considering* and *owing to*, and professional, rather than personal explanations.

- Tell students to exchange emails with their partner (or if they have typed them online, email their partner). Ask them to use the checklist to evaluate the emails.

- In whole-class round-up, ask students whether they would be satisfied receiving responses like the ones their partner has written, and if so, why. Ask whether the emails communicate their message effectively as well as politely and accurately.

▶ Set Workbook pages 80–81 for homework.
▶ Set Workbook Writing 4 on pages 82–83 for homework.

REVIEW 4 | UNITS 7 AND 8

LISTENING

1

• Ask students to read about the One World Play Project and answer the questions.

Answers
1 Through play we become stronger individuals and build better communities.
2 It donates footballs and cricket balls to disadvantaged communities.

2

• Prepare students for listening by having them read the notes. Ask them to think about the kind of information that is missing in each gap.

• 🔊52 Play the recording.

Transcript

I = Interviewer, J = Journalist

I: *So where did the idea for the One World Play Project come from?*

J: *Well, it started as the One World Futbol project. Back in 2006, a guy called Tim Jahnigen was watching a TV report about refugees in Darfur, Sudan. He saw some boys playing football with a ball they had made from old bits of rubbish tied together with string. He could see that they needed something better.*

I: *So he designed the One World football. What's it made of?*

J: *It's plastic and it can be used in any conditions – on roads, on beaches, on grass. The important thing is that it's very strong and never breaks or needs pumping up.*

I: *And how many of these footballs have they delivered to poor communities?*

J: *Over one million.*

I: *Wow! That's a lot. But who pays for them?*

J: *The project is sponsored by Chevrolet, the car brand – the balls have Chevrolet's name on them. They've supported the project since its launch at the 2010 football World Cup. One World Play Project sells the balls too. They promise that for each ball they sell, they will give another one free to a poor community.*

I: *That's interesting …*

• Give students time to read through their answers and check with a partner before checking as a class.

Answers
1 2006   2 report   3 rubbish (tied together with string)   4 plastic   5 strong   6 breaks or needs pumping up   7 one million   8 Chevrolet (a car brand)   9 name   10 (football) World Cup   11 sells   12 give

GRAMMAR

3

• Ask students to complete the text about Tim Jahnigen's background with the past simple and present perfect form of the verbs in brackets.

• Let them compare answers in pairs before eliciting answers from the whole class.

Answers
1 has enjoyed   2 has never played   3 swam   4 played   5 has also travelled   6 saw   7 already knew   8 started   9 suited

4

• Tell students to choose the correct option to complete the description.

Answers
1 will soon be   2 will encourage   3 will become   4 might feel   5 is going to continue   6 are going to look

VOCABULARY

5

• Tell students to complete the description with the correct verbs. Point out that the first letter of each verb is given.

Answers
1 measures   2 made   3 weighs   4 costs   5 comes   6 looks   7 need

6

• Explain that students don't need to use all the words to complete the text.

• Have them read their completed texts to a partner to check their answers.

Answers
1 enthusiastic   2 a team player   3 organized   4 reliable   5 sociable   6 ambitious   *easy-going* is not used.

DISCUSSION

7

• Put students in pairs or groups to answer the questions about sports they have done and how they have benefited them. Remind them to use the present perfect to start talking about it, but to use the past simple to add details. Give an example from your own life to show what you mean, e.g. *I've done a lot of running in the last few years. I started about five years ago.*

- For question 3, encourage them to think beyond the obvious answers. For example, other 'winners' of the OWPP idea could include football associations of the countries where the project is run for having more talented players to choose for their teams.

- Elicit some of these ideas in a whole-class summary discussion.

SPEAKING

8

- Put students in pairs. Tell them to read the conversations.

- Let them decide if they think they can complete the conversations without referring to their notes from Units 7 and 8, and whether they can say the conversations without first writing the expressions. Give them five minutes to prepare and practise the conversations. Go around the pairs offering advice and corrections where appropriate.

- Ask for volunteers to read out each dialogue in front of the class.

Answers
1 Please leave a message and I will call you back as soon as possible.
2 It's Kate here.
3 I'm just calling about the dinner on Friday.
4 I'd like to come, if that's possible.
5 Sorry I missed your call.
6 I'll be in the office this afternoon.
7 My name is Jake Edwards.
8 I'm interested in the job you advertised in the paper.
9 I'm keen to learn more about it.
10 I'll try to call you again later.
11 Sorry to bother you.
12 I just wanted to let you know that ...
13 I'll be good at getting people to donate money!
14 No need to call back.

WRITING

9

- Explain that the second gapped email is a response to the first. Tell students to read the email exchange and complete the second email with one word in each gap.

- Before they begin, ask the class whether the first gap should be *Dear* or *Hi*. Ask why to elicit that this is not an email between people who know each other personally.

- Have students read the email out one sentence by sentence to share answers.

Answers
1 Dear   2 do   3 will   4 in/within   5 will/should
6 on   7 let   8 Yours

10

- Tell students that this time they will write the reply to the enquiry without support. Ask the class for some possible responses before they write. Ask: *What possible reasons are there for the response to take so long? What action do you expect them to make in response to this letter?*

Suggested answer
Dear Ms Michaels/Dear Sasha,
Thank you for your email. Owing to the large number of applications, it is taking longer than expected to arrange the interviews. We will let you know by the end of the week.
Yours sincerely,
Fran Geavons

11

- Tell students to swap emails with a partner. They compare the solutions offered. Ask them which email the applicant would be happier to receive, and why.

9 Being effective

LEAD IN

• Ask students to look at the photo. Ask them the following questions:

Do people sell things in the street in your country? What sorts of things?

Do you think the woman in the photo would have success selling like this where you live? Why? Why not?

What are the advantages of selling in this way? What are the disadvantages?

How is she being effective?

TEDTALKS
BACKGROUND

1

• Put students in pairs. Tell the class to read the text about the TED Talk and the speaker, then to discuss the questions.

• Elicit feedback, allowing plenty of time for students to share ideas that they have picked up from other places or cultures. If you find ideas are not forthcoming at first, offer one or two examples of your own, or from the suggested answers list below.

> **Answers**
>
> 1 each other, including from different cultures
>
> 2 (suggested) It's easier to: cut pizza with scissors (like the Italians do), go to the beach in flip-flops rather than shoes (from Brazil), stop a cut from bleeding by rubbing half a lemon on it (like the Mexicans do) and wake up in the morning with yogic stretching, as many Indians do.

KEY WORDS

2

• Tell the class that the words in the box are used in the TED Talk. Ask students to match the words with definitions 1–6.

Explain that four of the words are illustrated by photos A–D, and they should match the photos with the words.

> **Answers**
>
> 1 shoe laces 2 tie 3 knot 4 loop 5 bow
> 6 to come untied
>
> A loop B bow C shoe laces D knot

• **Optional step.** Demonstrate the words with a shoelace to check understanding.

AUTHENTIC LISTENING SKILLS Word boundaries

3a

• Books closed. Tell students to write down three sentences that you will dictate. Read out the sentences two or three times each, but say them in normal fast speech, ignoring the word boundaries and including the assimilated sound /dʒə/ for *do you*.

Do you think it's OK? /dʒəˈθɪŋkɪtsəʊˈkeɪ/

What do you want to do? /ˈwɒdʒəˈwɒnəˈduː/

What do you think? /ˈwdʒəˈθɪŋk/

• In pairs, students compare what they have written and decide how many words are in each sentence.

• Write the sentences on the board and confirm the number of words in each. Ask students what they notice about the way the sentences are said. Point out that *do you* becomes /dʒə/ and *want to* becomes /wɒnə/.

• Tell students to read the Authentic listening skills box, then listen to sentences 1–4 from the talk, paying attention to the way the word boundaries merge.

• 🔊 **53** Play the recording.

▶ Teaching tip: Receptive or productive?, Unit 3.4, page 49.

3b

- Tell students to listen to the sentences again, this time practising saying them at the fast speed.
- 53 Play the recording again. Make sure everyone repeats the sentences.

3c

- Put students in pairs. Tell them to say phrases 1–4 with merged word boundaries. Before they start, point out that *give me* is often pronounced *gimme* /ˈɡɪmi/.
- Tell them to compare the way they pronounced it with the recording.
- 54 Play the recording.

9.1 How to tie your shoes

TEDTALKS

1

- Tell students that they are going to watch the TED Talk. At the end they will show each other Terry Moore's method of tying your shoes.
- 9.1 Play the whole talk.

Transcript

0.12 *I'm used to thinking of the TED audience as a wonderful collection of some of the most effective, intelligent, intellectual, savvy, worldly and innovative people in the world. And I think that's true. However, I also have reason to believe that many, if not most, of you are actually tying your shoes incorrectly.*

0.30 *(Laughter)*

0.31 *Now I know that seems ludicrous. I know that seems ludicrous. And believe me, I lived the same sad life until about three years ago. And what happened to me was I bought, what was for me, a very expensive pair of shoes. But those shoes came with round nylon laces, and I couldn't keep them tied. So I went back to the store and said to the owner, 'I love the shoes, but I hate the laces.' He took a look and said, 'Oh, you're tying them wrong.' Now up until that moment, I would have thought that, by age 50, one of the life skills that I had really nailed was tying my shoes. But not so – let me demonstrate.*

1.12 *This is the way that most of us were taught to tie our shoes. Now as it turns out – thank you. Wait, there's more. As it turns out, there's a strong form and a weak form of this knot, and we were taught to tie the weak form. And here's how to tell. If you pull the strands at the base of the knot, you will see that the bow will orient itself down the long axis of the shoe. That's the weak form of the knot.*

1.42 *But not to worry. If we start over and simply go the other direction around the bow, we get this, the strong form of the knot. And if you pull the cords under the knot, you will see that the bow orients itself along the transverse axis of the shoe. This is a stronger knot. It will come untied less often. It will let you down less, and not only that, it looks better.*

2.09 *We're going to do this one more time. (Applause) Start as usual, go the other way around the loop. This is a little hard for children, but I think you can handle it. Pull the knot. There it is: the strong form of the shoe knot.*

2.31 *Now, in keeping with today's theme, I'd like to point out – and something you already know – that sometimes a small advantage someplace in life can yield tremendous results someplace else.*

2.45 *Live long and prosper.*

- Note the differences in British English and North American English shown at the foot of the spread. In this unit, these focus on vocabulary differences. See Teaching tip 1 on page 6 of the Introduction for ideas on how to present and practise these differences.

> **Background information**
>
> **'Live long and prosper'**
>
> In the famous science-fiction movies and TV series, *Star Trek*, Dr Spock, an alien crew member of the *USS Enterprise*, salutes other characters with a strange hand gesture from his home planet, Vulcan, accompanied by their expression of good will, 'Live long and prosper'. It has become a comical but still friendly way of saying goodbye, recognizing the significance of sci-fi in popular culture.

- Put students in pairs. Encourage them to use a shoe with laces to actually try the strong and weak forms of the knot. If some pairs do not have a lace-up shoe between them, consider asking another student to lend his or hers, but only if appropriate!
- Give them plenty of time to try out the knots, and let students who have worked it out help those who have not.
- Ask for a volunteer to show the class the different ways of tying laces.

2

- Tell students to watch the first part of the talk again, indicating questions 1 and 2.
- 9.1 Play the first part of the talk from 0.00–0.31.
- Elicit answers from the class. (Accept just two or three of the adjectives for 1 if that's all they can recall.)

3

- Show them the summary of the second part of the talk. Ask them to watch and choose the correct option to complete the summary.

- ▶ 9.1 Play the second part of the talk from 0.31–1.12.

- Let them compare answers with a partner.

4

- Tell students to watch the third part of the talk in order to answer questions 1–3. Give them a minute to read them and predict the missing words in their heads.

- ▶ 9.1 Play the third part of the talk from 1.12–2.09.

- Go through the answers with the class.

5

- Ask students to look at the gapped sentence and think what the missing words might be.

- Tell them to watch the last part of the talk to confirm their ideas.

- ▶ 9.1 Play the fourth part of the talk from 2.09 to the end.

- Ask the class to paraphrase the sentence and say what they think it means or think of another example of where a small advantage makes a big difference.

VOCABULARY IN CONTEXT

6

- ▶ 9.2 Play the clips from the talk. When each multiple-choice question appears, students choose the correct definition. Discourage the more confident students from always giving the answer by asking individuals to raise their hand if they think they know.

Transcript and subtitles

*1 ... most of you are actually tying your shoes incorrectly. Now I know that seems **ludicrous**.*
   a strange
   b wrong
   c ridiculous

*2 I ... thought that by age 50 one of the life skills that I had really **nailed** was tying my shoes.*
   a got right
   b practised
   c forgotten

*3 This is a stronger knot ... It will **let** you **down** less ...*
   a injure
   b disappoint
   c annoy

*4 A small advantage some place in life can **yield** tremendous results someplace else.*
   a bring in return
   b hide
   c be the same as

*5 Live long and **prosper**.*
   a learn
   b be successful
   c eat well

▶ Extra activity: Ask for more!, Unit 7.1, page 93.

7

- In pairs, students think of examples to accompany points 1–3.

- Elicit a few examples from the class.

CRITICAL THINKING Understanding the main argument

8

- Put students in pairs to discuss what they think the main argument is. Ask them to agree on a one-sentence summary that begins: *Terry Moore is saying that ...*

- Let them compare their ideas with a neighbouring pair. If you see that students are struggling to come up with their own ideas, move on to Exercise 9.

9

- Tell students to read the messages about the talk and discuss the questions.

- Elicit feedback to Exercise 9 to find out whether any pairs wrote essentially the same points as any of the viewers did in their comments. Try to reach agreement on what points Terry Moore most wanted to make.

> **Answers**
>
> Students' own answers

10

- Tell students, still in pairs, to think of an example to illustrate two arguments made in the comments in Exercise 9.
- Elicit a few ideas for the class to hear and compare with their own ideas.

> **Suggested answers**
>
> 'It's important to do the basic things right before we try to do more complicated things.' Examples: children learn to walk before they can run; most people can use a simple spreadsheet program before they master design and maintenance of a more complex database.
>
> 'It's never too late to learn from other people.' Example: many adults, even in retirement, choose to study new things.
>
> 'There is no single correct way to do a task.' Example: people have their own way of holding a pen or pencil, or of holding a knife and fork or chopsticks.

PRESENTATION SKILLS Demonstration

11

- Books closed. Ask students to think back to a time when someone showed them how to do something. Ask them to consider how clearly they demonstrated and why it was successful or not.
- Put students in pairs to make a checklist of three important things to remember when giving a demonstration of how something works. If pairs are struggling to think of advice, prompt them by asking what you can do to prepare your demonstration beforehand.

> **Answer**
>
> Students' own answers

12

- Books open. Tell students to read the Presentation tips box and compare their answers from Exercise 11 with the tips for speakers.
- Elicit any extra tips that students thought of that are not mentioned in the box.

13

- ▶9.3 Tell students to watch the clips from the TED Talk again to find out which of the techniques from the Presentation tips box they think Terry Moore followed.

> **Answer**
>
> It is impossible to know how he practised before the talk, but he demonstrates confidently, indicating he did practise it until it felt easy. The only technical terms he uses are 'axis' and 'transverse', but these are clear from context. He gives the demonstration twice for clarity. He introduces the demonstration with a personal anecdote.

14

- **Optional step.** Prepare a small demonstration of an alternative way of doing something that you know. Do the demonstration in front of the class to encourage them to follow suit.
- Put students in pairs to prepare a demonstration. Make sure they follow the advice in the Presentation tips box. Monitor as they prepare, helping with any unknown vocabulary and making suggestions where appropriate.

15

- Put students in new pairs so that they can give their demonstrations.
- **Optional step.** Invite volunteers to the front of the class to demonstrate their alternative ways of doing things in front of the class. Alternatively, have them prepare a demonstration for the beginning of the next class.

Extra activity

'How to …' instructional videos

There are a huge number of professional and amateur *How to …* videos available online, for almost anything you may wish to learn. Ask students to choose something they would like to learn to do, find a video in English online and learn from it!

Useful sites include videojug, eHow, howcast, monkeysee and of course YouTube, or students can simply search *'How to'* and type what they want to learn. Indicate the range of areas that they can choose with some examples, e.g. *how to dance polka / fix a broken toilet / make a Harry Potter cake / play Happy Birthday on the piano*. Add examples that you think your students will like.

At the start of the following lesson, students share with each other what they wanted to learn and why, where they found a video to help and how useful it was.

▶ Set Workbook pages 84–85 for homework.

9.2 You'll find it useful

GRAMMAR Zero and first conditional

1

- Books closed. Put students in pairs or small groups. Ask them to make two lists: one of all the ways that speaking English (or another language) has been useful to them in their lives, and one of other ways that speaking other languages can benefit them. Offer an example for this second list, e.g. that the ability to speak a second language may help you feel good about yourself.

- Give the class five minutes for this task. Monitor groups carefully, prompting with suggestions and helping them express their ideas well.

- Books open. Tell the groups to compare their lists with the infographic. Ask whether they wrote any ideas that are not mentioned. Ask students to share with the class the most important benefits of learning English for them.

Background information

Learning a second language helps fight Alzheimer's!

There is scientific evidence that learning and using more than one language helps older people manage Alzheimer's disease better. A study at York University in Toronto found that bilingual patients with the disease started showing symptoms four to five years later than monolingual patients. We don't know why this is, but one theory suggests that brains get stronger working with two languages, so they are better able to cope with the mental problems the disease creates.

Alzheimer's is thought to affect between 21 and 35 million people worldwide. This is another good reason to learn English!

2

- Tell students to use the infographic to complete the sentences. Let them confer before fielding answers.

Answers

1 97%   2 job   3 tasks   4 2–4%   5 attractive

- Ask the class whether there are any ideas that they have never heard before or find hard to believe. Also ask who might be interested in publishing this data and why (e.g. schools, examination companies, publishers, teachers).

3

- Tell the students to answer questions a–d about sentences 1–4 in the Grammar box.

- Students can check their answers and overall understanding of the zero and first conditionals by turning to the Grammar summary on page 156. If students need more controlled practice before continuing, they could do some

or all of Exercises 1–3 in the Grammar summary. Otherwise, continue on to Exercise 4 in the unit and set the Grammar summary exercises for homework.

Answers

a Sentences 1–2 refer to something that is generally true.

b present simple

c In sentences 1–2 the present is used; in 3–4 the future with *will* is used.

d *unless: If you don't speak English, you will find it difficult to get a job …*

Answers to Grammar summary exercises

1

1 c   2 e   3 d   4 f   5 b   6 a

2

1 will feel   2 get   3 change   4 will discover
5 change   6 will probably forget   7 turn   8 will find
9 get   10 will stay   11 find   12 want   13 have to
14 don't write   15 always forget

3

1 when   2 If   3 If   4 if   5 when   6 If

TEACHING TIP

Grammar – when both options are possible

There is ambiguity in some grammar points such as zero and first conditionals, when in many situations both structures could be used. Students can be confused when this happens, and simply saying 'Both are possible' doesn't help clarify differences. Look for situations when both structures are possible and compare them with situations when only one structure works. By exploring these ambiguities with students, they can arrive at a deeper understanding.

4

- Tell students to choose the correct options to complete the text.

- Let them take turns to read out sentences to clarify the answers.

Answers

1 is   2 is   3 love   4 will find   5 offers   6 will have
7 don't   8 want   9 will make

- **Optional step.** Ask students which of the three factors in successful learning are most important in their opinion, and whether they can think of other essential factors.

5

- Put students in pairs or small groups. Ask students to look at the advertisement and discuss possible benefits as

---

well as disadvantages of e-learning compared with traditional classroom learning.

- Elicit their thoughts in a whole-class discussion.

Suggested answers

Benefits include: flexible study times, no need to travel to a school, ability to work at your own pace, may be cheaper than traditional classroom learning, lack of fear of getting things wrong.

Disadvantages include: lack of motivation that comes from a sense of class community, no teacher to ask questions to, lack of the pressure to study caused by the teacher's expectations, feedback and correction limited to right or wrong answers, little room for ambiguity and more complex learning.

6

- Tell students to put the words in order to write sentences. Remind them that there may be more than one way to order the clauses, but they may need to add punctuation.

Answers

1 If you join the e-learning course, you will be part of a large community. / You will … if you join …

2 If people enrol before 1 May, they get a 20% discount. / People get a … if they enrol …

3 They give people a free tutorial when they start.

4 They will give you your money back if you aren't satisfied. / If you aren't satisfied, they will …

7

- Put students in pairs. They use information in the infographic or their own ideas from Exercise 1 to make three more sentences with *when*, *if* or *unless* about the benefits of learning foreign languages. Remind them to use the zero and first conditional.

Suggested answers

If people study a foreign language for four or more years, they outperform their classmates.

You will find it easier to order food if you speak a country's native language when you are travelling.

When people with good language skills apply for work, they are more likely to get jobs as 30% of companies say these are the people they are looking for.

GRAMMAR Imperatives in conditionals

8

- Tell the students to read the sentences in the Grammar box and answer questions 1–3.

- Students can check their answers and overall understanding of imperatives in conditionals by turning to

the Grammar summary on page 156. If students need more controlled practice before continuing, they could do Exercises 4–6 in the Grammar summary. Otherwise, continue on to Exercise 9 in the unit and set the Grammar summary exercises for homework.

Answers

1 a   2 when   3 present simple

Answers to Grammar summary exercises

4

1 Serve the food when it is hot.

2 Please let me know as soon as she arrives. / Let me know as soon as she arrives, please.

3 Switch off the computer if it starts making a noise. / If the computer starts making a noise, switch it off.

4 Always check your emails before you send them. / Before you send your emails, always check them.

5 Don't do anything until I tell you.

6 Always read the instructions before you operate a new machine. / Before you operate a new machine, always read the instructions.

5

1 begin   2 switch   3 look   4 hurts   5 stand   6 go
7 will feel   8 come   9 do   10 will be

6

1 will come → comes   2 will be → are   3 will try → try
4 give → will give   5 When → If   6 will arrive → arrive

9

- Tell students to complete the sentences using verb in the correct form.

- Confirm answers with the class.

Answers

1 have   2 finishes   3 ends   4 Tell   5 are

- **Optional step.** After confirming answers, ask students where they imagine seeing or hearing the sentences. Sentence 1 could be a teacher talking to a student, 2 could be an on-screen message from an operating system or advice from a technician in a phone call, 3 could be on an advertisement or part of a promotional message, 4 could be someone speaking to a student about to start a new course and 5 could be someone with a car waiting to give a friend a lift somewhere.

10

- In pairs, students complete the commands in their own words. Encourage them to write more than one ending.

- Ask pairs to compare their answers with another pair before eliciting suggestions from the class.

• **Optional step.** Students write the beginning of a command
of their own on a piece of paper. They stand up, holding it in
front of them, and walk around the classroom, prompting each
other to end the commands in different ways. They report
back to the class with the most interesting or original endings
that they heard for their command.

SPEAKING Practical solutions

11 21st **CENTURY OUTCOMES**

• Ask students to think of solutions to the five everyday
problems in pairs. Have them write sentences using the first
conditional or an imperative. Make sure they know to use the
words *if*, *when*, *before* and *after*.

• Elicit some solutions for the first problem from the class
as a whole to ensure students know what to do and how to
do it, e.g.

*Every time you create a new password, write it in a special
place if you don't want to lose it. Make sure that you
disguise it if you want it to be secure.*

*If you use the same password for everything, you will
remember it but it won't be safe.*

• Monitor pairs carefully, offering suggestions and ensuring
good use of the target structures.

12

• Put pairs together in groups of four. Let them compare
their solutions to decide on the most useful.

• In whole-class feedback, elicit their ideas for each problem
and get them to vote on the most effective solutions given.

• Indicate the 21st CENTURY OUTCOME at the foot of the
page, and ask students to think of times in their professional
or academic lives when discussing practical solutions is

necessary. Ask them to write similar sentences they can
imagine saying at work or as part of their studies.

▶ Photocopiable communicative activity 9.1: Go to
page 225 for further practice of the zero and first
conditionals. The teaching notes are on page 241.

▶ Set Workbook pages 86–87 for homework.

9.3 Small details matter

READING Getting the basics right

1

• Books closed. Write the title of the article on the board.
Ask the class what the 'basics' are that you have to get right in
the tasks (1–3), which you can read out to them. Discuss each
separately.

2

• Books open. Tell students to read the article quickly and
choose the two correct messages that the article is saying
from the list of four (a–d).

• Let students confer before eliciting answers.

3

• Put students in pairs to read the article again to answer
questions 1–6.

• In feedback, make sure students justify their answers with
evidence from the article.

Answers

1 The tools weren't selling. (line 5)

2 They failed to make sure the website showed stock accurately, and to send the customer a catalogue. (paragraph 2)

3 the management (line 26)

4 It can increase sales by 10% or more. (lines 37–38)

5 Busy customers don't want to risk having a bad experience. (lines 40–42)

6 It has to be disciplined, have clear and simple goals and empower front-line managers. (lines 44–48)

4

• Tell students to find the words in bold in the article, then to answer questions 1–6 about them.

Answers

1 cheap   2 a short time   3 out of stock   4 connected / integrated / in touch with   5 strict   6 give the power to someone

5

• Put students in small groups. Ask them to think of at least one company that offers a consistently good experience. Encourage them to consider all types of company, from large multinationals to small local businesses. Ask them to identify reasons why they get things right.

• Regroup students so that they can share what they have discussed with students from other groups (see the Teaching tip below).

Answer

Students' own answers

TEACHING TIP

Taking the teacher out of the picture in feedback

The norm after any exercise is for students to tell the teacher their answers or ideas. After a free speaking activity such as a discussion, this isn't necessary. Consider allowing students the chance to give feedback to one another rather than telling you their ideas one by one. Regrouping students so that they can relay what they have discussed allows them to reformulate ideas and say them in a better, more fluent way, and gives them greater student talking time.

Let's say they discuss in groups of three or four: AAA, BBBB, CCCC, DDD, etc. Assign students in each group a number from 1 to 4: $A^1A^2A^3$, $B^1B^2B^3B^4$, C^1C^2 ... Then simply direct all the 1s to one corner of the room, all the 2s to another corner, and so on: → $A^1B^1C^1D^1$, $A^2B^2C^2D^2$, A^3B^3, etc. Now they can share what they have talked about.

VOCABULARY Being effective

6

• In pairs, students complete the sentences in their own words.

• Invite students to share their ideas with the class.

Suggested answers

1 ... listen to and read the language a lot. / ... use it before you lose it!

2 ... washes better than by hand. / ... saves water.

3 ... keep the doors and windows closed. / ... use renewable energy such as solar power.

7

• Ask students to match the verbs with the phrases to complete the expressions.

Answers

1 c   2 d   3 a   4 e   5 b

8

• Explain that the answers in Exercise 7 can help them choose the correct words to complete the sentences.

• Let students compare their answers before sharing the answers in class.

Answers

1 quick   2 worked   3 down, save   4 simple
5 wasted, economical, gets

SPEAKING Offering a good service

9   *21st* CENTURY OUTCOMES

• Ask students to look at the four categories and choose an organization that they know in each. Encourage them to choose companies that they don't think always give a good service.

• Make sure they have all made a note of four companies. Point out the 21st CENTURY OUTCOME at the foot of the page and explain that questions 1 and 2 give them the chance to demonstrate their business understanding. Students answer the questions for each company. If you don't think all of them can do this on their own, put them in pairs to support each other.

10

• Put students in small groups to discuss their ideas from Exercise 9. You could ask students to imagine that they are consultants hired by one of the companies in Exercise 9, and to decide what advice they should be given.

• Field their ideas in whole-class discussion. Find out which of the four industries mentioned in the categories list has the most to do to improve its service, according to the class.

Extra activity

Management consultants

Still in their groups, students decide which of the companies they have discussed in Exercise 10 has the most to do to provide a better service. They imagine they are management consultants who have been hired by this company to give them some advice and suggestions about how to improve.

Students hold a meeting to decide:

- what the problems facing the company are
- what the company should do about them
- which problem is the most important one to improve.

Students present the results of their meeting at the front of the class. For homework they could write a report addressed to the CEO of the company.

▶ Photocopiable communicative activity 9.2: Go to page 226 for further practice of the vocabulary in this lesson. The teaching notes are on page 242.

▶ Set Workbook pages 88–89 for homework.

9.4 Here's a trick that works

VOCABULARY Practical solutions (adverbial phrases)

1

- Ask students to look at the photo and explain the problem.

Answer
The shoes are on the wrong feet.

2

- Teach the phrases using realia and the board. Show the class an item of clothing *inside out* and *back to front*. Hold a bottle of water or a cup *upside down*. Then write that day's date with some numbers or letters *the wrong way round*. Finally, write the words *back to front*, as if seen in a mirror, like this:

ƚnoɿʇ oƚ ʞɔɒd

- Ask students to complete the sentences with the phrases in the box. (The answers are checked in Exercise 3.)

Answers
1 the wrong way round   2 inside out   3 upside down 4 back to front

Pronunciation Word stress

Where's the stress?

There are lots of ways of showing where the stress is in a word or phrase, but which is best? Look at the ways of marking stress below and answer the questions.

appli<u>ca</u>tion   **ma**nagement

coMMUnity

product   ● ●
detached

vo<u>ca</u>bulary

under'stand   ■ ☐ ☐
medical

- Which are quick and easy to mark on the board?
- Which are the clearest to see?
- Which don't distort the normal appearance of the word?
- Which do students need to understand to be able to see word stress in a dictionary?
- Which are often used in teaching materials?
- Which mark all the syllables, not just the stressed ones?

The system you use is up to you, but explain it to students and be consistent. And always ask students: *How many syllables? Where's the stress?*

3a

- Tell students to listen to the sentences in Exercise 2 to check their answers.
- 🔊 55 Play the recording.
- Ask students to listen again to mark the stress on the adverbial phrases (see Teaching tip above)
- 🔊 55 Play the recording again.

Answers
The stress always falls on the last word: *inside <u>out</u>, the wrong way <u>round</u>, upside <u>down</u>, back to <u>front</u>.*

3b

- In pairs, students practise saying the sentences. Tell them to check that their partner is stressing the phrases correctly.
- **Optional step.** Ask students to explain what sentence 3 means. Elicit that the phrase is used metaphorically to mean that the person's life was changed completely in a dramatic way. Write two more sentences on the board:

  *He knows that computer program **inside out**.*

  *No, you've got it all **back to front** – he didn't leave her, she left him.*

  Ask students to explain the metaphorical meaning of the phrases. Elicit that *inside out* here means *very well*, and *back to front* means here that the person has totally misunderstood the situation.

4

- Ask students to write four new sentences using the phrases. Monitor carefully as they write to check for clarity and accuracy.

- Let them show each other their sentences.

- **Optional step.** Tell students to stand up and move around the room talking to other students. They read out one or more of the sentences they have written, but replace the adverbial phrase with *beep*. The other student must try to 'fill the gap' with the correct phrase.

LISTENING Practical instructions

5

- Put students in pairs, and ask them to answer the questions about the phrases. Encourage miming the verbs.

- Ask students to share their answers and demonstrations with the class.

Answers
1 *fold* – bend an item of clothing and lay one part of it over another part, *pack* – put things into a bag so that you can take them somewhere, *roll* – wrap something around itself to form a tube
2 *un-* (*unfold*, *unpack*, *unroll*)

6

- Books closed. Explain to students that they are going to hear some instructions. Ask them to listen and say who the advice is for and what problem it solves.

- 🎧 56 Play the recording.

Transcript

So – here's some advice for all those people who travel to meetings and conferences and have to pack a smart suit or jacket in their bags. If you're like me, then you probably spend ages trying to get the jacket flat so that it looks OK and uncreased when you unpack it the other end. But here's a trick to avoid all that trouble.

Firstly, turn one half of the jacket inside out. Then fold the jacket in half, putting the sleeve that's not inside out into the inside out sleeve. Now roll the jacket, like you would do with a towel. But before you do that, put some other clothes – some socks, for example – inside the shoulder of the jacket. By doing this, you'll make sure that there are no lines or creases in the jacket when you unroll it. Finally, just to be sure, hang your jacket in the bathroom when you arrive at your hotel.

- Let students check in pairs before eliciting the answers from the class.

Answers
1 people who travel to meetings and conferences
2 the problem of keeping your jacket flat so that it looks OK

- Ask for a show of hands: *Who thinks this may be useful advice for you? Why?*

7

- Books open. Tell students to listen again to number instructions a–e in the order they are given.

- 🎧 56 Play the recording again.

- Elicit the steps one by one from the class.

Answers
1 e 2 d 3 c 4 a 5 b

- **Optional step.** Discuss possible reasons why it recommends hanging the jacket in the bathroom. If you have Internet access, get students to research this, at the same time looking for alternative methods and tips for avoiding creases in your jacket.

SPEAKING Giving instructions

8

- Put students in pairs. Ask them to cover Exercise 7 and repeat the instructions for packing a jacket. Show them the Useful language box.

- Alternatively, they take turns giving the instructions while their partner listens and looks at Exercise 7 to check.

9

- Explain that the students are going to give each other some practical instructions. Divide the class in two: As and Bs. Tell the As to turn to page 171 and Bs to page 172.

- Tell the students to memorize the instructions they find there. Give them a couple of minutes to do this.

- Put students A and B together in pairs: AAAAAA BBBBBB → AB AB AB AB AB AB. Remind them of the Useful expressions and tell them to give each other their instructions.

- Monitor carefully, listening for good use of English and clear instructions.

- When they have finished, ask the whole class whether they knew these tips, which they found most interesting and which they think they will use in future.

WRITING An email to a visitor

10

- Ask students to read the email and answer the questions.

Answers
1 They are coming to Brugg for a conference.
2 the conference centre and a restaurant

11

- Have the students identify various parts of the email in pairs. Tell them to underline the different parts.

- Put pairs together to compare answers.

Writing skill Giving directions

12a

• Tell students to complete the summary of the directions with the correct prepositions, using the email to help them.

12b

• Tell students to match the first half of the expressions (1–8) with their endings (a–f).

• Let them read them out to a neighbour to check.

• **Optional step.** In pairs, students practise giving directions in spoken form. Tell them to think of a location in the town near to the school. They take turns giving directions from the school to that location without saying the destination. Their partner listens to the direction and tries to identify the destination. Note the use of other verbs that are often used in directions, e.g. *get to / arrive at / reach your destination*. We don't need a preposition with *reach*.

13   *21st* CENTURY OUTCOMES

• Ask students to write an email to a visitor to their college or place of work, giving directions from the nearest station or bus stop. They should also invite them to lunch.

14

• Ask students to swap emails with a partner when they have finished so that they can use the checklist to evaluate each other's writing.

• Indicate the 21st CENTURY OUTCOMES at the foot of the page and ask whether their partner's written instructions were clear. If the directions described are familiar to the students who read the emails, ask them whether they think a stranger to the town could follow them easily.

▶ Set Workbook pages 90–91 for homework.

▶ Set Workbook Presentation 5 on pages 92–93 for homework.

10 The environment

UNIT AT A GLANCE

THEMES: Our relationship with the world around us, where we live and how we can survive, food

TED TALK: *How we can eat our landscapes.* Pam Warhurst talks about an urban renewal scheme that gets the community producing its own food.

AUTHENTIC LISTENING SKILLS: Understanding fast speech

CRITICAL THINKING: Recognizing tone

PRESENTATION SKILLS: Being straightforward

GRAMMAR: The passive, Phrasal verbs

VOCABULARY: Phrasal verbs, Food adjectives

PRONUNCIATION: Stress in passive forms, Intonation in questions

READING: *Big rise in greenhouse gas emissions*

LISTENING: In a restaurant

SPEAKING: Survey: How 'local' are you?, Expressing an opinion, Explaining what's on a menu

WRITING: A description of a system

WRITING SKILL: Explaining results

LEAD IN

• Ask students to look at the photo on page 106. Tell them to write a sentence that begins: *I think this unit is about …*

• When they have all finished the sentence, ask them to write a second sentence. Suggest the following stems:

  It will probably mention …

  I think we're going to read about …

  The themes include …

• Get the students to stand up and walk around the room, telling each other their predictions. After a minute, ask them to sit down.

• Ask students to raise their hand if they wrote anything about:

  the world we live in

  food and cooking

  city life

  pollution

  planning cities and urban spaces

  the city and the countryside

• Now tell students to look quickly through the unit to see if they were right.

• Ask them to choose one lesson that they are particularly looking forward to. Elicit a few students' preferences and ask why they like the look of that lesson.

TEDTALKS
BACKGROUND

1

• Explain that the students are going to watch an edited version of a TED Talk called *How we can eat our landscapes*. Ask them to read the text about the speaker, Pam Warhurst, and her talk, and answer questions 1–3 in pairs.

• Give them two minutes before eliciting answers.

Answers

1 edible

2 Students' own answers

3 Good reasons include: it's cheaper and fresher, you can control the chemicals you use, it's satisfying to grow your own food, you meet people in your community, you better understand where your food comes from.

Background information

Allotment gardening

In many countries, some people who live in cities grow their own fruit and vegetables by renting a small piece of land in or near the city. In Britain these are called *allotments* and in the US they are known as *community gardens*. Unlike other systems, such as the one described in the TED Talk, these plots of land are cultivated by one person or family rather than shared by a community.

KEY WORDS

2

• Ask students to cover the definitions (a–g), read the sentences and guess the meaning of the words in bold.

• Now tell them to look at the definitions and match them to the words in bold.

• Elicit answers from the class.

Answers

1 d 2 g 3 a 4 b 5 f 6 c 7 e

3

• Tell students to label the pictures with four words from Exercise 2.

AUTHENTIC LISTENING SKILLS
Understanding fast speech

3a

• Ask students if they sometimes have difficulty understanding people in English, and find out why. When a student mentions the speed with which some people talk, elicit phrases students can use to ask people to slow down. Teach and drill the phrases to the class, e.g. *Could you speak more slowly, please?, Sorry, you're talking too fast for me.*

• Tell students to read the Authentic listening skills box and identify which point the useful expressions they've just practised help to address. (the point about asking for clarification)

• While they listen to Pam Warhurst's introduction to her talk, students choose the main point she is making, a or b.

• 🔊 **57** Play the recording.

Transcript

This is where I come from, Todmorden. It's a market town in the north of England, 15,000 people, between Leeds and Manchester, fairly normal market town. It used to look like this, and now it's more like this, with fruit and veg and herbs sprouting up all over the place. We call it propaganda gardening.

• Elicit the answer, and congratulate the class on understanding the main point.

Answer
b

3b

• Tell students to listen again, and say what kind of plants they grow in Todmorden.

• 🔊 **57** Play the recording again.

• Elicit the answer, and congratulate the class on understanding some details.

Answer
They grow fruit and veg and herbs. (*Veg* is short for *vegetables*.)

• Ask them whether they think it will be easier or more difficult to understand when they watch the TED Talk rather than just listen to parts of it (as they have just done), and why. Refer them to the point in the Authentic listening skills box about making use of visual clues. Elicit some visual clues (e.g. the presentation slides, the speaker's gestures and facial expressions).

3c

• Tell them to listen to the next point Pam Warhurst makes about what has happened in her town.

• 🔊 **58** Play the recording. Play it again if students need to hear it twice.

Transcript

We've even invented a new form of tourism. It's called vegetable tourism, and believe it or not, people come from all over the world to poke around in our raised beds.

• In pairs, students describe what has happened. Elicit what has happened from the class. Celebrate what they *have* understood!

Answer
The town has become a tourist destination. People come to see their plants.

• Review the points in the Authentic listening skills box. Point out that:

– they listened first for the main idea and then for details (the first point)

– they understand that there will be visual clues to help them understand (the second point)

– they know how to ask for clarification, and that asking for help is a listening strength, not a weakness (the third point)

– they have succeeded in understanding some, not all of what they heard, and this is OK! (the fourth point)

10.1 How we can eat our landscapes

TEDTALKS

1

• Ask students to watch the edited version of the TED Talk and write one or two examples of the things mentioned in the list (1–3).

• ▶ **10.1** Play the TED Talk.

Transcript

0.13   The will to live life differently can start in some of the most unusual places. This is where I come from, Todmorden. It's a market town in the north of England,15,000 people, between Leeds and Manchester, fairly normal market town. It used to look like this, and now it's more like this, with fruit and veg and herbs sprouting up all over the place. We call it propaganda gardening. (Laughter)

0.42 Corner of our railway station car park, front of our health centre, people's front gardens, and even in front of the police station. (Laughter) We've got edible canal towpaths, and we've got sprouting cemeteries. The soil is extremely good. (Laughter)

1.04 We've even invented a new form of tourism. It's called vegetable tourism, and believe it or not, people come from all over the world to poke around in our raised beds, even when there's not much growing. (Laughter) But it starts a conversation. (Laughter)

1.20 And, you know, we're not doing it because we're bored. (Laughter) We're doing it because we want to start a revolution.

1.28 We tried to answer this simple question: Can you find a unifying language that cuts across age and income and culture that will help people themselves find a new way of living, see spaces around them differently, think about the resources they use differently, interact differently? Can we find that language? And then, can we replicate those actions? And the answer would appear to be yes, and the language would appear to be food.

1.58 So, three-and-a-half years ago, a few of us sat around a kitchen table and we just invented the whole thing. (Laughter) (Applause) We came up with a really simple game plan that we put to a public meeting. We did not consult. We did not write a report. Enough of all that. (Laughter) And we said to that public meeting in Todmorden, look, let's imagine that our town is focused around three plates: a community plate, the way we live our everyday lives; a learning plate, what we teach our kids in school and what new skills we share amongst ourselves; and business, what we do with the pound in our pocket and which businesses we choose to support.

2.39 We put that proposition to the meeting, two seconds, and then the room exploded. I have never, ever experienced anything like that in my life. And it's been the same in every single room, in every town that we've ever told our story. People are ready and respond to the story of food. They want positive actions they can engage in, and in their bones, they know it's time to take personal responsibility and invest in more kindness to each other and to the environment.

3.08 And since we had that meeting three and a half years ago, it's been a heck of a roller coaster. We started with a seed swap, really simple stuff, and then we took an area of land, a strip on the side of our main road, which was a dog toilet, basically, and we turned it into a really lovely herb garden. We took the corner of the car park in the station that you saw, and we made vegetable beds for everybody to share and pick from themselves. We went to the doctors. We've just had a six-million-pound health centre built in Todmorden, and for some reason that I cannot comprehend, it has been surrounded by prickly plants. (Laughter) So we went to the doctors, said, 'Would you mind us taking them up?' They said, 'Absolutely fine, provided you get planning permission and you do it in Latin and you do it in triplicate,' so we did — (Laughter) — and now there are fruit trees and bushes and herbs and vegetables around that doctor's surgery. And there's been lots of other examples, like the corn that was in front of the police station, and the old people's home that we've planted it with food that they can pick and grow.

4.11 And then there's the second plate, the learning plate. Well, we're in partnership with a high school. We've created a company. We are designing and building an aquaponics unit in some land that was spare at the back of the high school, like you do, and now we're going to be growing fish and vegetables in an orchard with bees, and the kids are helping us build that, and the kids are on the board, and because the community was really keen on working with the high school, the high school is now teaching agriculture . . .

4.39 And then there's the third plate, because if you walk through an edible landscape, and if you're learning new skills, and if you start to get interested in what's growing seasonally, you might just want to spend more of your own money in support of local producers, not just veg, but meat and cheese and beer and whatever else it might be.

4.55 But then, we're just a community group, you know. We're just all volunteers. What could we actually do? So we did some really simple things. We fundraised, we got some blackboards, we put 'Incredible Edible' on the top, we gave it every market trader that was selling locally, and they scribbled on what they were selling in any one week. Really popular. People congregated around it. Sales were up.

5.13 And then, we had a chat with the farmers, and we said, 'We're really serious about this,' but they didn't actually believe us, so we thought, OK, what should we do? I know. If we can create a campaign around one product and show them there is local loyalty to that product, maybe they'll change their mind and see we're serious.

5.29 So we launched a campaign – because it just amuses me – called Every Egg Matters. (Laughter) And what we did was we put people on our egg map. It's a stylized map of Todmorden. Anybody that's selling their excess eggs at the garden gate, perfectly legally, to their neighbours, we've stuck on there. We started with four, and we've now got 64 on, and the result of that was that people were then going into shops asking for a local Todmorden egg, and the result of that was, some farmers upped the amount of flocks they got of free range birds, and then they went on to meat birds, and although these are really, really small steps, that increasing local economic confidence is *starting to play out in a number of ways, and we now have farmers doing cheese and they've upped their flocks and rare breed pigs, they're doing pasties and pies and things that they would have never done before. We've got increasing market stalls selling local food, and in a survey that local students did for us, 49 per cent of all food traders in that town said that their bottom line had increased because of what we were actually doing. And we're just volunteers and it's only an experiment. (Laughter)*

6.31 *Now, none of this is rocket science. It certainly is not clever, and it's not original. But it is joined up, and it is inclusive. This is not a movement for those people that are going to sort themselves out anyway. This is a movement for everyone. We have a motto: If you eat, you're in. (Laughter) (Applause) Across age, across income, across culture.*

7.02 *Through an organic process, through an increasing recognition of the power of small actions, we are starting, at last, to believe in ourselves again, and to believe in our capacity, each and every one of us, to build a different and a kinder future, and in my book, that's incredible.*

7.25 *Thank you. (Applause) Thank you very much. (Applause)*

Note the differences in British English and North American English shown at the foot of the spread. In this unit, these focus on spelling and vocabulary differences. See Teaching tip 1 on page 6 of the Introduction for ideas on how to present and practise these differences.

- Let students compare with a partner before eliciting answers from the class. (Don't expect them to understand and note all of the answers given below.)

Answers
1 in the train station car park, in front of a health centre, in people's front gardens, in front of the police station, along the canal towpaths, cemeteries, at the side of the main road, on land at the back of the high school
2 fruit, vegetables, herbs, corn, fish, meat, cheese, beer, eggs
3 the local community, doctors, high school students, local producers, market traders, farmers

2

- Tell students to look at sentences 1–5 and guess the answers before watching the first part of the talk again.
- ▶10.1 Play the first part of the talk from 0.00–1.58.
- Elicit correct sentences from students.

Answers
1 15,000 2 police 3 vegetable 4 revolution 5 living

3

- Get students to predict the words they will need to complete the sentences. Elicit the words that they don't think they will need.
- ▶10.1 Play the second part of the talk from 1.58–3.08.
- Ask them whether they were right and elicit answers.

Answers
1 kitchen 2 plan, public 3 school, businesses 4 story

4

- Tell students to watch the third part of the talk and match sentence halves 1–5 with a–e.
- ▶10.1 Play the third part of the talk from 3.08–4.39.
- Let them discuss in pairs before asking for answers from the class.

Answers
1 d 2 e 3 a 4 c 5 b

5

- Tell students to read the summary and try to remember or guess the correct words to complete it.
- ▶10.1 Play the fourth part of the talk from 4.39 to the end for students to check.
- Students take turns reading out the text sentence by sentence.

Answers
1 producers 2 sales 3 serious 4 eggs 5 small 6 everyone

Extra activity

Incredible Edible *OUR* town

Write on the board three questions:

Where could you grow fruit and vegetables in your town or city? Make a list.

What would people like to grow? Why?

Who would you approach to put a similar scheme to Todmorden's into action? Who could get involved?

Put students in groups of four or five to plan a similar scheme to *Incredible Edible Todmorden* in their town. Give them time to discuss the questions.

Ask the class whether they can imagine it working in their town, where the best vegetable gardens might be, what they would grow and why.

VOCABULARY IN CONTEXT

6

- ▶10.2 Play the clips from the talk. When each multiple-choice question appears, students choose the correct definition. Discourage the more confident students from always giving the answer by asking individuals to raise their hand if they think they know.

Transcript and subtitles

*1 We **came up with** a really simple game plan that we put to a public meeting. We did not consult. We did not write a report.*

 a thought of

 b learned about

*2 People are ready and **respond to** the story of food.*

 a like to tell each other

 b have a positive reaction to

*3 And since we had that meeting three and a half years ago, it's been a heck of **a roller coaster**.*

 a an up and down journey

 b a difficult time

*4 … 49 per cent of all food traders in that town said that their **bottom line** had increased because of what we were actually doing.*

 a quality of their produce

 b the money they make

*5 Now, none of this is **rocket science**. It certainly is not clever, and it's not original.*

 a very complicated

 b very expensive

*6 It certainly is not clever, and it's not original. But it is joined up, and it is **inclusive**.*

 a a new idea

 b involving everyone

Answers
1 a 2 b 3 a 4 b 5 a 6 b

7

• Students finish the questions in any way they like. Monitor to help with language and provide suggestions.

• Pair them up to ask each other their questions.

Suggested answers
1 … global warming? / … cancer? / … Internet crime? 2 … food quality? / … caring for the environment? / … animal welfare? 3 … less meat? / … locally grown food? / … insects?

CRITICAL THINKING Recognizing tone

8

• Explain that a person's tone is the sound of their voice that shows how they are feeling, and it can have an effect on the way we feel about their argument. Ask students to think about Pam Warhurst's tone and how they would describe it. Tell them to choose two adjectives from the box, or come up with their own way of describing it.

• Ask them to compare their choices with a partner before eliciting ideas from the class.

Suggested answer
Her tone might be described as direct, down-to-earth (practical and not fanciful), funny or warm.

9

• Still in pairs, students discuss the way Pam Warhurst spoke and whether and how it helped her argument.

• Invite students to summarize their discussions for the whole class.

Suggested answer
Her humorous, direct, down-to-earth tone mirrors the message that Incredible Edible activities are direct and involve action more than words.

10

• Tell students to read the comments about the TED Talk to identify what they say about Pam Warhurst's tone and the effect the talk had on each viewer.

Answers
Leona says it's funny and easy to relate to. The talk makes her pupils enthusiastic about the idea of local action. Martin says the tone is practical and positive. He also responds to the 'just-do-it' attitude she has.

11

• Put students in pairs. Ask them to suggest the right tone for the two messages.

• In whole-class feedback, make sure they justify their ideas.

Suggested answers
An argument against cutting down forests could be given in an angry, emotional, factual or sarcastic tone. A presentation of a new electric vehicle could be given in a factual, direct, positive, optimistic or funny tone.

• **Optional step.** Review the TED Talk from Unit 8 with the students, or ask them to look at it at home, to identify the tone that Sanjay Dastoor takes when presenting his electric skateboard.

PRESENTATION SKILLS Being straightforward

12

• Remind students that in Exercise 8 they studied how tone affects how listeners feel about an argument and how they relate to it. Ask students, in pairs, to think about other ways speakers can help the audience relate to them and their ideas.

• Elicit students' answers for the class to listen and compare.

13

• Students read the Presentation tips box to further compare their ideas. Explain *straightforward* if necessary (not difficult or complicated, easy to understand).

14

• Tell students to watch clips from the talk and check which techniques Pam Warhurst follows.

• ▶ 10.3 Play the clips from the talk. Then let students compare their answers with a partner.

Answer

She follows all of the ideas in the Presentation tips box.

15

• Put students into pairs. Explain that they are going to present a practical idea to the local community. They should choose one of the given ideas or think of another idea.

• When pairs have decided, tell them to prepare a brief description. In order to help their audiences relate to the talk, they should follow the points in the box. Give them time to prepare some ideas and how to deliver them.

16

• When students have finished, put them in different pairs.

▶ Teaching tip: Three ways to pair up students, Unit 2.1, page 27.

• Students take turns giving their presentations to their new partners.

• When their presentations are over, ask the class how effective they thought the skill of being straightforward could be.

▶ Photocopiable communicative activity 10.1: Go to page 227 for further practice of the ideas and vocabulary from this lesson. The teaching notes are on page 243.

▶ Set Workbook pages 94–95 for homework.

10.2 A big sum of small actions

GRAMMAR The passive

1

• Put students in pairs to discuss which three things would make their town a better, happier place to live in. If ideas aren't forthcoming, elicit problems in the town and things people complain about. Write some typical problem areas on the board: traffic, parking, crime, pollution, rubbish, unemployment, lack of community spirit, lack of green space, etc.

• Write their ideas on the board and conduct a vote to see which ideas are most popular.

2

• Ask students to look at the infographic and answer the questions.

Answers

1 It's trying to help communities find new ways to live happily using fewer resources, starting with small, local action.

2 money and energy

3 They can improve community spirit and local economies, and reduce climate change and waste.

3

• Tell students to listen to examples of Transition town projects and match the projects (a–d) with the aims in the infographic (1–5). Point out there is one more aim than projects.

• ⒜ 59 Play the recording.

Transcript

So today I'm going to talk a little about Transition towns and what they are. The great thing about Transition towns is that they focus on simple, practical actions. Different ideas are tried and if they work, they're put into action. I'll give you some examples of Transition town projects.

There's a group in Brixton in London which has its own community power station. Electricity is produced by solar panels on top of people's houses.

In Deventer in the Netherlands, a group has set up 'repair cafés', where people teach each other how to mend broken household objects. In the past, broken things were often thrown away.

Then in Oxford in the UK, volunteers collect food that isn't wanted by supermarkets. Before, this food was put in the rubbish. Now it's taken by the volunteers to poorer members of the community.

In many Transition towns, street parties and festivals are organized by local residents. These are occasions when communities can get to know each other better. In the past events like these weren't organized unless it was a special national holiday.

• Elicit answers from the class.

Answers

a 1   b 4   c 3   d 5

4

• Ask students to discuss in pairs which ideas they like most and why. Also ask them to identify any similar schemes in their local area. If they don't know any, ask how they might find out about similar schemes.

- **Optional step**. If students have Internet access, they can look up 'Transition towns' in their country and community projects in their local area.

5

- Tell the students to answer questions a–e about sentences 1–5 in the Grammar box.

- Students can check their answers and overall understanding of the passive by turning to the Grammar summary on page 158. If students need more controlled practice before continuing, they could do some or all of Exercises 1–5 in the Grammar summary. Otherwise, continue on to Exercise 6 in the unit and set the Grammar summary exercises for homework.

Answers

a In sentences 1, 2 and 5 *are tried*, *is produced* and *is taken* refer to the present; in 3 and 4 *were thrown* and *was put* refer to the past.

b *be* (*is*, *are*, *was*, *were*) + past participle

c 1 different ideas   2 electricity   3 broken things
4 this food   5 the food

d 2 solar panels   4 the supermarkets   5 volunteers

e *by*

Answers to Grammar summary exercises

1

1 is made   2 were built   3 promoted   4 clean   5 was published   6 now drink   7 is given   8 Were they given

2

2 agent necessary   3 ~~by farmers~~   4 ~~by the firefighters~~
5 ~~by a driver~~   6 agent necessary

3

1 is made   2 are found   3 add   4 leave
5 is transformed   6 use   7 is made

4

1 was held   2 was invented   3 were built
4 was opened   5 were spoken   6 was written
7 was destroyed   8 was sold

5

1 ~~produce~~ → is / was produced   2 ~~were offered~~ →
offered   3 ~~from~~ → by   4 ~~arrest~~ → arrested   5 ~~Does~~ →
Is   6 ~~make~~ → are made

6

- Tell students to find two passive verbs in the text and to identify the agent of the first passive verb.

Answers

are organized, *weren't organized*; the agent is *local residents*.

Pronunciation Stress in passive forms

7

- Ask students to listen to the sentences to decide which part of the verb is stressed: *be* or the main verb.

- ⚏ **60** Play the recording. Elicit that the main verb is stressed.

- In pairs, students practise saying the sentences, paying attention to stress patterns. Point out that in sentence 4 the main verb is a phrasal verb, and that these are normally stressed on the second word.

TEACHING TIP

hmm HMM hmm hmm HMM

One way to focus attention on stress patterns is to take the lexical content away completely and to hum a phrase or sentence instead. For example, *Different ideas are tried* becomes 'HMM-hmm hmm-HMM hmm HMM. Here are three ways you can use this technique.

- Drill the hummed sentence before you drill the sentence spoken normally.
- Hum the sentences like this in random order. Students listen carefully to identify the sentence you said.
- Students hum the sentences in random order. A partner listens to identify the sentence.

8

- Students read about other Transition town ideas and rewrite the verbs in bold in the passive form.

- Elicit the passive sentences from the class. Encourage natural sentence stress to reinforce what they practised in Exercise 7. Drill the sentences if necessary.

Answers

1 was held   2 were made   3 is seen   4 are run
5 are taught   6 aren't thrown away

- **Optional step**. Ask students which idea (the 'Trashcatcher's Carnival' or 'Cycletastic') they think is more effective in communicating the ideas of Transition towns. Encourage them to justify their opinions.

Background information

-tastic

From *fantastic*, the informal suffix *-tastic* is often used to indicate that something is excellent or showing a lot of a particular quality. *Cycletastic* is a centre all about bicycles. A *goaltastic* football match is exciting with lots of goals. A *poptastic* new song has a pop style and is very good. A party could be described as *funtastic*. Would you say this lesson was *grammartastic*?

9

• Ask students to write sentences about the food industry using the prompts and the present or past passive. Remind students that if the agent is present, they will need *by*.

• Students compare their sentences with a partner before sharing them with the class.

Answers

2 In 2012, almost half of the food eaten in Britain was imported from other countries.

3 More bananas (1 million tons) are eaten by British people than any other imported food.

4 Thirty years ago nearly 100% of Chinese food was produced in China.

5 Now a lot of Chinese food isn't grown there but is imported.

6 In the USA 80% of all consumed water is used by the food industry.

7 15,000 litres of water are needed to produce 1 kilo of beef.

8 In 2012, 40% of the food produced in the USA was not eaten.

9 In the UK 60% of tomatoes are thrown away by consumers every year.

10 30% of the world's land is used by animal farmers.

• Ask the class which of the facts they find most surprising or shocking.

SPEAKING Survey: How 'local' are you?

10

• Ask students to look at the survey questions and to add two more questions of their own. To give them ideas, write the following prompts on the board: *clubs, newspapers, place of work, online shopping, entertainment, excursions*.

• Monitor as they write, checking clarity and accuracy in question formation.

11

• Explain that the students are going to ask their questions to three classmates and that they must note down their responses. Make sure they have the means to write notes as they move around the classroom.

• Tell them to stand up and ask three other students.

12 *21st* **CENTURY OUTCOMES**

• Put students in pairs to compare their findings from the survey. Ask them to summarize these in writing in four or five sentences. Remind them to practise passive forms where appropriate.

• Put pairs together in groups to report to one another their findings. Ask them to draw some conclusions about how involved people in the class are in the local area.

• Write on the board: 'Think globally, act locally'. Ask students what they think it means and how important they think it is to be involved in local matters.

▶ Photocopiable communicative activity 10.2: Go to page 228 for further practice of the passive. The teaching notes are on page 243.

▶ Set Workbook pages 96–97 for homework.

10.3 Running out of time

READING Big rise in greenhouse gas emissions

1

• Ask students, in pairs, to discuss the meaning of the four phrases about the environment.

Answers

1/2 *Global warming* and *climate change* refer to changes people think are affecting the world's weather, particularly an increase in the overall temperatures. Evidence suggests that these changes are caused by human activity. They are often used interchangeably, though climate change includes the idea that not all change is about a rise in temperatures (e.g. more extreme weather events).

3 CO_2 *emissions* refers to the release of carbon dioxide by industry, electricity production, cars and other forms of transport.

4 *Greenhouse gases* are gases that stop the heat in the atmosphere from escaping into space and so contribute to global warming. CO_2 is the best known example.

• Elicit answers from the class.

• **Optional step**. Invite a student or students to come to the board and explain the greenhouse effect to the class. Alternatively, if students have Internet access, ask them to find out about it and report back to the class.

2

• Students answer the question in pairs. Ask them for examples, such as support for green politics, the attention to green issues in national newspapers, recycling schemes and green incentives, to support their view.

3

• Ask students to read the article to determine whether the facts are true, possibly true or false. Make sure they know not to read the comments yet.

• Elicit answers from the students.

Answers

1 F (Global warming increased by 34%, but it does not state what the CO_2 levels were.)

2 F (The temperature is predicted to increase by 2–5 degrees.)

3 T (They are no longer able to absorb the greenhouse gases.)

4 T (These gases are making the world's oceans more acidic and this is happening faster …)

5 P (We are 'running out of time', so it may not be too late.)

4

• Tell students to read the comments and identify the correct name for each question. Explain that some questions may not correspond to anyone, and some may have two answers.

• Let students compare before eliciting answers from the class.

Answers

1 Phoenixman   2 Davina   3 N   4 Harry B, Greenjo
5 Davina   6 Kitesurfer

5

• Ask students to find the phrases in bold in the comments and choose the correct meaning for each.

Answers

1 b   2 a   3 a   4 b   5 a

• **Optional step**. Students choose two of the new words or phrases to learn. They write them up in their vocabulary books with the definition and an example sentence, from the text or their own lives, using the word.

VOCABULARY Phrasal verbs

6

• Ask students to discuss the meaning of the two phrasal verbs in pairs.

• Elicit their definitions to share and discuss with the rest of the class.

Answers

running out of: If you are running out of something, there is not very much left and soon you will have none left.

carry on: continue

• Ask students what the difference between *We're running out of time* and *We've run out of time*. Elicit that in the second sentence, there is none left.

• If you wish to present more information about the grammar of phrasal verbs, direct students to read the Grammar summary on page 158, and to do Exercise 6.

Answers to Grammar summary exercise

6

1 I'm picking him up from the airport at 10 a.m.

2 How many people turned up for the meeting?

3 He carried on working late into the night.

4 Freddy and I get along very well.

5 They took the company over in 2008. / They took over the company in 2008.

6 I had to look the word up in a dictionary. / I had to look up the word in a dictionary.

7 She set it up in 2012.

8 They just got on with it.

7

• Encourage students to first read the sentences in the exercise by asking them to identify sentences that concern the environment (these are sentences 1, 4 and 6).

• Tell students to match the phrasal verbs in bold with the expressions (a–f).

• Elicit answers from the class (see Teaching tip below).

Answers

1 f   2 c   3 a   4 b   5 e   6 d

TEACHING TIP

Encourage students to produce new language in feedback

When asking for answers from students, always encourage them to produce the language being studied. Let's say the new vocabulary is *turn up*, and students have to match it with its definition: *appear*. If you ask: *What's the meaning of 'turn up'?* Students will respond with the definition and you won't hear them say the word itself. Ask instead *Which phrase means appear?* and students get to say *turned up*. There are two reasons for doing it this way:

• it means students get a chance to practise saying the new vocabulary.

• it allows you to check any pronunciation issues, e.g. /tʊrn/ instead of /tɜːrn/.

8

• Students complete the sentences using one of the phrasal verbs from the previous two exercises. Point out they need to make sure verbs are in the correct form.

• Ask students to read out the completed sentences.

• **Optional step.** Students write one or more gapped sentences to test their classmates. Either get students working with other students and reading out their sentences to test them, or invite students to read them out to the class as a whole.

9

• In pairs, students complete sentences 1–6 in their own words. Monitor the pairs to help them express their ideas.

• When they have six sentences, join pairs together in groups to compare what they've written.

• Elicit some ideas for each sentence stem from the class.

SPEAKING AND WRITING Expressing an opinion

10

• Ask students to read the comments below the article again and to choose one where they have something more to add, either in agreement or disagreement with the comment. If you still have the students' opinions from Exercise 6 on the board, they can use those as a starting point.

• When they have chosen one, they write a response. Remind them that they can use ideas that they developed in Exercise 9.

11   *21st* **CENTURY OUTCOMES**

• Write on the board some questions that encourage students to make connections between arguments and to evaluate information critically:

Did you respond to the same comments?

Whose comments were most similar to your own? Whose were different?

Do you think that the comments addressed the issues correctly?

Would you say that your group share the same attitude towards environmental issues?

• Put students in small groups. Tell them to read out their comments to one another, and to discuss whether they agree or disagree with them.

• Conclude the lesson by inviting one student to read out a response to each of the five comments in the article.

• **Optional step.** Tell students their homework is to save the planet! Tell them to make one simple change in their lifestyle between now and the next lesson. You could, for example, tell them that leaving the TV and DVD on standby mode overnight can waste more than half the electricity that is used if they are left on, and that switching appliances off completely saves a lot of electricity. As well as making this change, they also need to think of other advice to share with the class in the next lesson. At the start of the next lesson, ask students to encourage each other with their ideas.

▶ Set Workbook pages 98–99 for homework.

10.4 Can you explain?

VOCABULARY Food adjectives

Extra activity

'Unique Leek'

The object of this game is to think of food items that no one else thinks of. Explain this to students and tell them that they will play six rounds of the game. In the first round they must write a vegetable of their choice. They write in large letters on a piece of paper without showing others. After twenty seconds tell them to hold up their paper. If any students have repeated the same vegetable, they are out of the game. Any non-English words, blank pages or invented vegetables are also grounds for disqualification, of course.

In subsequent rounds, remaining students have to think of unique food items in new categories, as given below. Repeated items disqualify, as in round 1. The two last remaining students are the winners.

Round 2 – a drink   Round 3 – meat or fish   Round 4 – a dessert   Round 5 – snacks   Round 6 – fruit

1

• Put students in pairs. Ask them to match foods a–f with the adjectives. Then elicit answers.

2

• In pairs, students use the six adjectives to describe other kinds of food they sometimes eat.

• Elicit different foods for each adjective.

LISTENING In a restaurant

3

• Explain the two conversations students are going to hear and tell them to complete the table. Check understanding of *dish*.

• 🔊 **61** Play the recording. Meanwhile, copy the empty table on the board with space for students to write their answers.

Transcript

1

A: So what are you going to have?

B: Um, there are a few things I'm thinking of, but what's this: 'Bigos'? Can you explain?

A: It's a kind of stew, made with meat and sauerkraut.

B: Sauer what?

A: Sauerkraut. You know pickled cabbage.

B: Oh, OK. So is it a local dish?

A: Not especially. But it is a traditional Polish dish. It means 'hunter's stew'.

B: Do you recommend it?

A: Well, how hungry are you?

B: Quite hungry.

A: Then yes, it's good. It's not a light dish.

B: You mean, it's very filling.

A: Yes it is …

2

W = Waiter, C = Customer

W: Are you ready to order?

C: Yes I'd like the pepper steak, please. Is it spicy?

W: Yes, it is quite spicy, but we can make it less spicy if you like.

C: No, that's OK. And, er, do any vegetables come with it?

W: Yes, French fries and a small salad.

C: OK.

W: And how would you like your steak?

C: Er, medium, please.

W: And can I get you anything to drink?

C: No, thanks. Just a jug of water would be great.

• Let students compare their tables in pairs before inviting volunteers to the board to fill in the table.

Answers

1 bigos (a stew); traditional, not light, filling

2 pepper steak; spicy, medium

• Ask students which of the dishes they would prefer and why.

4

• Students listen to the conversations again and complete the description of each dish.

• 🔊 **61** Play the recording again.

• Ask two students to read the descriptions out loud.

Answers

1 1 stew   2 traditional   3 meat   4 hungry

2 1 salad   2 medium   3 water

• **Optional step.** Students work in pairs to memorize and act out Conversation 2 between the waiter and the customer.

▶ Extra activity: Memorizing dialogues, Unit 3.4, page 49.

Pronunciation Intonation in questions

5a

• Ask students to look at the questions and decide whether the intonation rises or falls in each one. Then tell them to listen and check.

▶ Intonation in questions, Unit 1.4, page 20.

• 🔊 **62** Play the recording.

• Elicit answers from students.

Answers

1 fall   2 fall   3 rise   4 rise   5 fall*   6 fall   7 rise

*Note that the speaker's intonation rises on *recommend* but then falls on *it,* which is a slight deviation from the usual rise on the last syllable in *yes/no* questions.

5b

• In pairs, students ask and answer the questions in Exercise 5a, paying attention to intonation.

SPEAKING Explaining what's on a menu

6

• Ask students to write a short menu of four or five dishes. Encourage lesser-known local dishes, the sort they imagine having to explain to a foreign visitor.

• Explain that they are going to practise explaining dishes on a menu. Give them a minute to think about how they will explain their dishes to one another. Point to the Useful language box to help them.

▶ Teaching tip: Successful role plays, Unit 2.4, page 34.

• Read out situations 1 and 2 to the class. Ask them to silently imagine the conversations they are going to have. Let them listen to their own voice explaining, first as them talking to a guest, and then as a waiter in a restaurant.

• Put students in pairs so that they can take turns explaining their menus, the other student playing the roles of guest or restaurant customer.

• Listen carefully to their dialogues and make notes of interesting use of English. When they have finished, point out errors and corrections.

WRITING A description of a system

7

• Students read Eileen's email then get into pairs to discuss possible ideas for making her office more environmentally friendly.

• Elicit some ideas from students.

Suggested answers
Go 'paper-free'. Put signs up on people's computers saying: 'Do you need to print this?'
Switch off machines such as computers, photocopiers and printers when they aren't being used.
Use energy-saving bulbs in the lights.
Put signs in the bathrooms to use less paper for drying hands, or install electric hand driers.
Use the stairs rather than the lift.

8

• Tell students to read Lana's reply and compare her ideas with theirs.

• Ask students which of Lana's ideas they like the most.

9

• Ask students to read the email again to find the result of each action (1–3) that Lana suggests.

• Students compare what they've written with a partner.

Answers
1 people recycle more   2 plastic waste is reduced
3 you only use half the paper

Writing skill Explaining results

10a

• Tell students to look at the actions and results in Exercise 9, find them in the email and underline the phrases in the email used to introduce each result.

• Write the phrases on the board under the heading *Explaining results*. Note that *Like this* would also be possible.

Answers
In this way…   By doing this …   Like that …

10b

• Ask students to match actions 1–3 with results a–c. Students link the actions and results using one of the linking phrases from Exercise 10a.

• Ask students to read out their sentences. Note that the phrases are interchangeable.

Answers
1 b, e.g. Put a lot of plants in your offices. In this way, you will create better air …
2 c, e.g. The heating is set at a maximum of 18 degrees. Like that, we save on our energy bills.
3 a, e.g. Employees are encouraged to use the stairs … By doing this, they get more exercise …

11   21st CENTURY OUTCOMES

• Explain to students that they are going to write an email to Eileen with more ideas for making her office more environmentally friendly. They should use ideas 1–3 and one more of their choice, such as an idea from Exercise 7. Check understanding of *compost*.

• Point out the checklist in Exercise 12 as a means of checking that they are including what they need to in their emails. If they need reminding about how to introduce the reasons for writing, they should check back to Unit 6.4, page 71.

Suggested answer
Hi Eileen,
I'm just writing to suggest a few more ideas for making your office more environmentally friendly.
1) In our office employees are encouraged to read documents on the computer. We have signs up around the office which say: 'Do you need to print this?' In this way, paper and printer ink is saved, and the office is tidier, too.
2) You can fit automatic lights which switch off when no one is in the office or bathroom. Like that, you reduce energy bills, which saves money and electricity.
3) Some food can be recycled to make compost for the office plants. You need a special bin for the compost so that it doesn't smell. By doing this, food waste is reduced. The plants love it, too!
4) Another place to reduce the amount of paper is in the bathrooms. By encouraging people to shake their hands dry so that they only need one piece of paper to dry their hands, you can save a lot of paper. In this way, the company pays less and it makes the cleaners' job easier!
I hope this helps. Please let me know what you end up deciding to do.
Best regards,

12

- Tell students to swap emails with a partner, then read the email and check that it includes the points on the checklist.

- Point out the 21st CENTURY OUTCOME at the foot of the page, and ask them to evaluate overall how well their partner has used the information to address the issue at hand.

- **Optional step**. Show them the TED Talk by Joe Smith called *How to use a paper towel*.

Extra activity

How green is my office?

Ask students how environmentally friendly they think their offices are (or their homes if they aren't working) and why. Ask them how they think their colleagues and bosses (or other family members) would feel about encouraging greener practices. Ask them to consider whether they would be prepared to help introduce small changes at work. Put them in groups to discuss:

- what areas of office practice could be more environmentally friendly.

- which ideas could work and why.

- who they would talk to in order to help start the process.

- how much work it would involve.

Finally, ask them to decide whether they will actually make the changes they are discussing. If anyone decides to go ahead, be encouraging and follow up in subsequent lessons by asking how the plan is going.

▶ Set Workbook pages 100–101 for homework.

▶ Set Workbook Writing 5 on pages 102–103 for homework.

REVIEW 5 | UNITS 9 AND 10

READING

1

- Put students in pairs. Ask them to discuss clean alternatives to fossil fuels.
- Elicit the ideas of the class.
- **Optional step**. Conduct a class discussion about which alternative way of producing electricity is the best.

Suggested answers
nuclear power, solar energy, wind energy (onshore and offshore), wave energy, ethanol (from crops)

2

- Ask students to read the article about Pavegen quickly to find out where Pavegen's clean energy comes from. Set them only one minute for this.

Answer
'Footfall' energy comes from special flooring that converts the energy from people's footsteps into electricity.

3

- Ask students to read the article again and decide which of the sentences (a–c) is *not* true. Make sure they remember where they found the answers.
- Elicit answers from the class.

Answers
1 b   2 c   3 b

GRAMMAR

4

- Ask students to complete the description of how Pavegen flooring works with passive and active forms of the verbs in brackets. Make sure they understand that both past and present forms are used.
- Let them compare answers in pairs before eliciting answers from the whole class.

Answers
1 was developed   2 started   3 is kept   4 steps
5 bends   6 is stored   7 is converted   8 were used

5

- Tell students to complete the sentences using the zero or first conditional.

Answers
1 continue, will run   2 invent, will pay / pay   3 want, need / will need   4 are, involve   5 discuss, find out / will find out   6 will be, are
Note that both answers are possible in some of these.

▶ Teaching tip: Grammar – when both options are possible, Unit 9.2, page 122.

VOCABULARY

6

- Tell students to complete the notes about other PEA award winners with the correct verbs.

Answers
1 turned up   2 run out of   3 look after   4 keep   5 get
6 end up   7 works   8 saves   9 waste   10 set up

- **Optional step**. Hold a vote for the best idea represented by the PEA award winners.

DISCUSSION

7

- Tell students that they are going to discuss Pavegen and alternative forms of energy. Give them time before they speak to think of things to say, and how they could use a passive form and a conditional sentence in the discussion.
- Put them in pairs or small groups to discuss the questions. Explain that students get 'extra points' for imaginative ideas for questions 2 and 3.
- Elicit some of these ideas in a whole-class summary discussion. You may want to hold a vote for the most imaginative idea, the most realistic idea and so on.

Suggested answers
1 Students' own answers
2 on dance floors in discos; along city marathon routes; modified, it could be used on roads to exploit the energy of traffic driving over it
3 in gyms, people's exercise produces kinetic and heat energy; the steam from cooking and boiling water in the kitchen could be converted to electricity; while riding a bicycle you could charge up your mobile phone with a dynamo!

SPEAKING

8

- Put students in pairs. Tell them to read the conversations.
- Let them decide if they think they can complete the conversations without referring to their notes, and whether they can say the conversations without first writing the expressions. Give them five minutes to prepare and practise the conversations. Go around the pairs offering advice and corrections where appropriate.
- Ask for volunteers to read out the dialogue in front of the class.

Answers

1 what you are going to have …
2 Does it come with vegetables or salad?
3 Do you recommend it?
4 It's a kind of salad or dip.
5 It's made with tomatoes and onion and spices.
6 After you do that, …
7 make sure you leave it for two to three hours …
8 By doing that, …

WRITING

9

- Ask students to quickly read the email and complete it with one, two or three words in each gap.

- Let students compare their answers to encourage self- and peer-correction before reading the email out one sentence at a time to share answers.

Answers

1 you for your   2 are looking   3 'm attaching a
4 you / to get to   5 out of   6 'll come   7 (Just) cross /
(Just) go around / (Just) go across / (Just) walk across
8 out   9 along/down/up   10 will see / will come to
11 on your/the   12 to join   13 me know if
14 to meeting/seeing   15 regards/wishes

10

- Tell students to exchange emails with a partner and compare what they have written.

- **Optional step.** You could finish this review by asking students individually to write a reply to Marjorie.

11 Leaders and thinkers

LEAD IN

• Ask students to look at the photograph. Elicit the word for when people get together to discuss things, like the building of a school (*a meeting*). Put students in pairs to list reasons why the meeting in the photo is different to an equivalent meeting in the students' countries and reasons why it is similar.

Suggested answers

Reasons it may be different: it is being held outside while meetings in most countries would probably be held indoors; they are sitting on the ground, not on chairs; there may not be a written record of this meeting.

Reasons it may be similar: there is a leader of the meeting, who is standing while the others sit and listen; the leader is a man, not a woman; they seem to be dressed in smart clothes.

Background information

The Maasai

The Maasai people of southern Kenya and northern Tanzania are famous for their lifestyle alongside the safari wildlife of East Africa, for their colourful red clothes and their semi-nomadic existence. Maasai men travel on foot long distances to look after their cattle, which are the main signal of wealth in Maasai culture. It is a patriarchal society, and only men make up the senior decision makers in the community.

TEDTALKS

BACKGROUND

1

• Explain that the students are going to watch an edited version of a TED Talk called *Life at 30,000 feet* by Richard Branson. Ask them to read the text about the speaker and the talk, and answer questions 1–3 in pairs.

• Give them two minutes before eliciting answers.

Answers

1 They all carry the Virgin name.

2 He is interested in humanitarian issues, such as climate change.

3 No. His career has had 'ups and downs'. The text also mentions 'falling and picking yourself up again'.

KEY WORDS

2

• Books closed. Tell students they are going to study some vocabulary that is used in the TED Talk. Read out the six sentences and ask students to try to identify which word in each sentence is going to be the focus of study.

• Elicit the words that they think will be the focus of study.

• Books open. Students check their predictions and guess the meaning of the words in bold (which they should have identified). They then match the words with definitions a–f.

Answers

1 b 2 a 3 f 4 c 5 d 6 e

- To check comprehension further, ask follow-up questions: *Roughly what year was Facebook launched? What organizations do you think Richard Branson gives financial backing to? Why do oil companies need good PR departments? Do you think it's important to be ruthless in business to succeed? Which local companies have a good/bad reputation? Why? Which industry has Amazon shaken up?*

▶ Teaching tip: Concept check questions, Unit 12.3, page 163.

AUTHENTIC LISTENING SKILLS Fillers in conversations

3a

- Ask students to read the Authentic listening box. If students speak the same language and know each other well, ask what their classmates' favourite fillers are when speaking their first language, or even which fillers they tend to use. They may be able to identify your favourite fillers in English, too!

> #### Background information
> #### Modern fillers
> Other fillers that students may hear young people using in English include *like*, and *and stuff*, as in the following sentence:
>
> *Then she tried to, like, talk to him and stuff, but he didn't want to talk to her.*
>
> Some people find fillers like these annoying, even though most people have particular words that they use too much, often without realizing it.

- Tell them to listen to the extract from Richard Branson's talk and answer questions 1 and 2.
- 🔊 63 Play the recording. Elicit answers.

Transcript

No, I mean, I think I learned early on that if you can run one company, you can really run any companies. I mean, companies are all about finding the right people, inspiring those people, you know, drawing out the best in people. And I just love learning and I'm incredibly inquisitive and I love taking on the, you know, the status quo and trying to turn it upside down. So I've seen life as one long learning process. And if I see – you know, if I, you know, if I fly on somebody else's airline and find the experience is not a pleasant one, which it wasn't 21 years ago, then I'd think, well, you know, maybe I can create the kind of airline that I'd like to fly on. And so, you know, so got one second-hand 747 from Boeing and gave it a go.

> #### Answers
> 1 I mean, you know, well   2 you know

3b

- 🔊 64 Play the recording. Tell students to complete the sentence. Let them read it out to one another to check.

- Ask them to identify the point where he restarts his sentence.

> #### Answers
> 1 you know   2 you know   3 well   4 you know
>
> He restarts his sentence after the second *you know*, with *if I fly on somebody else's airline ...*

- Point out that unlike other TED Talks they have watched, Richard Branson is being interviewed. Ask students why this is relevant. (He isn't repeating a well-rehearsed script and has to think about what he is going to say, which is why he uses fillers.)

> **TEACHING TIP**
>
> #### Fillers for fluency
> All learners of a language would like to be more fluent, but fluency is not only about their competence in English; it is how other people perceive their English. Fillers are one of the ways that help learners sound more fluent, as long as they don't use them inappropriately. Let them practise using fillers by putting them in pairs, and having them take turns to speak for a minute on an easy topic, such as 'my family', 'my job', or 'where I live'.

11.1 Life at 30,000 feet

TEDTALKS

1

- Tell students to tick the sentences (1–5) that describe Richard Branson's business philosophy as they watch the edited version of his TED Talk. Let them read the sentences first.

- ▶ 11.1 Play the edited version of the TED Talk.

- Give students a minute to compare their answers and discuss which of his ideas they like before eliciting the answers.

> #### Answers
> Sentences 1, 2 and 3 describe Richard Branson's business philosophy.
>
> Students' own answers about which ideas they like.

Transcript

0.12 *CA: So, we're going to put up some slides of some of your companies here. You've started one or two in your time. So, you know, Virgin Atlantic, Virgin Records – I guess it all started with a magazine called Student. And then, yes, all these other ones as well. I mean, how do you do this?*

0.33 RB: I read all these sort of TED instructions: you must not talk about your own business, and this, and now you ask me. So I suppose you're not going to be able to kick me off the stage, since you asked the question. (Laughter)

0.43 CA: It depends what the answer is though.

0.46 RB: No, I mean, I think I learned early on that if you can run one company, you can really run any companies. I mean, companies are all about finding the right people, inspiring those people, you know, drawing out the best in people. And I just love learning and I'm incredibly inquisitive and I love taking on, you know, the status quo and trying to turn it upside down. So I've seen life as one long learning process. And if I see – you know, if I , you know, if I fly on somebody else's airline and find the experience is not a pleasant one, which it wasn't, 21 years ago, then I'd think, well, you know, maybe I can create the kind of airline that I'd like to fly on. And so, you know, so got one second-hand 747 from Boeing and gave it a go.

1.40 CA: Well, that was a bizarre thing, because you made this move that a lot of people advised you was crazy. And in fact, in a way, it almost took down your empire at one point. I had a conversation with one of the investment bankers who, at the time when you basically sold Virgin Records and invested heavily in Virgin Atlantic, and his view was that you were trading, you know, the world's fourth biggest record company for the twenty-fifth biggest airline and that you were out of your mind. Why did you do that?

2.12 RB: Well, I think that there's a very thin dividing line between success and failure. And I think if you start a business without financial backing, you're likely to go the wrong side of that dividing line. We had – we were being attacked by British Airways. They were trying to put our airline out of business, and they launched what's become known as the dirty tricks campaign. And I realized that the whole empire was likely to come crashing down unless I chipped in a chip. And in order to protect the jobs of the people who worked for the airline, and protect the jobs of the people who worked for the record company, I had to sell the family jewellery to protect the airline.

3.02 CA: Now, you use the Virgin brand a lot and it seems like you're getting synergy from one thing to the other. What does the brand stand for in your head?

3.10 RB: Well, I like to think it stands for quality, that you know, if somebody comes across a Virgin company, they –

3.15 CA: They are quality, Richard. Come on now, everyone says quality. Spirit?

3.19 RB: No, but I was going to move on this. We have a lot of fun and I think the people who work for it enjoy it. As I say, we go in and shake up other industries, and I think, you know, we do it differently and I think

that industries are not quite the same as a result of Virgin taking them on.

3.40 CA: So, now, you've always had this exploration bug in you. Have you ever regretted that?

3.47 RB: Many times. I mean, I think with the ballooning and boating expeditions we've done in the past. Well, I got pulled out of the sea I think six times by helicopters, so – and each time, I didn't expect to come home to tell the tale. So in those moments, you certainly wonder what you're doing up there or –

4.10 CA: Your companies have had incredible PR value out of these heroics. The years – and until I stopped looking at the polls, you were sort of regarded as this great hero in the UK and elsewhere. And cynics might say, you know, this is just a smart business guy doing what it takes to execute his particular style of marketing. How much was the PR value part of this?

4.40 RB: Well, of course, the PR experts said that as an airline owner, the last thing you should be doing is heading off in balloons and boats, and crashing into the seas. (Laughter)

4.59 CA: They had a point, Richard.

5.01 RB: In fact, I think our airline took a full page ad at the time saying, you know, come on, Richard, there are better ways of crossing the Atlantic. (Laughter)

5.11 CA: So seriously, is there a dark side? A lot of people would say there's no way that someone could put together this incredible collection of businesses without knifing a few people in the back, you know, doing some ugly things. You've been accused of being ruthless. There was a nasty biography written about you by someone. Is any of it true? Is there an element of truth in it?

5.35 RB: I don't actually think that the stereotype of a businessperson treading all over people to get to the top, generally speaking, works. I think if you treat people well, people will come back and come back for more. And I think all you have in life is your reputation and it's a very small world. And I actually think that the best way of becoming a successful business leader is dealing with people fairly and well, and I like to think that's how we run Virgin.

6.16 CA: Well, Richard, when I was starting off in business, I knew nothing about it and I also was sort of – I thought that business people were supposed to just be ruthless and that that was the only way you could have a chance of succeeding. And you actually did inspire me. I looked at you, I thought, well, he's made it. Maybe there is a different way. So I would like to thank you for that inspiration, and for coming to TED today. Thank you. Thank you so much. (Applause)

Note the difference in British English and North American English shown at the foot of the spread. In this unit, the difference is one of spelling only. See Teaching tip 1 on page 6 of the Introduction for ideas on how to present and practise these differences.

2

- Tell students to watch the first part of the talk again to answer the questions. Suggest that they try listening only so that they can focus on the exercise better.

- ▶11.1 Play the first part of the talk from 0.00–1.40.

- Let students compare answers with a partner before eliciting answers from the whole class.

Answers

1 No, it isn't difficult. He says 'if you can run one company, you can really run any companies.'

2 The key is finding the right people and drawing out the best in people.

3 He decided to start an airline because he had an unpleasant experience on one and thought he could do it better.

3

- While they watch the second part of the talk, students decide whether the sentences are true or false. Let them read the sentences first.

- ▶11.1 Play the second part of the talk from 1.40–3.40.

Answers

1 F (... his view was that ... you were out of your mind.)

2 F (... we were being attacked by British Airways.)

3 T (And in order to protect the jobs of the people who ..., I had to sell the family jewellery ...) Note that by 'the family jewellery' Branson is referring to his most important business at the time, i.e. Virgin Records.

4 T (I like to think that it stands for quality ...)

5 T (We have a lot of fun ... we do it differently ...)

4

- Students watch the third part of the talk and choose the correct answers to questions 1–3.

- ▶11.1 Play the third part of the talk from 3.40 to 5.11.

Answers

1 b 2 a 3 a

5

- Point to the interviewer's last question and ask students to complete Richard Branson's reply using the words in the box. Let them guess the answers before playing the talk for them to check.

- ▶11.1 Play the fourth part of the talk from 5.11 to the end. Elicit answers.

Answers

1 top 2 well 3 come 4 reputation 5 small
6 successful 7 fairly 8 run

Extra activity

Interview with a leader

In this activity, students prepare questions to ask a CEO or other type of leader that they know of, then discuss which questions are best and why.

Ask students to suggest leaders that they know of. These can be famous CEOs, dead or alive, such as Steve Jobs or Mark Zuckerberg, or from their country, business leaders from within their industry, or even other types of leaders, such as politicians, military commanders or spiritual leaders. Write their suggestions on the board.

Put them in pairs or small groups and tell them to choose one leader they would be interested in interviewing. When they have chosen, tell them to brainstorm and write down possible interview questions as if they were preparing for a special edition of TED Talks in your town or city. Monitor groups to check that questions are appropriate and mostly directed at their lives in positions of leadership.

When they all have a few questions, ask them to now imagine they are in the audience of the TED event and have the chance to ask just one question. Tell them to discuss in their groups which of their questions they should ask and why. They must reach an agreement.

When groups are ready, ask a spokesperson from each group to tell the class their leader, the question they have decided to ask them and why. Invite students from other groups to comment and to imagine the answers that the leaders would give.

VOCABULARY IN CONTEXT

6

- ▶11.2 Play the clips from the talk. When each multiple-choice question appears, students choose the correct definition. Discourage the more confident students from always giving the answer by asking individuals to raise their hand if they think they know.

Transcript and subtitles

*1 ... then I'd think, well, you know, maybe I can create the kind of airline that I'd like to fly on. And so, you know, so got one second-hand 747 from Boeing and **gave it a go**.*
   a tried it
   b gave it a new name

*2 ... and his view was that you were trading, you know, the world's fourth biggest record company for the twenty-fifth biggest airline and that you were **out of your mind**.*
   a not experienced
   b crazy

*3 Now, you use the Virgin brand a lot and it seems like you're getting synergy from one thing to the other. What does the brand **stand for** in your head?*
   a look like
   b represent

4 Well, I think that there's **a very thin dividing line between** success and failure.

    a not much difference between

    b a big difference between

5 ... we were being attacked by British Airways. They were trying to put our airline **out of business**, and they launched what's become known as the dirty tricks campaign.

    a not able to operate as a company

    b in another country

Answers
1 a   2 b   3 b   4 a   5 a

7

- Students discuss the questions in pairs. When they have finished, they share their answers with the rest of the class.

Answers
Students' own answers

CRITICAL THINKING Fact or opinion

8

- Put students in pairs to discuss whether sentences 1–5 are fact or opinion. Then discuss the answers, insisting that they give their reasons.

Answers
1 F (The companies he has started show that he is successful.)
2 F (clear from his business style and choice of balloon and boat adventure)
3 F (The interviewer says Branson has changed his approach to business.)
4 O ('cynics might say ...')
5 O ('You've been accused of being ruthless.')

9

- Students discuss, as a whole class, whose opinion the 'opinion' sentences in Exercise 8 are.

Answers
Sentence 4 – an opinion held by cynics
Sentence 5 – an opinion expressed in a biography

10

- Ask students to read Ulla's comment about the TED Talk and rate how much they agree with it (5 if they agree, 0 if they disagree). Ask for a show of hands of students who gave the post 5, 4, 3, 2, 1 and 0. Ask those who largely agree with Ulla what they agree with and those who largely disagree what they disagree with. Encourage a range of views.

Suggested answers
The viewer refers to the fact that Branson is successful and has achieved a lot. She expresses the opinion that he does not just do business to make money, and that he isn't proud.

PRESENTATION SKILLS Dealing with questions

11

- Ask students whether they are used to attending, listening to or giving presentations in interview format or where there is time for the audience to ask questions at the end.

- In pairs, students discuss how a speaker could deal with questions when they don't know the answer or with someone who strongly disagrees with them.

Answer
Students' own answers

12

- Students compare their ideas with the suggestions given in the Presentation tips box.

- Elicit those suggestions that answer the questions in Exercise 11.

Answers
All points except the penultimate one answer question 1 in Exercise 11. The fourth and fifth points answer question 2.

13

- Ask students to read questions 1–3 before watching the clip.

- ▶ 11.3 Play the clip. Give students a minute to compare answers before whole class discussion.

Answers
1 He says it stands for quality.
2 Because everyone says this about their company.
3 He says that he was going to say more after this. He is following the last point in the Presentation tips box, about bringing the conversation back to the point that you want to make.

14

- Put students in pairs and explain that they are going to practise answering questions at the end of a presentation they have given. Ask them to discuss how best to answer them.

- After a couple of minutes, elicit which approaches they have chosen.

15

• Tell students to take turns asking and dealing with the questions.

▶ Set Workbook pages 104–105 for homework.

11.2 Who are the CEOs?

GRAMMAR Modal verbs (1)

1

• **Optional step.** Books closed. Check students know what a CEO is (the Chief Executive Officer – or boss – of a company). If students have Internet access, ask them to do an image search for 'CEO' in pairs. Using the search results, ask them to describe a typical CEO according to the Internet. If only you have Internet access, do the search and ask students to guess what most CEOs are like. Invite observations and discussion.

• Books open. Students look at the infographic and answer the questions.

• Discuss the answers with the whole class.

2

• Tell students to listen to a journalist talking about the statistics in the infographic. Ask them to complete the conclusions that he makes.

• 🔊 65 Play the recording.

Transcript

So what does this data tell us about our business leaders? Well, first it's clear that we must get more women running companies. Ten per cent is a very low figure. In Germany company boards have to be at least thirty per cent female. We

also need to have more ethnic diversity. If there are so few women and people from different backgrounds at the top, how can you expect to find diversity in other parts of the company?

But it's good that a quarter of CEOs are under 35. You must involve young people, if you want things to change. Secondly CEOs work too much. Eight per cent of them never take a day off! I'm not saying you mustn't work hard. But you don't have to work all the time to be efficient. The information about parents is interesting. It seems you can run a business if your parents weren't entrepreneurs – that is, had no experience of running a business – but it certainly helps if they did. Forty-nine per cent of CEOs have parents who are or were entrepreneurs. And if you're interested …

• Let students compare answers with a partner before eliciting answers from the class.

3

• Tell the students to read sentences 1-7 in the Grammar box and answer questions a–d about them.

• Students can check their answers and overall understanding of modal verbs by turning to the Grammar summary on page 160. If students need more controlled practice before continuing, they could do one or both Exercises 1 and 2 in the Grammar summary. Otherwise, continue on to Exercise 4 in the unit and set the Grammar summary exercises for homework.

4

• Students look at the FAQs by new employees in a company and choose the correct options to complete the answers.

• Give them time to compare their answers with a partner before inviting students to read the passages to the class.

Background information

Flexible working rules

In many companies rules for employees aren't as strict as these. Companies in some industries adopt a more casual dress code, or allow their employees to dress casually on Fridays, a practice which is known as *dress-down Fridays* or *mufti days*. Some companies allow workers to start and finish at times to suit them, within limits, of course. If they want to start earlier in order to finish earlier, they may do so. This is called *flexitime*.

But what about Internet access? According to one survey, a third of employees spend two or more hours on non-work related websites every week, and some spend much more. Should companies restrict employees' access to websites like Facebook (responsible for 41% of non-work Internet use), or should they trust them to be responsible, and control their own use of company time for personal reasons? Some companies recognize the importance of letting staff feel comfortable in the workplace, and believe that hours lost to social media are more than made up for by a happier, more motivated workforce.

5

> **TEACHING TIP**
>
> **Office politics**
>
> If you are teaching to students who work in the same office or company, such as in in-company classes, be sensitive to issues surrounding office rules and the students' positions in the company relative to each other. Some ideas discussed in this lesson may be difficult for students to talk openly about in front of their superiors. Consider checking with one of them before you start. However, in most in-company classes you will find that students are more than happy to discuss their office rules and may want to adapt the activities to talk about their own company. If this is the case, let them personalize the lesson.

• Ask students to answer the questions about the company rules described in Exercise 4 in pairs.

• Let pairs share their opinions with their classmates in whole-class discussion.

Answer

Students' own answers

6

• Still in pairs, students read the three new FAQs and prepare answers, writing as if for the company website.

Suggested answers

1 Yes, of course you can. You will get your free parking card which you must put in the machine when you enter the car park. But you mustn't lend the card to friends or relatives to use the car park for personal reasons.

2 We understand that employees with part-time contracts may need to supplement their salaries with extra work. However, in your contract you will see it says that you have to do any extra work at times in the week that do not affect your work here. Also, you mustn't work for any competing companies.

3 You can claim your full salary if you are sick for up to five working days with illness but you must provide a doctor's note. If you are sick for more than five days, you will be paid at 70% of your full salary.

• **Optional step.** Ask students to write one more FAQ. Invite them to read them out and get other students to suggest answers orally, as part of a whole-class discussion.

GRAMMAR Modal verbs (2)

7

• Put students in pairs to discuss whether they would like to be their own boss and run their own business. Make sure they justify their answers. (But see the Teaching tip on the left!)

• Invite comments about the pros and cons of being your own boss.

8

• Before students listen to the conversation, put them in pairs to predict what Jane and her friend will say.

• 🅰66 Play the recording.

Transcript

A: *So how's work these days?*

B: *Well, it's OK, but I work really hard and I don't see much benefit from it. I'm thinking about leaving, actually. In fact I think I should start my own consultancy business. Do you reckon that's a good idea?*

A: *Well, hang on a minute. You really need to ask yourself why, first. You shouldn't start a business just because you don't like the company that you're working for.*

B: *No, that's not it. I've got a lot of contacts and I think I can make it work.*

A: *OK, well, good. But remember that it'll probably be more work and more stress too. The most stressful thing is not having the money to give your business a chance of success. Do you have any savings?*

B: *Well, I've got a bit of money, but perhaps not enough.*

A: *Right. So the first thing you should do is to write a business plan. Then you should find a financial backer – maybe go and see the bank. You know, if you start with that …*

- Elicit answers from students. Ask students if they think Jane's friend's advice is good.

Answers

1 She works hard but doesn't see much benefit from it. She has a lot of contacts and thinks she can make it work.

2 savings and a business plan

9

- Ask students to read the sentences in the Grammar box and answer the question.

- They can check their answers in the Grammar summary on page 160. If they need more controlled practice before continuing, tell them to do some or all of Exercises 3–5 on page 160. Otherwise, continue on to Exercise 10 in the unit and set the Grammar summary exercises for homework.

Answer

to give a recommendation or advice

Answers to Grammar summary exercises

3

1 shouldn't listen to / damage your ears by listening to
2 should get   3 shouldn't worry   4 should listen
5 should wear a hat   6 shouldn't regret / spend time regretting

4

1 mustn't   2 can   3 should   4 should   5 must
6 mustn't   7 should   8 mustn't

5

1 ~~to pay~~ → pay   2 ~~haven't~~ → don't have   3 ~~to see~~ → see
4 ~~don't have to~~ → mustn't   5 ~~don't must~~ → mustn't
6 ~~need finish~~ → need to finish

10

- Tell students to rewrite the sentences using *should* and *shouldn't* so that they have the same meaning.

- Let them compare sentences with a partner before eliciting answers.

Answers

2 You should employ people who have skills you don't have.

3 Should I keep my current job while I'm planning my new business?

---

4 You shouldn't expand your business too fast.

5 You shouldn't choose a business partner that you don't know well.

6 You should speak to other people who have their own company.

- **Optional step.** Ask students to discuss the question asked in number 3. Elicit the advantages to keeping your job while setting up a new business as well as the disadvantages.

SPEAKING Dilemmas

11 **21st CENTURY OUTCOMES**

- Explain to students that they are going to discuss a business dilemma in small groups. Before they do so, ask them to read the situation and write a question about it. Offer one question as an example, e.g. *How loyal is Harry to KPC?*

- Now instruct students to think of one thing that they would like to say during the discussion using one of the modal verbs they have been studying. Give them a minute to do this.

- Put students in small groups to discuss Harry's situation. Monitor groups while they talk, listening especially for appropriate use of modal verbs. At the same time, check that groups are exploring the dilemma in depth.

- Regroup students so that students from different groups are together. Ask them to listen to each group's ideas and decide to what extent they have solved Harry's problem.

- Conduct whole-class feedback to ascertain which groups have solved Harry's problem and to what extent. Mention any important questions that have been raised in the discussion. Ask whether the skill in this 21st CENTURY OUTCOME of solving problems is about finding the right answers or asking the right questions.

Extra activity

Business dilemmas

Put students in pairs or small groups. Tell them to write a situation similar to Harry's dilemma in Exercise 11 which involves a difficult decision for someone in a business setting. Write on the board some prompt questions:

Is it a decision for an employee or employer?

Does the dilemma centre around: relationships between colleagues? Unfair practice? Competition between companies? Secret information? Money?

When all groups have written their situation, they swap with another group who discusses and (hopefully) solves the dilemma. After the groups have discussed the situation for a few minutes, elicit whole-class feedback.

▶ Photocopiable communicative activity 11.1. Go to page 229 for further practice of modal verbs. The teaching notes are on page 244.

▶ Set pages 106–107 for homework.

11.3 Famous quotes

READING Words of wisdom

1

- Students discuss the questions in pairs.

- Elicit some of their ideas. Be prepared to translate their favourite quotes into English if you speak the students' first language well.

- **Optional step.** Find a famous quote of your choosing which was originally in English. Translate it into the students' first language or find a translation online. Write the translation on the board. Challenge students to translate it back into English and award a prize to the pair whose translation is closest to the original.

2

- Ask students to read the quotations on page 125 to match topic 1–5 with the person or people who talk about it.

- Let them compare with a partner before eliciting answers.

> **Answers**
> 1 Anita Roddick, Thomas Edison, Richard Branson
> 2 Prince Charles   3 Richard Branson, Mary Kay Ash
> 4 Gordon Bethune   5 Richard Branson, Henry Ford

3

- Ask students to tell the class their favourite quotes. Ask them why they like the quotes they do.

4

- Students read the quotations again and answer questions 1–10.

- Elicit answers from the class.

> **Answers**
> 1 entrepreneurs   2 they will treat customers better
> 3 proud   4 products that are going to make a difference in people's lives   5 the planet (i.e. green issues)   6 bad
> 7 to respond to change   8 employees   9 (possibly) his employees or himself!   10 it may be cheaper but no one will buy it

5

- Students look for words and phrases whose meaning corresponds to 1–5.

> **Answers**
> 1 shareholders   2 staff   3 launch   4 asset   5 royalty

- **Optional step.** Ask students to find one other word or phrase in the quotations that they would like to remember. Elicit a few ideas and ask why they want to learn those phrases. Ask them to write the word/phrase in their vocabulary notebooks.

6

- Put students in pairs to discuss questions 1–3.

- Elicit a range of different answers from the class for each question.

> **Suggested answers**
> 1 Students' own answers
> 2 clean water in oceans, seas, rivers and lakes; rainforests, corals, pristine polar regions, and other areas under threat of destruction or disappearance; the number of different species; clean air
> 3 Ryanair, Amazon, AirBnB, H&M

VOCABULARY *make* and *do*

7

- Ask students to look at sentences 1 and 2 and to elicit the basic meaning of *make* and *do*.

> **Answers**
> 1 b   2 a

- Reinforce these meanings by testing them on phrases and expressions that use this basic distinction between the two verbs. Say the phrase but replace either *make* or *do* with *beep*, e.g. *beep* some soup / a mess / a list (*make*), *beep* my homework / nothing / the gardening (*do*).

8

- Explain that like many frequent verbs in English, *make* and *do* are also found in a lot of common expressions where the meaning of *do* as *perform* and *make* as *create* are not present.

- Show the class the two columns and ask them to complete sentences 1–10 with the phrases.

- For variety, don't elicit the sentences in order from 1 to 10 but call out phrase from the columns in random order and elicit the sentence that goes with it, e.g. *Make a lot of money? – Five. You can make a lot of money as a lawyer, but it's hard work.*

> **Answers**
> 1 Do something   2 do my best   3 make a difference
> 4 do me a favour   5 make a lot of money   6 do my food shopping   7 make a suggestion   8 make a lot of progress   9 do business   10 make decisions

- **Optional step.** Students write three more sentences using *make* and *do* phrases from Exercise 8.

SPEAKING Life advice

9   `21st` **CENTURY OUTCOMES**

- Books closed. Ask students whether they are good at giving advice and receiving it from other people. Also find out about people at their workplaces or in their private lives who have guided and inspired them. Spend time talking about how these people guide and inspire, the lessons students have learned from them and why they think they are good at giving advice.

• Books open. Put students in pairs and ask them to choose three of the items from 1 to 6 about which they have advice to offer. Encourage them to use *should* and *shouldn't* when they write.

• Monitor closely, suggesting ideas and helping with language.

Suggested answers

1 You shouldn't expect progress to happen a little bit every day. Often no progress is made for weeks or months and then there is a lot of progress all of a sudden.

2 You should give each decision the time it deserves: big decisions need longer than small decisions. Don't be rushed into making big decisions too quickly.

3 Making money shouldn't be your first priority when choosing a career. You should choose a job according to how much you like it. Money is secondary.

4 Don't do favours for others if you are being forced to do them. Don't do favours because you hope they will return the favour one day. No, you should do favours for other people because you can.

5 You shouldn't mix doing business with friendships. Business should be impersonal, but it can quickly become personal if money and friends are involved.

6 You shouldn't ask: *Did I do my best?* Ask instead: *Did I do my best under the circumstances?* Don't ignore the obstacles in your life that stop you doing your very best.

10

• Reorganize students so that they are with different partners.

▶ Teaching tip: Three ways to pair up students, Unit 2.1, page 27.

• Ask them to tell each other their advice. Ask them to choose the piece of advice their partner gave them that they like best.

• Invite students to share their partner's advice with the class.

• **Optional step.** Ask students to look online for more famous quotes and bring their favourites to class the next lesson.

▶ Photocopiable communicative activity 11.2: Go to page 230 for further work on inspirational quotes. The teaching notes are on page 245.

▶ Set Workbook pages 108–109 for homework.

11.4 How did it happen?

LISTENING Problem solving

1

• Tell students to put the verbs in order. Students copy the completed problem-solving process on the board.

Answers

1 identify 2 analyse 3 tackle 4 solve

• Check students' pronunciation of the verb + problem collocations by drilling them. Point out the word stress on *ident*ify and *an*alyse.

2

• Ask students to read the tip about how to solve a problem. Explain that they will listen to two people in a university administration office who are discussing a problem. Tell them to answer questions 1–3 as they listen.

• 🔊67 Play the recording.

Transcript

C = Colleague, R = Roberto

C: *Hi, Roberto. Philip just called me. He hasn't received the programme for the open day.*

R: *No, that's right. I didn't send it to him.*

C: *Really? Why not?*

R: *It isn't finished.*

C: *Why isn't it finished?*

R: *I didn't feel confident about my English.*

C: *Why don't you get some English lessons?*

R: *Well, I want to but it's too expensive.*

C: *You should ask the university to pay. Or, another solution is to ask someone else to check it. You know, it's OK to ask for help.*

• Let students check their answers with a partner before checking with the transcript on page 170.

Answers

1 Philip hasn't received the programme.

2 Roberto didn't feel confident about his English.

3 He could get some English lessons – he could ask the university to pay for these lessons – or he could ask someone to check his English.

3

• Tell students to complete the replies without looking at the transcript.

- When they are ready, let them listen again to the conversation to check their answers.

- 🔊 67 Play the recording again.

Answers

1 not   2 isn't   3 don't   4 should

Pronunciation Positive and negative questions

4a

- Tell students to listen to the four questions and underline the words they hear.

- 🔊 68 Play the recording. Elicit the answers.

Answers

1 didn't   2 weren't   3 Did   4 was

- Let students hear and say the different versions of the sentences by leading them in choral drills of the two versions of the sentences, like this: ... *did you ask ... Why did you ask ... didn't you ask ... Why didn't you ask ... ... weren't the books ...* , etc.

4b

- In pairs, students take turns reading each sentence in Exercise 4a as either a positive or negative question. They must decide which question they heard and answer it appropriately.

SPEAKING Analysing problems and suggesting solutions

5

- Explain that students are going to discuss Problems 1 and 2. Put students in pairs and assign one student as Student A and the other as B. Instruct them to turn to their respective pages to read about the situations.

- Give them a couple of minutes to read and memorize the situation. Ask them to turn back to page 126.

- Point to the Useful language box and ask them to imagine instances in the conversations with their partner when they can use a few of the useful expressions. Encourage them to ask probing questions of each other to get to the root cause of each problem.

- Students discuss each problem in turn. Monitor carefully for good analysis of the problems and ways of suggesting solutions.

- When pairs have finished talking, elicit the root causes of the two problems and some possible solutions for each.

Suggested answers

Root causes of the problems: that the fire extinguishers have not been properly labelled, and that the council needs to save money.

Solutions: Students' own answers

6

- Encourage students to think of a problem they have faced recently. You may need to provide an example or two from your own life to prompt them to think of ideas for this exercise. For example, you could tell them that you have two friends who have had an argument and are not talking to each other. You want to invite both of them to a party but neither will come if they know the other is coming.

- Still in their pairs, they share the problems and analyse them in the same way as in Exercise 5.

WRITING Posting advice on a forum

7

- Lead students in whole class discussion. Ask them whether they ever go online in search of advice about the things listed 1–6.

- Find out as much as you can about students who respond to any of these types of advice. Ask them whether they post questions or just read others' questions and answers, which websites they recommend, how well they rate the advice they receive, and so on.

- Finish by asking how important the public's advice and recommendations are to businesses selling products online.

8

- Ask students to quickly read questions A–D, which have been posted on forums, and match each to one of the categories in Exercise 7.

- Elicit the answers.

Answers

A 2   B 1   C 6   D 3

9

- Students now match the suggestions (1–4) with the questions in Exercise 8.

Answers

1 D   2 B   3 A   4 C

- Put students in pairs to rate the advice.

10

• Ask students to use the question to analyse the format of a typical advice posting. Ask them if the suggestions include each of the four elements.

Answer

They include c, d and e.

Writing skill Features of online posts

11

• Put students in pairs to look at the posts and responses in Exercises 8 and 9 again. They choose the correct option to complete the sentences.

• Elicit the answers, asking for examples for each one.

Answers

1 They use short sentences, e.g. *He's really keen to go.*

2 The tone is conversational, e.g. *We'll never make it.*

3 Language is direct, e.g. *Any ideas?*

4 They don't use greetings or signing off expressions.

12 *21st* **CENTURY OUTCOMES**

• Tell students to each write a request for advice about something you'd like help with. Suggest they use the list in Exercise 7 to give them ideas. Monitor to make sure everyone has thought of something and support any who are struggling to come up with ideas.

• Mention the increasing importance of written communication in today's online existence and the need to instruct and advise clearly on platforms such as forums, in order to fulfil the 21st CENTURY OUTCOME at the foot of the page.

• Pair students up so that they can swap posts with each other. Ask them to reply in writing to their partner's request for advice. Write on the board some useful language: *I suggest you … You should probably/definitely … You shouldn't … You need to … Why don't you …? How about …?* Tell them to write directly under the request for advice.

13

• Let students swap back their posts with the responses. Ask them to read the advice and to decide whether it's good advice. Also get them to use the checklist to ensure their partner has followed convention.

• Invite students to nominate their partners for the best advice.

▶ Set Workbook pages 110–111 for homework.

▶ Set Workbook Presentation 6 on pages 112–113 for homework.

12 Well-being

LEAD IN

• **Optional step.** Books closed. If you know any quick yoga, tai chi or breathing exercises, or a similar meditative relaxation or mind-focusing technique, lead the class in it for five minutes or so. Otherwise, ask if a student can lead the class.

• Books open. Ask students to read the caption, and then ask whether any of them practise tai chi, yoga or similar mind and body relaxation activities (if you haven't done this in the optional step). Find out details such as how long they've been practising it, when and where they do it, whether they do it alone, and so on.

TEDTALKS
BACKGROUND

1

• Ask students to read the text about Arianna Huffington and her TED Talk. In pairs, they answer questions 1–3.

• Ask students to share their answers with the class.

> **Suggested answers**
>
> 1 She is interested in politics, current events, broadcasting, health and well-being. She has a busy and probably stressful working life.
>
> 2 & 3 Students' own answers

KEY WORDS

2

• Ask students to read sentences 1–6 and guess the meaning of the words in bold. Tell them to match the words with definitions a–f.

> **Answers**
>
> 1 f 2 e 3 c 4 a 5 d 6 b

• To consolidate understanding of the words, ask the following concept check questions:

*Why might somebody **faint**?* (they are hot, shocked, have not eaten or drunk water for a long time)

*What might someone living on the streets be **deprived** of?* (food, love, somewhere warm to sleep)

*Are any shops near where you live open **24/7**?* (e.g. a large supermarket, a convenience store)

*How much of an **iceberg** can you see above the water?* (approximately 10%)

*Was there much **one-upmanship** between you and your brother or sister? What did you do?*

*What technologies allow us to be **hyper-connected** these days?* (Internet, mobile networks)

▶ Teaching tip: Concept check questions, Unit 12.3, page 163.

AUTHENTIC LISTENING SKILLS
Discourse markers

3a

• Ask students to read the Authentic listening box and match the discourse marker with its function. Elicit answers.

> **Answers**
>
> 1 d 2 e 3 a 4 b 5 c

• Ask if students can think of any more discourse markers. If you have time, you can ask them to check in a couple of the reading texts in previous units to see if they can find any.

> **Suggested answers**
>
> Therefore, As a result, However, Alternatively, In addition, On the contrary, …

3b

- Ask students to read the three sentences from the TED Talk and decide which discourse marker they will hear in each one.

- Tell them to listen to confirm their answers.

- 🔊 69 Play the recording.

- Ask students to read out the sentences with the correct markers.

Answers
1 especially   2 So   3 In fact

3c

- Tell students to listen to and complete the conclusion from the end of the talk.

- 🔊 70 Play the recording. Elicit the completed sentence.

Answers
1 shut your eyes   2 discover the great ideas

12.1 How to succeed? Get more sleep

TEDTALKS

1

- Explain to students that they are going to watch an edited version of Arriana Huffington's TED Talk. Ask them to tick the reasons she mentions for the importance of getting more sleep.

- ▶12.1 Play the whole talk.

Transcript

0.13 *My big idea is a very, very small idea that can unlock billions of big ideas that are at the moment dormant inside us. And my little idea that will do that is sleep.*

0.28 *(Laughter)*

0.30 *(Applause)*

0.35 *This is a room of type-A women. This is a room of sleep-deprived women. And I learned the hard way, the value of sleep. Two-and-a-half years ago, I fainted from exhaustion. I hit my head on my desk. I broke my cheekbone, I got five stitches on my right eye. And I began the journey of rediscovering the value of sleep. And in the course of that, I studied, I met with medical doctors, scientists, and I'm here to tell you that the way to a more productive, more inspired, more joyful life is getting enough sleep. (Applause)*

1.23 *And we women are going to lead the way in this new revolution, this new feminist issue.*

1.33 *I was recently having dinner with a guy who bragged that he had only gotten four hours sleep the night*

before. And I felt like saying to him – but I didn't say it – I felt like saying, 'You know what? If you had gotten five, this dinner would have been a lot more interesting.' (Laughter)

1.51 *There is now a kind of sleep deprivation one-upmanship – especially here in Washington – if you try to make a breakfast date, and you say, 'How about eight o'clock?' they're likely to tell you, 'Eight o'clock is too late for me, but that's OK, I can get a game of tennis in and do a few conference calls and meet you at eight.' And they think that means that they are so incredibly busy and productive, but the truth is they're not, because we, at the moment, have had brilliant leaders in business, in finance, in politics, making terrible decisions. So a high IQ does not mean that you're a good leader, because the essence of leadership is being able to see the iceberg before it hits the Titanic. And we've had far too many icebergs hitting our Titanics.*

2.42 *In fact, I have a feeling that if Lehman Brothers was Lehman Brothers and Sisters, they might still be around. (Applause) While all the brothers were busy just being hyper-connected 24/7, maybe a sister would have noticed the iceberg, because she would have woken up from a seven-and-a-half- or eight-hour sleep and have been able to see the big picture.*

3.09 *So as we are facing all the multiple crises in our world at the moment, what is good for us on a personal level, what's going to bring more joy, gratitude, effectiveness in our lives and be the best for our own careers is also what is best for the world. So I urge you to shut your eyes and discover the great ideas that lie inside us, to shut your engines and discover the power of sleep.*

3.43 *Thank you.*

Background information
Lehman Brothers
Lehman Brothers was a large global investment bank, which declared itself bankrupt in 2008. It is generally thought that this played a major role in the global financial crisis that started around that time.

Note the difference in British English and North American English shown at the foot of the spread. In this unit, it is a grammatical difference, an unusual difference in past participle. See Teaching tip 1 on page 6 of the Introduction for ideas on how to present and practise these differences.

- When you elicit each answer from individuals, check with the rest of the class that they agree.

Answers
a, d
Students may also say that c is a reason because more sleep is 'good for us on a personal level', bringing 'more joy, gratitude, effectiveness in our lives', which suggests better relationships.

2

- Ask students to complete sentences 1–4 as they watch the first part of the talk again.
- ▶12.1 Play the first part of the talk from 0.00–1.23.
- Let students compare their answers before eliciting them from the class.

Answers

1 A   2 hard   3 fainted   4 productive

3

- Tell students to watch the second part of the talk again.
- ▶12.1 Play the second part of the talk from 1.23–1.51.
- Ask them to complete the summary using the words in the box.

Answers

1 revolution   2 women   3 sleep   4 four   5 interesting
6 five

4

- Tell students to read sentences 1–5 before watching the third part again. As they watch, they decide whether the sentences are true or false.
- ▶12.1 Play the third part of the talk from 1.51 to the end. Elicit answers.

Answers

1 F (She suggests people are in competition ('one-upmanship'), perhaps only men, but she doesn't mention women's competitiveness specifically.)

2 T (… we … have had brilliant leaders… making terrible decisions.)

3 F (She blames their hyperconnectivity: 'the brothers were busy just being hyper-connected 24/7'…)

4 T (… a sister would have noticed the iceberg, because she would have woken up from a seven-and-a-half- or eight-hour sleep …)

5 T (… what is good for us on a personal level … is also what is best for the world.')

VOCABULARY IN CONTEXT

5

- ▶12.2 Play the clips from the talk. When each multiple-choice question appears, students choose the correct definition. Discourage the more confident students from always giving the answer by asking individuals to raise their hand if they think they know.

Transcript and subtitles

*1 And we women are going to **lead the way** in this new revolution, this new feminist issue.*
  a be alone
  b show others the direction
  c have better jobs

*2 I was recently having dinner with a guy who **bragged** that he had only gotten four hours sleep the night before.*
  a said proudly
  b said loudly
  c said quietly

*3 So a high **IQ** does not mean that you're a good leader, …*
  a position
  b income
  c intelligence

*4 … maybe a sister would have noticed the iceberg, because she would have woken up from a seven-and-a-half- or eight-hour sleep and have been able to see **the big picture**.*
  a the overall view
  b the future
  c the real problem

*5 So I **urge** you to shut your eyes and discover the great ideas that lie inside us, …*
  a encourage
  b expect
  c need

Answers

1 b   2 a   3 c   4 a   5 a

6

- Ask students to complete the sentences in their own words. Monitor closely, helping with ideas and language.
- Students compare their sentences with a partner.

Suggested answers

1 … to study medicine. / … not to go to university but to get a job instead. / … to do the course I would enjoy the most.

2 … how much money they have. / … the number of friends they have on Facebook.

3 … global warming … greenhouse gas emissions are heating the world faster than ever. / … the financial crisis in 2007–8 … the banks were lending more money than they had to lend. / … fossil fuels … we will harm the planet if we keep taking them out of the ground.

Background information

Sleep facts and figures

Most adults need between seven and nine hours of sleep each night, but some can function normally after as little as six hours of sleep.

We naturally get tired twice during the day – at 2.00 am and 2.00 pm. This is why we often get sleepy after lunch, not because we've just eaten.

People who work irregular shifts, like nurses and taxi drivers are at greater risk of chronic illnesses like stomach and heart diseases. The body never gets used to shift work.

New-born babies sleep 14 to 17 hours a day.

It seems that light and colour play an important role in how sleepy or awake we feel. The red of sunrise can help to wake us up while the blue light of the sky during the day helps us stay awake. NASA has experimented with colour to regulate astronauts' sleep patterns.

CRITICAL THINKING Adapting an argument to an audience

7

- Read out the paragraph about adapting your argument to suit your audience.
- Put students in pairs to answer questions 1–3.
- When they have discussed for a couple of minutes, elicit ideas with the whole class.

Answers

1 She is speaking at a 'TED Women' event where the majority of the audience are women.

2 She described the culture of sleep deprivation as a male practice and stated that women were the ones to lead the revolution to better sleep patterns. She used humour directed at women.

3 They seemed to like it; they found it funny and applauded her at the end. (Students' own answers for the second part of the question.)

8

- Students read the comments about the TED Talk and decide what Arianna Huffington might say in response to each. They also discuss their own reactions to each comment.
- Conduct a brief survey of students' reactions about each comment to gauge opinion.

Suggested answers

Arianna Huffington may react in the following ways:

Mikel: I'm sorry the feminist angle made you want to stop listening. Of course, you're right, it isn't just a man's problem. Notice I started by saying how tired I had become. But I do think that women have a role in changing traditional business culture.

Jill: Exactly, Jill!

Megumi: While I like to think that you're right, Megumi, I'm not totally sure that women would get it right either. Perhaps we have the luxury of seeing the mistakes that men before us have made and a desire to be better than them. We also have more pressure to be good at work and at home, so we have to find that balance that perhaps men don't have.

PRESENTATION SKILLS Using humour

9

- In pairs, students discuss their answers to questions 1 and 2.
- Find out what the class thinks about humour and get pairs to read out their tips to the class.

Suggested answers

1 Humour may be a good way of engaging with your audience and persuading them. It may help you, and the audience, relax into your talk. It may generate a light-hearted tone. On the other hand, certain types of humour may be inappropriate, depending on the subject matter of the presentation.

2 Keep jokes simple and basic; try out your jokes on friends or colleagues first; avoid humour which may offend, such as sexist or racist jokes; don't try to be funny all the time – unless you are a comedian!

10

- Students read the tips in the Presentation tips box and compare them with their answers in Exercise 9.
- Ask students whether they have experience of using humour in presentations, either as a speaker or a member of the audience.

11

- Tell students to watch some clips from the TED Talk to identify the two jokes she makes.
- ▶ 12.3 Play the clips from the talk.
- Elicit the jokes.

Answers

1 He bragged about having only four hours' sleep. She said he would have been more interesting if he had had five. The implication is that he was a boring dinner partner.

2 The name of a company suggests that it is owned and run only by men. She suggests that 'Lehman Brothers and Sisters' would not have failed as a company.

12

- Ask the class if Arianna Huffington's humour follows the advice in the tips box.

13

• Elicit some effects of not having enough sleep from the class. Write their ideas on the board, e.g. *loss of bodily control, forgetfulness, bad moods, falling asleep in strange places and positions*.

• Tell students to think of a funny story about the effects of not having enough sleep. It could be a true story about them or someone they know, or invented if that isn't possible. They should make some notes. As they do so, monitor to help with ideas and language.

14

• Put students in small groups. Give them time to each present their stories to the group.

• Find out whether any stories they heard were similar and elicit a couple of the funniest ones if students are happy to tell them to the whole class.

Extra activity

Sleep questionnaire

Tell students that they are going to find out about all about their classmates' sleep habits. Put them in groups to write five questions to ask the rest of the class. Explain that they can ask any question as long as they are questions they would be willing to answer themselves!

Write some prompts on the board:

When you sleep, do you … ?	*Have you ever … ?*
When you were little, did you … ?	*What's the most/strangest/ best/worst/etc. … ?*
What time … ?	*Do you … ?*
How often do … ?	*Before you go to bed, … ?*
How many … ?	*In the morning, … ?*

Give groups five minutes to write their questions, and monitor to help groups with the expression of questions. Put any new night-time-related vocabulary that groups need on the board.

Regroup students so that they are now with people from other groups. Give them time to ask their questions to all the people in their new groups.

Bring students back to their original groups to share their findings. Instruct groups to decide on their three most interesting findings. A spokesperson from each group reports these to the class.

▶ Set Workbook pages 114–115 for homework.

12.2 If you walked every day …

GRAMMAR Second conditional

1

• Ask students to look at the list of items to do with well-being and to choose the three items they think are most important for their physical and mental well-being.

• Put them in pairs to compare their lists and discuss how well they look after themselves.

Answer
Students' own answers

2

• Tell students to look at the infographic and answer questions 1–3.

• Elicit the answers from the class.

Answers
1 walk for an extra 30 minutes each day for the rest of our lives
2 (the equivalent of) one-and-a-half times around the world
3 physical: decrease the chance of getting heart disease, lose weight, get fewer colds, sleep better, live longer; mental: be happier

3

• Tell the students to answer questions 1–4 about the sentences in the Grammar box.

• Students can check their answers and overall understanding of the second conditional by turning to the Grammar summary on page 162. If students need more controlled practice before continuing, they could do some or all of Exercises 1–5 in the Grammar summary. Otherwise, continue on to Exercise 4 in the unit and set the Grammar summary exercises for homework.

• If you want to extend this work to include the third conditional, you can use the final part of the Grammar summary and Exercise 6 to help you. There is a full Grammar extension lesson to teach this structure on the *Keynote* website. To access this lesson, go to ngl.cengage.com/keynote and use the password printed on the title page of this Teacher's Book.

Answers
1 the future   2 an imaginary situation   3 the past simple in the *if*-clause, *would* and *could* in the main clause   4 *would*

Answers to Grammar summary exercises

1

1 If she practised more, she would be a great piano player. / She would be a great piano player if she practised more.

2 We would have a better quality of life if we moved to the country. / If we moved to the country, we would have a better quality of life.

3 If you took the train, you would get there more quickly. / You would get there more quickly if you took the train.

4 He would feel less tired if he didn't go to bed so late. / If he didn't go to bed so late, he would feel less tired.

5 If the TV programme had a different presenter, it wouldn't be so popular. / The TV programme wouldn't be so popular if it had a different presenter.

6 I'd be very upset if I lost the match. / If I lost the match, I'd be very upset.

2

1 won't be   2 had   3 spoke   4 come   5 wouldn't need   6 rains   7 was/were, would touch   8 arrives, will you call

3

1 had   2 would you feel   3 was/were   4 wouldn't be   5 would feel   6 reduced

4

1 would be   2 would take   3 would give   4 wouldn't be

5

1 ~~would have~~ → had   2 ~~know~~ → knew   3 ~~was~~ → were   4 ~~went~~ → would go   5 ~~didn't~~ → doesn't or ~~She'll~~ → She'd

6

2 If I had been at the meeting, I would have said something.

3 I wouldn't have asked for a refund if the food hadn't been so bad.

4 If I hadn't stayed out late, I would have got more sleep.

5 We wouldn't have stayed for dinner if they hadn't insisted.

6 I wouldn't have bought the jacket if it hadn't been half price.

4

• Ask students to complete the sentences by putting the verbs into the sentences in the correct form.

• Students compare answers with a partner before sharing with the whole class.

> **Answers**
>
> 1 ran, would lose   2 became, would fall   3 ate, would save   4 drank, would look   5 slept, would be   6 understood, would all be

5

• Let students read the exchange between Nancy Astor and Winston Churchill. Ask whether the two people in the photos are married.

> **Answer**
>
> No, they aren't.

• Explain that the second conditional is often used to talk about present situations that are not the reality. Check that they understand the 'joke'.

6

• Tell students to underline the verbs in each sentence, then describe the reality of each situation.

• Let them compare in pairs before eliciting answers.

> **Answers**
>
> 2 *knew*, *'d write* I don't know the secret of happiness.
>
> 3 *lived*, *'d see* They don't live in Europe.
>
> 4 *wasn't*, *would be* He is a professional golfer.
>
> 5 *didn't like*, *wouldn't stay* She does like working here.
>
> 6 *were*, *could beat* I'm not ten years younger.

• **Optional step.** If students have Internet access, ask them to search for 'famous quotes second conditional'. Give them five minutes to find their favourite quote. After five minutes, students write their sentences on the board. Vote for the class favourite.

Pronunciation Contraction *'d*

7a

• Ask students to listen to the sentences from Exercise 6 and say what *'d* is a contraction of.

• ⟨🔊 71⟩ Play the recording.

> **Answer**
>
> *would*

7b

• In pairs, students practise saying sentences 2–4 in Exercise 6, paying special attention to the contraction *'d*.

▶ Teaching tip: Don't stress! (weak forms), Unit 4.2, page 56.

• **Optional step.** Read out the following sentences, with either the contracted *'d* or without. Students listen carefully to decide which they hear. *I('d) go there every day. We('d) love to see you. They('d) live here.* Then put them in pairs to practise by saying the sentences to one another.

8

• Ask students to complete the sentences using zero, first or second conditional structures. You may decide that students would benefit from a quick review of the zero and first conditional before attempting this exercise, in which case give them a few minutes to review the Grammar summary of Unit 9 on page 156 or do one or more exercises on page 157.

- They compare answers before sharing them with the class.

> **Answers**
>
> 1 could, would be   2 don't get, find   3 was/were, would pay   4 eat, helps   5 earned, would live   6 will retire, am   7 had, would spend   8 get, will try

SPEAKING Well-being and productivity

9   `21st` CENTURY OUTCOMES

- Ask students to read the case study. Ask them whether they are surprised the workers are feeling tired, stressed and bored.

- Point out the 21st CENTURY OUTCOME expected in this exercise. Ask whether the health and well-being of its employees should be a company goal, and if so, why.

- Put students in small groups. Indicate the ideas to start their discussion of the possible action the company could take. Encourage them to discuss alternative ideas if they think of them.

- Remind them that this exercise is an opportunity to practise the second conditional.

- While they are discussing what to do, monitor carefully, listening for instances of the second conditional in particular.

- Bring groups together to find out from each what they have decided to do and why. Allow groups to comment on each other's ideas.

TEACHING TIP

Differentiating students' roles in discussions

One way to encourage equal participation in speaking activities is to give students different responsibilities. If everyone approaches the problem from different angles, they may have things to say that others do not. In a discussion about business decisions it may be realistic to consider the problem from the point of view of different people within an organization, or of different companies.

For example, a management discussion about workers' morale might involve the CEO of the company (to chair the meeting), departments such as Human Resources (to present the options) and Finance (to worry about the cost of proposals), and a union representative (speaking for the employees' rights). If each student is asked to think about the problem from these positions, they may have more to say.

▶ Set Workbook pages 116–117 for homework.

12.3   Tell me what's good for me

READING   Health and well-being news

1

- **Optional step.** Books closed. Review the second conditional by asking students to use the structure to write sentences about healthy habits. Write one on the board as an example, but with the verbs missing, e.g. *If people ____ less sugary food, they ____ healthier hearts*. Elicit the correct verb forms (*ate, 'd have*). In pairs, students write three more, then they share them with other pairs.

- Books open. In pairs, students decide which things (1–5) are good and which are bad for you. Encourage them to discuss why.

- Elicit ideas from the class, encouraging different opinions for each point.

> **Answer**
>
> Students' own answers

2

- Continuing the class discussion, ask students what other things we have been told are good or bad for us. Ask them whether they usually follow the advice and if not, why not.

Background information

Health fads

The health industry is big business. Twenty billion dollars are spent in the US each year just trying to lose weight. But how to get healthier? Theories and ideas come and go. Here are some strange ones.

- Detox diets – published in the 1940s, the Master Cleanse recommends eating nothing and drinking only lemon juice with maple syrup and cayenne pepper for up to 45 days to lose weight. Without food, people quickly start to feel weak and get headaches. Not a good idea!

- Parasite diets – in the early 20th century, dieters were encouraged to eat meat infected with tapeworms (parasites that live in the digestive system and live on food that the person has eaten). You will be pleased to hear that this is now banned in most countries!

- Oxygen shots – oxygen is an essential chemical for life, right? Some people give themselves bursts of pure oxygen to help them feel younger and healthier and help combat tiredness. In fact, concentrated oxygen is toxic. There is no evidence it helps. Fresh air is better.

3

• Tell students to read news stories A–E about health and well-being so that they can match them with titles 1–5.

• Give them two minutes to encourage practice in skim reading, then elicit answers.

• Ask which news they had already heard or read. Find out where they heard it.

4

• Ask students to read the stories again to find out whether sentences 1–10 are true or false, or whether the information is not given.

• Let them confer in pairs before eliciting answers with the class.

Answers

1 T (... people ... have bought food because it had the label 'superfood' on it. ... [these] products ... are healthy ...)

2 F (They say that products like goji berries, coconut water, quinoa and pomegranate juice are healthy and have good nutritional benefits ...)

3 NG (The text doesn't say they are actually more expensive.)

4 T (... a fifty per cent increase in stress ... in the workplace in the last twelve years.)

5 NG (It mentions what companies wouldn't be allowed to do, but not employees.)

6 T (Some companies are allowing their workers a twenty-minute sleep at their desks ...)

7 NG (It says 'people often eat more after physical activity' but not why.)

8 T (The key is to make sure you burn more calories than you consume (exercise) and also to choose your food carefully (eating the right kind of food).)

9 T (... people who use online social networks have a better sense of emotional well-being.)

10 NG (There is no mention of the type of friends you have to be careful making.)

5

• Instruct students to find the words in bold in the text and to decide on their meaning from context if they don't already know.

• Go through the answers, and for each word, ask concept check questions: *Has smoking in bars been **banned** in your country? Have you ever been given **misleading** directions somewhere? What happened? What can people do to **combat** colds and flu in winter? What time of day do people often have a **nap**? Do you sometimes **nap**? How can you **cancel out** a debt? What's the name of one of your **close** friends? Why are you so **close**?*

Answers

1 a 2 b 3 b 4 a 5 b 6 a

TEACHING TIP

Concept check questions

One quick way to check understanding of new vocabulary or grammar is to ask students questions about it. It isn't always easy to come up with concept check questions on the spot, so they should form part of lesson planning. Concept check questions should:

• be easy to understand (keep them short and the vocabulary simple).

• be easy to answer (*yes/no* questions make good questions, for example).

• relate to students' lives if possible.

• provide the students who are listening to the question and answer with more information about the word and how it's used, to understand it better.

• show that the student understands the meaning of the word or structure!

Look at the concept check questions above. Do they conform to these criteria?

Try writing concept check questions for the following words from the reading text on page 135: *right* (line 15), *reachable* (line 15), *support* (line 42).

6

• Put students in small groups to discuss the conclusions to the five news stories and whether they agree with them.

• Elicit a variety of ideas and opinions from the class.

VOCABULARY Well-being adjectives

7

• Draw a picture on the board of a stick figure in a hammock reading a book. If you prefer, ask a student to draw it. Ask how the person feels and elicit *relaxed*. Ask what adjective you could use to describe the act of reading like this to elicit *relaxing*.

• Ask students to complete the two sentences in 1. Point out the distinct adjectives for describing the thing/activity (i.e. reading) and to say how it makes us feel.

• Get students to complete the sentences in 2–6 in the same way. Let them read their sentences in pairs to check their answers. Then ask them to share their answers around the class.

Answers

1 a relaxing, b relaxed   2 a welcoming, b at home
3 a stressful, b stressed   4 a tiring, b tired
5 a appreciative, b valued   6 a enjoyable, b happy

• Ask students what they notice about the words to describe how you feel. Point out that the -ed ending is a common feature of adjectives to describe feelings caused by other things. Elicit some more of these and show how often the thing that makes you feel that way can be described using the equivalent -ing form, e.g. frightened/ing, bored/ing, surprised/ing, exhausted/ing.

8

• Ask students to complete the questions with the correct option.

Answers

1 relaxing   2 stressed   3 welcoming   4 tiring
5 valued   6 enjoyable

• Students ask each other the questions in pairs.

SPEAKING Proposals for well-being

9 21st **CENTURY OUTCOMES**

• Put students in small groups to discuss various risks to public health. Ask them, as if they were a government committee, to identify specific ways to improve the well-being of the population in the areas given.

• Give the class ten minutes to come up with a few proposals. When each group has a few proposals, join groups together into larger groups to share their ideas. (Alternatively, keep the groups apart and start the Extra activity below.)

• Finally, bring the class together to air the most interesting proposals for each area of public health. Discuss the extent to which each proposal recognizes the real public health issues and the means to deal with them.

Extra activity

Hustings

Hustings are events before an election where the candidates and parties have the opportunity to present their policies to the public. Explain that the groups are going to take part in one of these to decide which group, or 'political party' has the best health policies.

Point out that hustings are a type of presentation and therefore the presentation tips they have learned over the course may be useful, especially the tips in Unit 3 about persuasion, Unit 6 about engaging with your audience and about dealing with questions in Unit 11.

Give groups plenty of time to prepare their presentations. Write some useful structures on the board for presenting policies, e.g.

If we are elected, we will …
We are going to …
We need to …

Invite groups to come to the front of the class to deliver their election speeches. Explain that at the end each student will be able to vote for just one party, but that they cannot vote for their own party.

When all the parties have spoken, hold the election! Congratulate the winning party.

▶ Photocopiable communicative activity 12.1: Go to page 231 for further practice of the second conditional. The teaching notes are on page 246.

▶ Set Workbook pages 118–119 for homework.

12.4 What are the options?

LISTENING Time wasting

1

• Put students in small groups to answer questions 1 and 2.

• Elicit ideas from the whole class about what activities they think are a waste of time and how much time they think they waste.

• **Optional step.** Conduct a survey to find out the top ten time-wasting activities in the class. Ask students to call out their time-wasting activities so that you can write them on the board. Each student then writes their top three on a piece of paper. Tell them to come to the board and put one tick next to the activity they decided was the third biggest time waster, two ticks for the second and three ticks for the biggest. Rank the activities from the most to the fewest ticks. If students all have their own mobile devices, you could do this using an online survey tool.

2

• Tell students to listen to the conversation. Give them a minute to prepare for listening by reading questions 1–3.

• 🎧 72 Play the recording.

Transcript

A = Andy, L = Leanne

A: *So, Leanne, I think you wanted to say something?*

L: *Well, yeah, just briefly, 'cos I was at a management conference last week and I went to a talk about productivity – how much time people spend working productively, and how much time they waste. And, actually, some really interesting points were made – points which I thought, maybe … some are ideas that could be applicable here.*

A: *OK, great. Let's hear them.*

L: OK, well, the main point the speaker made – and it seems like a simple thing, really – was that most people aren't aware of their own level of productivity. They don't really know how much time they're wasting. And the idea is that if you make them more aware of this, they will become more productive.

A: I see. And how would you do that?

L: OK, well, one way would be to ask them to keep a record of how they spend their time. So, the time they spend at their desk working, the time they spend at their desk looking at other things on the Internet, the time they spend away from their desk – at the coffee machine or going outside to have a cigarette. So you could give them a kind of time sheet and they could fill it in.

A: Would that work? I mean, most people wouldn't answer honestly, would they? Rather than telling them, why don't we just watch them without telling them? Then you'd really find out how much time they were wasting.

L: No, no – that's not the point. We're not checking on people. The point is that we just want people to think about how they're using their time. If people are aware, they waste less time. You don't actually have to spy on anyone. Apparently, if you …

- Put students in pairs to compare their answers, then elicit answers from the class.

Answers

1 By making people more aware of how much time they're wasting, you help them reduce wasted time.

2 To watch them without telling them – then they'd really find out how much time they wasted.

3 It isn't about checking on people but about making them think about how they're using their time.

3

- Ask students to complete the sentences using the verbs in the correct form.

- When they have completed the sentences, let them listen to the conversation again to check their answers.

- [△72] Play the recording again.

Answers

1 will become   2 do   3 to ask   4 wouldn't answer
5 telling, telling   6 to think

Pronunciation Stress in suggestions

4

- Tell students to listen and repeat the sentences.

- [△73] Play the recording. Pause between sentences and replay them to allow students time to listen well and repeat enough times to be confident.

- Students underline the stressed syllables in the sentences. Then in pairs they practise saying them. To further consolidate this pronunciation point, do a substitution drill (see Teaching tip below).

▶ Teaching tip: Pronunciation – backchaining, Unit 1.2, page 17.

TEACHING TIP

Substitution drilling

Students benefit from repeated practice of grammatical structures, lexical chunks and phonological patterns. They also need practice manipulating language for themselves. Substitution drills achieve both goals: repeated practice but with variations that they need to think about to adapt.

For example, students need to become fluent in making suggestions, using phrases like

1 One way would be to … ,

2 You could try … ,

3 Another alternative would be to … , and

4 Why don't you … ?

Number them on the board as above, then give a suggestion in infinitive form, e.g. talk to him about it. Show that you can use all four structures to make the suggestion, i.e. One way would be to talk to him about it. You could try talking to him about it. Another alternative … , and so on. Think of more suggestions to fire at the students so that they have to manipulate them to fit the structures, e.g. make a list, email the company, outsource the work, look for another job, etc.

Drill chorally first to give students a secure, anonymous space to practise, then nominate individuals so that you can check all students are getting it right. Finally, let students test each other in pairs.

Answers

1 One way would be to use a different company.

2 You could try phoning him.

3 Another alternative would be to eat here.

4 Rather than taking the bus, why don't you take the train?

SPEAKING Discussing options

5 21st CENTURY OUTCOMES

• Explain that the aim of this speaking activity is to brainstorm ideas in response to question 3. Refer students to the 21st CENTURY OUTCOME at the foot of page 137. Elicit what brainstorming is and why it can be useful. It is a way of responding to a problem by thinking of lots of possible solutions, which are all accepted and recorded. It is believed to encourage creative solutions through free and spontaneous thinking.

• Put students in small groups to discuss questions 1–3 and brainstorm possible solutions to the problem of time-wasting at work. Remind them that this is an opportunity to practise making suggestions in English, and indicate the Useful language box to help them.

Suggested answers
1 They all are but using the Internet for personal reasons wastes a lot of time.
2 Other possibilities include: following sport or news events online, checking emails too often and unnecessarily, taking smoking breaks and attending unnecessary meetings.
3 Students' own answers

• While groups are talking, monitor, listening in to their brainstorming sessions and making a note of ways that they make suggestions. Before they finish, set up three columns on the board:

Possible solutions / Advantages / Disadvantages

• Get the students' attention. Elicit from each group their favourite answers for question 3. Write them in the first column. When you have a number of ideas on the board, hand out board pens to students and invite them to make some notes in the second and third columns.

• Gauge popularity of each suggestion by asking the class to discuss them. Conclude by getting consensus on which suggestions should be considered seriously by the company.

WRITING A reply to an enquiry

6

• Explain the situation. Tell students to read the email and answer the questions.

• Elicit answers from the class.

Answers
1 She offers paying for each individual class, paying for a cheaper package of ten classes or an even cheaper package of unlimited classes for six months.
2 Her tone is friendly.
3 Rashmi can come along one day, try a class and chat to the club instructors and other members.

• Find out if anyone in the class attends yoga classes, where they do it and the payment options. Find out what Vinyasa yoga is from the students if possible.

7

• In pairs, students read the email again and match elements a–c with sentences in the email.

• When they have found the sentences, get students to read them out to the class.

Answers
a Thank you for your enquiry about yoga classes … You mentioned that …
b For payment, there are three options …
c What new members often do is … If you did that, you could also have a chat …

WRITING SKILL Listing options

8

• In pairs, students compare the listed options in the email with the spoken version and find the differences.

Answer
Instead of numbers, each option is organized by discourse markers: *One option would be to …* , *Another possibility would be to …* , *Or lastly you could …* . Another difference is that the details are introduced with words, not a colon: *That means …* , *That would give you …* , *With that option …*

9

• Ask students to imagine that they work for a gym and fitness centre and they receive an email from someone who wants to join the gym. Students read the email.

• Ask them to write a reply.

▶ Teaching tip: Writing 'workshop-style', Unit 7.4, page 102.

10

• When they have finished, put students in pairs. Tell them to exchange emails and to read them, using the checklist to evaluate them.

• Give the class any general feedback on their writing that you think is useful.

Suggested answer

Dear Devon,

Thank you for your enquiry about the gym and fitness centre. You would be very welcome to join, of course. You mentioned that you are not sure how often you can use the gym and swimming pool. They are open every day from 7.00 am to 10.00 pm. There are three payment options if you don't want to commit for one year:

1 Ten-visit pack: 10 visits to use any facilities, any time ($65)

2 One-month package: as many visits as you like for one month ($80)

3 Six-month package: as many classes as you like for six months ($400)

Why don't you try the ten-visit pack to start? When you have finished, you could decide whether to repeat the ten-visit pack or try a one-month or six-month package.

We look forward to seeing you here soon.

Best regards,

▶ Photocopiable communicative activity 12.2: Go to page 232 for further practice of discussing options. The teaching notes are on page 246.

▶ Set Workbook pages 120–121 for homework.

▶ Set Workbook Writing 6 on pages 122–123 for homework.

REVIEW 6 | UNITS 11 AND 12

LISTENING

1

• Ask students to read the article about CHG Healthcare and choose the correct options to complete the sentences.

• Elicit answers from the class.

> **Answers**
>
> 1 relatively young   2 temporary   3 being a good employer

2

• As students listen to the interview about what makes CHG a great place to work, they should tick the items that the speaker mentions.

• 🔊 **74** Play the recording.

Transcript

I = Interviewer, E = Employee

I: *So what makes CHG a good company to work for?*

E: *Wow! There are so many things. Obviously the nature of the work is important. When your job is to help people who are in bad health to get better, then naturally you get a lot of job satisfaction. Ninety-eight per cent of the staff say they enjoy the challenge of their work and feel that it's making a difference to society. And over ninety per cent say that CHG gives them responsibility for their work – in other words, trusts them to do their job – and supports them when they need training or professional development.*

I: *OK – and what about benefits for employees?*

E: *Employees get eleven paid days of holiday in the year, which sounds very little but this is pretty normal for the USA. However, after one year of working, they can take a further eighteen days a year unpaid if they want or need to. The company is very sensitive to workers' home-work balance. So if an employee's child was sick, for example, they would either help them with time off or allow them to work from home, if that was possible. There is also a very friendly atmosphere among the staff – almost like a family, so employees often help each other out in this kind of situation. Oh, and the company pays for employees to do volunteer days in the community too – like helping out in a local school.*

I: *And well-being? I guess as it's a healthcare company, they promote employee health too?*

E: *Oh sure, absolutely. There are free health checks, there's an onsite fitness centre and massage therapy is available. They also have a lot of onsite services at the headquarters such as pharmacies and a wellness clinic that mean that staff can easily access ...*

• After listening, students check their answers with a partner before you elicit the answers.

> **Answers**
>
> a, c, e, f, h, i

• **Optional step.** In pairs, students rank the items in the list in order of what matters to them as employees.

3

• In pairs, ask students to discuss which words from the interview complete the notes. Students listen again and complete the notes.

• 🔊 **74** Play the recording again.

• Elicit answers from the class.

> **Answers**
>
> 1 challenge   2 trust   3 support   4 eleven   5 eighteen   6 home   7 friendly   8 family   9 volunteer   10 checks   11 fitness

GRAMMAR

4

• Ask students to complete the sentences about CHG with the modal verbs in the box.

• Let them compare answers in pairs before eliciting answers from the whole class.

> **Answers**
>
> 1 don't have to   2 can   3 needs to   4 shouldn't   5 should   6 must

5

• Tell students to complete the comments using the zero, first or second conditional and the verbs in brackets.

> **Answers**
>
> 1 had, would be   2 weren't, wouldn't be   3 ask, always get   4 stay, will use

VOCABULARY

6

• Tell students to complete the text about *Fortune* magazine using the correct form of *make* and *do*.

> **Answers**
>
> 1 make   2 make   3 do   4 make   5 do   6 do   7 do

7

• Students choose the correct option to complete the statements.

> **Answers**
>
> 1 welcoming, relaxed   2 valued   3 stressful   4 tiring, enjoyable

DISCUSSION

8

- Tell students that they are going to discuss CHG Healthcare as an employer. Give them time before they speak to think of things to say, and how they could use modal verbs and conditional sentences in the discussion.

- Put them in pairs or small groups to discuss questions 1 and 2.

- Elicit some of these ideas in a whole-class summary discussion.

SPEAKING

9

- Put students in pairs. Tell them to read the conversation about a problem in the workplace.

- Let them decide if they think they can complete the conversations without referring to their notes, and whether they can say the conversation without first writing the expressions. Give them five minutes to prepare and practise the conversation. Go around the pairs offering advice and corrections where appropriate.

- Ask for volunteers to read out the conversation in front of the class.

Answers

1 What kind of noise did they complain about?

2 Has anyone else ever said (that) this is a problem?

3 Then we need to do something about it.

4 What do/would you suggest?

5 if those people wore headphones, they wouldn't be bothered

6 Another alternative would be to put partitions up

7 Wouldn't that be expensive?

8 rather than spending money on the problem, why don't we (just) ask people

9 we need to / must be careful here.

10 If we ask/asked people not to talk, it will/would create a bad feeling.

WRITING

10

- Ask students to read the post and reply to it, offering recommendations.

- Monitor carefully, making sure they are using suitable structures to give suggestions and striking a friendly tone.

11

- Tell students to exchange emails with a partner and compare what they have written. Find out how similar their ideas were and elicit some of the best ones.

Suggested answer

Hi Jean-Baptiste,

A lack of time for learning is a common problem but there are many ways to practise English. One way to practise at times that suit you is to study online. That way you can study from home, and online courses aren't as expensive as classes. Also, why don't you take advantage of short periods of time such as when you're on the bus? Use your phone to study vocabulary or practise listening. You could even practise when you're walking in the street. Talking to yourself in your head helps with spoken fluency – try having imaginary conversations in English. I hope these ideas help!

Extra activity

Beyond the book!

At the end of a course of study, it is important to help students think about and plan their ongoing study now that one course is coming to an end and a new one is unlikely to start for a few weeks or months.

Start a discussion about the students' plans for English now that the course is coming to an end. Find out how much English they plan to use, in what contexts, and how they feel about studying alone. Be sensitive to the fact that students may like a break after studying for so long, but be sure to encourage them to keep practising.

Get students to brainstorm things that they could do to practise English without the classes. Encourage a variety of types of ideas, and activities of different lengths. Ensure there are ideas for all four skills. Here are some suggestions:

- Read graded readers.

- Read an interesting article on a website of your choice every day.

- Listen to podcasts and watch visual media designed for learners.

- Watch a favourite TV series in English.

- Keep a diary or blog to practise writing.

- Find a conversation exchange partner online to practise speaking.

- Go to language exchange events in your town or city.

- Re-read articles.

- Visit the *Keynote* website and do activities there. (ngl.cengage.com/keynote)

- Put vocabulary studied during this course on a smart phone flashcard app to study in spare moments.

Ask students to fill in a diary for the next few weeks or months with activities for each week or month. Suggest they tick the activities they have done at the end of each week or month.

TEST 1 | Units 1 and 2

Name: _____

Total score: _____

VOCABULARY

1 Read the text and choose the correct word for each space. The first one is done for you.

Working from home

If you're like me, there's a pretty good **(0)** _B_ that you sometimes think about **(1)** _____ your job from home. Perhaps you know people in your company who you never see except when they **(2)** _____ meetings via Skype. 'Telecommuting' is becoming more **(3)** _____ , but is it the right move for you?

First, is your job suitable? If you work in a team, don't think you can get **(4)** _____ on the work action by emailing your **(5)** _____ every day. You may need to **(6)** _____ with difficult situations that need face-to-face communication. Second, can you work independently and **(7)** _____ tasks without your **(8)** _____ there to manage you? And can you balance home and working life? For example, will your other **(9)** _____ be happy with you at home all the time? And what's to stop you **(10)** _____ fun when you should be working?

0	**A** opportunity	**B** chance	**C** hope	**D** probability
1	**A** earning	**B** having	**C** working	**D** doing
2	**A** attend	**B** watch	**C** make	**D** visit
3	**A** often	**B** widespread	**C** wide	**D** increasing
4	**A** by	**B** through	**C** at	**D** in
5	**A** partners	**B** subjects	**C** colleagues	**D** friends
6	**A** treat	**B** solve	**C** deal	**D** sort
7	**A** make	**B** attend	**C** solve	**D** prioritize
8	**A** trainee	**B** boss	**C** apprentice	**D** assistant
9	**A** half	**B** partner	**C** part	**D** wife
10	**A** taking	**B** doing	**C** having	**D** making

Marks (out of 10): _____

2 Complete the sentences with the correct form of the word in CAPITAL LETTERS. The first one is done for you.

0	In some countries nurses are qualified after only two years as a _trainee_ .	**TRAIN**
11	The Indira Gandhi National Open University in India has 3.5 million _____ .	**STUDY**
12	The _____ will be pleased to listen if you have any problems.	**MANAGE**
13	I wanted a _____ contract but they only gave me 12 hours a week.	**TIME**
14	I always think I can decorate a room in one day, but I _____ how long it takes paint to dry.	**ESTIMATE**
15	There is a fashion among runners to stop wearing shoes and run _____ .	**FOOT**
16	Don't waste time on the Internet: _____ what is important to you when you go online.	**PRIORITY**
17	A degree in history can help you find work in museums or as a historical _____ .	**RESEARCH**
18	My workload was becoming too much so I had to advertise for an _____ .	**ASSIST**
19	You will deal with international clients, so a good understanding of _____ differences is essential.	**CULTURE**
20	It was a _____ to meet you.	**PLEASE**

Marks (out of 10): _____

GRAMMAR

3 Complete the text with a suitable word in each gap. Use only one word in each gap. The first one is done for you.

Seventeen-year old Harry Bestwick **(0)** _____*is*_____ learning to be a plumber. Although the local adult education college runs a course in plumbing, Harry is **(21)** _____ doing academic studies. Plumbers **(22)** _____ not usually study formally; instead, they train on the job as apprentices. Harry **(23)** _____ a job with a small plumbing company in the area. He works five days **(24)** _____ week with Francesco, the boss of the company.

Harry is very busy at **(25)** _____ moment. He isn't **(26)** _____ this busy, but Francesco is away on holiday, so Harry is doing a lot more work, including **(27)** _____ the weekend. Francesco **(28)** _____ not really like Harry doing jobs on his own, but Harry is pleased to have some more responsibility.

(29) _____ days, with the economic situation as it is, the number of apprentice schemes is **(30)** _____ down, so Harry is lucky to have a job.

Marks (out of 10): _____

4 Complete the second sentence so that it means the same as the first. Use no more than three words. The first one is done for you.

0 Most of the time Tricia's work is in the main office in London.
Tricia _____*usually works*_____ in the main office in London.

31 Tricia travels abroad for work every six months.
Tricia travels abroad for work _____ year.

32 She's currently on a business trip in China.
At _____, she's on a business trip in China.

33 She always calls her boss in the evening to tell her how the trip is going.
She calls her boss _____ to tell her how the trip is going.

34 This trip is unusual because she normally travels alone.
This trip is unusual because she _____ with a colleague this time.

35 Tricia asked her Chinese colleague to recommend a good restaurant.
Tricia: 'Can _____ if there's a good restaurant near here?'

36 Tricia prefers travelling from Monday to Friday to travelling Saturday or Sunday.
Tricia: 'I don't like travelling _____ as much as during the week.'

37 Tricia: 'I hate it when I have to leave my family for long periods.'
Tricia _____ like leaving her family for long periods.

38 Tricia tries to get at least one day off each trip. Today, she is at the Great Wall of China.
Tricia tries to get a day off at least _____ each trip. Today, she is at the Great Wall of China.

39 Tricia wanted to know the length of the Great Wall.
Tricia: _____ to know how long the Great Wall is.

40 There are more online meetings now than there were before.
Online meetings are _____ common now than they were before.

Marks (out of 10): _____

READING

5 Read the article and choose the correct answers A, B, C or D, according to the writer. The first one is done for you.

Five reasons to work for nothing

What is it that gets us out of bed every morning to go to work? Job satisfaction? A feeling we can make a difference to people's lives? Sure, these things matter, but the bottom line? Money. Would you work if you didn't earn a salary? Well, here are four reasons people work for free.

1 A lucky few can devote their lives to a good cause without asking for a penny. Jennifer Nightingale is a shop assistant in a charity shop which sells second-hand goods donated by members of the public. The proceeds go to children with cancer – Jennifer lost a niece to leukaemia eight years ago, so the charity is important to her and her sisters. Her husband earns enough so she feels justified spending twenty hours a week helping to raise money for the sick.

2 Some jobs are so popular that a single position – on a movie or an Internet start-up, for example – gets hundreds of applicants. Many companies in creative fields like arts and media exploit their popularity and take on people for up to six months for no pay. In exchange, these workers (interns) get valuable work experience, a more interesting CV and the chance to get in the door. But there are no promises, and most hopeful film makers or games designers end up no closer to their dream job than before. Internships are usually filled by wealthy middle-class people whose can support themselves financially.

3 In Britain, many unemployed people must do work for which the employer does not pay them. This is to claim their Job Seekers' Allowance (the money that the government gives to people with no job). Otherwise, it can be cut. The work they are given does not always reflect their interests or help them follow their career paths. One young woman was happy volunteering in a museum but had to stop this when the Job Centre made her work in a shop for no wages. She took legal action against the government, saying that forcing her to do work she did not want to do was against her human rights.

4 Since the 1970s feminist groups have argued that stay-at-home mothers should receive wages. While millions of women, and some men, do housework and raise children for nothing, many people disagree that it is really 'work' in the way that accounting, teaching and mining is work. Recent research compared what stay-at-home mums do with professional cleaners and childcare givers, and calculated the worth of their work as £30,000 a year. Although many countries award benefits and tax cuts to families with children, no countries pay for housework.

0 The motivation people have to work comes from
   A helping other people. ☐
   B making money to live. ☐
   C feeling satisfied and part of a community. ☐
   D all of these motivations. ☑

41 The writer describes volunteers as 'lucky' because
   A they have a good reason to get out of bed in the morning. ☐
   B they can afford to work for free. ☐
   C they have jobs that give them a lot of satisfaction. ☐
   D they believe in good causes. ☐

42 Jennifer Nightingale
   A gives things that belonged to other people to sick children. ☐
   B raises money for a charity by donating her salary to it. ☐
   C raises money for a charity by selling used things. ☐
   D raises money for her niece. ☐

43 Jennifer's work
   A is full-time. ☐
   B is not important. ☐
   C means a lot to her family. ☐
   D makes life difficult for her husband. ☐

44 Companies that employ interns for no salary usually
   A make more money than other companies. ☐
   B only employ rich people. ☐
   C promise them a job at the end of the internship. ☐
   D use their popularity as employers to attract volunteers. ☐

45 Interns who work for free
   A do so because they want to be more attractive to future employers. ☐
   B don't have money to give to their families. ☐
   C know that it won't help them get their perfect job. ☐
   D always work for six months. ☐

46 One of the problems with internships is that
   A the work experience is not of good quality. ☐
   B many are not open to poor people. ☐
   C they give young people false dreams. ☐
   D there is no guarantee of a job at the end. ☐

47 Unemployed people in Britain
   A must volunteer to work for charities to receive Job Seekers' Allowance. ☐
   B can receive money from the government. ☐
   C don't want to work in shops. ☐
   D are given jobs working for the government. ☐

48 One young woman
   A was offered volunteer work at a museum by the local Job Centre. ☐
   B wants to work in a museum in the future. ☐
   C wasn't happy with the choice of unpaid job she was given. ☐
   D didn't want to work for free. ☐

49 Housework
   A is only paid a salary in a few countries worldwide. ☐
   B shouldn't be paid as much as accountants, teachers or miners. ☐
   C is recognized as valuable by governments across the world. ☐
   D can be compared to similar paid jobs to calculate how much it is worth. ☐

50 Some governments
   A pay families to clean their own houses. ☐
   B tax families with children less money than families without children. ☐
   C have started paying women to work from home. ☐
   D encourage men to do the housework by paying them. ☐

Marks (out of 10): _____

LISTENING

6 🅐 **75** Listen to the book review and fill in the missing information. The first one is done for you.

0 The book is by Joanna Biggs and is called *All Day Long: A Portrait of Britain at* _____*Work*_____ .

51 As well as being a journalist and writer, Biggs is also a book _____ .

52 Catherine didn't read _____ the book.

53 Gareth was interested in the way the book compares different people's _____ lives.

54 The writer estimates that most of us work a total of _____ hours in our lives.

55 The first area of work that the author looks at in the book is _____ .

56 These days, robots do most of the work in Britain's _____ industry.

57 Some manufacturers of _____ objects, e.g. ballet shoes, still survive in Britain.

58 Company directors and poor people who do several jobs to survive both have to work _____ .

59 The company director and the coffee shop barista both have to _____ their customers.

60 The writer thinks that in the future many jobs will change because the world will be more _____ .

Marks (out of 10): _____

SPEAKING

7 Talk in pairs, A and B.

Step 1

Student A: look at the first photograph. Talk about the woman's job.
Student B: look at the second photograph. Talk about the man's job.

Make sure you both:
- describe the job and say what you think it is like to do it.
- describe a typical day for someone who does the job.
- say what skills are needed to do the job well.
- talk about any trends that you think are happening in the industry.

You have two minutes to think about what you are going to say. Student A: you go first.

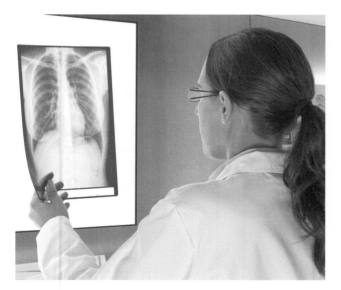

Step 2

You are going to ask your partner about the job they do, have done or would like to do.

Make sure you ask about:
- the job, what it involves, if they like it and why.
- the organization they work for or would like to, its size, etc.
- the skills that are important in the job.

Student A: you ask Student B questions first.
Student B: now you ask Student A.

You can receive ten marks for including all the points above and using a range of language.

Marks (out of 10): _____

WRITING

8 You are looking for a temporary job over the summer in an English-speaking country to improve your English and get some work experience. You see this job advertisement.

GOLDENFIELDS CAMP SITE, DEVON, UK

We are a large, popular campsite on the south coast of England.

We are looking for friendly, hardworking people to work with us between July and September.

Please send CVs and enquiries to jackie@goldenfields.co.uk

Write an email to the campsite asking for more information. Write about 100 words. Ask a minimum of two questions.

You can receive ten marks for including all the necessary points and the conventions of email writing.

Marks (out of 10): _____

TEST 2 | Units 3 and 4

Name: _____

Total score: _____

VOCABULARY

1 Read the text and choose the correct word for each gap. The first one is done for you.

Parents pay daughter to do sports

Veronica is a sporty girl who swims very fast, but she also has cystic fibrosis, a life-threatening disease. Sport is important in keeping her healthy but she finds it hard to **(0)** __D__ herself to do exercise every day. Her parents **(1)** _____ her for her efforts, but this doesn't always **(2)** _____ in making her feel positive about having to work so hard.

So this summer holiday, they've decided to give her a financial **(3)** _____ , and Veronica is **(4)** _____ money by swimming, **(5)** _____ exercise into a summer job. Her parents have decided to **(6)** _____ her for staying healthy. She has **(7)** _____ herself a target of twenty lengths (or 500 metres) of the local pool every day. Veronica is proud of the **(8)** _____ she has earned: 'I'm making **(9)** _____ money doing this – £120 so far. If I **(10)** _____ it to 20 km by the end of the summer, I'm going to spend it on a surfboard!'

0	**A** make	**B** set	**C** let	**D** motivate
1	**A** congratulate	**B** praise	**C** push	**D** tell
2	**A** act	**B** achieve	**C** pass	**D** succeed
3	**A** incentive	**B** debt	**C** saving	**D** achievement
4	**A** borrowing	**B** lending	**C** affording	**D** earning
5	**A** getting	**B** turning	**C** doing	**D** moving
6	**A** invest	**B** owe	**C** give	**D** reward
7	**A** put	**B** set	**C** passed	**D** made
8	**A** income	**B** savings	**C** loan	**D** finances
9	**A** good	**B** big	**C** lots	**D** high
10	**A** reach	**B** get	**C** make	**D** achieve

Marks (out of 10): _____

2 Complete the text with the words in the box. There are three extra words you do not need. The first one is done for you.

~~afford~~	all	borrow	debts	hurry	invest	lend
loan	matter	owe	salaries	savings	spend	work

Advice for students

British university students now have to pay for degree courses themselves. These are normally about £8,600 a year for first degrees, so they must decide whether they can **(0)** ___afford___ to **(11)** _____ up to £30,000 on a three-year course. Most undergraduates have to either **(12)** _____ the money from their parents or take out a **(13)** _____ from a government agency, since young people don't usually have the **(14)** _____ necessary to pay for their time at university **(15)** _____ by themselves.

Clearly, when you pay for your education, you **(16)** _____ in your future; people with a degree usually have better **(17)** _____ than people with only school qualifications. However, starting your working life with such big **(18)** _____ probably means you will have to prioritize money over personal interest when making career choices. Otherwise, you might find that you can't pay back the loans no **(19)** _____ how hard you work. It looks as if young people in the UK might not be in such a **(20)** _____ to go to university without giving it serious thought.

Marks (out of 10): _____

GRAMMAR

3 Complete the text with a suitable word in each gap. Use only one word in each gap. The first one is done for you.

Give directly

Bernard Omondi received the text message early in the morning. In Kenya, where Bernard and his wife live, a
(0) _____*lot*_____ of people use mobile phones to send money with a payment system called M-Pesa. When Bernard read
the message to his wife, she **(21)** _____ not understand at first because he **(22)** _____ laughing so
much. A few days before, some strangers **(23)** _____ given him a mobile phone and told him they wanted to give
him **(24)** _____ money. In this world, not even family and friends have **(25)** _____ money to give each
other, so why should strangers do it? Naturally, Bernard didn't believe the message at first. But he soon did, when a second
message appeared. It said: 'CONFIRMED. YOU HAVE RECEIVED $1000'.

The founders of Give Directly **(26)** _____ looking at ways to reduce poverty **(27)** _____ they came up
with the idea of just giving money to people who need it. And it works – only a **(28)** _____ of the money they raise
is wasted on administration. Kenyans don't seem to waste the money, either. Bernard used his to buy **(29)** _____
old motorcycle and start a taxi service. Before, he had sometimes worked for other people, but often couldn't find
(30) _____ work at all.

Marks (out of 10): _____

4 Complete the second sentence so that it means the same as the first. Use no more than three words. The first one is done for you.

0 I only realized how competitive I was when I started to play Monopoly.
I _____*hadn't realized*_____ how competitive I was until I started to play Monopoly.

31 I'm sure most people play Monopoly as children.
There can't be _____ who don't play Monopoly as children.

32 However, I played the game for the first time last week.
Before last week, though, I _____ played the game.

33 I didn't realize how many rules there are in the game.
I didn't realize that there are a _____ rules in the game.

34 However, you don't need to know many rules to start playing.
However, you only need to know _____ rules to start playing.

35 You get a small amount of money from the bank at the start of the game.
You get _____ from the bank at the start of the game.

36 Landing on streets that other people own means you have to pay 'rent'.
If you land on _____ street that another person owns, you have to pay 'rent'.

37 At the beginning, I wasn't very enthusiastic about the game.
At the beginning, I didn't have _____ enthusiasm for the game.

38 I didn't manage to buy a single street for more than half an hour.
I didn't manage to buy _____ streets for more than half an hour.

39 When I bought a hotel on an expensive street, I started winning and having fun.
I _____ much fun until I bought a hotel on an expensive street and started winning.

40 Now I play every day. My wife thinks I play far more than necessary.
Now I play every day. My wife thinks I play far _____.

Marks (out of 10): _____

READING

5 Read the article and decide if each sentence is correct (C) or incorrect (I).

The world's top cities

Standard of living is partly dependent on where we live. Every year, surveys are published that claim to identify the best cities to live in globally. For a city to reach the top ten, it must score highly across a range of criteria, such as crime, education and the environment. Predictably, the winners are all found in the developed countries of Europe, North America and Australasia. More surprising is the fact that the USA fails to appear in any top ten. In one survey the first US representative is at number 25: Portland in Oregon, a city famous for its low crime rate.

To assess living standards, you have to decide what to measure. The three most important surveys share most of the same criteria: safety, schooling, health care and political–economic stability, for example. They may differ on other factors, like public transport, climate and leisure facilities. This is one reason their results vary quite a lot. Another is that it's difficult to measure many of these factors accurately; one survey might score a place highly for leisure while another gives it a low score. Opinions differ, after all. As a result, the surveys are often criticized. The New York Times claimed that 'The Economist Intelligence Unit's liveability survey' focuses too much on the English-speaking world, for example. Eight of its ten top in 2014 were in Canada, Australia or New Zealand.

Cities move up and down the charts surprisingly often due to current events. Vancouver was knocked off the number one spot in one survey when an important road there was temporarily closed. And last place in 2014 was occupied by Damascus in Syria, the scene of terrible human suffering and political upset at a time of civil war in that country.

So which cities are the best places to live? The clear winner is Vienna in Austria, which appears in either first or second position on all three main surveys. It seems that anywhere in and around the German-speaking world is an excellent place to live; Switzerland and Germany are also up there in the rankings. Elsewhere, Australia and Japan are well represented, with Melbourne, Sydney and Tokyo scoring highly.

These surveys may be of interest, but perhaps they are basically incorrect. What do they mean if they don't take into account the things that really matter most to us: family, friends, cultural familiarity and friendly communities? After all, the best city in the world is probably your own.

0 The place you live can affect the quality of your lifestyle. ___C___
41 There is more than one survey each year that measures cities' 'liveability'. _____
42 The surveys only evaluate cities on three continents. _____
43 Cities in the United States do not normally do very well. _____
44 The surveys measure how good a city is by looking at the same things. _____
45 The article gives two reasons why the different surveys say different cities are best. _____
46 Most of the factors for evaluating cities are easy to measure. _____
47 The position of cities in the surveys doesn't change much because standard of living is a stable quality. _____
48 Vienna holds the number one position in three of the main surveys. _____
49 Cities in Europe dominate the rankings. _____
50 The writer doesn't think these surveys are the only way to evaluate a city. _____

Marks (out of 10): _____

LISTENING

6 Ⓐ 76 Listen to five people talking about the 'sharing economy'. Choose the correct option.

Speaker 1

0 Where does the man live?
   A in a village ☑   B in a city ☐   C in the countryside ☐

51 What do the people share?
   A their jobs ☐   B their cars ☐   C their train tickets ☐

52 What advantage does the man mention?
   A He makes friends. ☐   B It is faster. ☐   C He doesn't like driving. ☐

Speaker 2

53 How does the 'Borrowing Shop' help the woman?
   A She does less work. ☐   B She saves money. ☐   C She saves time. ☐

54 What did the woman borrow?
   A some books ☐   B some music ☐   C some tools ☐

Speaker 3

55 What does the man like doing?
   A shopping on the Internet ☐   B buying used things ☐   C buying presents for his family ☐

56 Where did he buy a video camera?
   A from a friend ☐   B online ☐   C in a shop ☐

Speaker 4

57 Who does the woman share the cooking with?
   A her family ☐   B her neighbours ☐   C her colleagues ☐

58 What advantage *doesn't* she mention?
   A She has more time. ☐   B It's a friendly thing to do. ☐   C It costs less. ☐

Speaker 5

59 Why does the man like buying food this way?
   A He can choose what he wants. ☐   B It is grown locally. ☐   C It's good value for money. ☐

60 What other advantage is there?
   A People are friendly. ☐   B The food is clean. ☐   C The food is fresher than in a supermarket. ☐

Marks (out of 10): _____

SPEAKING

7 Talk in pairs, A and B.

Step 1

Student A: look at the first photograph. Talk about the reasons the man may be doing this.
Student B: look at the second photograph. Talk about the reasons the woman may be doing this.

Make sure you both:
- describe what they are doing.
- talk about the reasons they may be doing these things and what incentives there are for people like this.
- say whether you would be motivated to do something similar.

You have two minutes to think about what you are going to say. Student A: you go first.

Step 2

Student A: ask Student B questions about something they had some success in doing.

Make sure you ask:

- why the thing they did was a success.
- what motivated them to do it.
- whether they found it easy or difficult, and why.

Student B: now you ask Student A.

You can receive ten marks for including all the points above and using a range of language.

Marks (out of 10): _____

WRITING

8   You see this notice in your language school.

> ## HELP WANTED
>
> The school director is asking each student to write a report about their country or a country that they know well. The best entries will appear in a special travel article in next month's school magazine. Send us a report of about 100–200 words about the country giving some basic information about the place and the people. Make sure you include some information and advice for visitors.
>
> **Please send your report to editor@beaconsmag.ac.uk.**

Write your report. Write about 100 words.

You can receive ten marks for including all the necessary points and the conventions of report writing.

Marks (out of 10): _____

TEST 3 | Units 5 and 6

Name: _____

Total score: _____

VOCABULARY

1 Read the text and choose the correct word, A, B, C or D, for each gap. The first one is done for you.

Don't trust what you read online!

I don't get to the shops very often, so I usually **(0)** _D_ things on the Internet, especially if I'm **(1)** _____ for time. Like most people, I understand that the **(2)** _____ to sensible online shopping is to read other consumers' product reviews; that's how we measure customer **(3)** _____ , right? Wrong. It turns out that one in seven reviews might not be genuine; companies pay people to write positive **(4)** _____ for them. I read about a student who is paid to **(5)** _____ lots of comments on many consumer websites with different names every day. This may be a cheap way to **(6)** _____ products, but it is against the law.

So **(7)** _____ of the reviews you read. Not knowing whether a review is genuine is a real **(8)** _____ to trust when it comes to Internet shopping. At the end of the **(9)** _____ , we only have the opinions of others to help us decide. Companies should be **(10)** _____ to their customers, not speaking for them.

0	**A** invest	**B** cost	**C** pay	**D** purchase
1	**A** pressed	**B** late	**C** occupied	**D** busy
2	**A** tip	**B** method	**C** key	**D** advantage
3	**A** agreement	**B** pleasure	**C** satisfaction	**D** happiness
4	**A** comments	**B** notes	**C** sayings	**D** explanations
5	**A** give	**B** use	**C** send	**D** post
6	**A** help	**B** promote	**C** launch	**D** support
7	**A** care	**B** beware	**C** warn	**D** watch
8	**A** barrier	**B** wall	**C** block	**D** border
9	**A** book	**B** day	**C** story	**D** road
10	**A** going	**B** watching	**C** listening	**D** hearing

Marks (out of 10): _____

2 Complete the text with the words in the box. There are three extra words you do not need. The first one is done for you.

campaigns	emails	launch	meetings	messages	needs	~~oceurs~~
peak	presentations	products	research	satisfaction	set	trick

What matters in branding

Here at *WhatMatters* we understand that the branding process **(0)** _occurs_ at all levels of your business activity, from the advertising **(11)** _____ you run all the way down to the text **(12)** _____ you send. We help companies keep their brand in mind right from the start – when developing new **(13)** _____ and doing market **(14)** _____ . That way you can **(15)** _____ your product at the **(16)** _____ of the brand's commercial potential.

We know that every business is different, so the **(17)** _____ is to understand our customers' **(18)** _____ before we begin. That's why we ask to attend important **(19)** _____ you have and key **(20)** _____ you give about the company. Then we let *you* decide: how can your company make the most of a partnership with *WhatMatters*?

Marks (out of 10): _____

GRAMMAR

3 Complete the text with a suitable word in each gap. Use only one word in each gap. The first one is done for you.

These days, **(0)** _____ *more* _____ and more people are listening to podcasts. If you haven't started, I'd consider **(21)** _____ the same. As well as being one of **(22)** _____ most entertaining ways to use your mobile phone, this year the choice of shows has been greater **(23)** _____ ever. *Serial*, a crime documentary, became the **(24)** _____ popular podcast in the world, reaching five million downloads.

Podcasts aren't the same **(25)** _____ radio programmes. For one thing, the time you want to listen to a programme may be different **(26)** _____ the scheduled time – podcasts let you choose when to listen. Also, podcasts are a lot **(27)** _____ varied – I enjoy **(28)** _____ to many different types of podcast, from storytelling to science. So they allow you **(29)** _____ listen to what you want at the **(30)** _____ time for you.

Marks (out of 10): _____

4 Complete the second sentence so that it means the same as the first. Use no more than three words. The first one is done for you.

0 There have never been this many cars on the roads.
There _____ *are more cars* _____ than ever on the roads.

31 But in London, traffic has decreased in recent years.
But in London, there _____ now than a few years ago.

32 If you've travelled in the city for any time, you'll know about the congestion charge.
If you've spent _____ in the city, you'll know about the congestion charge.

33 This means you have to pay £11.50 a day if you drive through the centre of London.
This means that by driving through the centre of London, you agree _____ £11.50 a day.

34 So don't go by car through the city centre if you want to save money.
So to save money, avoid _____ by car through the city centre.

35 However, it's quicker to drive through the city centre than it was a few years ago.
However, a few years ago, it _____ quick to drive through the city centre as it is now.

36 This is because people are now more likely to take public transport instead.
This is because it has encouraged _____ public transport instead.

37 Understanding the underground is easier than the bus routes.
It's _____ the underground than the bus routes.

38 But of course nothing is cheaper than walking or cycling when getting around town.
But of course _____ way to get around town is walking or cycling.

39 Personally, I really want to see the sights, so I walk everywhere if possible.
Personally I hate _____ the sights, so I walk everywhere if possible.

40 Many people think London wasn't as pleasant before the congestion charge was introduced.
Many people think London _____ now that the congestion charge has been introduced.

Marks (out of 10): _____

READING

5 These people all want to study German. Below them are descriptions of eight language courses (A–H). Decide which two courses would be suitable for each person.

Briony's company is sending her to work in Germany in three months. Fortunately, the company operates in English, but she doesn't even have the basic German to talk to people. For this reason, she wants to learn with other students. The company will give her time off if necessary.
41 _____   **42** _____

Francine lives in the countryside, and must make the most of her time when her children are asleep. She wants to start learning German to be able to speak it on holiday and she doesn't want to spend a fortune.
43 _____   **44** _____

Geoff learned German living in Switzerland. A French teacher, Geoff has to teach a new German class, but he doesn't feel confident teaching grammar. He thinks aiming for an exam would motivate him, but he only has a couple of hours a week free after work.

45 _____   46 _____

Philippa is out of work, so she can't afford many hours. She can study mornings and evenings (not afternoons), and wants to work hard. She has a high level of Spanish, and having already learned some German is motivated to perfect all areas of her German independently, with a little guidance.

47 _____   48 _____

Paul can't find work so he's decided to look in Germany. He studied German grammar at school but he'll need to communicate better to get a job. He looks after his grandfather every morning so classes make a sociable change.

49 _____   50 _____

Marks (out of 10): _____

A AudioLab

Did you learn to speak and listen in your language from a grammar book? No. Learn to speak, from zero to confident, using our new techniques centred on listening and speaking. Students say they feel more confident in everyday situations: shops, restaurants, interviews … Classes evenings and weekends.

B Berlin School

Do you need travel and survival German fast? Our '4 × 4' courses provide an intensive General German immersion experience four hours day, four days a week. Classes are run in 100% German, with expert teachers. Elementary-advanced levels. Mon-Thurs mornings, 9.00–1.00.

C Einstein Language Institute

We offer challenging, fun and affordable evening classes at higher levels for students of German who want a solid mastery of the formal aspects of the language as well as communication, whether to pass exams, impress at interview or just to feel happy with their progress.

D Get ready for Germany

This year-long course is for people considering moving abroad to improve their career prospects. As well as interview practice and Business German, students will learn everyday phrases for a range of situations. Previous knowledge of German is required. Classes 4.00–6.00 pm Monday and Wednesday afternoons. Maximum 10 students per class.

E GoGerman.com

Our online General German courses have the edge over traditional face-to-face classes – flexible hours and competitive prices wherever you are. You'll be matched to your personal native-German teacher to practise vocabulary, grammar and pronunciation. We specialize in beginner and low-level classes.

F Language Coach

I offer online, personalized and small group guidance in language learning. This style suits people who already have some German and know how to learn but need help setting goals and getting organized and motivated. With few contact hours it's great for people on a budget. Lessons Sat and Sun am only.

G Private lessons

Personalized German classes for people in a hurry. I am a qualified teacher specializing in German grammar. I have experience teaching business German and exam preparation. I can come to you, wherever you are in the city, and at a time to suit.

H Telephone German

Our courses are perfect for people who cannot commit to travelling long distances because of work, family or disability. Improve your conversation skills with our friendly qualified teachers in real conversations over the phone, at all hours. Private class quality at group class prices.

LISTENING

6 🄰77 Read the sentences below. You will hear a conversation between a woman, Rachel, and her friend, Stephen, about an art exhibition. Decide if each sentence is correct (C) or incorrect (I).

  0 Only one of them saw the exhibition. _____C_____

51 Rachel didn't go because she was sick that day. _____

52 She won't get another chance to see the exhibition. _____

53 Stephen recommends going. _____

54 Stephen disagrees with the exhibition's definition of art. _____

55 Stephen didn't like the appearance of some of the pictures. _____

56 The images show that things that are normally invisible can be attractive. _____

57 Stephen was impressed by some photos of parts of trees. _____

58 Some images came from studying humans. _____

59 The exhibition is free. _____

60 Stephen persuades Rachel to go to the exhibition. _____

Marks (out of 10): _____

SPEAKING

7 Talk in pairs, A and B.

Step 1

Imagine you are both staying at a hotel but you do not know each other. You sit together at breakfast because there are no free tables. You have two minutes to decide together:
- why you are at the hotel (work, holiday, etc.)
- what you can talk about
- who will begin the conversation and how they will start

Have your conversation.

Student A: start the conversation.

Step 2

You are now going to ask each other for your opinions and give your views on one of these topics:
- a film, TV programme or book you have seen or read
- a place you have visited
- an advert you have seen

Decide what you would like to tell each other about.

Student A: ask Student B for their opinion about one of the topics.
Student B: when you have finished your conversation, ask Student A for their opinion about another of the topics.

You can receive ten marks for including all the points above and using a range of language.

Marks (out of 10): _____

WRITING

8 You recently went to a new restaurant in town. You decide to write a review about it on a customer review website. Read your notes and write your review.

Business: Luigi's Pizzeria

Location: central, with good parking ✓

Decoration: colourful, very bright lights – not very romantic atmosphere ??

Service: very friendly staff ☺ service a bit slow – 40 minutes' wait for food!!

My dish: mushroom pizza – best I've had ✱

My friend's dish: pasta – nice, but too much tomato sauce. And very spicy!

Overall: _____

Write your review. Write about 100 words.

You can receive ten marks for including all the necessary points and the conventions of review writing.

Marks (out of 10): _____

TEST 4 | Units 7 and 8

Name: _____

Total score: _____

VOCABULARY

1 Read the text and choose the correct word, A, B, C or D, for each gap. The first one is done for you.

The Xivo Sol-R9

Even if you're not **(0)** __C__ in underwater photography, consider buying a camera that **(1)** _____ you to relax about getting it wet or damaged. For readers who aren't familiar **(2)** _____ the history of underwater cameras, prices have come down fast – a cheap model **(3)** _____ little more than a normal one these days. And **(4)** _____ this – they are **(5)** _____ of tough materials so there's no need to be **(6)** _____ of the kids breaking it. The Sol-R9 is no exception, apart from one thing: unlike other cameras, it **(7)** _____ on solar power. This **(8)** _____ addition extends battery life, but the solar panel, **(9)** _____ 30 × 80 mm, means it's heavier than similar models. It **(10)** _____ in blue, red and silver.

0	**A** keen	**B** good	**C** interested	**D** excited
1	**A** tells	**B** allows	**C** makes	**D** lets
2	**A** with	**B** about	**C** to	**D** in
3	**A** charges	**B** costs	**C** pays	**D** spends
4	**A** get	**B** listen	**C** think	**D** take
5	**A** produced	**B** created	**C** made	**D** manufactured
6	**A** afraid	**B** concerned	**C** worried	**D** anxious
7	**A** uses	**B** goes	**C** performs	**D** runs
8	**A** novel	**B** rare	**C** unoriginal	**D** first
9	**A** stretching	**B** sizing	**C** weighing	**D** measuring
10	**A** goes	**B** appears	**C** shows	**D** comes

Marks (out of 10): _____

2 Complete the sentences with the correct form of the word in CAPITAL LETTERS. The first one is done for you.

0 Applicants for the position must be __ambitious__ but can also work well in a team. **AMBITION**
11 We're looking for an affectionate, _____ person to look after the children. **CARE**
12 I want a phone with a _____ battery that won't die after three hours. **RELY**
13 This helicopter is no toy, and can reach a _____ of 80 metres above the ground. **HIGH**
14 The new office assistant is keen and extremely _____ . **WORK**
15 Our dog likes people but she's not very _____ with other dogs. **SOCIETY**
16 I spend all my time charging gadgets: phones, tablets, cameras. It's _____ ! **END**
17 The new job is extremely _____ but it's a great experience. **CHALLENGE**
18 I'm not much of a _____ . I'm better at working alone. **PLAY**
19 It's good to be _____ but you also need to recognize when you need help. **DEPEND**
20 The fact that she has so much experience is a _____ reason to employ her. **COMPEL**

Marks (out of 10): _____

GRAMMAR

3 Complete the text with a suitable word in each gap. Use only one word in each gap. The first one is done for you.

Have you **(0)** _____ever_____ thought you were going to die? We all have scary moments in our lives, but for my brother Josh, his scuba diving trips **(21)** _____ brought him more near-death experiences than most hobbies. Although he's **(22)** _____ practising this sport all his life, he's **(23)** _____ dived deeper than 25 metres. However, even from those depths you **(24)** _____ get an illness called 'the bends' if you come up too fast. Once, Josh panicked and **(25)** _____ not come up slowly enough. Luckily, he didn't get the bends, but when he came out of the water he was very scared. His buddy, diving with him, said she thought he **(26)** _____ had a lucky escape!

I don't think Josh will go diving again until he **(27)** _____ attended a course in underwater safety. I'm sure he **(28)** _____ go back in the water one day, but he says he's **(29)** _____ to think more carefully before he does, and his family **(30)** _____ all going to make sure he does!

Marks (out of 10): _____

4 Complete the second sentence so that it means the same as the first. Use no more than three words. The first one is done for you.

0 Carrie Thule has decided to apply for the job of station manager at the fire station where she works.
Carrie Thule is _____*going to apply*_____ for the job of station manager at the fire station where she works.

31 Carrie started working at the fire station over ten years ago and she's still working there.
Carrie _____ working at the fire station for over ten years.

32 She hasn't had any serious injuries so far although it's a dangerous job.
She hasn't had any serious injuries _____ although it's a dangerous job.

33 She said, 'I'm ready to take the next step in my career.'
She said that _____ ready to take the next step in her career.

34 Before she became a firefighter, she worked for the fire service in administration until 2009.
She _____ in fire service administration since 2009, when she became a firefighter.

35 Her experience in both roles is likely to make her a stronger candidate.
She expects that her experience in both roles _____ her a stronger candidate.

36 Also, she thinks being a woman is unlikely to be a disadvantage.
Also, she doesn't think the fact that she's a woman _____ a disadvantage.

37 So it's possible that Carrie will get the job, but she doubts it. She's still very young to manage the team.
So Carrie _____ the job, but she doubts it. She's still very young to manage the team.

38 It's as unusual to have women in senior positions in the British fire service as it ever was.
There _____ been many women in senior positions in the British fire service.

39 Carrie's manager said, 'I'll give you a good reference.'
Carrie's manager said he _____ a good reference.

40 If she doesn't get the job her plan is to keep firefighting. She loves it too much to stop.
If she doesn't get the job _____ going to stop firefighting. She loves it too much to stop.

Marks (out of 10): _____

READING

5 Read the article and choose the correct answers A, B, C or D, according to the writer. The first one is done for you.

When the experience of age meets the enthusiasm of youth

It's Friday, and eighteen of Eileen Madson Primary School's youngest children take the yellow school bus to their other school in town. Just like every day, they bring lunch boxes and favourite toys. It's a fun day out they look forward to. They're off to spend time with their 'grandmas and grandpas'.

These aren't their real grandparents, however. They are residents at the Columbia Garden Village retirement home in Invermere, in Canada. Normally a place of peace and quiet, every Tuesday and Friday the atmosphere is brought to life for the residents, all of them in the later stages of life. With the arrival of the youngsters this old people's common room is turned into a classroom. All of a sudden, there is singing, laughter and movement as the activities change from knitting and talking about the weather to lessons and play time.

This collaboration between school and retirement home is unusual but not unique. Kindergarten teacher Barbara Carriere had the idea when she read of a similar scheme in Oklahoma. She was so impressed that it seemed to benefit both the children and the elderly people that she wanted to try it herself. She and her husband got their scheme started in 2011. Similar programmes exist in other places. In Toronto, for example, high-school students consult senior citizens about aging and death as part of their philosophy classes. 'Intergenerational learning', as the idea has been called, could be an advantage in a variety of ways and at different education levels.

It was an immediate hit with the children in Invermere, who feel comfortable mixing with people sometimes 80 years older than them. The residents help the children with reading and writing and with art projects. According to the teachers, the children's reading has improved due to the individual time the old people can spare their students.

The children learn about aging, too. Not all of them have grandparents, or see them very often if they do, so this contact with old people helps them understand what it means to get old. Real relationships between the generations are made. One boy who normally doesn't play with his classmates happily interacts with the residents and asks them to read to him. A little girl even asked to have her birthday party in the retirement home.

As for the older members of the class, they appreciate getting back the motivation that comes from being needed. Not only do they report an improved quality of life, it has also had the surprising effect in some of reducing the amount of medical treatment they need. Barbara Carriere is enthusiastic about the programme, and emphasizes that it costs very little and can really make a difference.

0 What do the children take with them on the bus?
- **A** something to write with and something to eat ☐
- **B** something to play with and something to eat ☑
- **C** something to wear outside and something to eat ☐
- **D** something to play with and something to wear outside ☐

41 Where are the children going?
- **A** on a school trip to a new place ☐
- **B** to visit their grandparents ☐
- **C** to another school ☐
- **D** to a place for retired people ☐

42 How often are these special lessons?
- **A** once a week ☐
- **B** twice a week ☐
- **C** twice a month ☐
- **D** every day ☐

43 What changes do the old people experience?
- **A** Their living space becomes noisy. ☐
- **B** The furniture in the common room is moved. ☐
- **C** They have lunch with the children. ☐
- **D** They spend more time outside. ☐

44 Why was Barbara Carriere interested in the idea?
- **A** She was impressed by the programme in Toronto. ☐
- **B** She wanted the children to learn about philosophy. ☐
- **C** She did it before in Oklahoma and it worked there. ☐
- **D** She thought it could help two groups of people. ☐

45 What does the programme in Toronto show about using old people in schools?
- **A** Old people can teach philosophy. ☐
- **B** Children of all ages can benefit from interacting with old people. ☐
- **C** Old people are better with teenagers than young children. ☐
- **D** You are never too young to learn about philosophy. ☐

46 Why do the children enjoy the company of the residents?
- **A** They don't feel stressed with the older people. ☐
- **B** The residents are enthusiastic readers. ☐
- **C** They can play more than at school. ☐
- **D** They can write to them and enjoy reading their replies. ☐

47 What advantage do the old people have over the teachers?
- **A** They are more patient than the teachers. ☐
- **B** They can spend longer with each student. ☐
- **C** They are more experienced readers. ☐
- **D** They have more authority in the children's eyes. ☐

48 What other benefit does visiting the retirement home have for the children?
- **A** They can have their birthday parties there. ☐
- **B** Some of them can see their grandparents more often. ☐
- **C** They meet old people and understand aging better. ☐
- **D** They can listen to stories. ☐

49 How do the residents benefit?
- **A** They enjoy being useful again. ☐
- **B** It saves the retirement home money. ☐
- **C** They feel younger. ☐
- **D** They live longer. ☐

50 Why is the idea a good one, according to Barbara Carriere?
- **A** It doesn't use the school's financial resources. ☐
- **B** It improves everyone's quality of life. ☐
- **C** It works very well but isn't expensive. ☐
- **D** It brings down medical costs. ☐

Marks (out of 10): _____

LISTENING

6 ⚙ **78** You will hear a conversation in a computer shop. Tick the correct answer, A, B or C.

0 How is the woman feeling?
- **A** She is thankful that Adam is helping her. ✔
- **B** She is feeling bad for wasting Adam's time. ☐
- **C** She is worried that she has made the right decision. ☐

51 Why have they come to the shop?
- **A** to buy a memory stick for a printer ☐
- **B** to buy a printer ☐
- **C** to get a printer repaired ☐

52 Why is the man qualified to help the woman?
- **A** He has a degree in computer science. ☐
- **B** He recently had to do the same thing as her. ☐
- **C** He has a good memory. ☐

53 What does he need the hard disc drive for?
- **A** to store e-books ☐
- **B** to store songs ☐
- **C** to store movies ☐

54 Why doesn't the man want a memory stick?
- **A** They cost more than he has right now. ☐
- **B** It will take too long to choose one. ☐
- **C** They are too small for what he wants. ☐

55 What size does the man need?
- **A** 1,000 megabytes ☐
- **B** 1,000 gigabytes ☐
- **C** 1,000 terabytes ☐

56 Why is the woman surprised?
- **A** The man makes a joke about her mobile phone. ☐
- **B** The hard disc drive is so small. ☐
- **C** The drive reminds her of her first computer. ☐

57 What did the woman use her first computer for?
- **A** having fun ☐
- **B** writing documents ☐
- **C** studying ☐

58 What was her opinion about her first computer when she used it?
- **A** She didn't think it was very good. ☐
- **B** She thought it was too slow. ☐
- **C** She thought it was really good. ☐

59 Why does she think early programmers were good?
- **A** They were able to do so much with basic machines. ☐
- **B** They did things no one had done before. ☐
- **C** The games they made were as good as modern games. ☐

60 Why does the man choose the hard drive?
- **A** He doesn't have enough money for the others. ☐
- **B** He doesn't want a black one. ☐
- **C** It's more convenient for his office. ☐

Marks (out of 10): _____

SPEAKING

7 Talk in pairs, A and B.

Step 1

Student A: look at the first photo. Talk about the skills, personal qualities and interests that are needed to do this job.
Student B: look at the second photo. Talk about the skills, personal qualities and interests that are needed to do this job.

Make sure you both:
- say what job the people are doing.
- say what kind of person would be good at the job and why.
- talk about the skills and interests you need to do this job.
- say whether you would be good at a job like this and why.

You have two minutes to think about what you are going to say. Student A: you go first.

Step 2

Work in pairs, A and B. You are going to leave voicemail messages. Read about the messages, then make the calls. You have two minutes to think about what you are going to say.

Student B: you go first. Choose from 1–4 and leave your message.
Student A: now you choose from 1–4 and leave your message.

Repeat with the other two messages.

Message 1: You are a friend. Call and invite Student A to the cinema on Saturday. Ask them to let you know if they can come.

Message 2: You work at InterMotor, a car hire company. You want to know if Student B booked a car for Monday 14th July or Monday 21st July.

Message 3: You make a business call. You work for an office equipment company. You want to arrange a meeting with Student A. You will send an email with more information.

Message 4: You are a colleague of Student B. You have a meeting with them at 10.00 a.m. this morning, but you cannot attend it. Explain why and suggest a different time.

You can receive ten marks for including all the points above and using a range of language.

Marks (out of 10): _____

WRITING

8 You receive these emails in your inbox.

1

TO: *Click here to add recipients*   CC:

SUBJECT:

Hi darling,

I'm trying to organize a dinner for the family to celebrate Jasmine's birthday. I'd like us to buy her a present from everyone, but so far I haven't got many ideas. Can you think of something?

I wanted to do it next weekend, but Sarah tells me you can't come then. Why? What are your plans? Anyway, I'd really love it if everyone can be there. Can you suggest another time?

Love Mum

2

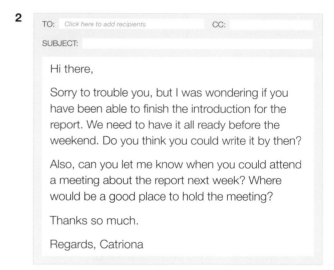

TO: *Click here to add recipients*   CC:

SUBJECT:

Hi there,

Sorry to trouble you, but I was wondering if you have been able to finish the introduction for the report. We need to have it all ready before the weekend. Do you think you could write it by then?

Also, can you let me know when you could attend a meeting about the report next week? Where would be a good place to hold the meeting?

Thanks so much.

Regards, Catriona

Write short replies to the emails, answering all the questions in each email. Write 35–45 words for each reply.

You can receive ten marks for including all the necessary points and the conventions of email writing.

Marks (out of 10): _____

Name: _____

Total score: _____

VOCABULARY

1 Read the text and choose the correct word, A, B, C or D, for each gap. The first one is done for you.

The best way to learn a language?

I **(0)** _D_ a lot of time trying to learn Japanese before I finally **(1)** _____ out of patience and decided to stop. My teacher used an absolutely **(2)** _____ method, so stupid, we had to repeat lots of sentences none of us understood, which seemed the wrong way **(3)** _____ to me, because surely understanding comes before speaking. I remember thinking that teaching languages isn't **(4)** _____ science; it can't be that complicated to do. But I was wrong: no one has yet come **(5)** _____ with one simple way to teach a language that gets **(6)** _____ .

One problem is that what **(7)** _____ for me may not be good for you. People **(8)** _____ to different techniques of teaching, so a challenge for teachers is to create **(9)** _____ lessons. But more important in my opinion is that teachers worry too much about lessons and not enough about how they can help students **(10)** _____ on with the job of learning on their own, when the teacher isn't around.

0	**A** took	**B** used	**C** passed	**D** wasted
1	**A** ran	**B** came	**C** fell	**D** let
2	**A** unusual	**B** ludicrous	**C** alternative	**D** logical
3	**A** out	**B** round	**C** back	**D** down
4	**A** rocket	**B** nuclear	**C** natural	**D** medical
5	**A** through	**B** out	**C** up	**D** on
6	**A** results	**B** solutions	**C** products	**D** outcomes
7	**A** serves	**B** makes	**C** does	**D** works
8	**A** respond	**B** return	**C** reply	**D** react
9	**A** full	**B** wide	**C** inclusive	**D** complete
10	**A** continue	**B** hang	**C** let	**D** get

Marks (out of 10): _____

2 Complete the text with the words in the box. There are three extra words you do not need. The first one is done for you.

down	ending	filling	get	~~getting~~	letting	light
line	looking	on	saving	setting	turn	up

The importance of customer service

At the centre of any business are the people who use your service, so **(0)** _getting_ the details right for your clients has to be as important to you as your bottom **(11)** _____ if you want to avoid **(12)** _____ up in trouble. Sandra Milligan understands the importance of **(13)** _____ after her customers. Since **(14)** _____ up a fast food delivery service that provides **(15)** _____ sandwiches and **(16)** _____ snacks to factory workers on the Slough Trading Estate in southern England, she has worked hard to build up relationships. 'It's important that I **(17)** _____ along with my regular customers. My biggest fear is **(18)** _____ them down.' Sandra doesn't employ anyone else to do her deliveries for her for that reason. This has the added benefit of keeping costs **(19)** _____ but she doesn't think it is sustainable: 'If the business carries **(20)** _____ growing like this, I'll need an assistant soon.'

Marks (out of 10): _____

GRAMMAR

3 Complete the text with a suitable word in each gap. Use only one word in each gap. The first one is done for you.

How to prepare a mango

Mangoes **(0)** _____*are*_____ known as the King of Fruits in Pakistan. Throughout Southern Asia, where mangoes **(21)** _____ originally farmed, if you go to a wedding or important cultural event, you **(22)** _____ probably see its leaves used as decoration. The fruit has spread to other tropical countries now so that mangoes in supermarkets are as likely to be grown **(23)** _____ farmers in Latin America as in Asia.

People come **(24)** _____ with all sorts of interesting ways to consume mango – as juice, milkshake or ice-cream – but we're going to learn a simple way to prepare the fruit on its own, so **(25)** _____ you don't like mango, stop reading now! Mangoes are very juicy, so **(26)** _____ you want to make a mess, you will need to use the sharpest knife you have. Look at the mango. There is a large flat stone inside which **(27)** _____ removed by cutting along it and around it. However, if you want to avoid the stone, **(28)** _____ not cut down the exact middle, but cut a centimetre on either side of it. Now you have two circular pieces of fruit. Cut lines through the fruit (but not through the skin) across and down two centimetres apart **(29)** _____ you have lots of squares. Then push from underneath so that the fruit is turned inside out. Now you can get on **(30)** _____ eating your mango!

Marks (out of 10): _____

4 Complete the second sentence so that it means the same as the first. Use no more than three words. The first one is done for you.

0 China is the world's biggest burner of coal, with ten billion tonnes of emissions each year.
More coal _____*is burned*_____ in China than any other country, with ten billion tonnes of emissions each year.

31 But last year the Chinese brought down their emissions for the first time to reduce pollution.
But last year emissions in China _____ down for the first time to reduce pollution.

32 Power companies in countries with high levels of pollution experience great pressure to clean up their act.
When levels of pollution in countries _____, power companies there experience great pressure to clean up their act.

33 Last year environmentalists like Greenpeace made a huge effort to stop companies from drilling for oil in the Arctic.
Last year a huge effort _____ environmentalists like Greenpeace to stop companies from drilling for oil in the Arctic.

34 For oil companies to stop bringing oil up from the ground, global demand needs to slow down.
Oil companies _____ bringing oil up from the ground only if global demand slows down.

35 Farming meat and dairy products produces about 14.5% of all greenhouse gas.
About 14.5% of all greenhouse gas _____ farming meat and dairy products.

36 Governments should not encourage people to eat meat if they want to reduce emissions.
To all governments! _____ people to eat meat if you want to reduce greenhouse emissions.

37 Industry won't want to spend money reducing its waste if governments don't provide incentives.
Industry won't want to spend money reducing its waste _____ incentives.

38 For people to recycle more in the future, governments need to provide more motivation.
People _____ more in the future if governments provide more motivation.

39 In developing countries, many people recycle glass bottles because they are worth something.
Glass bottles _____ in developing countries because they are worth something.

40 So, everyone, unless we act now, it will be too late.
So, everyone, act _____ it is too late.

Marks (out of 10): _____

READING

5 These people are all looking for good restaurants to eat in. Below them are descriptions of eight restaurants (A–H). Decide which two restaurants would be suitable for each person.

Graham and eight friends from university are going out on Sunday evening for his birthday. They love spicy food, as long as they don't have to spend too much.

41 _____   42 _____

Andrea is celebrating her new job with a friend. She wants a night out on Thursday with no restrictions on cost, somewhere that caters for wheelchair users. She doesn't eat meat or spicy food.

43 _____   44 _____

Karen, her husband and their two children need a restaurant on Saturday evening that will keep everyone happy. The children enjoy eating meat and would like somewhere that plays interesting music.

45 _____   46 _____

Phillip and Jane are saving money to buy a house. They want a romantic dinner for two at a restaurant that takes environmental issues seriously. They don't enjoy spicy food.

47 _____   48 _____

Theo needs a table for his boss and an important client for Friday lunchtime. Price is not an issue, but it must be somewhere smart. Theo doesn't know what kinds of food the client likes.

49 _____   50 _____

Marks (out of 10): _____

A *El Dorado* boasts an ambitious menu that includes 'world' food, from Latin American chilli to Indian curry. This cheap venue is great for parties so it can get very crowded. Open Monday to Sunday, lunch and dinner. Children aren't permitted after 7.00 pm.

B On weekend evenings, the *Aquarium* turns into a restaurant where diners can watch fish swimming past as they eat and listen to gentle music inspired by the sea. Served in a truly magical atmosphere, the food is reasonably priced and organic, if a little unexciting – hamburgers and chicken are popular. Reservations limited to a maximum of four people.

C *The Lemon Tree*, although expensive, is worth every penny for its quality vegetarian dishes, and friendly service. A spacious lift takes you to this third-floor restaurant with views of Greenvale Forest. Closed lunchtimes.

D The reasonably priced *Bougie Bistro* in the front room of the Gaunard family home is open from Friday evening to Sunday lunchtime. The menu? Whatever Madame Gaunard has cooked that day, but it is always classic French cuisine with locally-grown organic ingredients in an intimate setting most suitable for adult groups.

E The *Pad-Thai Curry House* welcomes groups, with tables for up to 12 people, so you can celebrate in style. If you're looking for hot dishes there are traditional curries from Thailand and other chilli dishes. A popular venue for people on a budget.

F The *Rive Gauche* is criticized for being over-priced, but location and quality of food always makes eating here a special occasion. Choose from a wide range of sophisticated meat and fish dishes while admiring the view of the city across the river, which is impressive at lunchtime, romantic at night.

G The *Shardlake*, right in the centre of town, caters for professionals with a wide range of classic menus for all tastes. This up-market and rather pricey venue is on the ground floor with easy access for disabled people.

H This busy venue is the city's only wood-fire grill serving barbecued meat. If you can afford the bill, the smoke-flavoured dishes at *Smokey Joe's* are a must. The lively atmosphere of this family-friendly restaurant is strengthened when, on most nights, the resident guitarist plays country and western songs. Closed on Sunday and Mondays.

LISTENING

6 🔊 **79** Listen to an interview about buying fruit and vegetables. Fill in the missing information. The first one is done for you.

0 Francesca talks about 'Pick Your Own' _____*farms*_____ .

51 At a pick-your-own farm, you can pick _____ .

52 Francesca thinks that farmers get _____ on the farm.

53 The food bought this way is cheap and _____ .

54 The children prefer going to the farm than to _____ .

55 Days out to the farm make the children feel _____ .

56 Their friends benefit if they pick _____ .

57 Typical fruit they pick: cherries, gooseberries and _____ .

58 Typical vegetables include: peas, beans and _____ .

59 Francesca thinks this experience means that her children _____ food better.

60 To find a pick-your-own farm, search online or look for _____ when you are in your car.

Marks (out of 10): _____

SPEAKING

7 Talk in pairs, A and B.

Step 1

Tell each other about a dish that you sometimes make.

Make sure you both:
- describe the dish in detail.
- say what kind of food it is.
- say what's in it.
- explain how to make it. Describe any special techniques you use to make it.

You have two minutes to think about what you are going to say.

Student A: tell Student B about your dish first.
Student B: ask questions about Student A's dish. Then tell him/her about your dish.

Step 2

Recommend a restaurant that you have visited to your partner.

Make sure you both say:
- the name of the restaurant and where it is.
- the kind of food it serves.
- why you would recommend it, giving any negative points.

Student B: make your recommendation to Student A.
Student A: when Student B has finished, recommend a different restaurant.

You can receive ten marks for including all the points above and using a range of language.

Marks (out of 10): _____

WRITING

8 You receive this email from a friend. Read the email and think about your answer.

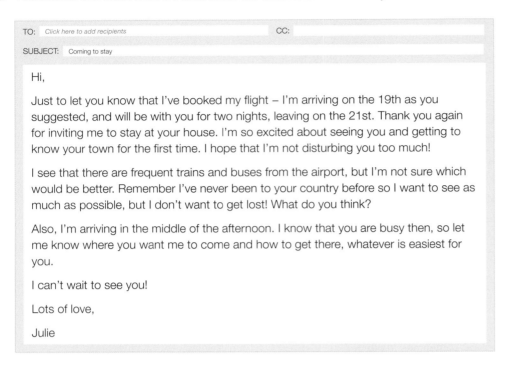

TO: *Click here to add recipients*   CC:

SUBJECT: Coming to stay

Hi,

Just to let you know that I've booked my flight – I'm arriving on the 19th as you suggested, and will be with you for two nights, leaving on the 21st. Thank you again for inviting me to stay at your house. I'm so excited about seeing you and getting to know your town for the first time. I hope that I'm not disturbing you too much!

I see that there are frequent trains and buses from the airport, but I'm not sure which would be better. Remember I've never been to your country before so I want to see as much as possible, but I don't want to get lost! What do you think?

Also, I'm arriving in the middle of the afternoon. I know that you are busy then, so let me know where you want me to come and how to get there, whatever is easiest for you.

I can't wait to see you!

Lots of love,

Julie

Reply to Julie's email. Write about 100 words.

You can receive ten marks for including all the necessary points and the conventions of email writing.

Marks (out of 10): _____

TEST 6 | Units 11 and 12

Name: _____

Total score: _____

VOCABULARY

1 Read the text and choose the correct word, A, B, C or D, for each gap. The first one is done for you.

A new approach to management

Adam Warwick is leading the **(0)** ___D___ in the management of Internet businesses. He saw how many online companies were going out of **(1)** _____ and he realized he needed to do **(2)** _____ different. Like in many new Internet businesses, his employees were feeling **(3)** _____ . Warwick heard about a company in Brazil that **(4)** _____ business by putting its employees first, giving them more freedom in how they worked. He decided to give it a **(5)** _____ . He let his workers choose their own hours and whether to work at home. Friends and colleagues thought he was **(6)** _____ of his mind, but then the company started **(7)** _____ a lot of money. More important to Warwick is the fact that his employees feel **(8)** _____ where they are: 'I want everyone to feel **(9)** _____ home in the company. I **(10)** _____ other leaders to forget about financial success and hand over control to the employees. It works!'

0 A path	**B** direction	**C** road	**D** way
1 A business	**B** success	**C** money	**D** action
2 A nothing	**B** anything	**C** something	**D** everything
3 A hard	**B** reliable	**C** stressed	**D** tiring
4 A made	**B** set	**C** created	**D** did
5 A drive	**B** push	**C** go	**D** run
6 A crazy	**B** out	**C** off	**D** away
7 A affording	**B** making	**C** producing	**D** doing
8 A happy	**B** pleasing	**C** enjoyable	**D** agreeable
9 A by	**B** at	**C** to	**D** in
10 A imagine	**B** say	**C** suggest	**D** urge

Marks (out of 10): _____

2 Complete the sentences with the correct form of the word in CAPITAL LETTERS. The first one is done for you.

0 Have you had another ____stressful____ day at the office, darling? Come and sit down. **STRESS**

11 Bonuses are important in making employees feel _____ by the company. **VALUE**

12 Can I make a _____? Why don't we move the meeting to the conference room? **SUGGEST**

13 Has changing Internet provider made a big _____ to your connection speed? **DIFFER**

14 I hate having nothing to do; I find working hard much more _____. **ENJOY**

15 I need to do something _____ when I get home from work, like read a book. **RELAX**

16 In setting up new companies, there's always a thin _____ line between being brave and being stupid. **DIVIDE**

17 The conference organizers were very _____ to us. They invited us to a wonderful meal. **WELCOME**

18 All the staff are feeling _____ after a week of really hard work. **TIRE**

19 We're going with the cheaper client, and that's final. We've made our _____. **DECIDE**

20 You're doing really well, and it's clear that the boss is _____ of your work. **APPRECIATE**

Marks (out of 10): _____

GRAMMAR

3 Complete the text with a suitable word in each gap. Use only one word in each gap. The first one is done for you.

Business lessons from nature

Harvester ants live in dry deserts where it **(0)** _____*can*_____ be hard to find water, so they must **(21)** _____ careful not to spend too much time outside, where they quickly lose water from their bodies. But they have **(22)** _____ leave their nests, of course; the ant colony **(23)** _____ die if they stayed in the nest and **(24)** _____ not look for food, which also contains the water they need. The decision is a difficult one: when there is lots of food available outside, the colony **(25)** _____ to send many ants out, but they must **(26)** _____ go unnecessarily. So who decides? Ant colonies have queens, but these don't advise the workers about what they **(27)** _____ do. Instead, ants have a simple system that controls their behaviour. An ant **(28)** _____ only go out if another one comes back with food. This way, they don't **(29)** _____ to communicate complex messages from one to the other. Humans **(30)** _____ learn a lot about how to organize systems from these insects if they paid more attention to the natural world.

Marks (out of 10): _____

4 Complete the second sentence so that it means the same as the first. Use no more than three words. The first one is done for you.

0 Doctors recommend getting between seven and nine hours of sleep each night.
Doctors say you _____*should get*_____ between seven and nine hours of sleep each night.

31 Only a few adults can function normally after as little as six hours of sleep.
Most adults need _____ for more than six hours in order to function normally.

32 It isn't usually necessary for people who do regular exercise to sleep for as long.
People who do regular exercise don't _____ to sleep for as long.

33 If you can't sleep, I advise not eating large meals for three hours before bedtime.
If you can't sleep, you _____ eat large meals for three hours before bedtime.

34 You should buy good pillows – bad pillows are one of the most common causes of neck pain.
If I _____, I'd buy good pillows to prevent neck pain.

35 I changed my pillow recently and all my neck pain disappeared.
If I _____ my pillow recently, my neck pain wouldn't have disappeared.

36 Actually, if we chose to stay awake for longer, we wouldn't be able to get more done.
Actually, if we chose to stay awake for longer, we _____ more done.

37 Lorry drivers have to take a break every four and a half hours to avoid accidents.
You _____ a lorry for more than four and a half hours without taking a break, to avoid accidents.

38 One lorry driver went to prison for driving for more hours than he should.
If the lorry driver had stopped driving after four and a half hours, he _____ gone to prison.

39 And nurses are more likely to get heart disease because they work irregular hours.
If nurses _____ irregular hours, they wouldn't be as likely to get heart disease.

40 We get so stressed about sleeping, but we need to see it as a solution to life's problems.
If we saw sleep as a solution to life's problems, we _____ so stressed about it.

Marks (out of 10): _____

READING

5 Read the interview and decide if each sentence is correct (C) or incorrect (I).

Ask the doctor

With so much information in the media about nutrition at the moment, you'd think that we'd all know how to eat healthily. But a recent survey reveals confusion is widespread, with a lack of understanding of even basic ideas about eating right. We interviewed nutrition specialist, Dr Anan Singh about the problem.

Dr Singh, do you believe we aren't eating well?
Yes and no. I think we're doing a lot of good: lots of choice in the shops, and cooking has never been more popular, which you can see from all the TV shows. So people are caring more about food, but it's no good cooking something special on Saturday if the rest of the week you eat hamburgers. What worries me is that being overweight is becoming normal. Patients underestimate how unhealthy their weight is because they look around and see everyone else looks the same as them. So we're losing sight of our goals.

So what's the problem with nutrition?
The main issue for me is education. What we teach kids at school is simplified and doesn't prepare them for all the confusing information they hear on television. Sugar is a great example of the message not being communicated clearly. Ninety per cent of people would still say sugar is just 'bad', when in fact it is as essential as water. A better, but more complicated, answer would involve discussing sugar in natural foods like fruit and wheat and how it is processed by the body.

Much of the confusion is down to marketing. Companies work hard to persuade us to eat more and more of their products, and they've succeeded. The way certain important terms are used commercially – words like 'healthy eating' and 'organic' – doesn't help much, either. They don't really mean what they should. Take 'healthy eating' for instance. It's used by the food industry to sell special low-calorie products that people eat when they're dieting and losing weight. But healthy eating is something we should all be doing over the long-term, by eating normal nutritionally-balanced meals. 'Organic' food is widely believed to provide nutritional benefits, even though it's really about the effect the farming techniques have on the environment. The best way to tell if something is good for you is to read the nutrition information on the back of the packet.

Lastly, if you could change anything, what would it be?
I'd make food companies put the nutritional information for each product in big writing on the front of their packets to let the numbers speak for themselves. And I'd teach children how to understand the information so they can decide for themselves.

0 The results of some research shows that, in general, people understand about nutrition. ___/___

41 There is more interest in ways of preparing food than before. _____

42 People's perception of what a healthy body size should be is changing. _____

43 Dr Singh believes the real facts about sugar are too complicated for children to learn. _____

44 He believes it would be better to avoid sugar in fruit. _____

45 He says we eat more than we need to because of what we are told. _____

46 Food companies have invented phrases to market their products which don't mean anything. _____

47 Healthy eating is about losing weight, according to Dr Singh. _____

48 He believes eating organic products is good for your health. _____

49 He advises shoppers to avoid reading what is written on food packaging. _____

50 If Dr Singh was in charge, food packaging would look quite different. _____

Marks (out of 10): _____

LISTENING

6 🔊 80 Listen to five people talking about their health and well-being. Choose the correct option.

Speaker 1

51 How often does the woman practise yoga?

   A about once a week ☐   **B** about twice a week ☐   **C** about three times a week ☐

52 What is one problem she has?

   A The teacher isn't good at yoga. ☐   **B** The woman gets stressed. ☐   **C** There is no one to look after her son. ☐

Speaker 2

53 How does the man feel about running?

   A disappointed ☐   **B** surprised ☐   **C** tired ☐

54 Why did he start the sport?

   A He had a bad back. ☐   **B** He wasn't sleeping well. ☐   **C** He was overweight. ☐

Speaker 3

55 Which reason for playing football is the least important for the girl?

   A sporting success ☐   **B** the health benefits ☐   **C** the social life ☐

56 According to her, how can sport help her with regard to university?

   A Sport helps keep your brain healthy. ☐   **B** It will give her something to do at university. ☐
   C It will help her get a place at university. ☐

Speaker 4

57 What reason does the woman give for walking?

   A to keep fit ☐   **B** to feel better emotionally ☐   **C** to study nature ☐

58 Where's the woman's favourite place to walk?

   A around the village ☐   **B** through the forest ☐   **C** along the coast ☐

Speaker 5

59 Why is the man not sure of long-term success?

   A It's difficult for him to do. ☐   **B** He's had one or two cigarettes. ☐   **C** It hasn't lasted a long time yet. ☐

60 Why is the man successful?

   A He sees the positive side. ☐   **B** He's keeping away from cigarettes. ☐   **C** He wants to please his sister. ☐

Marks (out of 10): _____

SPEAKING

7 Work in pairs, A and B.

Step 1

Read the situation, then look at the options below.

> A person who works for your company in another country will be working at your office for a few days. While she is here, you have been asked to plan her visit. You need to decide on a good place for her to stay; some good restaurants where she can eat; a social event that you could organize to help her get to know the staff; other practical aspects of her stay (e.g. transport).

Make sure you both:
- discuss each point in the situation.
- discuss a few options for each point.
- decide on the best option(s) for each point and say why you think they are good.

You have two minutes to think about what you are going to say.

Talk about the situation.

Step 2

You are going to ask each other questions about something you have had to organize.

Make sure you ask:

- what your partner organized.
- the things they had to consider.
- whether there were any problems and how they solved them.
- whether it was a success.
- whether they found it easy or difficult, and why.

Student A: start by asking Student B questions.
Student B: when Student A has finished, ask your questions.

You can receive ten marks for including all the points above and using a range of language.

Marks (out of 10): _____

WRITING

8 You read this comment online.

I'm preparing for an important exam this summer but I'm not finding it easy. I planned to spend three hours each day studying and then stop, but I get bored very quickly and end up daydreaming or checking for messages on Facebook. Then, because I waste so much time, I need to study all day! I'm really stressed, but I know it shouldn't be this stressful. Does anyone have any suggestions?

Write a reply to the comment with your suggestions. Write about 100 words.

You can receive ten marks for including all the necessary points and the conventions of posting comments.

Marks (out of 10): _____

Answer key

To score each test as a percentage, take the total mark (e.g. 60), divide by 80 (e.g. 0.75) and multiply by 100 = 75%.

Test 1 (Units 1 and 2)

VOCABULARY

1

1 D   2 A   3 B   4 D   5 C   6 C   7 D   8 B   9 A   10 C

2

11 students   12 manager / management   13 full-time
14 underestimate   15 barefoot   16 prioritize
17 researcher   18 assistant   19 cultural   20 pleasure

GRAMMAR

3

21 not   22 do   23 has / got   24 a   25 the   26 usually / normally / often   27 at / on / during   28 does   29 These
30 going

4

31 twice a   32 the moment / present   33 every evening   34 is travelling   35 you tell me   36 at/on the weekend   37 doesn't / does not   38 once
39 I'd like / I would like   40 becoming more

READING

5

41 B   42 C   43 C   44 D   45 A   46 D   47 B   48 C
49 D   50 B

LISTENING

6

51 reviewer   52 all of   53 working   54 100,000
55 manufacturing   56 car   57 specialist
58 (really) long hours   59 smile at / be friendly to
60 dangerous

Transcript 75

Interviewer:	So Gareth. Hi.
Reviewer:	Hello, Catherine.
Interviewer:	As usual, Gareth and I are talking about a book. Which book did you choose for us?
Reviewer:	It's called 'All Day Long: A Portrait of Britain at Work', by Joanna Biggs.
Interviewer:	I don't know her.
Reviewer:	She's a writer and journalist. She's also a book reviewer and edits the London Review magazine.
Interviewer:	I should say I didn't finish reading it. I read most but not all of the book.
Reviewer:	Tut tut! That's no good! (laughs)
Interviewer:	(laughs) What I read I found really interesting. What did you think, Gareth?
Reviewer:	I enjoyed it. It was fascinating comparing people's working lives with each other. The main idea is that we all do this thing called 'work' – we spend about 100,000 hours of our lives doing it – but we don't stop to really think about it.
Interviewer:	About 100,000 hours sounds rather depressing!
Reviewer:	(laughs) I know. So each chapter covers a different theme. She starts with manufacturing, you know, the traditional idea of work, making things in a factory. But actually, very little manufacturing happens here any more, it's generally done by robots. The car industry, for example, still exists but most of the work is automated.
Interviewer:	But there are specialist manufacturers still …
Reviewer:	Yes. She visits a place in Britain where they make specialist ballet shoes. Businesses like that sell small amounts of goods that don't interest the big global manufacturers.
Interviewer:	I enjoyed reading the similarities between work at the top of the work ladder and the people working at the bottom.
Reviewer:	What? Like the company director who has to work really long hours …
Interviewer:	… she can't find time to eat breakfast …
Reviewer:	Right, not very different from the poor man with three jobs because he doesn't earn much money.
Interviewer:	Also working for very little are the baristas in coffee shops. They were like the director, too …
Reviewer:	Right, because they are forced to smile at the customers, even though they don't feel like it, and the director needs to do the same – be friendly to her rich clients at business dinners. That comes across very clearly in the book – how we're all trapped by work.
Interviewer:	This wasn't the only negative conclusion, was it?
Reviewer:	No. She describes the future of work. All these children who want to be vets and football players are probably going to be climate change specialists or emergency workers as the world becomes a hotter, more dangerous place.
Interviewer:	Not a happy ending then?
Reviewer:	Not really, no. But interesting even so.
Interviewer:	Well, Gareth, let's finish there. Thanks for coming on the show.
Reviewer:	Always a pleasure, Catherine.

SPEAKING

7

Put students in pairs to talk about the photos and then discuss them. Tell students to follow the instructions and give them two minutes to prepare their brief presentation about the photos. Then ask them to discuss the points in Step 2. As they are speaking, monitor their English and award marks up to ten according to the criteria in the table below. Give two marks if the student meets each criterion well, one mark if their performance is satisfactory, and no marks if they do not meet the criterion at all.

Did the student …?	Marks
complete the task, i.e. talk about everything they were asked to?	
speak fluently, i.e. without too much hesitation?	
speak accurately, with correct grammar and vocabulary, and a clear pronunciation?	
ask questions and interact with their partner naturally and appropriately? (Step 2 only)	
use language presented in the unit for talking about jobs?	
Total marks out of 10	

WRITING

8

Use the following table to award ten marks. Give two marks if the student's writing meets each criterion well, one mark if their writing is satisfactory, and no marks if they do not meet the criterion at all.

Did the email include …?	Marks
a reference to the advertisement? (e.g. *I saw your advertisement …*)	
a reason for writing? (e.g. *I am writing to ask …*)	
accurate grammar, vocabulary and good punctuation, paragraphing, etc.?	
a suitable polite and formal style? (e.g. polite greeting, indirect questions, etc.)	
at least two questions about the job that show good understanding of the situation?	
Total out of 10	

Test 2 (Units 3 and 4)

VOCABULARY

1

1 B 2 D 3 A 4 D 5 B 6 D 7 B 8 A 9 A 10 C

2

11 spend 12 borrow 13 loan 14 savings 15 all
16 invest 17 salaries 18 debts 19 matter 20 hurry

GRAMMAR

3

21 did 22 was 23 had 24 some 25 enough
26 were 27 when / and 28 little 29 an 30 any

4

31 many people 32 had never / hadn't / had not 33 lot of 34 a few 35 a little money 36 a / any 37 very much / a lot of 38 any 39 wasn't having / was not having / didn't have / did not have 40 too much

READING

5

41 C 42 I 43 C 44 I 45 C 46 I 47 I 48 I
49 I 50 C

LISTENING

6

51 B 52 A 53 B 54 C 55 B 56 C 57 B
58 B 59 B 60 A

Transcript 76

Speaker 1: There's a scheme in my village where people save money by travelling to work together. Lots of people here work in the city, but the trains are very expensive, so driving makes sense. Whoever's turn it is to drive picks the others up from their houses. It's quite sociable as well; I know people here much better since I started commuting with them.

Speaker 2: There's a shop I sometimes go to called The Borrowing Shop. It's actually more like a library, but you don't borrow books, you borrow things. Say you need something but you're only going to use it once or twice, instead of buying it, you borrow it. It's really simple, and completely free. Last week I needed a few things to decorate my bedroom – a hammer, some paint brushes, that sort of thing, and they had all the tools I needed.

Speaker 3: I hate it when people throw things away that still work, so I try to find second-hand stuff. It's easier these days with the Internet, but I don't always get things online though. I got my *daughter a video camera for her twelfth birthday from a local second-hand shop.*

Speaker 4: *In our street there are a few of us that share the cooking. We began just taking cakes and biscuits – that sort of thing – around to each other's houses, but we enjoyed it so much we started cooking meals for one another. Well, none of us has much money. Also, it means I don't have to rush home from work to cook for the family. Except for today – it's my turn to cook!*

Speaker 5: *We get most of our fruit and vegetables from a local grower these days. It's much better than a supermarket if you don't want your food to come from a long way away. Mind you, there isn't much choice – just what's in season at the time, but it's always really fresh and green. It's not cheap either, but then, that's the price for saving the planet! I also love the social side – everyone stops to chat when they collect their food – you don't see that in a supermarket!*

SPEAKING

7

Put students in pairs to talk about the photos. Tell students to follow the instructions and give them two minutes to prepare their brief presentation about the photos. When they have finished this, give them two minutes to prepare Step 2 and tell them to ask and answer questions as instructed. As they are speaking, monitor their English and award marks up to ten according to the criteria in the table below. Give two marks if the student meets each criterion well, one mark if their performance is satisfactory, and no marks if they do not meet the criterion at all.

Did the student …?	Marks
complete the task, i.e. talk about everything they were asked to?	
speak fluently, i.e. without too much hesitation?	
speak accurately, with correct grammar and vocabulary and a clear pronunciation?	
ask questions and interact with their partner naturally and appropriately? (Step 2 only)	
use language presented in the unit for talking about motivations, incentives and rewards?	
Total out of 10	

WRITING

8

Use the following table to award ten marks. Give two marks if the student's writing meets each criterion well, one mark if their writing is satisfactory and no marks if they do not meet the criterion at all.

Did the report …?	Marks
give appropriate facts about one country?	
use short sentences and not exceed or fall short of the given length?	
use accurate grammar, vocabulary and good punctuation, paragraphing, etc.?	
write numerical information correctly?	
give suitable advice for a visitor to the country?	
Total out of 10	

Test 3 (Units 5 and 6)

VOCABULARY

1
1 A   2 C   3 C   4 A   5 D   6 B   7 B   8 A   9 B   10 C

2
11 campaigns   12 messages   13 products
14 research   15 launch   16 peak   17 trick
18 needs   19 meetings   20 presentations

GRAMMAR

3
21 doing   22 the   23 than   24 most   25 as   26 from / to   27 more   28 listening   29 to   30 best

4
31 is less traffic   32 any time travelling   33 to pay
34 going   35 wasn't as / was not as   36 people to take
37 easier to understand   38 the cheapest   39 not seeing / missing   40 is more pleasant

READING

5
41 A   42 B   43 E   44 H   45 C   46 G   47 C
48 F   49 A   50 D

LISTENING

6

51 I   52 I   53 C   54 C   55 I   56 C   57 I
58 I   59 C   60 I

Transcript 77

Rachel: Did you manage to see that exhibition at the town hall in the end?

Stephen: Yes, I went on Sunday. You saw it last weekend, didn't you?

Rachel: I never got there in the end. Noreen and I wanted to go but then she wasn't feeling well.

Stephen: Oh dear. Well, you don't want to miss out. It finishes on Friday.

Rachel: Really? The only chance I've got is if I pop in during my lunch break. So you think I should go?

Stephen: Absolutely. I wouldn't exactly call it art, though.

Rachel: No?

Stephen: It's fascinating but it's photography about science and they advertised it as art.

Rachel: Photos can be art.

Stephen: I know, but I mean, these were all taken with microscopes.

Rachel: (disappointed) Oh, I didn't know that.

Stephen: I mean, I don't know if technical photos like that can be called artistic, but don't get me wrong, they were all very beautiful.

Rachel: They don't sound it!

Stephen: No, what I mean is, they were chosen for their visual impact. I definitely found them attractive.

Rachel: What do you think they communicated?

Stephen: I guess the whole point of the exhibition is about the beauty of things we can't see. How can I explain? OK, so there was a series of really large photos of these brain cells that looked like enormous trees or something. The detail was amazing – every branch of these cells was visible, a bit like the branches in a dark forest. That's what I thought, anyway.

Rachel: And were some taken from the human body, the images?

Stephen: Erm, no I don't think so. I don't think any of them were, which is a shame – that would have been interesting.

Rachel: Sounds, er, interesting. I'm not sure I want to spend my hour off work looking at brain cells, though.

Stephen: Look, you might as well go. You don't do anything else in your lunch hour except eat, and it won't cost you anything.

Rachel: I might do.

SPEAKING

7

Put students in pairs to have the conversations. Tell students to follow the instructions and give them four minutes to read and prepare both steps. As they are speaking, monitor their English and award marks up to ten according to the criteria in the table below. Give two marks if the student meets each criterion well, one mark if their performance is satisfactory, and no marks if they do not meet the criterion at all.

Did the student …?	Marks
successfully keep up a natural conversation?	
successfully give their opinion? (Step 2 only)	
show interest in what their partner said and interact with them naturally and appropriately?	
speak fluently, i.e. without too much hesitation?	
speak accurately, with correct grammar and vocabulary and a clear pronunciation?	
Total out of 10	

WRITING

8

Use the following table to award ten marks. Give two marks if the student's writing meets each criterion well, one mark if their writing is satisfactory, and no marks if they do not meet the criterion at all.

Did the review …?	Marks
give all the necessary information?	
include a balance of positive and negative points connected with contrasting linkers?	
give a clear recommendation at the end that makes sense according to the notes?	
include accurate grammar and a good range of vocabulary?	
show good organization and paragraphing?	
Total out of 10	

Test 4 (Units 7 and 8)

VOCABULARY

1

1 B 2 A 3 B 4 A 5 C 6 A 7 D 8 A 9 D 10 D

2

11 caring 12 reliable 13 height 14 hard-working
15 sociable 16 never-ending 17 challenging
18 team-player 19 independent 20 compelling

GRAMMAR

3

21 have 22 been 23 never / not 24 might / can
25 did 26 had 27 has 28 will 29 going 30 are

4

31 has been 32 yet 33 she was 34 hasn't worked
35 will make 36 will be 37 might get
38 have never / haven't / have not 39 would give her
40 she isn't / she's not / she is not

READING

5

41 D 42 B 43 A 44 D 45 B 46 A 47 B
48 C 49 A 50 C

LISTENING

6

51 B 52 B 53 B 54 C 55 B 56 B 57 A
58 C 59 A 60 C

Transcript 78

Rebecca: Thanks for helping me, Adam. I'm pleased with this one. I think it will cope with all the documents I need to produce. I'm glad I had your advice. I know you're busy.

Adam: It's a pleasure. I know you think I'm a computer expert, but I'm not. It's only because I bought a printer not long ago that I know which questions to ask.

Rebecca: Oh, come on!

Adam: I only asked if you can return it if it's broken from using cheap ink cartridges.

Rebecca: Yes, but you also know about connecting memory sticks to printers.

Adam: You don't need a degree in computer science to know that! Which reminds me, I do need to get something while we're here, an external hard disc drive. It's so I can make a copy of my music library. I think I've got enough money. Have you got time for this?

Rebecca: Yes, of course. Is an external hard drive like a memory stick?

Adam: Yes, except they're much bigger, and can store more music or films. Ah, here we are. Hard drives. I'm looking for a terabyte.

Rebecca: A 'terabyte'? See, you are a tech wizard!

Adam: A terabyte is just a memory size. Like a gigabyte, but it's a thousand gigabytes. Here we are. You could get about, ooh, 250 films on that.

Rebecca: (surprised) On that? You're joking! It's smaller than my mobile phone. You know, I remember our first computer we had at home. It was about fifty times bigger than that. I think it had 32 kilobytes.

Adam: Really? You couldn't fit a Word document on that!

Rebecca: (laughs) I know. But we played video games on it. They were terrible compared to today, and very slow. But my brother and I thought they were great – we used to fight about whose turn it was.

Adam: I can't believe it's possible to make games that small. I'm sure they were really simple.

Rebecca: Oh, they were. They were always just one screen and the graphics were basic – nothing like today's games! It's amazing really – I suppose the programmers were very clever to make any games at all with those limitations … So, have you chosen one?

Adam: Yes, I think I'll get this one. It's got a short cable, see, and I already have too many cables in my office. I don't want any more!

Rebecca: They're a pain, aren't they? It's not a very nice colour, though. Can't you get that black one?

Adam: I don't really care what colour it is. Anyway, this is cheaper.

Rebecca: OK. Come on then. Let's pay for our things.

SPEAKING

7

Put students in pairs to talk about the photos and to 'leave' the voicemail messages. Tell students to follow the instructions and give them two minutes to prepare their brief presentation about the photos. Once they have finished talking about the photos, allow them two minutes to prepare the voicemail messages. As they are speaking, monitor their English and award marks up to ten according to the criteria in the table on page 205. Give two marks if the student meets each criterion well, one mark if their performance is satisfactory, and no marks if they do not meet the criterion at all.

Did the student ...?	Marks
complete the task, including everything necessary?	
speak fluently, i.e. without too much hesitation?	
speak accurately, with correct grammar and vocabulary and a clear pronunciation?	
use suitable language for telephoning? (Step 2 only)	
use suitable language to talk about skills, personal qualities and interests?	
Total out of 10	

WRITING

8

Use the following table to award ten marks. Give two marks if the student's writing meets each criterion well, one mark if their writing is satisfactory, and no marks if they do not meet the criterion at all.

Did the emails ...?	Marks
start and end appropriately?	
keep within the stated word limits?	
address the three points in each email?	
use phrases suitable for short emails?	
use accurate grammar, a good range of vocabulary and good punctuation, spelling, etc.?	
Total out of 10	

Test 5 (Units 9 and 10)

VOCABULARY

1

1 A   2 B   3 B   4 A   5 C   6 A   7 D   8 A   9 C   10 D

2

11 line   12 ending   13 looking   14 setting   15 filling
16 light   17 get   18 letting   19 down   20 on

GRAMMAR

3

21 were   22 will   23 by   24 up   25 if   26 unless   27 is
28 do   29 until / so   30 with

4

31 were brought   32 are high   33 was made by   34 will stop   35 is produced by   36 Don't encourage
37 unless governments provide   38 will (only) recycle   39 are recycled   40 now before

READING

5

41 A   42 E   43 C   44 G   45 B   46 H   47 B
48 D   49 F   50 G

LISTENING

6

51 fruit and vegetables   52 lonely   53 fresh   54 the supermarket   55 excited   56 too much
57 strawberries   58 tomatoes   59 understand   60 pick your own / PYO signs

Transcript 79

Interviewer:	*I'm joined in the studio by Francesca, who's here to talk about 'pick-your-own' farms. Thanks for coming in.*
Francesca:	*It's a pleasure.*
Interviewer:	*Now you go to pick-your-own farms with your children, don't you? What exactly is a 'pick-your-own' farm? How is it different from a normal farm?*
Francesca:	*It is a normal farm. The only difference is that the farmer lets members of the public harvest the fruit and vegetables they want as well as harvesting the produce him or herself.*
Interviewer:	*And why would they do that? Isn't it annoying having ordinary people like you marching all over the place?*
Francesca:	*No, I don't think so. I think they enjoy our company, to be honest. It must be quite lonely working all on your own. Summer is a busy time for farmers, so they appreciate the extra help from outside. And you have to pay, of course, though it's not very expensive.*
Interviewer:	*And what do you get out of it?*
Francesca:	*Well, food, for a start! For me, it's a very cheap way to do the shopping! Also, I love produce that is so fresh. When we bring it home you can smell the difference in the kitchen.*
Interviewer:	*Mmm, the smell of the countryside! Wonderful. And the kids? Do they enjoy it?*

Francesca:	Oh, yes. For them it's a day out in the countryside, and it's one of the only ways I can get them to help with the shopping – I mean, they hate going to the supermarket!
Interviewer:	(laughs) Yes, I'm sure!
Francesca:	In fact, they get so excited that we have to be careful not to pick too much. I often end up giving away tons of fruit to friends! And that's really nice, you can afford to be generous with strawberries when you've got three kilos in the fridge!
Interviewer:	I was going to ask what sort of things you pick.
Francesca:	Oh, all sorts. Strawberries and cherries, that sort of thing, as well as less common fruit you don't get in the shops, like gooseberries. And on the vegetable side, we usually come home with peas, beans … lots of tomatoes, of course.
Interviewer:	It sounds wonderful.
Francesca:	It really is. For me, too, I'm happy that my boys get some time really, you know, connecting with the country because otherwise I don't think they would really understand where their food comes from.
Interviewer:	So how can listeners find out where to find a pick-your-own farm?
Francesca:	Well, I'm sure you've seen signs at the side of the road saying 'Pick your own', or 'PYO'. We found one farm like that when we were driving around one day. Of course nowadays you can look it up online – there are websites with lots of information about each place.
Interviewer:	So there you go. Another idea for what to do this summer. Thanks Francesca.

SPEAKING

7

Put students in pairs. Tell them to follow the instructions in Step 1 and give them two minutes to prepare their brief presentations about the dishes they make. When they have finished Step 1, they should move on to Step 2 and recommend a restaurant to their partner. As they are speaking, monitor their English and award marks up to ten according to the criteria in the table. Give two marks if the student meets each criterion well, one mark if their performance is satisfactory, and no marks if they do not meet the criterion at all.

Did the student …?	Marks
complete the task, i.e. talk about everything they were asked to?	
speak fluently, i.e. without too much hesitation?	
speak accurately, with correct grammar and vocabulary and a clear pronunciation?	
ask natural questions and interact with their partner appropriately?	
use language presented in the unit for talking about food and restaurants?	
Total out of 10	

WRITING

8

Use the following table to award ten marks. Give two marks if the student's writing meets each criterion well, one mark if their writing is satisfactory, and no marks if they do not meet the criterion at all.

Did the email …?	Marks
start with a greeting and positive comment?	
include a clear suggestion about travel plans?	
give directions to a named destination (e.g. home) using correct prepositions?	
include a friendly ending that refers to Julie's visit?	
use accurate grammar, vocabulary and good punctuation, paragraphing, etc.?	
Total out of 10	

Test 6 (Units 11 and 12)

VOCABULARY

1

1 A   2 C   3 C   4 D   5 C   6 B   7 B
8 A   9 B   10 D

2

11 valued   12 suggestion   13 difference   14 enjoyable
15 relaxing   16 dividing   17 welcoming   18 tired
19 decision   20 appreciative

GRAMMAR

3

21 be   22 to   23 would   24 did   25 needs /
has   26 not   27 should / must   28 will / may /
can   29 need / have   30 could / would

4

31 to sleep   32 usually need / have   33 shouldn't /
should not   34 were you   35 hadn't changed / had not
changed   36 couldn't get / could not get
37 mustn't drive / must not drive   38 wouldn't have /
would not have   39 didn't work / did not work
40 wouldn't get / would not get

READING

5

41 C   42 C   43 I   44 I   45 C   46 I   47 I
48 I   49 I   50 C

LISTENING

6

51 A   52 B   53 B   54 A   55 B   56 C   57 B
58 C   59 C   60 A

Transcript 80

Speaker 1: Well, I needed a bit of 'me' time so about three months ago I joined a yoga class. It's on Tuesdays and Thursdays, after I've dropped my son off at the babysitter's. The teacher understands that we aren't all that fit. It isn't always relaxing, though. What with one thing and another I can't always get there, I usually miss a class every week. And of course, the pressure to go is quite stressful for me!

Speaker 2: I never thought I'd hear myself say this, but I just love running! My brother encouraged me to start after I kept getting these back problems – you know, just general aches and pains. Well, they're all gone now and I find I need less sleep, too. I've actually put on a few kilos since starting, which I didn't expect, but I'm not too worried – the chocolate reward at the end is the best bit!

Speaker 3: I'm currently training for a big match we've got next week. I guess football for me is about being with my friends and about winning more than keeping fit or anything like that. At the moment, I think the fact that I'm in a team improves my chance of getting into a good university because they say it looks good on my application. I mean, I won't stop once I've got in – I'll keep playing there if I'm not too busy.

Speaker 4: I find that as I get older I appreciate more the good that a walk in the country can do me, not so much physically as mentally. Even though the village where I live is very pleasant, it's important to get out into nature and let the trees and the smells and the green spaces do their thing. I especially like driving down to the sea – the sound of the waves just makes me incredibly happy.

Speaker 5: Have I stopped smoking? I'm still not totally convinced I've managed it yet because it's only been six months since I had a cigarette. Not that I'm finding it hard – most days I don't even think about them. I wasn't even tempted at my sister's wedding and there were one or two other smokers there. I think it's working because I keep reminding myself of the health benefits and the fact that I am doing it for no one else but me.

SPEAKING

7

Put students in pairs. Tell them to follow the instructions in Step 1 and give them two minutes to prepare their discussion about the situation. When they have finished Step 1, they should move on to Step 2 and ask each other questions about something they have had to organize. As they are speaking, monitor their English and award marks up to ten according to the criteria in the table on page 208. Give two marks if the student meets each criterion well, one mark if their performance is satisfactory, and no marks if they do not meet the criterion at all.

Did the student ...?	Marks
complete the task, i.e. talk about everything they were asked to?	
ask questions and interact with their partner naturally and appropriately?	
use language presented in the unit for talking about problems and solutions?	
speak fluently, i.e. without too much hesitation?	
speak accurately, with correct grammar and vocabulary and a clear pronunciation?	
Total out of 10	

WRITING

8

Use the following table to award ten marks. Give two marks if the student's writing meets each criterion well, one mark if their writing is satisfactory, and no marks if they do not meet the criterion at all.

Did the reply ...?	Marks
give appropriate suggestions and answer the query in suitable detail?	
provide an explanation of why this is good advice?	
use appropriate language for making suggestions and giving advice?	
follow the conventions for posting comments (short sentences, a direct tone, no greeting or signing off)?	
use accurate grammar, vocabulary and good punctuation, paragraphing, etc.?	
Total out of 10	

Communicative activities

1.1 What's my job?

Take a card from the pile. Show it to the other students but do not read it yourself! Use the key words below to ask questions in order to find out which job is on your card.

Key words

work alone	work in a team	talk to customers or clients	work regular hours	work from home
work in an office	work in a factory	work in a shop	use machines	use tools
need special qualifications	need special skills	wear a uniform	wear special clothes	write emails
write reports	travel	help people	get a good salary	have a lot of stress

> Do I work in an office?

> You sometimes work in an office, but you also visit customers.

TRAIN DRIVER	ACCOUNTANT	SCHOOL TEACHER
POLICE OFFICER	ACTOR	CAR MECHANIC
YOGA INSTRUCTOR	SALES REPRESENTATIVE	DENTIST
ELECTRICIAN	IT SPECIALIST	STORE MANAGER
MARKETING EXECUTIVE	CHILDREN'S NANNY	PILOT
GARDENER	RESTAURANT MANAGER	TRAVEL AGENT

1.2 Job interviews

1 Read this job advertisement.

> **WANTED**
> **Island Caretaker**
>
> Bored with the office? Looking for something different?
> Do you like the natural world and enjoy working outdoors?
>
> Then **THIS** is the job for you!
>
> The job is for a period of one year, on a small island in the
> South Pacific. There you will study the wildlife, take
> photographs and write reports for social media.

2 Work with a partner. Choose roles and read the information for your role below.

Student A – HR Officer

You are the HR officer who wrote the job advertisement.
Before you interview the candidate for the job:

- Make a note of the qualities and skills you expect a candidate for this job to have.
- Decide what training and support you are able to offer the successful candidate.
- Make a list of questions that you want to ask the candidate during the interview.

Student B – Candidate

You really want this job! You have been invited to attend a job interview with the HR Officer. In preparation for the interview:

- Make a note of the qualities and skills that will be needed in this job. Think about your past experiences and find an example for each one that will help you convince the HR officer that you are the best candidate for the job.
- Make a list of questions you want to ask the HR Officer during the interview.

Qualities & skills

1 _____
2 _____
3 _____
4 _____
5 _____

Questions

_____
_____
_____
_____
_____

3 Carry out the job interview.

2.1 A questionnaire

1 Add these time expressions and adverbs to the questions below.

at the moment	currently	every day / week / month	now
sometimes	this week / month / year	usually	

Question	Answers and more information
Which language do you _____ speak with your family and friends?	
Are you learning another language _____ ?	
Do you watch TV _____ ?	
Are you _____ watching a TV / DVD series?	
What are you doing at work _____ ?	
Do you go to work _____ ?	
Are you _____ looking after a relative?	
Do you have any children at home _____ ?	
Do you read a newspaper _____ ?	
Which magazines do you _____ read?	
Are you reading a book _____ ?	
Do you go on holiday _____ ?	

2 Talk to other students and write the information they give you in your questionnaire.

Are you currently watching a TV series?

Yes, I am. It's called *Breaking Bad*.

Nunzio is watching a TV series called Breaking Bad.

2.2 A week away

1 Decide on the details of the situation.

You won first prize in a competition. The prize is a week's holiday on a boat trip / at a yoga villa / on a coach tour / walking in the mountains / on a train journey / on safari.

The holiday starts in (country) _____ , and there are (number) _____ people in your holiday group.

The weather is _____ .

2 Complete the details about you.

Name:...

Nationality:...

Who (if anyone) you're on holiday with:...

Your job:...

Your interests:..

....

How you feel about the holiday:...

....

3 Your group leader has just welcomed everybody and told you about the holiday. Now there are food and drinks, and it is time to meet the other people in your holiday group.

Hi, I'm George and this is Nina.

Pleased to meet you. I'm Natalie.

Where are you from, Natalie?

I'm from Russia but I live in Germany.

Oh, that's interesting. What do you do in Germany?

I work for a car company. We have a lot of work at the moment, so I'm very happy to be here and not at work. What about you?

3.1 What does it look like?

1 Draw a simple sketch of any of the following: your office, your kitchen, your desk or your fridge. Include all the things that are usually in, around and next to your office or kitchen; on, under and around your desk; or in and around your fridge. Do not show your drawing to anyone!

2 Use the key expressions in the Useful language box to get information about your partner's sketch.

USEFUL LANGUAGE

How much … ?   How many … ?   Do you have …   (any / much / many)?
Could you … ?   some …   a lot of …   a few …   a little …

3 As you get the information, start to draw a sketch of what your partner is describing. Ask about items, quantity, space, dimensions and position of items.

Communicative activities

3.2 Group story-telling

1 Complete sentence 1. Then fold the page back along the dotted lines (so that sentences 2–8 are still visible) and pass the page to the student on your left. On your new page, write sentence 2. Then fold and pass the page to the next student. Continue until you have finished the story.

1 As a child Jonathan had a dream to be a/an _____ (job) when he grew up. But growing up in _____ (country) with no money, this seemed unlikely.

- -

2 couldn't afford (to do something – what?) _____

_____

- -

3 borrow (how much money? from where or who?) _____

_____

- -

4 buy (a possession to help him do his job) _____

_____

- -

5 earn (how much?) _____

_____

- -

6 save (per cent) _____

_____

- -

7 can afford (to do something – the same as in sentence 2?) _____

_____

- -

8 Next he hopes to _____

_____

2 Work in pairs to create a full story. Read your two stories and decide which one you prefer. Rewrite the story together so that it flows smoothly and makes sense.

4.1 Interrupted mini-stories

1 Student A: give the other students roles or verbs from your chart as they say a number.
Student B: choose a number from 1–10 = this is the main character in your story.
Student C: choose a number from 11–20 = this is what they were doing.
Student D: choose a number from 21–30 = this is what happened.

2 Make a basic sentence that includes the character and the two verbs. Add any further information to improve the sentence.

_____ was / were _____ when _____ .

3 Set the scene. What information can you add about the weather, the time, the occasion, the place, and any other characters that are there?

4 Think of a reason for the interruption in the basic sentence. Use the past perfect tense.

5 Combine all three parts: the basic sentence, the scene and the reason, and write up the story.

 -

	Character		Past continuous verb		Past simple verb
1	I	11	write	21	crash
2	My mother	12	go	22	return
3	My father	13	eat	23	leave
4	My grandparents	14	argue	24	explode
5	My brother / sister	15	buy	25	arrive
6	My best friend	16	watch	26	collapse
7	My partner	17	train	27	ring
8	My next door neighbour	18	work	28	shout
9	My boss / teacher	19	travel	29	end
10	My colleagues / classmates	20	practise	30	fall

Communicative activities

4.2 A successful race

Student A

Read the text and talk about it with your partner. How many differences can you find between the two texts? What are they?

I lost my job at the bank at the end of the financial crisis. After 15 years of office work, I wasn't in a hurry to find another indoor job and so I decided to take a few weeks off. While I was watching the New York marathon on TV, I decided that I would like to start running. I joined a running club in March last year. At first I went running once a week with the other new club members and I enjoyed it very much. Very soon I felt stronger and healthier and I even got a suntan, something I had never had while I was working in an office!

Last autumn I ran my first 5-kilometre race. It was difficult but I kept going. I was running with other club members and that helped. I did my best and was so happy when I passed the finishing line in just over 30 minutes. It was my first ever running race, and I was hooked!

I started to train more regularly; often going out for a run four times a week. I wasn't interested in finding a new job; I was only interested in achieving my next goal – running a half marathon. Earlier this year I entered the Atlantic City race.

Finally, the big day arrived. I didn't feel right but I decided to do the run anyway. The race began at 10 a.m. Within 15 minutes, I knew I was having an off day. My head hurt and I felt dizzy. I don't really know what happened, but suddenly I was on the ground and a paramedic was looking after me. It was the end of the race for me, but the beginning of the next stage of my life. I now work at the running club and last week I married the lady who looked after me when I fell during the race. Next year I plan to run the race together with my new wife.

✂ -

Student B

Read the text and talk about it with your partner. How many differences can you find between the two texts? What are they?

I lost my job at the hospital at the start of the financial crisis. After 20 years of office work, I wasn't in a hurry to find another indoor job and so I decided to take a few months off. While I was watching the New Orleans marathon on TV, I decided that I would like to start running. I joined a running club in April last year. At first I went running twice a week with the other new club members and I enjoyed it very much. Very soon I felt stronger and happier and I even got a suntan, something I had never had while I was working in an office!

Last autumn I ran my first 10-kilometre race. It was tiring but I kept going. I was running with other club members and that helped. I did my best and was so happy when I passed the finishing line in just over an hour. It was my first ever running race, and I was hooked!

I started to train more regularly; often going out for a run six times a week. I wasn't interested in finding a new job; I was only interested in achieving my next goal – running a marathon. Earlier this year I entered the Dodge City race.

Finally, the big day arrived. I didn't feel right but I decided to do the run anyway. The race began at 11 a.m. Within 15 minutes, I knew I was having an off day. My legs hurt and I felt sick. I don't really know what happened, but suddenly I was on the ground and a volunteer was looking after me. It was the end of the race for me, but the beginning of the next stage of my life. I now work at the running club and last month I married the lady who looked after me when I fell during the race. Next year I plan to run the race together with my new colleagues.

5.1 The best flower delivery service

1 Go online to find out about three flower delivery services. Make notes about each of the headings in the chart.

Information	Company 1 _____	Company 2 _____	Company 3 _____
average price of flower arrangement / bouquet			
starting price			
going up to ... (price)?			
delivery costs			
delivers to ...			
delivery time			
other products, e.g. chocolates, soft toys			
promotions / special offers			
payment options			
promotional videos / ads			
other services			

2 Make a general comparison of the companies and their services, e.g. *X is cheaper than Y for a basic bouquet.*

3 Which of the companies would you use for the following?
- sending a Mother's Day bouquet
- sending flowers to a friend in hospital
- sending flowers to a colleague who has just had a baby
- sending flowers to someone in another country

5.2 A day out

1 Complete the missing information in whole-class discussion.

Number of people: _____

When (month / day of the week?): _____

Duration (whole day / half day / plus evening?): _____

Cost per person: _____

2 In small groups, brainstorm your ideas.

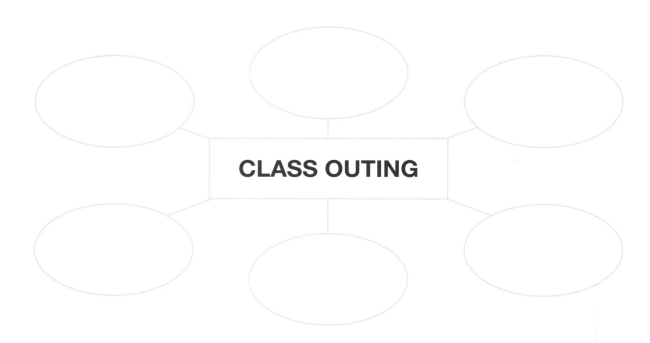

CLASS OUTING

3 Choose your favourite suggestion and write up a plan for the day out. Include information on the points below and anything else you think is important.

- meeting place and time _____

- transport _____

- destination _____

- food and drink _____

_____

_____

- what we will do and / or see _____

_____

_____

_____

- return time _____

- cost _____

4 Present your suggestion to the class. Ask for other students' opinions about your suggestion. Answer any questions they have.

What do you think of …?
Is … a good …?
It's fantastic / great / good / all right / OK / so-so.
I think it's a dreadful idea! / I don't think it's that great.
In my experience …
It depends on …
I imagine …

5 After the presentations, chose one of the suggestions. Say why you think it's the best one.

6.1 Coffeepotting

1 Brainstorm everyday normal tasks that need to be done at home or at work.

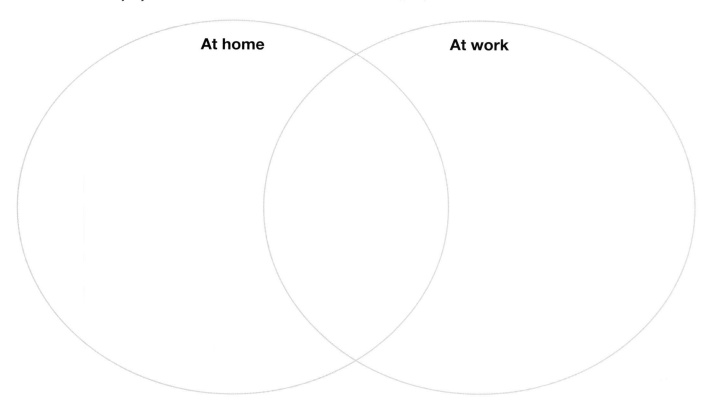

At home   **At work**

2 Complete the sentences for yourself. Write either about the everyday tasks you do at work or those you do at home (not both places).

I hate _____ .

but I don't mind _____ .

When possible, I try to avoid _____ .

Usually, I'm quite happy to _____ .

I prefer (not) to _____ .

I spend a lot of time _____ .

I often need to _____ .

I sometimes try to _____ .

I don't allow myself to _____ .

It's easier to _____ than to _____ .

_____ is the most _____ .

Most of all, I love _____ .

3 In pairs, tell each other about the tasks you have described above, but don't say what you are talking about!

6.2 Hidden agendas

You've just returned from a conference in _____ where you held a talk about _____ .

Yesterday you bought a _____ ; you are very excited about it. You need to sell your old one.

You are very happy because your _____ has just had a baby. You don't know what kind of present to buy.

You've just spent a lot of money on a _____ , but you are not sure whether it was the right thing to do.

You're trying to decide where to go on holiday next _____ . You're hoping to get advice from everyone you talk to.

You've been offered a fantastic promotion, but it means moving to the office in _____ . Should you take the job?

You've just won _____ and you want to share the good news.

Your _____ has broken down. You need a good mechanic and a lift home.

You are looking for a place to live. It must have a garden for your _____ .

Your partner has just opened a _____ and you're trying to find customers / clients.

It's your _____ 's birthday. You need to make them a special cake, but you hate baking.

Your _____ wants to learn to play the _____ . You're looking for a teacher.

7.1 Experiences we've had

1 Underline four experiences from the list that you'd like to ask other students about. Then write your own fifth question below.

miss a flight
get on the wrong train

win a prize
come first in a competition

give a presentation to more than ten people
fall asleep in a presentation

publish something
keep a blog for more than six months

find something that was stolen
lose something that was important, e.g. your
    credit card, passport or ID card

be on the radio or television
meet someone famous

live or work abroad
learn another foreign language (not English)

drive a racing car
go skiing or snowboarding

[your own idea]

_____

2 Talk to as many other students as you can and ask them your questions. Write the name of anyone who answers *Yes, I have* next to the question.

3 Report your findings to the class.

4 Ask at least one student about their experience.

Alison, you've missed a flight, haven't you?

Yes, I have.

Where were you going?

I was in Istanbul on business last year but the taxi broke down on the way to the airport.

What happened?

Well, I missed the flight by about an hour, and it was evening, so I had to go back to the hotel and get a flight the next day.

7.2 Personal qualities

1 Take a 'quality' card and talk about someone you know, someone you have read about or heard of who has this quality.

2 Talk about the qualities that are most important for these jobs.

accountant	cabin crew	charity volunteer	doctor	dog walker
electrician	hairdresser	IT support	lawyer	musician
police officer	schoolteacher	shop manager	sports coach	waiter

3 Talk about other qualities that a person in these jobs should have, using these phrases: *good at ... , interested in ... , keen on ... , not afraid of ... .*

---

honest	ambitious
caring	positive
easy-going	organized
enthusiastic	reliable
hard-working	sociable
independent	a team-player
knowledgeable	confident
practical	patient

1

2

3

4

5

6

7

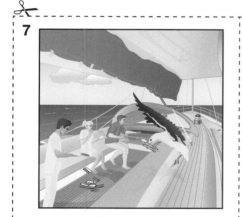

8

9

10

11

12

a gas fire for camping

an electric toothbrush

a pencil sharpener

a battery-powered cordless hand drill

a two-person tent

mini speakers for a smart phone

a petrol-driven lawn mower

a smoke alarm for the ceiling

a Swiss army penknife

a car satnav

a burglar alarm for a house

an electric-powered bike

a fridge with a freezer compartment

a stairlift for an old or disabled person

a battery-powered torch

a TV remote control

a movement-sensitive outdoor security light

solar panels for a house roof

a tumble dryer

a desk electric fan

kitchen scales

9.1 Conditional mix and match

If you're hungry,	When you are hot and have no energy,	If you don't drink enough water when it's hot,	If someone steals your camera while you're on holiday,
If you lose your credit card,	Unless you leave now,	If you miss your train,	If your suitcase is too heavy,
If you want to check your emails,	If you don't call her when you get there,	Many people believe that if they get a good job,	You won't get good marks
If you don't go to bed before midnight,	Unless you help me,	When Cindy's not here,	If you see Joan,
don't panic – you can get the next one.	she'll worry.	they'll be happy.	I sit at her desk.
go to the local police station.	you''ll miss your flight.	you'll be tired in the morning.	give her my best wishes.
it's difficult to concentrate.	eat something salty and drink something sweet.	connect to the free wi-fi.	unless you do your homework.
you feel very tired.	you have to pay more money.	contact your bank immediately.	I won't be able to do it.

Communicative activities **225**

9.2 Information-gap crossword

Student A

With a partner, take turns to define and describe your missing words so that you can both complete the crossword.

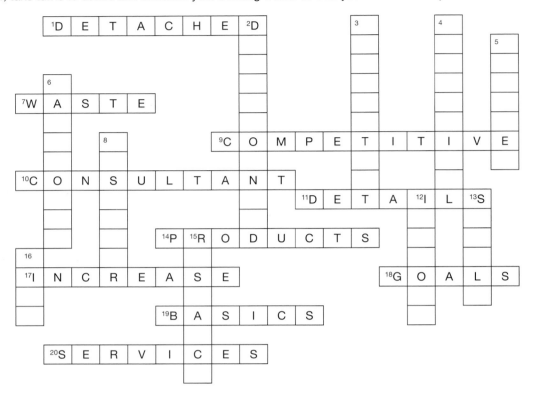

- -

Student B

With a partner, take turns to define and describe your missing words so that you can both complete the crossword.

10.1 Town meeting

1 Read the situation and the seven proposals. Then discuss which is the best one.

Situation

You are attending a public meeting to decide what to do with a 400-square-metre unused plot of land in your town (i.e. the size of two tennis courts). There used to be a small paper factory on the land. Now the area is empty apart from one large old tree in the middle. The area is bordered by a main road, a nursery school, an old people's residential home, and a church. Your town has approximately 25,000 inhabitants.

Proposals

A Special garden for elderly people

The manager of the residential home for old people next to the land would like to make a garden for the old people with lots of places to sit, and wide paths for wheelchair access. It would be a place of peace and quiet for the 38 women and 12 men who are spending their last days in the home. It could also be opened to the public, but for adults only.

B Outdoor play area for the nursery school

At the moment there is just a concrete yard for the forty pre-school children to play in. To keep the children safe, there would be a tall fence or wall built between the land and the main road. The nursery school is run by the town – it isn't private.

C A vegetable garden for everyone

The new Urban Gardeners' Association would like to plant the land with fruit, vegetables and herbs. It would be a place for the whole community, where local people can take and use the produce that is grown there. They would construct a small building where gardening workshops and cookery classes could take place. The association is a charity run by volunteers.

D Boutique hotel

The owner of a small chain of boutique hotels wants to build a small hotel on the land. The town needs a new hotel that would attract more tourists. They would build a large underground car park. The car park would be bigger than the hotel needs so they would be willing to rent out some spaces.

E Car park for the church

In the last year there has been an increase in the number of people attending the church on Sundays and at special times of the year. They have recently started a very successful youth club on Saturdays and would like to offer a school holiday programme too. As the church does not have a car park, this is causing a problem with the residents in the area. The church would like to buy the land and turn it into a car park.

F A new café

The owner of the most popular café in the town wants to open a second café. He would build an outdoor seating area and a stage for music and cultural events. He would also like to set up a big screen so that customers could watch special sports events such as the Football World Cup and the Olympic Games.

G Market place

The local traders association would like the area to be used for a twice weekly farmers' market. This would be a place for local farmers and other traders to sell their home-grown organic fruit, vegetables, flowers and other produce. The town does not currently have a market.

2 Now vote for your favourite proposals.

Communicative activities

✂ -

A Around a third of all the food in the world is wasted. In the UK, 50% of food waste happens at

- -

B Crude oil is a thick, black liquid that is found underground and under the sea. Crude oil is

- -

sent to the government, who want to reduce the waste by 20% within the next three years. *[end]*

- -

spill and the clean-up costs were said to have been more than 40 billion US dollars. *[end]*

- -

a result of the disaster. Additionally, the company's reputation was damaged greatly by the oil

- -

diesel and gas. These fuels are used to help power engines in machines and vehicles

- -

gallons of crude oil were pumped into the Gulf of Mexico and over 1000 km of coastline from

- -

the food is ruined on farms and during transportation and in stores. Greenhouse-gas emissions

- -

such as cars, trucks and aeroplanes. As a result of the BP oil spill in 2010, more than 200 million

- -

transport it. A meeting was held last month between major supermarkets and the farming

- -

home, where 7.2 m tonnes of food and drink is thrown away annually by households. The rest of

- -

industry to decide how to deal with this waste problem. A 200-page report from the meeting was

- -

Texas to Florida was affected. Many birds, fish and other animals such as dolphins were killed as

- -

changed at oil refineries into different fuels that we all use in our daily lives such as petrol, oil,

- -

from the food waste are produced in rubbish sites and from the vehicles that are used to

- -

11.1 Do I have to?

1 In pairs, use the modal verbs in the box and your own ideas to complete the sentences.

must / mustn't	have to / don't have to	need to / don't need to	can / can't	should / shouldn't

a You _____ have a big party on important birthdays, e.g. 30th or 50th.

b You _____ tell your boss before you apply for another job.

c You _____ blow your car horn between midnight and 6.00 a.m.

d When there is a fire, you _____ use the stairs.

e You _____ drive the wrong way down a one-way street.

f You _____ be rich to be happy.

g If you are afraid of flying, you _____

_____

_____

h When you find money on the street, _____

_____

_____

i Before you start a company you _____

_____

j If you want to run a marathon, _____

_____

_____

k When you are very tired, you _____

_____

l To improve your English, you _____ and _____

_____

_____

2 Compare your sentences in groups. Which do you like best?

11.2 Quotation game

Set A

I don't like the word 'businesswoman'. Perhaps …	You can't use up creativity. The more you use, …	It does not matter how slowly you go as long as …	You cannot have a positive life and …
The most common way people give up their power is …	You have to learn the rules of the game. And then you have to …	A leader is one who knows the way, goes the way, and …	Your time is limited, so don't waste it living …
You only live once but if you do it right, …	He who has great power should …	Do what you feel in your heart to be right – for you'll be …	How wonderful it is that nobody need wait a single moment before …

Set B

… by thinking they don't have any. *Alice Walker*	… once is enough. *Mae West*	… shows the way. *John Maxwell*	… starting to improve the world. *Anne Frank*
… play better than anyone else. *Albert Einstein*	… use it lightly. *Seneca*	… 'committed mother' would be the best description. *Steffi Graf*	… criticized anyway. *Eleanor Roosevelt*
… someone else's life. *Steve Jobs*	… the more you have. *Maya Angelou*	… a negative mind. *Joyce Meyer*	… you do not stop. *Confucius*

12.1 Dilemmas

1 Read the dilemmas in the speech bubbles. Choose two that you think you could give advice on.

2 In pairs, discuss your four dilemmas and decide what advice you would give.

3 Write a piece of advice for each of the four dilemmas.

4 Write your advice in the form of an email or a post on a forum.

A My boss has sent me a Facebook friend request. I don't want to offend him by not accepting it, but I also don't want him to see posts and photos from my private life. I don't know what to do.

B I went to my doctor because of my constant headaches and tiredness. She recommended taking at least two weeks off work. I know she's right, but it's a very busy time of year, and I work with some very competitive people, so I'm worried about losing my job.

C A friend wants to take a year off to go travelling and she's asked me to go with her. I'd love to go on the trip – I've been thinking about doing it for a while – but I don't know if our friendship is strong enough for us to spend so much time together. We had a big argument last month and we've only just started talking to each other again.

D Our son (aged 16) is getting less than average grades at school. University education is so important these days but with these grades he will not get a place. We're worried about his future although he doesn't seem to be worried himself.

E I think we eat too much meat. It's expensive and not good for our health, and eating so much of it is also bad for the planet. I'd really prefer to be a vegetarian and only cook vegetarian food at home but my partner doesn't want to give up meat.

F Our neighbour's dog has had puppies and my husband has already chosen the one he wants. I like animals, but we have two small children and my husband often goes away on business trips. I'm already tired all the time and I just know that I will have to train and walk the dog every day.

G My 70-year-old father is no longer well enough to live by himself. We do not have a spare room for him in our small house and I don't think it is fair that my partner should have to care for him. My brother, who lives on the other side of the world, doesn't want our father to go into a care home.

H I get so sad when I watch TV reports about children in war zones or see pictures on the Internet of all the poor and hungry children around the world. I'd like to do something to help, but I don't know what.

12.2 Life choices, lifestyle

1 Read the actions in the box. Think about your own life and write actions in the circle that best describes you.

2 Show your lifestyle choices to your partner, and discuss your options together.

sit in the direct sun	go cycling	talk to your neighbours
regularly do further training courses	go jogging	watch TV every day
read a daily newspaper	do yoga or a similar mind and body exercise	spend time in the fresh air every day
meet colleagues socially	have a yearly health check	play a musical instrument
use the stairs (not the lift)	go to bed early	recycle bottles, paper, plastic
keep a diary	take naps during the day	regularly use public transport
cook your own meals rather than buying packaged food	get 8 hours sleep a night	eat fruit every day
take time to have a proper lunch every day	back up your computer every month	eat at your desk
do exercise three times a week	drive fast	have an Internet-free day every week
	spend time alone	sit all day
		stand all day

A

I don't do it although it's good for me.

B

I do it because it's good for me.

C

I do it although it's bad for me.

D

I don't do it because it's bad for me.

Communicative activities | Teacher's notes

1.1 What's my job?

A small group game in which students ask and answer questions in order to find out which job is written on their card.

Language

Job titles and positions

Present simple questions and answers, adverbs and expressions of frequency

Preparation

You need a copy of the top half of the worksheet for each student, but only enough copies of the bottom half for one per group of three–six students. Once you have enough copies of the cards for each group, you could cut down the copying by placing two top halves on the photocopier and copying two per page. Prepare the job cards by cutting them out.

In class

1 Divide the class into groups of three–six students; give each student a copy of the top half of the photocopiable page containing the key words, example and blank cards.

2 Place the cut-up job cards face down (so the jobs cannot be seen) in a pile in front of the students in each group. Tell them not to read the cards yet!

3 Explain that they are going to use the key words to make questions that will help them discover which job is written on a card.

4 Ask students to read the example exchange in the speech bubbles. Elicit other questions they might ask using the key words, e.g. *Do I work shifts? Is my job dangerous?* Encourage use of adverbs of frequency – primarily in the answers, but also in the questions if appropriate.

5 Students take it in turns to pick up the top card from the pile and show it to the others in their group. The student who picked up the card should **not** read the job on the card, but should ask questions in order to guess which job is on the card.

6 Tell students to keep a record of how many questions they each needed to guess their job correctly. The game ends when all the cards have been used, and the winner is the student who guessed the most jobs correctly using the fewest questions.

7 To extend the game, students write other jobs on the blank cards (without letting the others know what they have written), cut them out, shuffle them, place them face down in a pile, and play the game again.

1.2 Job interviews

A paired role-play activity in which students prepare for and carry out job interviews.

Language

Vocabulary for qualities and skills

Asking and answering direct and indirect work-related questions

Preparation

Make one copy of the worksheet for each student.

In class

1 Set the scene by asking questions to introduce the theme of possibly working on an island as a caretaker, e.g. *Have you ever been to a very small island? Do you like peace and quiet? Are you interested in wildlife?*

2 **Exercise 1.** Write *caretaker* on the board. Explain what the job of a caretaker usually is, i.e. = someone whose job is to look after a large building such as a school, office building or block of flats. Explain that this is a job advertisement for a very special kind of caretaker. Ask students to read the job advertisement and deal with any vocabulary questions that arise.

3 Divide the class into pairs. Explain that in each pair there will be an HR (Human Resources) Officer (Student A) and a job candidate (Student B). Students decide which they would prefer to be.

4 **Exercise 2.** All Student As sit together, read the role card in Exercise 2, and prepare for the role play. They should do this by brainstorming their ideas and talking about questions they might expect to ask or have to answer during an interview, writing them on the worksheet. All Student Bs sit together and do the same. Allow twenty minutes for this step.

5 **Exercise 3.** In their original A/B pairs, students carry out the role play (Exercise 3). Suggest a further 15 minutes for the interview.

6 If you have time, change the pairs so that the HR Officers interview two further candidates.

7 The HR Officers should decide which candidate they would like to offer the job to, or, if they only interviewed one person, decide whether they would offer them the job.

8 Hold a class feedback and reflection session, allowing students to discuss freely how the interviews went, what they liked and disliked, and what they would do differently another time. Encourage them to talk about the language they used and whether they were lacking any specific words or phrases.

9 To extend this activity, have students write a different job advertisement and prepare for role plays in which they should take the opposite role to the one they had in the first activity.

2.1 A questionnaire

A pairwork and mingling activity in which students complete questions using time expressions and then talk to other students about what they do / are doing.

Language

Present continuous and present simple

Time expressions and adverbs: *at the moment*, *currently*, *every day / week / month*, *now*, *sometimes*, *this week / month / year*, *usually*

Preparation

Make one copy of the worksheet for each student.

In class

1 **Exercise 1.** Give each student a copy of the worksheet. Ask them to work in pairs and complete the questions in the questionnaire with time expressions and adverbs. Check that these are correct before you move onto the next stage.

   Suggested answers

   Which language do you usually speak with your family and friends?
   Are you learning another language at the moment?
   Do you watch TV every day?
   Are you currently watching a TV / DVD series?
   What are you doing at work this week / month / at the moment?
   Do you go to work every day?
   Are you currently looking after a relative?
   Do you have any children at home now / at the moment / this week?
   Do you read a newspaper every day?
   Which magazines do you usually read?
   Are you reading a book at the moment?
   Do you go on holiday every year?

2 Give students five minutes to decide for themselves how they would answer each of the questions. Deal with any questions they have about vocabulary or grammar. They shouldn't complete the questionnaire for themselves.

3 **Exercise 2.** Ask them to look at the conversation in the speech bubbles. Tell them that their task now is to talk to as many students as possible and make notes of the answers and information in the second column of the questionnaire. They should ask each student they talk to one question after another (in any order) until they receive a positive answer. At this point they should find out further information and make a note of it, *e.g. I speak German with my husband, but I speak Spanish with my parents.* The notes would then say: *Maria speaks German with her husband and Spanish with her parents.*

4 When they have spoken to as many other students as possible and made notes next to all the questions, stop the activity and ask them to sit down again in their original pairs.

5 In their pairs, the students should now use their notes to tell their partner about the information they received, e.g. *Sami watches TV every day. He watches the news at 8 p.m.*

2.2 A week away

A group activity in which students decide on the details of a social situation before they meet and greet each other and find out what they have in common.

Language

Language of meetings and introductions

Preparation

Make one copy of the worksheet for each student.

In class

1 **Exercise 1.** Before they meet and greet each other, students should decide as a class on the details of the situation. First, they should circle one type of holiday from the choices given, then they should discuss and write details of where the holiday begins, how many people are in the group (this should be more than the number of students in the class), and what the weather is like. Ask them to elaborate and talk about each of these points further, e.g. *You won first prize in a competition. The prize is a week's holiday walking in the mountains. The holiday starts in Austria, and there are 18 people in your holiday group. The weather is warm and cloudy. It snowed last week, but now it's around 20 degrees in the day.*

2 **Exercise 2.** Once students have all agreed on the situation, get them individually to fill out the personal information. Tell them that they do not have to be themselves – they may invent a new character and personality – but to avoid confusion they should keep their gender and age! Allow 5–10 minutes for this task.

3 **Exercise 3.** Explain the social situation: the group leader has introduced herself and has told them about the programme for the week. Now that the official greeting is over, the tourists have the first first opportunity to meet and talk to the other people in their holiday group. Finger food and drinks are provided, and they are encouraged to mingle and talk to as many people as possible.

4 Tell students to stand up and mingle. They should introduce themselves, make a little bit of small talk, and then move on, as they should talk to as many people in the class as possible in the time you allow – 15 or 20 minutes, depending on the size of the group. They should try to find people who they have something in common with, and who they could imagine sitting next to at breakfast or dinner tomorrow on the first 'real' day of the holiday. When they find someone with whom they have something in common, they can move around together, introducing each other to other students.

5 After the allotted time, or when the mingling task has reached its natural conclusion, ask the students to sit down and decide who they hope to share the breakfast /dinner table with tomorrow, and why.

3.1 What does it look like?

A pairwork activity to practise asking questions and giving detailed information.

Language

countable and uncountable nouns

some, any, much, many, a lot of, a little, a few

Preparation

Make one copy of the whole worksheet per student.

In class

1 Students work in pairs, sitting opposite each other. They each fold their paper in half along the fold line so that they can only see their first empty picture frame.

2 **Exercise 1.** In the first frame, each student draws a sketch of any one of their office, their kitchen, their desk or the inside of their fridge. Ask them to include as many items as possible – especially small ones such as bottles of milk in the fridge, pens and pencils on the desk, etc. No great artistic skill is necessary! Give the students ten minutes to draw their sketches individually – they should not show anyone their sketch at this stage.

3 Student A tells Student B what, in general, they have sketched: my office, my kitchen, etc.

4 **Exercise 2.** Student B asks Student A questions about what they think Student A's sketch might contain, e.g. *How many different items are on your desk? Are there any windows in the room? How much milk is in the fridge?* If Student B cannot think of many questions, Student A should help with prompts, *e.g. There are a lot of papers next to my computer.* The questions and prompts should concentrate on items, quantity, space required, dimensions and position of items.

5 **Exercise 3.** As soon as Student B has obtained a few pieces of information, they should start to draw what Student A is describing into the picture frame at the bottom of their page. The paper should stay folded.

6 When Student B has run out of questions, Student A looks at B's picture (still without unfolding their papers). A should tell B what is still missing. B should draw these things into the picture.

7 Students A and B now swap roles: A asks questions and draws what B describes in their second picture frame. Afterwards, they compare pictures again in the same way as in Step 6. Finally, they unfold their papers and compare the sketches they made.

8 To complete the task, the pairs should exchange more general information about the place they sketched, e.g. how many people work there, how much time, or how many hours a day, they spend there, what could be done to improve the area.

3.2 Group story-telling

A whole-class and pairwork activity in which students write and tell stories similar to the one on the TED Talk.

Language

Financial vocabulary, e.g. *buy*, *earn*, *save*, *afford*, *lend*, *borrow*

Revision of *How much …?* and *How many …?*

Preparation

Make one copy of the worksheet per student.

In class

1 Give each student one copy of the worksheet and tell them that they are going to write stories together, but without knowing what the others are writing.

2 **Exercise 1.** Explain that they will write one sentence at a time, from 1–8. After completing sentence 1, they fold back the paper so the first sentence can no longer be seen, and so that sentence 2 is at the top of the page. Tell them that the story should be chronological, i.e. start in the past and continue up to the present. Tell them that the final sentence is slightly different in that they can finish it in whichever way they like.

3 The students then pass their paper to another student (if possible, to the student on their left). Without looking at sentence 1, students should write sentence 2 of the story. Remind them that as they have written a version of the previous sentence they know roughly what they story might be about. Each sentence must contain the key word(s) given and relate to the prompts in brackets.

4 After writing sentence 2, the students fold the page back so that sentence 2 can no longer be seen and sentence 3 is at the top of the page. The page is then passed on again.

5 Continue in this way until all eight sentences have been written. Then get the students to pass on the paper one last time.

6 **Exercise 2.** Students now work in pairs to unfold and read the two stories on the papers they hold. They should decide which one they like best / which one they think will make the best story.

7 Give them time to tweak, change, improve the story so that it reads smoothly and makes sense, e.g. they may need to add connecting sentences, improve the grammar or add one extra point. Then they could either read it out to the other students, or turn it into a presentation, illustrating it with free images from the Internet. (To find these, you can just type 'free images' into a search engine, or go directly to websites such as http://www.freeimages.com/ or http://pixabay.com.)

8 In pairs, the students can write up the whole story as if it were the transcript of a TED Talk.

4.1 Interrupted mini-stories

A small-group activity involving discussion and writing leading to written short stories.

Language

Past simple, past continuous and past perfect

Preparation

Make a copy of the top half of the worksheet for each student in the class and a copy of the bottom half of the page for each group of four students.

In class

1 If possible, divide the class into groups of four. Give each student a copy of the top half of the page. Ask the groups to nominate their members A, B, C and D. Give Student A in each group a copy of the bottom half of the page. This student should not show the paper to the others in their group.

2 **Exercise 1.** Student B says a number between 1 and 10. Student A says which character this number refers to. All the students write this down. Student C chooses a number between 11 and 20. All the students write down which verb this number refers to. Student D chooses a number between 21 and 30 and everyone writes down the verb it refers to.

3 **Exercise 2.** Make sure that students know that Student C's verb should be in the past continuous and Student D's verb in the past simple. All four students in the group make suggestions as to how best to combine the three elements they have. If possible, they should try to relate the story to something that really happened to them or to people that they know, e.g. *My mother was eating when the phone rang.*

4 **Exercise 3.** When they have agreed their basic sentence, they should find ways to improve it by adding more information, *e.g. My mother was eating a cream cake with her best friend when her mobile phone rang.*

5 **Exercise 4.** Now the basic sentence has been written, the groups discuss how to expand the story by adding information to set the scene and a reason for the interruption. Here they should try to use the past perfect, by asking themselves questions such as *Why did that happen?* and answering in the past perfect, e.g. *Because her husband had forgotten that it was her birthday.*

6 **Exercise 5.** When they have decided on the whole story, the students write it up. They should now have mini-stories with two or three sentences, e.g. *It was my mother's birthday and she was in a cafe in the afternoon. She was not very happy. She was eating a cream cake with her best friend when her mobile phone rang. It was my father – he had forgotten that it was her birthday and he was calling to wish her a happy birthday, and to say that he had booked a restaurant for dinner that evening, so my mother suddenly cheered up!* Help them with any corrections before they pin it to the wall for the other class members to read.

4.2 A successful race

A pairwork activity to spot the differences between two texts.

Language

Expressions from Unit 4.4, e.g. *be in a hurry*, *have an off day*

Revision of past simple and past continuous

Preparation

Make one copy of the worksheet for each pair of students and cut the page along the dotted line.

In class

1 Divide the class into pairs with Student A and Student B in each pair. Give each Student A a copy of the first text and give each Student B a copy of the second text. Tell them to read through their text quietly. Write *I was hooked!* on the board and elicit what it means (= if you are hooked on something, you find it so interesting that you want to do it as much as possible).

2 Explain to the students that they are going to talk about what they read in the text by retelling the story to each other. While doing so they will realize that there are certain differences in the story. Without showing their partner their text they should write down all the differences they come across while talking. Make sure that each pair has found all twenty differences before they move onto the next part of the activity.

3 Each pair should now decide which differing information they prefer, i.e. do they want the story to be about a man who worked in a bank or a hospital? They should change their texts accordingly. Tell them they can change any other information in the text as long as it still makes sense.

4 Finally, students work in new pairs and read their new adapted stories to their new partner.

Answers

*I lost my job at the **bank / hospital** at the **end / start** of the financial crisis. After **15 / 20** years of office work, I wasn't in a hurry to find another indoor job and so I decided to take a few **weeks / months** off. While I was watching the **New York / New Orleans** marathon on TV I decided that I would like to start running. I joined a running club in **March / April** last year. At first I went running **once / twice** a week with the other new club members and I enjoyed it very much. Very soon I felt stronger and **healthier/ happier** and I even got a suntan, something I never had while I was working in an office!*

*Last autumn I ran my first **5 / 10** kilometre race. It was **difficult / tiring** but I kept going. I was running with other club members and that helped. I did my best and was so happy when I passed the finishing line in just over **30 minutes / an hour**. It was my first ever running race, and I was hooked!*

*I started to train more regularly; often going out for a run **four / six** times a week. I wasn't interested in finding a new job; I was only interested in achieving my next goal – running a **half marathon / marathon**. Earlier this year I entered the **Atlantic City / Dodge City** race.*

*Finally, the big day arrived. I didn't feel right but I decided to do the run anyway. The race began at **10 am / 11 am**. Within 15 minutes, I knew I was having an off day. My **head / legs** hurt and I felt **dizzy /sick**. I don't really know what happened, but suddenly I was on the ground and a **paramedic / volunteer** was looking after me. It was the end of the race for me, but the beginning of a the next stage of my life. I now work at the running club and last **week / month** I married the lady who looked after me when I fell during the race. Next year I plan to run the race together with my new **wife / colleagues**.*

5.1 The best flower delivery service

A small-group webquest in which students go online to research the services and products of three flower delivery services and compare their findings.

Language

Comparatives and superlatives

Preparation

Make one copy of the worksheet for each student.

Note: If you do not have Internet access in your classroom, the research stage of this task can be set as homework in preparation for the comparison stage, which can be done in class.

1 Students choose three large flower delivery companies that are active online, e.g. Interflora, Floraqueen, 1-800-flowers, Teleflora, Fleurop, and work together as a group to find out about their services, using the headings in the chart. If they are doing this at home, they can either work in their study groups or individually. In either case, the aim would be for the students to bring a completed worksheet to class in order to work on the comparison and other tasks together.

2 **Exercise 1.** Students should make notes in the chart about the information they find. Some headings are more subjective, e.g. what students think about the company's ads and videos. To watch advertising videos, the students may have to leave the company website (maybe via a direct link) and go to YouTube.

3 **Exercise 2.** When they have completed the chart, students make general comparisons of the companies and their products and services in small groups. They can do this orally or in writing. In either case they will need to use comparatives and superlatives. Either elicit the type of language they might use, or write examples on the board, e.g. *X is cheaper than Y for a basic bouquet. X's delivery costs are less expensive. X's delivery service isn't as efficient/fast as Y's Y. X's videos are more interesting than Y's. Z has the funniest video.*

4 **Exercise 3.** Students decide which company they would use in specific situations. Ask them to discuss this in their groups and select one company for each situation. They should then present their answer to the whole class, justifying their decision, again using comparatives and superlatives.

5 Finally, discuss as a class whether any groups have selected the same flower delivery service for any of the situations.

5.2 A day out

A whole-class and small-group activity in which students make and discuss suggestions for a class outing.

Language

Giving your views and adjectives of opinion (*all right*, *amazing*, *awful*, *dreadful*, *fantastic*, *so-so*)

Comparatives and superlatives

Preparation

Make one copy of the worksheet for each student.

In class

1 Tell students their task is to plan a day out for the class. Explain that this will be done in stages and that at the end of the activity they should come to a group decision.

2 **Exercise 1.** Students discuss the basics of their day out as a class. Make sure that all the students are working to the same parameters by getting them to agree on, and write down, a few solid facts. Do this by discussing and filling in the missing information in the box, e.g.

Number of people: *e.g. 22 (= number of students, plus teacher / family?)*

When (month / day of the week?): *e.g. Friday 10th May*

Duration (whole day / half day / plus evening?): *e.g. afternoon and evening*

Cost per person: *e.g. maximum €25 per person*

3 **Exercise 2.** When the basic information has been agreed on, divide the class into small groups of three or four students. Give them five minutes to brainstorm ideas for a class outing and write their notes on the page in the mind map.

4 **Exercise 3.** Then tell students to choose their favourite idea and develop it further using the prompts provided. Allow another ten minutes for this task. If you have the equipment in your classroom, get them to prepare an overview of their favourite suggestion on flip-chart paper which they can then use in their mini-presentations in the next stage of the activity. (Or they can do this on laptops / mobile devices for presentation on the interactive whiteboard.)

5 **Exercise 4.** The groups now present their suggestions to the rest of the class. While they are doing this, encourage them to elaborate on the ideas and to get and give opinions using the language in the speech bubbles.

6 **Exercise 5.** After all the suggestions have been presented, hold a whole-class discussion in which students say why they think one suggestion is better (or worse) than the others. Encourage them to use comparatives and superlatives here, *e.g. Maria's suggestion is better than Karim's because … / The third group's suggestion is the most expensive …*

7 Finally, get the class to vote for their favourite suggestion. And … why not actually go on the outing?

6.1 Coffeepotting

A pairwork activity in which students write about and discuss everyday tasks and how they feel about them.

Language

Verb patterns with infinitive and -ing

Infinitive and -ing clauses

Preparation

Make one copy of the worksheet for each student.

In class

1 **Exercise 1.** Individually, students brainstorm everyday, mundane tasks that they do at work or at home and write them into the appropriate sections on their worksheets, e.g. *ironing, washing, filing, photocopying*. Elicit tasks that can be done both at home or at work, e.g. *answering the phone, writing emails, making tea* and have them write these into the overlapping section.

2 **Exercise 2.** Each student now decides whether they want to talk about everyday tasks that they do at home or at tasks that they do at work. Then, without talking to other students, they complete the sentences for themselves, paying attention to whether they need the infinitive or an -ing form in each sentence.

3 **Exercise 3.** When most students have finished writing, put them in pairs to read out or tell their partner what they have written. However, instead of reading out the sentences exactly as they are written, they should substitute the verb or task they have written with the word *coffeepot* or *coffeepotting*, e.g. *When possible I try to avoid coffeepotting in the evening because there's no hot water left. I'm usually happy to coffeepot in the evening because I can do it in front of the TV.*

Note: *coffeepotting* is a nonsense word and not a real activity! If you feel uncomfortable with this word, you can ask students to use *beep/beeping* instead.

4 The student who is listening should guess what their partner is talking about from the context of the sentence. They can ask questions to find out extra information, using the chosen substitute word, e.g. *When you coffeepot in front of the TV, do you use a machine?* The listener then states the task and whether it's a home or a work task. In the example, the partner guesses that these are home everyday tasks, probably washing up and ironing. Finally, they can offer some advice (using the grammar points from the unit), e.g. *I think you should try to avoid washing up in the evening … .*

5 Get students to swap roles in their pairs and repeat the activity again.

6 Finally, put two pairs together in groups of four, and then ask them to split into two new pairs so that each student can tell their new partner what they found out about their previous partner.

6.2 Hidden agendas

A class or large-group speaking activity in which students hold small talk conversations, with each student having specific information that that they want to bring into each conversation.

Language

Small talk expressions and phrases

Preparation

Make one copy of the worksheet per 12 students in the class and cut out the cards, i.e. if there are up to 12 students in the class, you only need one set of the cards. For between 13 and 24 students you need two sets, or three sets if you have more than 24 students.

In class

1 In a small class, this can be done with the whole class. In larger classes, divide students into groups of ten or twelve. Give each student one hidden agenda card. They should not show anyone else what is on their card. Ask them to write in the missing information in any way they choose, although it must make sense.

2 Explain to students that they are at a conference or party – choose and discuss the location and the reason that they are all there in order to set the scene – and that they are going to make small talk with as many other people as possible in the time you allow for the task. Tell them that they should try to bring the information on their card into each conversation in as natural a way as possible.

3 Students look at the Useful language box on page 70 of their Student's Books and decide how they are going to start (and continue) their conversations, e.g. *Is it your first time here? Are you enjoying the conference/party?*

4 Tell students to stand up and find a partner in their group / the class and to start the conversation. Remind them that they must try to get their hidden information into the conversation.

5 After the conversation has continued for a little while, or the small talk has reached its natural conclusion, the students should try to guess what is on their partner's card and write it down before moving on to talk to someone else and repeat the task. At this stage, students should not confirm what their hidden information is to anyone they talk to.

6 After the activity has finished (how long this takes will depend on the number of students there are), hold a class/group feedback session in which they say what they have guessed was the hidden agenda of each student. Discuss how easy or difficult it was to get this information into a conversation in a natural way, and which students did it most successfully.

7.1 Experiences we've had

A mingling activity in which students ask questions of as many other students as possible and then discuss what they have found out and ask for further information.

Language

Have you ever … ? (present perfect to describe experiences, contrasted with past simple)

Preparation

Make one copy of the worksheet for each student.

In class

1 Give each student a copy of the worksheet. Explain that they are going to ask as many other people as possible five questions, and then as a class discuss the number of people who answered the questions positively or negatively.

2 **Exercise 1.** Ask them to read through the experiences and decide how to turn them into present perfect questions. Elicit a couple of examples, e.g. *Have you ever missed a flight? Have you ever got on the wrong train?* Now elicit what answers they could expect to hear / give, e.g. *No, I haven't. Yes, I have.*

3 Tell students to underline four of the sixteen experiences from the list that they would like to ask other students about. They should write a fifth idea of their own (something not on the list) and make this their fifth question.

4 **Exercise 2.** Ask students to stand up and mingle and ask all the students in the class all of their questions. Explain that this is a 'quick-fire activity' and that at this stage they do not need to ask more details (this is done later in the discussion stage). Whenever someone answers positively with *Yes, I have*, they should put a tick next to that point on their paper and note the name of the person.

5 Stop the activity when the students have all spoken to each other and asked their five questions, or beforehand if you see that it is ending of its own accord.

6 **Exercise 3.** Get the students to talk about their findings in a class feedback session, e.g. *Five students have missed a flight. Only one student has been on the television.*

7 **Exercise 4.** Students should ask at least one other student from their notes some further questions after they have reported the basic facts, e.g. *Alison has missed a flight.* (question directed at Alison) *Alison, where were you going? What happened?* (Alison gives details.)

7.2 Personal qualities

A small group two-part activity in which students talk about personal qualities in people they know and that are needed for specific jobs.

Language

Personal qualities: *honest, ambitious, sociable*, etc.

Prepositional phrases: *good at … , interested in … , keen on … , not afraid of …*

Preparation

Make one copy of the worksheet for each group of three to five students. Cut out the cards for each group.

In class

1 Divide the students into groups of three to five. Give each group a set of personal quality cards and the top part of the worksheet.

2 Tell the groups to spread the cards out in front of them and read the qualities out loud. Make sure they all know what the words mean before they start the first activity.

3 **Exercise 1.** Ask students to take turns to pick up a card and talk about someone they know, have read about or heard of (e.g. on the TV) who possesses this quality. Make sure they give examples of why they think this is, e.g. *My colleague is a very reliable person. She always answers my emails within 24 hours.*

4 When a card has been picked up, and the quality talked about, the students should put this card to one side. The next student then takes another card and talks about someone who has that quality. Continue until all the cards have been used or the students are unable to think of any more examples.

5 **Exercise 2.** Groups use the same cards and spread them out again in front of them. In any order, they should discuss the jobs in the box and the qualities they think people who do them should have.

6 As they do this, students write down and rank and the qualities needed for each job, e.g. *Police officers should be firstly, … secondly, … and also …*

7 **Exercise 3.** Write these prepositional phrases on the board: *good at … , interested in … , keen on … , not afraid of …* and ask students to use them to add to what they have already written, e.g. *Police officers should not be afraid of dogs. They should be interested in helping people*, etc. The students should use a dictionary where necessary.

8 In the final stage of this activity, two groups sit together and compare what they wrote. Ask them if there were any jobs that they found it difficult to discuss / write about.

8.1 I think …

A small-group activity in which students talk about scenes in pictures and predict what they think is going to happen.

Language

Future predictions with *will* and *might*

Preparation

Make a copy of the worksheet for each pair of students, enlarging the pictures if possible. Cut out the cards and separate them into two piles: the first set of six picture cards and the second set of six picture cards.

In class

1 Put students into groups of three or four and give each group a set of the first six picture cards. Tell them to look at the cards and describe the situations to each other. Deal with any vocabulary questions they might have at this stage.

2 Once students have described the pictures, tell them that their next task is to make suggestions about what will/might happen next. (If they already know that *going to* can be used for predictions based on evidence, they can use that too.) Allow them five minutes to think of ideas in their groups and then take class feedback. Write these headings on the board: *picnic, fishing, sailing boat, gardener, walkers, motorway*, and get one member of each group to come up and write their group's prediction under the headings.

3 Now write these six phrases on the board: *a storm with thunder and lightning, a coach of American tourists, an old bicycle, an emergency helicopter, hundreds of bees, a hungry bird*. Tell students that each phrase goes with one of the pictures. They should talk in their groups about the situations again and then tell the whole class about any changes they'd like to make to their suggestions, e.g. *For picture 5 we think there will be a storm and the walkers will get really wet. For picture 6, there might be a coach of American tourists on the motorway.*

4 Now hand out the second set of picture cards to each group and tell students to match them with the first set of cards. How many (if any) of the situations on the second cards did they guess correctly? As a whole class, the students can decide which group made the most 'correct' predictions.

5 Finally, ask the students as a whole class to make suggestions about what might happen after each situation that is shown on the second set of cards. e.g. (for cards 2 and 9) *The boy and his father might fall into the sea* (and for cards 4 and 8) *The gardener might become famous in the USA.*

Answers

These cards match: 1–11, 2–9, 3–7, 4–8, 5–12, 6–10

8.2 Gadgets and devices

A group activity in which students describe a gadget or device without saying exactly what it is.

Language

Language of description, measurement and function, e.g. *it allows you to … , it weighs … , it measures … , it looks …*

Preparation

Copy and cut out one set of cards for each group of three to four students.

In class

1 Choose one card and use it as an example so that the students know how the activity works. Tell the students you have a gadget or device on your card (do not show them what is on the card) and that you will give them a maximum of six clues as to what the device is and does but that you will not say exactly what it is. They should listen carefully and after you have given them your first clue, they can start to guess what the device is. Your task is to describe the device as well as you can without actually saying what it is; their task is to decide what is written on your card. For example, if you select the two-person tent: *Clue 1: You can sleep in it. Clue 2: It's made of material/fabric. Clue 3: It comes in many different colours and sizes.*

2 Divide the class in groups of three to four students. Give each group a set of cut-out cards. The cards should be placed in a pile, face down (so the text and pictures cannot be seen) in the middle of each group.

3 The students take it in turns to take a card, silently read what is on it and look at the illustration, and describe it to the others in their group in the way that you just modelled. Remind them to use the language of describing objects that they have learned in Unit 8.

4 The student who guesses the device correctly gets to keep the card. If the students think they know what the object is, but do not know the word in English, allow them to look it up in a dictionary, or as a last resort, in a mono-lingual class – say it in their own language.

5 If, after a student has given six clues, the others in their group still have not correctly guessed what is on the card, then the card should be placed back at the bottom of the pile.

6 The next student takes the card at the top of the pile and the activity continues in the same way until the time is up or all the cards have been used.

7 At the end of the activity, the student with the most cards is the winner.

9.1 Conditional mix and match

A paired activity in which students match up conditional sentence halves and think of other ways to finish the sentence halves.

Language

Zero conditional sentences, e.g. *When/If Cindy's not here, I sit at her desk.*

First conditional sentences, e.g. *Unless you leave now, you'll miss your flight.*

Imperatives in conditional sentences, e.g. *If you lose your camera while you're on holiday, go to the local police station.*

Preparation

Make one copy of the worksheet per pair of students. Cut out the cards into a set for each pair and ensure that they are mixed up.

In class

1 Divide the class into pairs and give each pair of students one set of cards. Tell them they have to match the sentence beginnings with the most appropriate endings. Point out that more than one ending might be possible in some cases, but in order to make 16 complete conditional sentences, there is only one correct solution.

2 When each pair has matched all the cards, ask them to read out their complete sentences to check the answers.

Answers

If you're hungry, it's difficult to concentrate.
When you are hot and have no energy, eat something salty and drink something sweet.
If you don't drink enough water when it's hot, you feel very tired.
If someone steals your camera while you're on holiday, go to the local police station.
If you lose your credit card, contact your bank immediately.
Unless you leave now, you'll miss your flight.
If you miss your train, don't panic – you can get the next one.
If your suitcase is too heavy, you have to pay more money.
If you want to check your emails, connect to the free wi-fi.
If you don't call her when you get there, she'll worry.
Many people believe that if they get a good job, they'll be happy.
You won't get good marks unless you do your homework.
If you don't go to bed before midnight, you'll be tired in the morning.
Unless you help me, I won't be able to do it.
When Cindy's not here, I sit at her desk.
If you see Joan, give her my best wishes.

3 Now tell them to remove the second card (the ending) of each sentence and put these to one side. The pairs should now decide on an alternative way to finish each of the sentences and write their ideas down.

4 Ask the pairs to read out their new sentences. Award a point for each grammatically correct sentence. When all the sentences starting with the same beginning have been read out, ask the class to vote on the best/funniest sentence and award one extra point to the pair who wrote it. In a large class / if you don't have much time, you can do this for a limited number of sentences.

5 The game can be played again using the cards that were put to one side. This time the students should create new sentence beginnings to fit with the endings on the cards.

9.2 Information-gap crossword

A paired information-gap activity to revise vocabulary.

Language

Vocabulary from Unit 9.3

Preparation

Make one copy of the worksheet for each pair of students. Cut the page in half so that each student gets one half-completed crossword.

In class

1 Divide the class into pairs. Student A gets the half-completed crossword from the top half of the page, and Student B gets the one from the bottom half. Explain that Student A has all the words that are needed to complete the 'across' part of the crossword, and Student B has all the 'down' words. Tell the students that all the words can be found in Unit 9.3.

2 Give the students two minutes to quietly read through the words in their half of the crossword. If there are any they aren't sure of, tell them to find the words in Unit 9.3 and work out the meaning from the context.

3 Remind your students that they should not show their crossword to their partner, and explain the crossword terms they will need, such as 1 across and 2 down.

4 In their pairs, students ask each other to give them clues for their missing words, e.g. What is 10 across? Their partner should offer an answer, e.g. It's a word for an expert or a professional person who gives help and advice. They should not just give the word needed!

5 Once you've set up the activity, it will run by itself. Use the time to go around the class and listen in to the students, giving help and prompts where required.

6 The aim of the activity is for all students to complete their crossword.

Answers

10.1 Town meeting

A whole-class activity in which students decide what to do with an unused area of land.

Language

Topic and vocabulary from Unit 10.1, e.g. *community, local, area of land, public garden, business, environment, residents, car park, local traders, unused*

Preparation

Make one copy of the worksheet for each student. Prepare one voting slip per student, i.e. a piece of paper on which you should write:

> *1st choice (3 points)*
> *2nd choice (2 points)*
> *3rd choice (1 point)*

You could fit this five or six times on a sheet of A4 paper and cut the sheet into slips.

In class

1 Tell the students that they all live in the same town and that they are attending a meeting about an unused plot of land in their town. At the meeting they will be able to discuss the seven different proposals for making use of the land and vote for their favourites.
2 **Exercise 1.** Give students time to read through the situation and all the proposals. Answer any vocabulary questions they may have at this point, but not questions about the content of the proposals.
3 Explain to the students that they have 15 minutes to discuss what they think the pros and cons / benefits and negative aspects might be. For example, *Proposal C, the vegetable garden, is something that could help everyone in the town, but I don't know how it will work. / Who will benefit from proposal E, the car park?* Allow more time if necessary and encourage students to try to persuade each other if they disagree.
4 **Exercise 2.** After they have discussed the proposals, hand out one voting slip per student. Tell them to write their top three choices on their voting slip. Now collect the slips in. Choose one student to read out the slips and another to write the number of votes on the board.
5 If there is no clear winner, ask the students to vote again, but this time just for their one favourite proposal out of the two or three that got the most votes in the first round. This can be done on another voting slip or simply by a show of hands, e.g. *Raise your hand if you would like to vote for proposal XX.*
6 Hold a short feedback session in which the group discusses how happy they are with the decision and whether it was a difficult or easy one to make (and accept).

10.2 Environmental reports

A pairwork activity in which students piece together sections of two reports and then find all the passive forms before writing their own texts.

Language

Present and past passive forms, e.g. *is found, are used, were said, was damaged*

Preparation

Make one copy of the worksheet for each pair or group of three students. Cut along the dotted lines so that you have 15 strips of paper in each set.

In class

1 Divide the class into pairs or groups of three. Give each pair or group a complete set of 15 strips of paper containing the two mixed up texts.
2 Point out that there are two texts, A and B. The first part of each is labelled *A / B* and the final sentence of each text is marked *[end]*.
3 First, students decide which ending goes with which beginning. After that, they should divide up the remaining 11 strips of paper according to which report they think each one belongs to. Then they work out the correct order. Explain that each strip is just a line of the report and not a complete sentence, which should help them to put the strips in the correct order.
4 When they have put the strips in the right order they should check their solution with that of another pair or all together in class.
5 When they all have the correct solution, ask them to find and underline seven passive forms in each text.

Answers

A *Around a third of all the food in the world is wasted. In the UK, 50% of food waste happens at home, where 7.2 m tonnes of food and drink is thrown away annually by households. The rest of the food is ruined on farms and during transportation and in stores. Greenhouse-gas emissions from the food waste are produced in rubbish sites and from the vehicles that are used to transport it. A meeting was held last month between major supermarkets and the farming industry to decide how to deal with this waste problem. A 200-page report from the meeting was sent to the government, who want to reduce the waste by 20% within the next three years.*

B *Crude oil is a thick, black liquid that is found underground and under the sea. Crude oil is changed at oil refineries into different fuels that we all use in our daily lives such as petrol, oil, diesel and gas. These fuels are used to help power engines in machines and vehicles such as cars, trucks and airplanes. As a result of the BP oil spill in 2010, more than 200 million gallons of crude oil were pumped into the Gulf of*

Mexico and over 1000 km of coastline from Texas to Florida was affected. Many birds, fish and other animals such as dolphins were killed as a result of the disaster. Additionally, the company's reputation was damaged greatly by the oil spill and the clean-up costs were said to have been more than 40 billion US dollars.

6   Now the students should choose one of these environmentally-related topics: *elephants or rhinos in danger, recycling, wind or solar power, packaging, bottled water, plastic bags, sea pollution.* They should write their own short reports, either alone or in their pairs, about the topic of their choice. Remind them to include passive forms. Help out where required and make any necessary corrections. The students' own (corrected) reports can be pinned up for the other students to read.

11.1 Do I have to?

A pair and group activity in which students complete and discuss sentences.

Language

Modal verbs: *must / mustn't, have to / don't have to, need to / don't need to, can / can't, should / shouldn't*

Preparation

Make one copy of the worksheet for each student.

In class

1   Put students into pairs and give them each a copy of the worksheet. Some students may prefer to work alone for the first part of the activity but it is best to encourage them to work in pairs as this will force them to communicate more and they are likely to produce a greater variety of suggested answers and modal verbs.

2   **Exercise 1.** Tell them to complete all 12 sentences with their own ideas (or ideas that they can agree on in their pairs). The first six sentences only need modal verbs; for the second six they will need to write more information. Explain that there is no one correct solution to any of the sentences (but that there are some 'wrong' ones!). They should concentrate on getting their own ideas onto the paper, using a variety of modal verbs, and making as few (grammatical) errors as possible.

3   Give them approximately 15 minutes to complete the sentences. While they are writing, go around and provide grammar, vocabulary or spelling help where required.

4   **Exercise 2.** When the sentences are all complete, the students should sit together in groups and compare and discuss what they have written, justifying their opinions and different points of view.
    Suggested answers (i.e. which modals)
    a   *should / don't have to / don't need to*
    b   *should / shouldn't*
    c   *mustn't*
    d   *should / must*
    e   *mustn't*
    f   *don't have to / need to / don't need to*
    g   *should / need to / can*
    h   *should / can't*
    i   *have to / should*
    j   *need to / should / need to*
    k   *shouldn't / mustn't*
    l   *should / can*

5   To round off the activity, write completed sentence d on the board: *When there is a fire, you shouldn't use the stairs.* Get the whole class to suggest further safety instructions, which can then be written up and pinned to the wall or classroom door, e.g. *When you hear the fire bell, you don't need to panic.*

11.2 Quotation game

A pairwork or small group activity in which students think of ways to finish quotes, then find out what the complete quotes really are. This is also a 'memory' game.

Language

Motivational language, leadership and life quotations

Preparation

Make one copy of the worksheet for each pair or small group of students. Cut out the quote cards – don't mix the first 12 cards (Set A) with the second 12 (Set B). If possible, copy the cards onto thick paper or card so that the text does not show through when you turn them over.

In class

1 Divide the class into pairs or small groups of three or four students. Give each pair or group the Set A cards – don't give them the Set B cards yet.

2 Tell students to spread the cards on the table in front of them. Explain that each card contains half or more of a quote from a well-known person. Give them ten minutes to think of ways of finishing the quotes so that they are grammatically correct and make sense. Students should write these down on a piece of paper for later reference. Ask them to read out their favourite 'completed' quotes before moving onto the next stage.

3 Give each group the Set B cards. Explain that these contain the end of each quote and that their next task is to match the endings with the beginnings to make 12 complete quotes. Go through the answers in class and compare the answers to the students' own suggestions from the previous stage. How close are their ideas to the original quotes?

Answers

Your time is limited, so don't waste it living someone else's life. **Steve Jobs**

You cannot have a positive life and a negative mind. **Joyce Meyer**

It does not matter how slowly you go as long as you do not stop. **Confucius**

You have to learn the rules of the game. And then you have to play better than anyone else. **Albert Einstein**

A leader is one who knows the way, goes the way, and shows the way. **John Maxwell**

Do what you feel in your heart to be right – for you'll be criticized anyway. **Eleanor Roosevelt**

He who has great power should use it lightly. **Seneca**

You only live once but if you do it right, once is enough. **Mae West**

How wonderful it is that nobody need wait a single moment before starting to improve the world. **Anne Frank**

The most common way people give up their power is by thinking they don't have any. **Alice Walker**

You can't use up creativity. The more you use, the more you have. **Maya Angelou**

I don't like the word 'businesswoman'. Perhaps 'committed mother' would be the best description. **Steffi Graf**

4 Now get the students to turn over all 24 cards so they are face down on the table, and to mix them up. The cards are now a memory game. Students take turns to turn over two cards so that they can read the writing. When they turn over two that match, i.e. make up a complete quote, they keep them and have another turn. If the cards they turn over do not match, they should turn them back over so the words cannot be read, and the next student should take their turn. At the end of the game, the student who has found the biggest number of complete quotes is the winner.

12.1 Dilemmas

A pairwork activity leading into whole-class work in which students read and discuss and report on life dilemmas.

Language

Second conditional and giving advice, e.g. *If you … , you could … and If I were you, I'd …*

Preparation

Make a copy of the worksheet for each student.

In class

1 **Exercise 1.** Put students into pairs and give them each a copy of the worksheet. Give them approximately five minutes to read the dilemmas (but they shouldn't discuss them yet). Each student selects two dilemmas which they think they would be able to offer some advice on. Deal with any vocabulary questions before continuing.

2 **Exercise 2.** In pairs, students discuss the advice they might give on the four dilemmas. If both students have chosen the same dilemma, they should select another one.

3 **Exercise 3.** Bring the class together and elicit how people give advice in written form, e.g. by email or letter, on an Internet forum, in the comments section of a website or blog. Put an example on the board, e.g. (for dilemma D) *If I were you, I'd talk to his teacher.* or *If you talked to his teacher, she would tell you whether she's worried about his grades.* Tell students to write a reply for each dilemma in their pairs, using whichever form they prefer. The task is intended to be collaborative and should therefore involve discussion and agreement between the students. Offer help where required and check that they are correctly using the second conditional in their replies.

4 Now ask individuals students to get up, take their written advice with them and find another student who has written advice for one of the same problems. They should compare their advice and, if they like what the other student has written, add this advice to their own. They do this for all four dilemmas.

5 **Exercise 4.** After about 15 minutes, or when you see that the mingling task is naturally coming to an end, get the students to sit down with their original partner and compare what extra advice they have gathered. In their pairs they now write all the advice for each dilemma in the form of an email or a post on a forum. They should write four separate emails / posts. If possible, they can display their writing so that everyone else in the class can read it. Give them time to read the others' work.

6 Hold a class feedback session in which students discuss how similar (or different) their advice was to that given by the others, especially in response to the same dilemma. Ask them to choose the most useful piece of advice for each dilemma by getting them to say which was the most helpful, as well as how they would feel if it was their personal life dilemma and they received this advice.

12.2 Life choices, lifestyle

Individual work, followed by pairwork in which students talk about their lifestyles and give each other suggestions as to how to improve.

Language

Well-being adjectives

Discussing options, e.g. *You could … / One way would be to … / Another alternative would be to … / Rather than … , why don't you … ?*

Preparation

Make one copy of the worksheet for each student.

In class

1 **Exercise 1.** Hand out the worksheets. Tell the students to read the actions in the box and, thinking about their own life, write some of them into the relevant circles. For example, if they think that cycling is good for them but they don't do it, then they write *go cycling* into circle A. If they watch TV every day and they think this is probably bad for them, they write *watch TV every day* into circle C. Not all of the actions in the box are clearly good or bad for you and so where students write them will depend not only on their lifestyle but also on their own point of view. Allow only ten minutes for this task (so that they do not have too much time to think but instead are forced to make quick decisions).

2 **Exercise 2.** Put students into pairs and ask them to compare their completed worksheets. After five minutes ask for quick feedback about how similar each pair is in lifestyle choices. They should ask each other questions and answer them using the well-being adjectives from Unit 12.4, e.g. *What do you find most enjoyable? – I love doing yoga. I find it very relaxing.*

3 Now tell them they are going to talk to each other and offer advice and discuss options about how they can 'improve' their lifestyle. They should start by looking at what their partner has written in circle A, e.g. if their partner has written *spend time in the fresh air every day*, then they could say something like: *One way would be to go out during your lunch break. Rather than going to the canteen at lunchtime, why don't you eat a sandwich in the park?*

4 They should then look at what their partner has written in circle C and give suggestions and advice as to how to stop these activities. The idea is that their partner could one day write them in Circle D (and the actions from A in B).

5 Stop the task when you notice that it is reaching its natural conclusion. Hold a further feedback round in which students talk about the advice they were given, the options and alternatives their partner came up with, and whether they think they will follow the advice and suggestions and change their lifestyle and life choices in a positive way.

6 Finally, tell each student to write a resolution, i.e. one way they will try to improve their lifestyle and well-being.